Scripture and Other Artifacts

Scripture and Other Artifacts

Essays on the Bible and Archaeology in Honor of Philip J. King

Edited by

MICHAEL D. COOGAN
J. CHERYL EXUM
LAWRENCE E. STAGER

Managing Editor
JOSEPH A. GREENE

WESTMINSTER JOHN KNOX PRESS
Louisville, Kentucky

©1994 Westminster John Knox Press

Book design by Publishers' WorkGroup

Cover design by Drew Stevens

*Cover illustration by Carl Andrews,
courtesy of the Leon Levy Expedition*

First edition

Published by Westminster John Knox Press
Louisville, Kentucky

This book is printed on acid-free paper that meets the
American National Standards Institute Z39.48 standard.

PRINTED IN THE UNITED STATES OF AMERICA

2 4 6 8 9 7 5 3 1

Library of Congress Cataloging-in-Publication Data

Scripture and other artifacts : essays on the Bible and archaeology in
    honor of Philip J. King / edited by Michael D. Coogan, J. Cheryl
    Exum, Lawrence E. Stager : managing editor Joseph A. Greene. — 1st
    ed.
        p.   cm.
    Includes bibliographical references and indexes.
    ISBN 0-664-22036-3 (alk. paper)
    1. Bible—Antiquities.   I. King, Philip J.   II. Coogan, Michael
David.   III. Exum, J. Cheryl.   IV. Stager, Lawrence E.
BS621.S37   1994
220.9'3—dc20   94-9998

Contents

Preface

At first glance Phil King's life seems typically Bostonian in its insularity. His home has always been in the Boston area, as has his academic career, first at St. John's Seminary (1958–1974), and, since 1974, at Boston College, where he has been Professor of Hebrew Bible and Biblical Archaeology. Even the offices of the American Schools of Oriental Research were in nearby Cambridge when he was its president. Yet his life has been far from parochial. His studies in Rome at the Pontifical Biblical Institute (S.S.L., 1957) and the Pontifical Lateran University (S.T.D., 1959) have made that city one of his favorites. He has spent much time in the libraries and universities of England. And his trips to the Middle East since he was first a fellow at the then American School (now the Albright Institute) in Jerusalem in 1966–67 have been innumerable. He has worked on excavations at Tell es-Sa'idiyeh and Tell er-Rumeith in Jordan, at Taanach on the West Bank, at Gezer and Tell el-Hesi in Israel, and in the Wadi al-Jubah in Yemen. In addition, he has served as a consultant for the Carthage excavations in Tunisia, as an advisor to the Tel Miqne/Ekron and Ashkelon projects in Israel, and as an informal counsel to countless others.

One measure of Phil's standing and esteem among both biblical scholars and archaeologists is that he is the only person to have been elected president of the three major scholarly societies in North America in the interrelated disciplines of biblical studies and archaeology: the American Schools of Oriental Research (1976–1982), the Catholic Biblical Association of America (1981–1982), and the Society of Biblical Literature (1988). Phil's tireless and unselfish efforts on behalf of these organizations have benefited many scholars working in the fields of archaeology and biblical studies. Throughout his academic career, he has generously supported and promoted the work of others, especially younger scholars.

In the course of his travels and work, Phil has accumulated an international and broad circle of friends, and to make this collection of essays manageable in size, we decided to restrict contributors to practicing archaeologists and biblical scholars who have been active in fieldwork. Regrettably this has meant that many people, especially in the wider biblical field, could not participate in this celebration of Phil's life and work in anticipation of his seventieth birthday on March 26, 1995.

The title of our volume makes use of Bill Dever's apt characterization of the Bible as a curated artifact and reflects the two foci of Phil King's career, the Bible and archaeology. In recent years he has been especially concerned with the integration of biblical and archaeological data, resulting in his books *Amos, Hosea, Micah: An Archaeological Commentary* (Westminster Press, 1988) and *Jeremiah: An Archaeological Companion* (Westminster John Knox Press, 1993). These volumes have not only helped to bring the often unpublished results of archaeologists and the technical studies of biblical scholars to a broader audience; they have also served as models of synthesis. With his encyclopedic and firsthand knowledge of excavations and his expertise in exegesis, Phil has demonstrated how archaeological data can be used to illuminate the Bible, and at the same time how that anthology of the writings of ancient Israel and early Judaism and Christianity is part of a larger cultural continuum—is itself, as it were, an artifact that can be understood only in the light of its context. The Bible and archaeological data, then, are complementary, and our understanding of both is heightened by our consideration of both. Such a synthesis is the theme of this volume, and we have asked contributors to follow the model Phil has provided in integrating the results of excavation and the conclusions of exegesis.

Many of the contributors wrote in their original submissions of Phil's generosity, friendship, and scholarship, tributes with which we fully concur but have curtailed in the interests of consistency and brevity. It is our hope that the volume in its entirety expresses those sentiments, both for those whose essays are included here and for the many more who wanted to contribute but were unable to do so because of other commitments. One indication of the widespread nature of these feelings is that others too had wanted to sponsor a Festschrift such as this, and several publishers were eager to publish it when all we had was an idea. In the end we chose Westminster John Knox because of its association with Phil, especially in his most recent work.

We are grateful to Dr. Cynthia Thompson of Westminster John Knox Press for her support and counsel from proposal to publication. Thanks are also due to Dr. Joseph A. Greene of the Semitic Museum, who coordinated the project—corresponding with authors, converting manuscripts to a uniform format, preparing the index, and carrying out innumerable other indispensable tasks—with an unfailingly sunny disposition and consistent skill, scholarship, and tact. We especially thank Leon Levy and Shelby White, whose generous subvention enabled our idea to become a book.

We are delighted to present this volume to Phil as a partial expression of gratitude to our mentor, colleague, and friend. Happy birthday, Phil!

Michael D. Coogan
J. Cheryl Exum
Lawrence E. Stager
July 1994

Abbreviations

GENERAL

AT	Alalakh Text
BCE	Before the Common Era
BP	Before Present
ca.	circa
CAD	*Chicago Assyrian Dictionary*
CE	Common Era
cm	centimeter(s)
chap.	chapter(s)
col(s).	column(s)
CTA	*Corpus des Tablettes en Cuneiformes Alphabetiques Découvertes à Ras Shamra-Ugarit*
EB	Early Bronze
fig(s).	figure(s)
ft	foot; feet
ha	hectare(s)
HE	*Historia Ecclesiastica*
Hebr.	Hebrew
in	inches
kg	kilogram(s)
km	kilometer(s)
l	liter(s)
LB	Late Bronze
lb	pound(s)
LTK	*Lexikon für Theologie und Kirke*
LXX	Septuagint

m, mm	meter(s), millimeter(s)
MB	Middle Bronze
MT	Masoretic Text
NEB	New English Bible
NIV	New International Version
NRSV	New Revised Standard Version
n(n).	note(s)
no(s).	number(s)
p(p).	page(s)
PG	*Patrologia Graeca*
pl(s).	plate(s)
REB	Revised English Bible
RSV	Revised Standard Version
v(v)	verse(s)

BOOKS OF THE BIBLE

1-2 Chr.	Chronicles
1-2 Cor.	Corinthians
Dan.	Daniel
Deut.	Deuteronomy
Exod.	Exodus
Ezek.	Ezekiel
Gen.	Genesis
Hag.	Haggai
Hos.	Hosea
Isa.	Isaiah
Jer.	Jeremiah
Josh.	Joshua
Judg.	Judges
1-2 Kgs.	Kings
Lam.	Lamentations
Lev.	Leviticus
Matt.	Matthew
Mic.	Micah
Nah.	Nahum
Neh.	Nehemiah
Num.	Numbers
Ps. (pl. Pss.)	Psalms

1-2 Sam.	Samuel
Tob.	Tobit
Zech.	Zechariah

Contributors

Avraham Biran
Hebrew Union College-Jewish
  Institute of Religion
Jerusalem, Israel

Elizabeth Bloch-Smith
151 Stoneway Lane
Bala Cynwyd, Pennsylvania

Edward F. Campbell
McCormick Theological Seminary
Chicago, Illinois

Dan P. Cole
Lake Forest College
Lake Forest, Illinois

Robert Cooley
Gordon-Conwell Theological
  Seminary
South Hamilton, Massachusetts

Frank Moore Cross
Harvard University
Cambridge, Massachusetts

Graham I. Davies
University of Cambridge
Cambridge, England

Philip R. Davies
University of Sheffield
Sheffield, England

William G. Dever
University of Arizona
Tucson, Arizona

Israel Finkelstein
Tel Aviv University
Tel Aviv, Israel

David Noel Freedman
University of California-San Diego
La Jolla, California

Richard S. Hess
Glasgow Bible College
Glasgow, Scotland

Nancy Lapp
Pittsburgh Theological Seminary
Pittsburgh, Pennsylvania

Burton MacDonald
St. Francis Xavier University
Antigonish, Nova Scotia, Canada

Amihai Mazar
Hebrew University
Jerusalem, Israel

Carol L. Meyers
Duke University
Durham, North Carolina

Eric M. Meyers
Duke University
Durham, North Carolina

Alan Millard
University of Liverpool
Liverpool, England

Jerome Murphy-O'Connor, O. P.
Ecole Biblique
Jerusalem, Israel

Robert North, S. J.
Pontifical Biblical Institute
Rome, Italy

Gary D. Pratico
Gordon-Conwell Theological
    Seminary
South Hamilton, Massachusetts

Anson F. Rainey
Tel Aviv University
Tel Aviv, Israel

Walter E. Rast
Valparaiso University
Valparaiso, Indiana

James A. Sauer
Semitic Museum
Harvard University
Cambridge, Massachusetts

Ephraim Stern
Hebrew University
Jerusalem, Israel

David Ussishkin
Tel Aviv University
Tel Aviv, Israel

Andrew Welch
University of California-San Diego
La Jolla, California

Sources of Illustrations

Grateful acknowledgement is given to the following for illustrations used in this book:

Chapter 1

Illustrations reproduced courtesy of HUC-JIR Nelson Glueck School of Biblical Archaeology, Jerusalem.

Chapter 3

Fig. 3-2: Reproduced with permission from Scholars Press; from *Shechem II: Portrait of a Hill Country Vale*, Edward F. Campbell.
Other illustrations reprinted with permission from the author.

Chapter 4

Fig. 4-1: Drawing by Judith Dekel. From *The Conquest of Lachish by Sennacherib*, David Ussishkin, 1982; reproduced with permission from the author.
Fig. 4-2: Reproduced with permission from the author.
Fig. 4-3: Reproduced courtesy of Carta's *Historical Atlas of Jerusalem*, Dan Bahat.

Chapter 5

Illustrations reproduced with permission from the authors.

Chapter 6

Illustrations reproduced with permission from the author.

Chapter 13

Illustrations reproduced with permission from the author.

Chapter 14

Illustration reproduced with permission from the author.

Chapter 15

Illustrations reproduced with permission from the author.

Chapter 17

Figs. 17-1, 17-2a-b: Photographs reproduced courtesy of the Trustees of the British Museum.
Fig. 17-3: Reproduced with permission from the author.

Chapter 19

Fig. 19-1: Reproduced with permission from the Department of Antiquities, Republic of Cyprus, from the "Report of the Department of Antiquities, Cyprus," 1984.
Fig. 19-2: Reproduced with permission from the Museo Arqueologico Nacional, Madrid, Spain.
Figs. 19-3, 19-4: Reproduced with permission from *Latomus: Revue d'Etudes Latines*.
Figs. 19-5, 19-6: Reproduced with permission from the Römisch-Germanische Kommission des Deutschen Archäologischen Instituts.

Chapter 20

Photographs by Avrahan Hay, reproduced with permission from the author.

Chapter 21

Illustrations reproduced with permission from the author.

Chapter 22

All images computer-generated by C. Andrews.
Fig. 22-1: Reproduced courtesy of the Royal Meteorological Society, Berkshire, England.
Fig. 22-2: Reproduced with permission from *Nature* 364, copyright 1993, Macmillan Magazines Limited.

Fig. 22-3: Reproduced courtesy of Academic Press, *Quaternary of Israel*, Aharon Horowitz, 1979.

Fig. 22-4: Reproduced with permission from Gustav Fischer Verlag, *Geobotanical Foundation*, M. Zohary, 1973.

Fig. 22-5: Originally appeared in an article by Aharon Horowitz in *Expedition*. Reproduced courtesy of A. Horowitz.

Fig. 22-6: Reproduced courtesy of A. M. Rosen.

Fig. 22-7: Reproduced with permission from *Nature* 296, copyright 1982, Macmillan Magazines Limited.

Fig. 22-8: Reproduced courtesy of K. W. Butzer.

Fig. 22-9: Reproduced courtesy of Gordon and Breach Science Publishers. Originally published in "Gulf War Disruption" in *Gulf War and the Environment*, F. El-Baz, 1994.

Fig. 22-10: Reproduced courtesy of State Organization of Antiquities and Heritage, Republic of Iraq.

Fig. 22-11: Reproduced courtesy of British School of Archaeology in Iraq.

Chapter 23

Illustrations reproduced with permission from the author.

Chapter 24

Illustrations reproduced courtesy of The Oriental Institute of The University of Chicago.

PHILIP J. KING

Philip King:
An Appreciation

Philip King's contributions as scholar, author, archaeologist, and professor are well known, and are the occasion for this volume. We wish to speak here of him as a friend. He came into our lives in 1978, shortly after assuming the presidency of the American Schools of Oriental Research (ASOR) at a low point in its history. A mutual friend had invited us to an ASOR meeting, which it would be an understatement to describe as chaotic. In accepting the presidency of the organization at this meeting, Phil said with characteristic modesty and perhaps realism that the job was his because no one else wanted it—and no wonder: the treasury was virtually empty, publications were over a year behind, and the membership was fractious. With the patience of a consummate diplomat, Phil presided over stormy meeting after stormy meeting to make the changes necessary for ASOR's survival.

Over the years we have come to know Phil much better. In 1980 we traveled with Phil and a group of ASOR trustees to Syria, Jordan, and Israel. Wherever we went, we were amazed at his vast network of friends. From the cultural attaché in Damascus to the cab driver in Jerusalem, Phil knew their families and their troubles. It was Phil who introduced us to the world of field archaeology in general and to Larry Stager in particular. Each year we have journeyed to Israel with Phil to visit the excavations at Ashkelon. In the early years of the dig, Phil often acted as a gofer; more recently, after a long apprenticeship, he has graduated to elder statesman. In fact, Larry considers Phil the dig's patron saint.

We have even managed to coax Phil into joining us on boats cruising the Aegean, despite his natural inclination to stay on land and his claim that he becomes seasick even in the bathtub. On one particularly rough trip, Phil sat rigid in a chair and never complained as the chair moved slowly across the cabin and then slid back just as slowly in the other direction. Nor was this his last trip!

Phil's remarkable ability to understand and to listen, to accept people's differences, has made it possible for him to know a large number of people very well. This includes the relatively young; as one teenager said, "I really like Dr. King. He's cool!"

The world of archaeology will be enhanced for future generations because of the important role that Phil King has played throughout his long career. And the lives of all of us who call him friend have also been enriched by our association with this generous man.

Leon Levy
Shelby White

Publications by Philip J. King

A Study of Psalm 45. Rome: Pontifical Lateran University, 1959.

The Book of Judges. New York: Paulist Press, 1960.

Matthew and Epiphany. *Worship* 36 (1962): 89 95.

The Bible Today. *The Current* 3 (1962): 226–31.

The Book of Psalms, 2 parts. New York: Paulist Press, 1962.

When Israel Was a Child. *The Bible Today* 1 (1963): 286–93.

Elizabeth, Zachary, and the Messiah. *The Bible Today* 2 (1964): 992–97.

Jonah, Book of (vol. 6, pp. 56–57), Theology of Law (vol. 6, p. 307). In *Catholic Encyclopedia for School and Home*. New York, 1965.

The Book of Numbers. Old Testament Reading Guide. Collegeville, Minn.: Liturgical Press, 1966.

Life at the American Schools in Jerusalem. *The Bible Today* 6 (1968): 2353–58 (with M. McNamara).

Amos. *The Jerome Biblical Commentary*, ed. R. E. Brown; J. Fitzmyer; and R. E. Murphy. Englewood Cliffs, N.J.: Prentice-Hall, 1968, 242–52.

Micah. *The Jerome Biblical Commentary*, ed. R. E. Brown; J. A. Fitzmyer; and R. E. Murphy. Englewood Cliffs, N.J.: Prentice-Hall, 1968, 283–89.

In Memoriam: G. Ernest Wright. *Catholic Biblical Quarterly* 36 (1974): 568–70.

The American Archaeological Heritage in the Near East. *Bulletin of the American Schools of Oriental Research* 217 (1975): 55–65.

Archaeology at the Albright Institute. *Biblical Archaeologist* 38 (1975): 79–88.

Through the Ancient Near East with ASOR. *The Bible Today* 17 (1979): 2113–20.

Hosea's Message of Hope. *Biblical Theology Bulletin* 12 (1982): 91–95.

American Archaeology in the Mideast: A History of the American Schools of Oriental Research. Philadelphia: American Schools of Oriental Research, 1983.

The Contribution of Archaeology to Biblical Studies. *Catholic Biblical Quarterly* 45 (1983): 1–16.

Die Archaologische Forschung zur Ansiedlung der Israeliten in Palästina. *Bibel und Kirche* 2 (1983): 73–76.

Sharing the Results of Scholarly Research. In *The Word of the Lord Shall Go Forth*, ed. C. Meyers and M. O'Connor. Philadelphia: American Schools of Oriental Research, 1983, 1–12.

Edward Robinson: Biblical Scholar. *Biblical Archaeologist* 45 (1983): 230–32.

Revealing Biblical Jerusalem: An Introduction. In *Biblical Archaeology Today*. Proceedings of the International Congress on Biblical Archaeology, Jerusalem, 1984, ed. J. Aviram. Jerusalem: Israel Exploration Society, 1985, 435–39.

The Contribution of Archaeology to Biblical Studies. In *Companion to the Bible*, ed. M. Ward. New York: Alba House, 1985, 137–59.

ASOR at 85. *Biblical Archaeologist* 47 (1984): 197–205.

Archaeology, History, and the Bible (pp. 44–52), Lachish (pp. 537–52), Palestine (pp. 740–46), Zobah, Zorah (p. 1167). In *Harper's Bible Dictionary*, ed. P. J. Achtemeier. San Francisco: Harper and Row, 1985.

Teaching the Bible and Living Its Message. *Bible Review* 3, no. 1 (1987): 4–5.

The Influence of G. Ernest Wright on the Archaeology of Palestine. In *Archaeology and Biblical Interpretation*, ed. L. Perdue, L. Toombs, and G. Johnson. Atlanta: John Knox Press, 1987, 15–30.

American Archaeologists. In *Benchmarks in Time and Culture*, ed. J. Drinkard, G. Mattingly, and J. M. Miller. Atlanta: Scholars Press, 1988, 15–35.

Amos, Hosea, Micah: An Archaeological Commentary. Philadelphia: Westminster Press, 1988.

The Marzeaḥ Amos Denounces: Using Biblical Archaeology to Interpret a Biblical Text. *Biblical Archaeology Review* 15, no. 4 (1988): 34–44.

Judges, Book of. In *The Books of the Bible*, ed. B. Anderson. New York: Charles Scribner's Sons, 1989, vol. 1, 113–21.

Biblical Archaeology. In *The New Jerome Biblical Commentary*, ed. R. Brown, J. Fitzmyer, and R. Murphy. Englewood Cliffs, N.J.: Prentice-Hall, 1989, 1196–218.

The Great Eighth Century. *Bible Review* 5, no. 4 (1989): 22–33, 44.

Biblical Archaeology: Old Testament Examples. *The Bible Today* 27 (1989): 270–77.

The Marzēaḥ: Textual and Archaeological Evidence. In Yigael Yadin Memorial Volume of *Eretz-Israel: Archaeological, Historical, and Geographical Studies*, ed. A. Ben-Tor, J. Greenfield, and A. Malamat. Jerusalem: Israel Exploration Society, vol. 20 (1989), 98–106.

The Eighth, the Greatest of Centuries? *Journal of Biblical Literature* 108 (1989): 3–15.

Studies on the Mesha Inscriptions and Moab. Archaeology and Biblical Studies Series, ed. P. J. King. Atlanta: Scholars Press, 1989.

An Outline of Biblical History (p. 3135), Biblical Archaeology, Geography of the Holy Land (pp. 467–77). In *The Catholic Study Bible*, ed. D. Senior. New York: Oxford University Press, 1990.

Frederick Jones Bliss at Tell el-Hesi and Elsewhere. *Palestine Exploration Quarterly* 122 (1990): 96–100.

Survey of the Geography, History, and Archaeology of the Bible Lands. In *The New Oxford Annotated Bible with the Apocrypha*, ed. B. Metzger and R. Murphy. New York: Oxford University Press, 1991, 407–24.

Bible Lands: Exploring the Valleys of Jerusalem. *Bible Review* 7, no. 2 (1991): 28–33, 52.

Archaeology and the Book of Jeremiah. In Avraham Biran Volume of *Eretz-Israel: Archaeological, Historical, and Geographical, Studies* ed. E. Stern and T. Levy. Jerusalem: Israel Exploration Society, vol. 23 (1992), 95–99.

History of the American Schools of Oriental Research (vol. 1, 186–88); Jerusalem (vol. 3, 747–66). In *The Anchor Bible Dictionary*, ed. D. N. Freedman. New York: Doubleday, 1992.

The American Schools of Oriental Research. In *Biblical Archaeology Today, 1990: Proceedings of the Second International Congress on Biblical Archaeology*, ed. A. Biran and J. Aviram. Jerusalem: Israel Exploration Society, 1993, 13–16.

Micah, Book of. *HarperCollins Study Bible*, ed. W. A. Meeks. San Francisco: Harper and Row, 1993, 1379–90.

Jeremiah: An Archaeological Companion, Louisville, Ky.: Westminster/John Knox Press, 1993.

1 | Tel Dan: Biblical Texts and Archaeological Data

AVRAHAM BIRAN

Dan is first mentioned in the Bible in Genesis 14:14: "When Abram heard that his kinsman had been taken captive, he led forth his trained men . . . and went in pursuit as far as Dan" (RSV). At that time, the city was called Laish or Leshem, as we are told in Joshua 19:47 and Judges 18:29; a city by that name whose king is Horon-Ab appears in the Egyptian Execration Texts of the eighteenth century BCE. Nothing else is known about the early history of the city or its inhabitants.

The identification of Dan-Laish with Tel Dan, formerly Tell el-Qadi ("mound of the judge") at the source of the River Jordan, was made by Edward Robinson in 1838 and has never been seriously disputed. Moreover, archaeological excavations at Tel Dan, conducted by the author since 1966, have uncovered a bilingual inscription in Greek and Aramaic specifically mentioning Dan, definitively confirming the identification.

It is not my purpose in this essay to prove or disprove the accuracy of the references to Dan or Laish in the Bible. Rather, I wish to present the results of our archaeological research on the one hand and the related textual information on the other, affording a more comprehensive picture than is possible if the biblical evidence and the archaeological results are discussed separately.

The traditional date for the patriarchs is the first half of the second millennium BCE. The excavations of Tel Dan have revealed that by that time Dan-Laish was already a city with a long history. Founded in the fifth millennium BCE, it was a relatively large and prosperous city in the second millennium BCE, defended by a formidable sloping earth rampart and at least one impressive mud-brick triple-arched gate. This, I imagine, was the gate Abraham saw when he reached Dan-Laish (Gen. 14:14, fig.

FIG. 1-1. Eastern arch of the Laish gate.

1-1). If, as is likely, Abraham entered the city, he would have done so by going up the stone steps from the east through the three arches of the gate passage and down the stone steps west of the entrance to the street below.

Although we did not excavate the houses near the street, we found houses elsewhere in the town, built of stone and mud brick, with infant jar burials under the floors. We also found elaborate stone-built tombs in which several interments took place. The large assemblage of funerary offerings found in the tombs represents a rich material culture (fig. 1-2). The fact that we found houses and tombs built into the inner slope of the rampart indicates that the inhabitants had to seek living quarters beyond the limited space available within the crater at the foot of the inner ramparts.

The city Dan is next mentioned in the Bible in connection with the settlement of the tribe of Dan in the north of the country. The reference in Joshua 19:47 is brief: "the Danites went up and fought against Leshem, and after capturing it and putting it to the sword they took possession of it . . . , calling Leshem, Dan, after the name of Dan their ancestor." A more detailed account is given in Judges 18:27–29: "The Danites came to Laish . . . and smote them with the edge of the sword, and burned the city with fire. . . . And they rebuilt the city. . . . And they named the city Dan; . . . but the name of the city was Laish at the first." Earlier we are told that the land was "very fertile" (Judg. 18:9); indeed, the abundant waters

FIG. 1-2. Finds in one of the Middle Bronze Age tombs.

at the foot of Mount Hermon and the surrounding rich soil corroborate such a description. Furthermore, the inhabitants of Laish are described as "living in security . . . and unsuspecting" (18:7), implying that the people felt secure in their defenses. We may assume that this sense of security was due to the conviction that the formidable sloping earth ramparts were impregnable. The people seemed justified in their belief, for according to the archaeological evidence it had been a long time since calamity had befallen their city. While a destruction level of the sixteenth century BCE was found, this disaster must have been at best a dim memory at the time of the Danite conquest. This false sense of security of the people of Laish no doubt contributed to their downfall.

The archaeological evidence for the conquest of Laish by the Danites is circumstantial. In the sequence of occupation levels uncovered at Tel Dan, the excavation revealed a layer (Stratum VI) characterized by pits or silos, some of which are stone-lined and over 2 m deep. The pits are dug into earlier settlement strata of the end of the Late Bronze Age in the thirteenth century BCE. In some places they were dug into a deep pebble layer. Here and there a thin layer of ash could be detected. The pits contained large storage jars, or pithoi, and cooking pots dated to the twelfth century BCE, the Iron I period (fig. 1-3). Collared-rim jars, well

FIG. 1-3. Twelfth-century BCE pit with vessels.

known in the northern hill country and Judah, make their first appearance at Tel Dan in these pits. Neutron activation analysis of the collared-rim jars shows that some were made in Tel Dan and some in other parts of the country. The material culture represented by the pits is distinctly different from the one represented in the earlier strata of occupation, and the profusion of the pits indicates a change in the settlement pattern. Unlike the population of the previous settlement with its Mycenaean imports and urban character, a seminomadic population living in tents and huts is indicated by the pits in this stratum.

To identify this seminomadic people I return to Judges 18. On its way north, the tribe of Dan "encamped at Kiriath Jearim in Judah . . . called Mahaneh-dan to this day" (v 12). Mahaneh-dan, meaning "camp of Dan," indicates a seminomadic tribe who put the "cattle and the goods in front of them" (v 21). It is reasonable to conclude that the twelfth-century Stratum VI at Tel Dan represents the first settlement of the Danites at the site. That the change of population may not have been entirely peaceful is indicated by a very thin ash layer covering some of the remains of the Late Bronze Age city of Laish. If forced to choose between the references to the conquest of Laish in Joshua and in Judges, I would have to say that on the archaeological evidence the account in Joshua describes the event more accurately.

We know little of the activities of the Danites once they had settled at Tel Dan. The references to Dan in the blessings of Jacob (Gen. 49:16–17) and Moses (Deut. 33:22) and in the Song of Deborah (Judg. 5:17) may reflect the variety of occupations engaged in by the Danites, but the excavations have not as yet shed any light on these activities. However, the discovery of crucibles, copper slag, blow pipes, and furnaces in the pits of Stratum VI leads me to conclude that the new inhabitants engaged in metalwork (fig. 1-4). Whether metalwork was indigenous to the Danites, as may be inferred from the fact that a member of the tribe is said to have assisted in the construction of the Tabernacle (Exod. 31:6; 35:34; 38:23), or they learned the art from the original inhabitants of Laish is impossible to say. The latter is suggested by the remains of metalwork at Tel Dan already in the LB I period. The Danites' reputation as metalworkers may also be implied by 2 Chronicles 2:12–14, where it is reported that the king of Tyre, in response to Solomon's request, sends to Jerusalem an artisan whose mother is a Danite. That metalwork at Dan continued well into the eleventh–tenth centuries BCE is indicated by the results of our excavation.

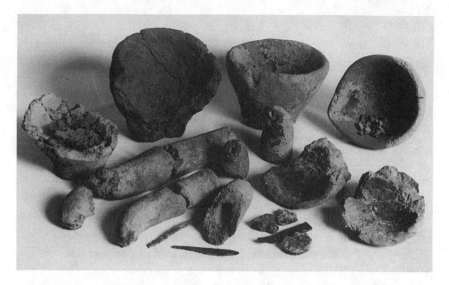

FIG. 1-4. Crucibles and blow pipes of tenth–eleventh centuries BCE.

The seminomadic character of the Danites did not last more than a generation or two. Our next level of occupation is represented by houses built of stone and mud brick, indicating that the Danites had become sedentary and urbanized. Their town, however, was destroyed in a violent conflagration in the middle of the eleventh century BCE, according to the evidence uncovered in every area excavated. There is no direct textual information about this destruction, but it may be alluded to in Judges 18:31. The statement that the *pesel* ("statue," "idol," "graven image"?) lasted as long as the house of God was in existence at Shiloh points to a destruction of Dan at the same time as that at Shiloh, in the mid–eleventh century BCE.

Judges 18 also states that the Danites brought cultic objects with them from the land of Benjamin. Whether they built a temple is not told. The fact that priests officiated at Dan (v 30) suggests the existence of a temple, but so far no remains of such a sanctuary have come to light. Possibly these lie beneath the considerable cultic remains uncovered in the northern part of the town near the spring. The earliest of these remains are dated to the late tenth–early ninth century BCE and consist of stone structures, altars, seven-spouted oil lamps, large pithoi with snake motifs, incense stands, a burnished bowl incised with a trident containing the bones of small animals, faience, and ceramic figurines. It is reasonable to suggest that these remains belong to a sanctuary built by Jeroboam I.

According to 1 Kings 12:28–29, Jeroboam I set a golden calf at Dan and at Bethel. The reason for doing so is explicitly stated in the text, but why Dan and Bethel? Probably because of their location at the northern and southern borders of Jeroboam's kingdom and because of their association with cultic tradition. The text does not indicate where at Dan the golden calf was set, but it was probably within the confines of the sanctuary, where the cult objects mentioned above were found.

In the days of Jeroboam the sanctuary at Dan extended over a relatively large area, at least 45 by 60 m. Such an area, with its various structures, storerooms, and open spaces paved with stone, may be the "houses on high places" mentioned in 1 Kings 12:31. Perhaps it was here that an altar or altars stood where the priests offered sacrifices and burned incense. That the sanctuary at Dan was of considerable importance may be adduced from 1 Kings 12:30, which states that the people went "as far as Dan." It appears, however, that the sanctuary built by Jeroboam did not last long. Evidence of conflagration on the stone blocks indicates that sometime in the first quarter of the ninth century BCE it was destroyed, possibly by Ben-hadad of Aram-Damascus, who "smote" Dan and other cities of northern Israel (1 Kings 15). The word "smote" may imply a limited punitive action rather than total destruction. If so, this is borne out in the excavations of Dan. No overall destruction of the city was uncovered, and the archaeological evidence from the sanctuary area seems to confirm a small incursion. A relic from this Aramaean attack may be the accidental discovery of the base of a pottery vessel with an Aramaic inscription dated on epigraphic grounds by Nahman Avigad to the ninth century BCE.

Following Ben-hadad's attack, a flurry of building activity took place at Dan. In the north, above the remains of Jeroboam's sanctuary, an almost square stone structure roughly 18.5 by 18.5 m was built, surrounded on three sides by a large courtyard of thick yellow travertine. The fine ashlar masonry laid in courses of headers and stretchers is a beautiful example of construction known from the royal buildings in Hazor, Samaria, and Jerusalem. One detail at Dan is of special interest. A number of ashlars were found in a slanting position. This was because originally wooden beams had been placed beneath the stones. When the wood decayed, the stones lost their supporting base and fell. According to 1 Kings 7:12,

Solomon's great court "had three courses of hewn stone round about, and a course of cedar beams." Many centuries later, Cyrus, king of Persia, decreed that the house of God at Jerusalem be rebuilt "with three courses of great stones and one course of timber" (Ezra 6:4). The method of construction found at Dan thus serves to illustrate the written text.

The square ashlar construction and other remains of this stratum are dated on archaeological grounds to the mid–ninth century BCE. There is no record in the biblical text of this extensive construction, but then there is no mention either of the complex city gate and fortifications discovered at the southern slope of the mound, also dated to the mid–ninth century BCE. The excavations revealed over 70 m of a wall 4 m thick, strengthened by buttresses, an outer gate, and an inner or main gate. In front of the entry gate is a flagstone pavement of which 140 m² have so far been exposed. Proto-Aeolic capitals found in the debris may have adorned the door jambs of the threshold (fig. 1-5). The flagstone pavement extends through the outer gate to the main gate of the city and continues to the top of the mound (fig. 1-6). The gate and city wall were destroyed in the second half of the eighth century BCE.

The discovery of a gate at Dan was not surprising; similar gates have been found elsewhere in Israel. Of special interest were some unique features, especially in the area between the outer and main gates. David sat "between the two gates" (2 Sam. 18:24). Here at Dan are two gates with a flagstone pavement between them, which vividly illustrates this verse. On another occasion David sat "in the gate . . . and all the people came" (2 Sam. 19:8). Boaz and the elders of Bethlehem "sat at the gate" (Ruth 4:1–2). The bench found at Dan along the northeastern tower of the main gate may have served the elders of the city, but where did the king sit? Jehoshaphat and the king of Israel "were sitting on their thrones, arrayed in their robes, at the threshing floor at the entrance of the gate of Samaria" (1 Kgs. 22:10). Where then did Hezekiah sit when he gathered his combat commanders in "the square at the gate of the city" (2 Chr. 32:6)?

I suggested early in the course of the excavations that the stone structure with four decorated column bases found at the entrance to the main gate of Dan could be the place where the king sat (fig. 1-7). The unusual capital with spiral leaf decoration found in 1992 in the debris covering the pavement may have belonged to this structure (fig. 1-8). The intriguing discoveries of 1992 suggest another possibility, however.

In the course of conservation and restoration work carried out by the

FIG. 1-5. Proto-Aeolic capital.

FIG. 1-6. Part of the royal processional pavement of the Israelite period.

FIG. 1-7. Structure with decorated bases at the right of the main Israelite gate.

FIG. 1-8.
Decorated capital.

Israel Antiquities Authority, an installation was uncovered consisting of five standing stones (*maṣṣēbôt?*) immediately to the right of the outer gate's entrance (fig. 1-9), together with many pottery vessels (fig. 1-10). This assemblage deserves special consideration because of the quantity—some fifteen whole vessels and fragments of ten others—and the nature of the vessels: oil lamps, small bowls, and incense cups, but no cooking pots or storage jars as found elsewhere on the pavement. Furthermore, these vessels show traces of fire on the inside, indicating that they had probably been used for burning incense. If, as is likely, the five standing stones are *maṣṣēbôt*, the whole installation may then be assumed to have cultic significance. The standing basalt monolith at the right of the threshold of the main gate, found early in the excavation (fig. 1-11), and the travertine monolith in front of the outer gate lend support to this suggestion. While I hesitate to ascribe religious significance to undefined architectural remains, we cannot entirely dismiss the idea, especially in view of 2 Kings 23:19, that as part of his religious reformation, Josiah "remove[d] the high places of the gate."

I believe I am justified in assuming the existence of a sanctuary at the gate of Dan. Whatever the case, the flagstone area of the gate complex at Dan, be it street, square, threshing floor, or high place, was much in use. The archaeological discoveries made at the Israelite gate of Dan are an important contribution to our comprehension of what took place at the ancient city gates of Israel and cannot be ignored when researching the meager textual references available.

The considerable building activities at Dan in the first half of the ninth century BCE should be ascribed to Ahab. This, of course, is based on indirect evidence. The continuous wars with the Aramaeans would have called for strengthening the defenses of Dan, the northern outpost of Ahab's kingdom. As a result of his victories, Ahab won the right to establish "bazaars in Damascus" (1 Kgs. 21:34). This, in turn, brought considerable prosperity and enabled him to engage in rebuilding and also enlarging the sanctuary, which had been destroyed by Ben-hadad.

In the first half of the eighth century BCE, Jeroboam II (2 Kgs. 14:25, 28) extended the boundaries of Israel as far north as Lebo-hamath and Damascus. No mention of Dan is made, but excavations at Dan have uncovered monumental steps built in the sanctuary area in the first half of the eighth century BCE, the time of Jeroboam's reign. A courtyard with a central altar was also erected, west of which was a room with an altar, three iron shovels, and a sunken jar containing ashes. Two incense altars

FIG. 1-9. Side view of the five standing stones.

FIG. 1-10. Vessels found next to the five standing stones.

FIG. 1-11. Basalt pillar at the entrance of the main gate.

were uncovered at the southern end of the room (fig. 1-12). It appears that the sanctuary of Dan had become even more important. The castigation of the people by Amos for following the cult there (Amos 8:14) may reflect the centrality of the cult of Dan at that time (fig. 1-13).

FIG. 1-12. Five-stone altar with two iron shovels.

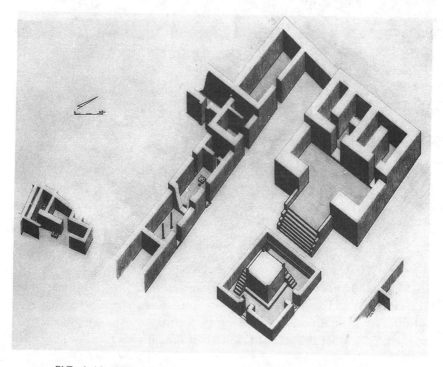

FIG. 1-13. Isometric cutaway view of eighth-century sanctuary.

FIG. 1-14. Seal impression of *zkryw*.

The building activities at Dan were not limited to the sanctuary area. In the center of the city a flagstone piazza was built on the way leading from the gate to the sanctuary. At the same time the defenses were strengthened. A wall was built halfway up the royal processional route to force would-be attackers to make an indirect approach. A gate and tower were built with the new wall, and an additional upper gate was built on top of the ridge. Again, no biblical text is available to tell who is responsible for these new fortifications. Possibly it was Jeroboam II, in anticipation of the Assyrian attack. An intriguing footnote may be added: a stamped jar handle with the name *zkryw* was found in 1991 (fig. 1-14). It is tempting to identify this individual with Jeroboam's son, Zechariah, who ruled for only six months (2 Kgs. 15:8).

Dan is not mentioned among the cities conquered by Tiglath-pileser III, but the excavations have revealed the total destruction of the defenses of the city in the second half of the eighth century BCE. A meter of burnt mud brick and stone collapse was found in the gatechambers, on the flagstone pavement, and in the upper gate area. Only one other area to the west of the sanctuary suffered the same fate, as is evident from a fierce conflagration layer. While it is clear why Tiglath-pileser could not allow the fortifications of Dan to remain intact, the reason for destroying the houses near the sanctuary remains a mystery. Dan as a whole was not affected by the Assyrian conquest, and the city continued to flourish.

Hezekiah's call (2 Chr. 30) to come and celebrate the Passover feast in Jerusalem may reflect a new relationship of Dan with the kingdom of Judah. Excavations have revealed that seventh-century BCE Dan was a city of well-built private houses and large public buildings, possessing a rich cosmopolitan material culture but no fortifications whatsoever. The prophet Jeremiah, at the end of the seventh century BCE, when warning the people of Jerusalem that the enemy was already at Dan (Jer. 4:15; 8:16), does not speak of Dan figuratively. He knew, and so did his listeners, that Dan at that time was a large and prosperous and undefended city. The Babylonian army, on their way south toward the conquest of Jerusalem, apparently left it in peace. There is no evidence of destruction at Dan from the beginning of the sixth century. Dan ceased to be a metropolis, however, and gradually declined. Only the sanctuary continued to function through the Hellenistic and Roman periods, probably to serve the needs of the population in the surrounding area.

SELECT BIBLIOGRAPHY

Biran, A.

1970a   A Mycenaean Charioteer Vase from Dan. *Israel Exploration Journal* 20:92–94.

1970a   Une Tribune Anarchique: Dan. *Bible et Terre Sainte* 125:8–15.

1974a   Tel Dan. *Biblical Archaeologist* 37, no. 2:25–51.

1974b   An Israelite Horned Altar at Dan. *Biblical Archaeologist* 37, no. 4:106–7.

1975   Dan, Tel. *Encyclopedia of Archaeological Excavations in the Holy Land*, ed. M. Avi-Yonah, 1:276, 313–21. Jerusalem: Israel Exploration Society and Massada Press.

1980   Tel Dan: Five Years Later. *Biblical Archaeologist* 43:168–82.

1981a   The Discovery of the Middle Bronze Age Gate at Dan. *Biblical Archaeologist* 44:139–44.

1981b   To the God Who Is in Dan. In *Temples and High Places in Biblical Times*, ed. A. Biran, 142–51. Jerusalem: Nelson Glueck School of Biblical Archaeology of Hebrew Union College–Jewish Institute of Religion.

1982   The Temenos at Dan. *Eretz-Israel* 16:15–43 (Hebrew).

1984a   The Triple Arched Gate at Tel Dan. *Israel Exploration Journal* 34:1–19.

1984b   Die Wiederentdeckung der alten Stadt Dan. *Antike Welt* 15:27–38.

1986   The Dancer from Dan, the Empty Tomb, and the Altar Room. *Israel Exploration Journal* 36:168–78.

1988 Histoire de Deux Villes. In *Archéologie, Art, et Histoire de la Palestine*, ed. E.-M. Larrousaz, 55–64. Paris: Les Editions du Cerf.
1989a The Collared-rim Jars and the Settlement of the Tribe of Dan. *Annual of the American Schools of Oriental Research* 49:71–96.
1989b The Evidence for Metal Industry at Dan. *Eretz-Israel* 20:120–34 (Hebrew).
1989c Prize Find: Tel Dan Scepter Head—Belonging to Priest or King? *Biblical Archaeology Review* 15, no. 1:29–31.
1990 The Middle Bronze II Ramparts at Tel Dan. *Eretz-Israel* 21:56–65 (Hebrew).
1992 *Tel Dan: 25 Years of Excavations at Tel Dan.* Tel Aviv (Hebrew).
1993 Dan. In *The New Encyclopedia of Archaeological Excavations in the Holy Land*, ed. E. Stern, 1:323–32. Jerusalem: Israel Exploration Society and Carta; and New York: Simon and Schuster.
Schulman, A. R.
1990 An Enigmatic Egyptian Presence at Tel Dan. In *Festschrift Jürgen von Beckerath*, ed. B. Schmitz and A. Eggebrecht, 235–44. Hildesheimer Ägyptologische Beiträge 30.
Tzaferis, V.
1977 A Bilingual Dedicatory Inscription from Tel Dan. *Qadmoniot* 10, no. 4:114–15 (Hebrew).
Wapnish, P.; B. Hesse; and A. Ogilvy
1977 The 1974 Collection of Faunal Remains from Tell Dan. *Bulletin of the American Schools of Oriental Research* 227:35–62.
Yellin, J., and J. Gunneweg
1989 Instrumental Neutron Activation Analysis and the Origin of Iron Age I Collared-rim Jars and Pithoi from Tel Dan. *Annual of the American Schools of Oriental Research* 49:133–41.

2 | "Who Is the King of Glory?" Solomon's Temple and Its Symbolism

ELIZABETH BLOCH-SMITH

Solomon's Temple, as described in 1 Kings 6—7, has exercised the ingenuity of both archaeologists and biblical scholars.[1] Archaeological studies have tended to concentrate on the constituent elements and minutiae, providing ancient Near Eastern parallels for architectural features, furnishings, and decorative motifs. In contrast, biblical scholars have focused on the general religious significance of the structure. Solomon's Temple is considered by many biblical scholars to be a symbolic representation of the heavenly abode and of creation, the paradisiacal garden of Eden (e.g., Levenson 1988:90–99; Smith 1992:160–61). The symbolism of the aggregate structure and its uniquely Israelite aspects are rarely emphasized in either archaeological or biblical discussions. In this essay, archaeological and biblical evidence will be used to reconstruct the Temple and to explicate its symbolism, for which Israelites needed no explanation.

THE OUTER COURTYARD

According to the account in 1 Kings, the outer courtyard at the Temple entrance contained an immense tank called "the molten sea," ten "lavers" or stands, and two towering pillars, all of which Hiram of Tyre cast in bronze (1 Kgs. 7:13–40). The lavers were positioned five to the right of the entrance and five to the left, and the tank was placed on the right, at the southeast corner (1 Kgs. 7:39). Though not specified, it is presumed that "the bronze altar" constructed during the reign of David or Solomon (1 Kgs. 8:64; 9:25; 2 Kgs. 16:14–15; 2 Chr. 6:13) also stood in the Temple's outer court (Busink 1970:321–24; Paul and Dever 1973:58; Meyers 1992d:359).

18

Archaeological parallels have been cited for each of the courtyard objects. The columns Jachin and Boaz (1 Kgs. 7:15–22) have been compared to flanking freestanding columns, column bases, or *maṣṣēbôt* from the Shechem Migdal temple (Middle Bronze), the Hazor temple of Stratum I (Late Bronze), and the Tell Tainat temple (Iron Age) (Ottosson 1980; Fritz 1987:40), as well as the Melqart temple of Tyre (Busink 1970:318).

The two freestanding pillars flanking the Temple porch entrance (1 Kgs. 7:15–22, 41–42) are generally agreed to attest to Yahweh's presence and power, although they have also been regarded as phalloi, stylish ornaments, fire altars, imitation Egyptian obelisks, and symbols for Yahweh (see Busink 1970:13–17 for a review of the literature). The twin pillars have been interpreted as gateposts or mythological "trees of life," symbolically announcing the indwelling of the god (Wright 1941:21; Paul and Dever 1973:257; Meyers 1992a:597–98; 1992d:360).

R. B. Y. Scott (1939) suggested that *yākîn* and *boʿaz* were the initial words of sentence-long dynastic oracles or prayers inscribed on the columns. In support of this interpretation, Victor Hurowitz (1992:257–58 n.2) cites several Mesopotamian and biblical examples. One Assyrian example, apparently composed for the dedication of several wooden columns to a temple in the city of Kar Tukulti-Ninurta (second half of the thirteenth century BCE), describes and provides measurements for the columns and their capitals, erected upon orders from the king, and mentions royal dedicatory inscriptions. In the following section on the Temple interior, it will be suggested that the Phoenician pillars are an adaptation of an earlier Mesopotamian practice of erecting flowering trees or branches to represent an attribute or symbolize the power of the deity resident in the temple. Seen from a distance, the ornate capitals atop the Jerusalem pillars may have given the columns a floral appearance. In Solomon's Temple, however, the inscriptions would have made explicit the blessings that were once implicit in the pillar/post representation.

The lavers, wheeled carts decorated with reliefs of lions, oxen, cherubim, and palm trees (1 Kgs. 7:27–38), have been reconstructed on the basis of similarly decorated bronze wheeled stands from Ras Shamra, Megiddo, Enkomi, and Kition (Busink 1970:338–48, 350–52; Paul and Dever 1973:258).

The explanation of the function of the so-called lavers is based upon a Chronicles text explaining that the wheeled stands supported basins used for rinsing parts of the burnt offering (2 Chr. 4:6). Each of the ten lavers consisted of a square wheeled stand or base supporting a basin. In relating the objectionable practices of Eli's sons at the shrine in Shiloh, the basin is mentioned in the context of boiling sacrificial meat (1 Sam. 2:12–16). The exaggerated size of the Temple stands has been argued to have precluded their daily use for boiling sacrificial meat (for a review of the literature, see Busink 1970:348–50); they may have served, however, as functioning or mimetic "hot carts," in conjunction with the altar where the sacrificial meat was roasted for the deity. It is not coincidental that ten carts stood in the outer courtyard, five to each side of the Temple entrance, and ten lampstands stood in the *hêkāl*, five to each side of the entrance of the *dĕbîr* (1 Kgs. 7:49). Perhaps the ten carts represented ten constituent groups or tribes, much as ten tribes formed the premonarchic confederation recorded in the Song of Deborah (Judges 5).

Assyrian, Cypriot, and Syrian parallels are cited for the immense "molten sea," which rested on the backs of twelve cast-bronze oxen (1 Kgs. 7:23–26). An Assyrian relief of Sargon II (last quarter of the eighth century BCE) depicts two huge cauldrons resting upon bulls' forelegs at the entrance to the temple of Musasir. Two large stone bowls, approximately 2 m (ca. 6 ft) in height and diameter, one of which had four handles on which bulls were carved in relief, have been reported from the vicinity of Amathus in Cyprus (Paul and Dever 1973:258). Additional bases rendered as oxen were uncovered in excavations from ninth-century BCE Tell Halaf and eighth-century BCE Tell Tainat (Busink 1970:332).

By the time of the Chronicler, the molten sea functioned in priestly ablutions (2 Chr. 4:6). The great size of the tank, however, in conjunction with the fact that no practical application is offered for the "sea" during the time of Solomon, supports the supposition that the tank served a symbolic purpose. Either the "cosmic waters" or the "waters of life," which emanated from below the garden of Eden, or the "great deep" of chaos is most often cited as the underlying symbolism for the molten sea (Meyers 1992c:1062). Another possibility consonant with Jerusalem cultic theology is that the molten sea symbolized the conflict between Sea and the other gods, a conflict attested in West Semitic literature. At Ugarit, Baal fought Sea and River in the first major section of the Baal cycle (CTA 2.4) (Cross 1973:118–19; Smith 1990:55). More speculative is Avraham Malamat's (1989:107) tracing back into early Mesopotamian tradition of the theme of the god or ruler defeating divine Sea, with an early second-millennium BCE king of Mari, Yahdun-Lim, claiming victories at the sacred sea and in the sacred forest.

The political function of the conflict story between the storm god and the cosmic sea has been recognized by Mark Smith (1990:56). Smith cites an early-eighteenth-century BCE letter from the prophet Nur-Sin of Aleppo to Zimri-Lim of Mari in which the god defeats Sea and then bestows the weapons upon the earthly king. The storm god Adad proclaims, "I s[et] you on the th[rone of your father]; the weapons with which I had battled against Sea I gave to you" (Durand 1993:45; Bordreuil and Pardec 1993). Just as Adad provided Zimri-Lim with the weapons to defeat Sea, so Yahweh empowered David to subdue Sea and River, "I will set his [the king's] hand upon the sea, his right hand upon the rivers" (Ps. 89:26 [NRSV 25]). The molten sea may have symbolized Yahweh's cosmic victories and extension of divine powers to the king.

Each of the courtyard items was of unusually great size, and, in the case of the tank and stands, significantly larger than the adduced ancient Near Eastern parallels. Jachin and Boaz rose a total of 23 cubits (ca. 12.2 m), consisting of a 5-cubit-high capital atop an 18-cubit-high stem. The immense tank, 10 cubits in diameter (ca. 5.3 m), held nearly 38,000 liters. Including the height of the wheels and the band that supported the basin, each stand/"laver" measured 4 cubits square (ca. 2.1 m) and 7 cubits high (ca. 3.7 m). The basin supported by each of the ten stands had a capacity of forty baths (ca. 920 liters).

Cosmic dimensions attributed to cities, temples, and gods convey temporal and spatial magnitude (Smith 1988; Hurowitz 1992:337). A god of cosmic size is omnipotent, omnipresent, and reigns for eternity. The immense cherub throne in the Temple *děbîr*, 10 cubits high and 10 cubits wide (ca. 5.3 by 5.3 m), attests to the Israelites' vision of their god as superhuman in size. Baal's throne of superhuman size (see below) and the meter-long footsteps carved into the portal and thresholds leading into the cult niche of the temple at ᶜAin Dara (Abu Assaf 1990:15–16) are further examples of late-second- to early-first-millennium Syrian conceptions of gods of superhuman size. Accordingly, the exaggerated size of the structures in the Solomonic Temple courtyard would suggest that they were not intended for human use, but belonged to the realm of the divine. As a hypothesis, it may be proposed that the courtyard symbols conveyed Yahweh's triumphant enthronement. Upon defeating the chaotic forces of nature, as represented by the molten sea, the god of the Israelites accepted the sacrificial offerings of the ten constituent groups or tribes and entered the Temple bestowing blessings on the king and the people, as recorded on the pillars flanking the Temple entrance.

THE TEMPLE INTERIOR

Like the courtyard, the Temple proper incorporated symbolism associated with the divine king. If the *'ûlām*, "porch," is reconstructed with a porticoed opening (1 Kgs. 7:19, 21), worshipers may have dimly perceived the gilded carved-wood reliefs of cherubim, ornamental palms, and calyxes that adorned the doors leading into the *hêkāl*. Identical gilded carvings adorned the shrine doors and interior walls as well. The exact configuration of the cherubim, palms, and calyxes is uncertain. Ezekiel describes wainscotcd walls decorated with a pattern of "cherubim and palm trees, with a palm between every two cherubim" (Ezek. 41:18). The lotus chain and guilloche border design of a Kuntillet Ajrud wall painting may echo the decorative borders of the Temple carvings (Beck 1982:56–58; see Strange 1985 for a discussion of the symbolism of the decoration including the floral border).

Ancient Near Eastern art predating and postdating Solomon's Temple is filled with composite creatures such as cherubim (winged felines with human faces) or griffins (winged felines with bird faces) that are subdued by and serve the deities. In carved stone wall reliefs, painted murals, and cylinder sealings, these composite creatures characteristically flank palms or stylized trees, either feeding from the tree or perhaps guarding it. Among later representations, an actual deity occasionally replaces the tree, or a divine emblem, such as the winged disc, hovers above. This scene of a "sacred tree" with flanking mirror-image creatures was usually incorporated into a larger scene that included deities with subservient priests, kings, or servants. Extensive studies treat both the tree motif (Meyers 1976) and cherubim (Pfeiffer 1922; Albright 1938; Busink 1970:267–72; Keel 1977:16–35). In this discussion of Solomon's Temple, only earlier and contemporary examples of cherubs associated with trees will be cited.

Date palms, stylized trees, cherubim, and a decorative border are all elements of a Mari palace mural. While the palace may date back to the reign of Yahdun-Lim, the murals are probably to be attributed to Zimri-Lim, who enlarged and rebuilt the palace in the early eighteenth century BCE. Miraculously preserved, the mural was painted on a thin layer of mud plaster just to the right of the entrance into the throne room (in Courtyard 106). Initially called "l'investiture du roi," the central scene is now thought to depict a different royal ritual or ceremony, perhaps the annual induction of the statue of Ishtar into the palace (Malamat 1989:23).

A two-storied rectangular structure fills the center of the mural. On the upper floor, the king stands before a goddess, and below, two mirror-image figures each hold a vase into which flow streams of water with fish. Stylized trees and date palms flank the structure, and an ornate decorative border frames the entire composition. Three tiers of animals stand alongside the stylized trees: at the bottom, an anthrocephalic(?) bull standing with forelegs on a mountain, above which is a griffin feeding from the tree, and on top, a winged sphinx or cherub wearing a feathered tiara. Human figures climb the date palms to harvest the fruit, and mirror-image figures with horned caps and arms raised as if in adoration stand beyond the palm trees facing the central scene (Parrot 1958:53–64).

On the basis of the stylized trees flanking the Temple, M.-T. Barrelet explained the scene as a ceremony taking place in the cella and antecella of a temple, which he interpreted as continuing the tradition of posts or emblems set up to frame the entrance to temples or animal stalls. Date palms flanking the entrance to the Sin Temple at Khorsabad and depictions on cylinder seals from Tell Billa and Tell Agrab, and on the stele of Gudea, provide additional examples of this practice (Barrelet 1950:9–15; see also Busink 1970:318–21). Such temple pillars or posts, which resemble flowering trees or branches, may have symbolized the divine attributes of longevity and fruitfulness, or virility and fertility, which could be bestowed upon supplicants or animals in the stalls (cf. Gen. 30:37–39). The Phoenician practice of erecting inscribed pillars flanking the temple entrance, such as at the Jerusalem, cAin Dara, and Tainat temples, may have replaced the early palm or stylistic tree representations.

Several elements of the Solomonic Temple are also found in the contemporary Level II temple at cAin Dara, in northwest Syria not far from Tell Tainat. The temple was constructed according to the Phoenician tripartite plan, with two immense columns flanking the entrance. Monstrous lions and cherubs depicted with stylized palms guarded the entrances to the temple platform and into the temple proper and the cella. The deity inhabiting the temple, in this case the goddess Ishtar, was also of superhuman size. "Divine" footprints, about one meter long, stand in the portico entrance, and then tread on the thresholds, first left and then right, leading into the cella. The single reported outer courtyard object was a large, though not immense, sacrificial basin found in the courtyard of the Level III temple (a temple virtually identical to its predecessor), which measured approximately 1.6 by 3.5 m (Abu Assaf 1990).

The motif of composite creatures such as the cherub in association

with palms or "sacred trees" is also well attested in the ancient Near
Eastern minor arts, especially glyptic art. On Mesopotamian cylinder
sealings, a deity or divine emblem usually appears in the scene.[2] The
greatest number of representations of trees and composite winged creatures without deities originate in Mittanni, Syria-Palestine, and Cyprus
(e.g., Porada 1947:52, figs. 63, 107; Vollenweider 1967: pl. 59.4, 5, 7;
Frankfort 1970:135, 248, 260, fig. 296; Collon 1982:12; 1987: figs. 271,
383; Schaeffer-Forrer 1983: R.S. 23.001, Chypre A12; Buchanan and
Moorey 1988: pl. IX.281). As expected, the nonglyptic representations of
winged sphinxes with "sacred trees" derive from the same regions: a gold-
leaf relief from the Late Bronze–early Iron Age Enkomi-Alasia Tomb 2, a
Gezer cylinder seal, and the Samaria ivories (Keel 1977:18).

Cherubim in association with trees were common elements in royal
and cultic contexts in ancient Near Eastern art. The extensive Israelite
literature permits speculation on the meaning of this motif and the constituent elements for the Jerusalem cult. Cherubim were stationed by
Yahweh to guard the way to the tree of life in the garden of Eden (Gen.
3:24), and they served as the divine chariot (1 Sam. 4:4; 2 Sam. 22:11=Ps.
18:11). While "tree" evokes the tree of life from the garden of Eden,
timōrâ, a tree related to the date palm, is specified in the Temple decoration. This variant form of the word for date palm may simply refer to an
ornamental tree or palmette, and not *Phoenix dactylifera*. Date palms
became a symbol for the righteous adherents of Yahwism who remained
vital and virile even into old age, like the date palm that sustained the
Israelites during their wandering in the desert (Exod. 15:27=Num. 33:9,
cf. Ps. 52:8). Psalm 92:13–16 expresses a conventional symbolic value of
the date palm (perhaps postexilic, see Kraus 1989:228), while nostalgically
evoking the date palm ornamentation on the Temple doors and walls:

> The righteous bloom like a date palm;
>   they thrive like a cedar in Lebanon.
> Planted in the house of the Lord,
>   they flourish in the courts of our God.
> In old age they still produce fruit;
>   they are full of sap and freshness,
> attesting that the Lord is upright,
>   my rock, in whom there is no wrong.
>   (New Jewish Publication Society translation)

As Ezekiel describes the configuration of palm trees and cherubim, the
tree is the focus of attention, flanked by cherubim (Ezek. 41:18–20). In

Mesopotamian sealings with this same configuration, a deity occasionally replaced the tree, demonstrating that the tree represented either the god personified by a symbol for an attribute (the tree as a symbol of longevity and fruitfulness) or divine powers and blessings (virility/fertility). Therefore, according to the conventional meaning of the motif as employed in Mesopotamia, the tree symbolized divinity or divine powers. Solomon probably adopted the motif of tree with flanking cherubim on the strength of its representation of the cherubim guarding the tree of life in the garden of Eden. The Temple itself thus represented the garden of Eden, Yahweh's residence and audience hall on earth, and the cherubim transported Yahweh down into the garden, formed his throne, and protected him.

In the innermost section of the Temple, Yahweh "enthroned upon cherubim" received supplicants (1 Sam. 4:4; 2 Kgs. 19:15=Isa. 37:14–16 and Ps. 99:1; 1 Kgs. 6:23–28). The earliest representations of cherub thrones are unique to the region of Syria-Palestine. William F. Albright (1938:2) cited examples from Byblos (Ahiram sarcophagus), Hamath, and Megiddo. Othmar Keel (1977:25, 29–30 n. 33, figs. 9, 15–17) added later examples: a figurine from Ayia Irini in Cyprus, Egyptian depictions in the tomb of Panchesi and on an ostracon in the Gayer-Anderson collection in Stockholm, and Phoenician sealings of Melqart on a cherub throne.

A telling feature of Yahweh's cherub throne was its magnitude. Great size signified importance, sovereignty, and, ultimately, divinity. Among men, Saul's great height marked him for kingship (1 Sam. 10:23; see Keel 1977:35). In the realm of the gods, according to the Ugaritic myths, Baal's throne was of superhuman size, so Athtar was denied Baal's throne for failing to measure up to the size of the throne that the king of the gods was to occupy (CTA 6.1.56–65) (Greenfield 1985). Ishtar's meter-long footsteps carved on the thresholds of the cAin Dara temple provide an indication of her imagined size. As mentioned in connection with the courtyard objects, the enormous size symbolized the spatial and temporal magnitude of the deity.

Greater Egyptian influence might have been expected in the Temple architecture, since Pharaoh's daughter was provided with a palace within the temple-palace complex (1 Kgs. 7:8). But a survey of archaeological parallels suggests that Egyptian features such as the sphinx were mediated through the Phoenicians. Although our knowledge of tenth-century BCE Phoenician art is limited, the winged sphinx, for example, while rare in Egypt (Dessenne 1957) is common in the art of Phoenicia and northern

Israel (e.g., Crowfoot and Crowfoot 1938). Even the literary genre of
building accounts follows Mesopotamian rather than Egyptian conven-
tions "in overall structure and in numerous linguistic and ideological
details" (Hurowitz 1992:26).

When the Temple wall reliefs are compared to Mesopotamian examples, the most striking feature is the absence of the deity and the king
from the Solomonic depictions. An aniconic proscription prevailed
(Mettinger 1979:24). Even in the "cult niche," the dēbîr, there was no
representation of the deity, only the "vacant throne" and the divine manifestation in the form of the ark (Keel 1977:37–45).

HUMAN AND DIVINE KINGSHIP
IN THE TEMPLE

Although explicit royal imagery was absent from the Temple decoration,
the construction of the Temple nonetheless conveyed divine endorsement
of Solomon's kingship. The proximity of the Temple and the royal palace
together with the carefully chosen symbols in the Temple courtyard com-
municated to the assembled worshipers Yahweh's sponsorship of the
human king.

Solomon adopted a prevalent architectural plan that served to bolster
his ideological position. The palace-temple complex or citadel was a common Near Eastern architectural feature. M. Ottosson (1980:51) noted
that "langhaus-type [temples] always seem to share their courtyards with a
'palace.'" Syro-Palestinian examples have been excavated at Megiddo,
Hazor, Beth Shan IX, and Shechem from the Bronze Age, and at Tell
Qasile and Beth Shan Lower V from the Iron Age (62). Solomon's Temple was an imposing structure, bigger than its contemporaries in Syro-
Palestine (112), but the national shrine was built in the shadow of the
larger, adjacent palace, prompting T. A. Busink (1970:161) to claim that
Solomon built a "Palastburg, keine Tempelburg."

Symbols and images are effective only when their meaning is known.
The monarchy needed a mechanism for instructing worshipers in the
explicit and implicit meanings of the cult symbols. Hebrew cultic texts
may have served to articulate and transmit the symbolic meaning of the
courtyard objects and their relationship to the Temple proper. The cultic
repertoire, exemplified by 2 Samuel 22:8–16 (= Ps. 18:8–16), Psalm 29,
and early elements of Psalms 89 and 93 (Cross 1973:135, 152, 158–62;

but see Kraus 1988:258; 1989:201–2, 232–33 for difficulty in dating these psalms), recounted Yahweh's victories over the earth and its creatures, including the sea, concluding with a description of the warrior god enthroned in his Temple for eternity. This overall progression is matched by Exodus 15:1–18. Verses 1–2, devoted to the victory over the Egyptians, use the mythic language of divine conflict with Sea. Verses 13–18 culminate in the creation of the residence for god and people alike.

As the Temple represented the garden of Eden, the molten sea perhaps symbolized secondarily the primordial waters issuing forth from Eden (Gen. 3:10), and the twin pillars modeled the trees (of life and knowledge) planted in the garden. This interpretation of the pillars and tank symbolizing Eden, while consistent with the interior decoration, needs to account for the stands/lavers and the great size of all the courtyard objects. Conflict followed by enthronement and empowering of the king is a preferable interpretation of the Temple architecture since it supports the monarchy more explicitly than the themes of Yahweh as creator and the garden of Eden.

The outer courtyard symbols in conjunction with the Temple proper were constructed as a public display to convey Yahweh's triumphant enthronement and endorsement of the monarchy. After defeating the chaotic forces of nature, symbolized by the molten sea, Yahweh extended his powers to the monarch (Ps. 89:26) and designated Zion, the holy mountain won in battle, to be the seat of eternal divine (and human) sovereignty (Exod. 15:1–18; 2 Sam. 22:8–16; Pss. 29; 89; 93). Sated with offerings, Yahweh entered his Temple, thereby bestowing blessings on the king and the people, as recorded on the pillars flanking the Temple entrance. Solomon's choice of palmette and cherubim motifs to adorn the walls and doors conveyed to Temple visitors that the Temple proper recreated or incorporated the garden of Eden, Yahweh's terrestrial residence.

Whereas Mesopotamian building accounts were written in general, poetic language to glorify the building and the builder, the account in 1 Kings is "striking in the exact details given, and especially the fact that dimensions are provided. . . . The information provided by the biblical inscriptions seems to be intent on enabling the reader actually to visualize the building or object described" (Hurowitz 1992:246). Scrutinizing the literary record of Solomon's Temple in light of the material culture, and vice versa, produces a revised image of the temple and its symbolic function in the Israelite cult.

NOTES

1. I am deeply indebted to my husband, Mark S. Smith, of St. Joseph's University, for the ongoing discussions and careful editorial hand that enabled this wedding of archaeology and text.

2. The competing cherub and calf representations of Yahweh in Israelite tradition may derive from the two different iconographic traditions depicting storm gods which are preserved on Syro-Mesopotamian cylinder seals. D. Collon (1987:170) has noted the change in animals attending the storm god beginning with second-millennium BCE representations. It was during the third-millennium BCE Akkadian period that the winged composite creature was introduced as a chariot or throne for the god and goddess. In cylinder sealings of the period, the storm god and goddess stand on the backs of winged lion-griffins (e.g., Amiet 1980: #769, Appendix 5, "Images of Gods and Goddesses"). First Dynasty Babylonian seals continue use of the motif (e.g., Frankfort 1939: pl. 27*i*) and introduce a variant form, in which the storm god, standing in his chariot, cracks a whip over a winged monster spitting fire or lightning, on the back of which rides the nude storm goddess (e.g., Frankfort 1939: pl. 22*a*). Beginning in the second millennium BCE, the storm god and goddess were also depicted with an attendant bull. First Dynasty Babylon sealings show the storm god both with the winged-lion and with the bull or calf (Amiet 1980: Appendix 5, "Images of Gods and Goddesses"). Second-millennium Syrian cylinder seals also depict the storm god with a bull or calf, on the back of which occasionally stands a nude goddess (e.g., Porada 1947: fig. 101; Amiet 1980: Appendix 5, "Images of Gods and Goddesses"). On an Akkadian seal from about 1500 BCE, the storm god brandishes a mace and holds a flail and the leash of his bull (e.g., Collon 1987: fig. 787). The Israelite (storm) god was eventually divorced from the nude goddess or consort present in both the winged creature and bull/calf iconographic traditions.

WORKS CITED

Abu Assaf, A.
1990   *Der Tempel von ʿAin Dara*. Damaszener Forschungen, 3. Mainz: Philip von Zabern.

Albright, W. F.
1938   What Were the Cherubim? *Biblical Archaeologist* 1:1–3.

Amiet, P.
1980   *Art of the Ancient Near East*. Translated by J. Shepley and C. Choquet, from French. 1977. New York: Harry N. Abrams.

Barrelet, M.-T.
1950   Une Peinture de la Cour 106 du Palais de Mari. *Studia Mariana* 4:9–35.

Beck, P.
1982   The Drawings from Ḥorvat Teiman (Kuntillet ʿAjrud). *Tel Aviv* 9:3–68.

Bordreuil, P.; and D. Pardee
1993   Le combat de *Ba'lu* avec Yammu d'après les textes ougaritiques.
              Mari Annales Recherches Interdisciplinaires 7:63–70.
Buchanan, B., and P. R. S. Moorey
1988   *Catalogue of Ancient Near Eastern Seals in the Ashmolean Museum,
              Vol. III: The Iron Age Stamp Seals.* Oxford: Clarendon.
Busink, T. A.
1970   *Der Tempel von Jerusalem von Salomo bis Herodes. Band I: Der Tem-
              pel Salomos.* Leiden: E. J. Brill.
Collon, D.
1982   *The Alalakh Cylinder Seals: A New Catalogue of the Actual Seals
              Excavated by Sir Leonard Woolley at Tell Atchana, and from Neighbor-
              ing Sites on the Syrian-Turkish Border.* BAR International Series,
              132. Oxford: British Archaeological Reports.
1987   *First Impressions: Cylinder Seals in the Ancient Near East.* Chicago:
              University of Chicago Press.
Cross, F. M.
1973   *Canaanite Myth and Hebrew Epic: Essays in the History of the Religion
              of Israel.* Cambridge, Mass.: Harvard University Press.
Crowfoot, J. W., and G. M. Crowfoot
1938   *Samaria-Sebaste I: Early Ivories from Samaria.* London: Palestine
              Exploration Fund.
Dessenne, A.
1957   *Le Sphinx. Etude iconographique, I: Des origines à la fin du second
              millénaire.* Bibliothèque des écoles françaises d'Athènes et de
              Rome, 186. Paris: Boccard.
Durand, J. M.
1993   Le mythologème du combat entre le dieu de l'orage et la mer en
              Mésopotamie, *Mari Annales Recherches Interdisciplinaires* 7:41–61.
Frankfort, H.
1939   *Cylinder Seals: A Documentary Essay on the Art and Religion of the
              Ancient Near East.* London: Macmillan and Co.
1970   *The Pelican History of Art: The Art and Architecture of the Ancient
              Orient.* 4th rev. Middlesex: Penguin Books.
Fritz, V.
1987   Temple Architecture: What Can Archaeology Tell Us about
              Solomon's Temple? *Biblical Archaeology Review* 13:38–49.
Greenfield, J.
1985   Ba'al's Throne and Isa. 6:1. In *Mélanges bibliques et orientaux en
              l'honneur de M. Mathias Delcor,* ed. A. Caquot, S. Légasse, and M.
              Tardieu, 193–98. Alter Orient und Altes Testament, 215. Keve-
              laer: Butzon and Bercker, and Neukirchen-Vluyn: Neukirchener
              Verlag.
Hurowitz, V. (A.)
1992   *I Have Built You an Exalted House: Temple Building in the Bible in*

Light of Mesopotamian and Northwest Semitic Writings. Journal for the Study of the Old Testament Supplement Series, 115/American Schools of Oriental Research Monograph Series, 5. Sheffield: JSOT Press.

Keel, O.
1977   *Jahwe-Visionen und Siegelkunst: Eine neue Deutung der Majestätsschilderungen in Jes 6, Ez 1 und 10 und Sach 4.* Stuttgarter Bibelstudien 84/85. Stuttgart: Verlag Katholisches Bibelwerk.

Kraus, H.-J.
1988   *Psalms 1–59: A Commentary.* Translated by H. C. Oswald, from German. 1978. Minneapolis: Augsburg.
1989   *Psalms 60–150: A Commentary.* Translated by H. C. Oswald, from German. 1978. Minneapolis: Augsburg.

Levenson, J. D.
1988   *Creation and the Persistence of Evil: The Drama of Divine Omnipotence.* San Francisco: Harper and Row.

Malamat, A.
1989   *Mari and the Early Israelite Experience.* The Schweich Lectures of the British Academy, 1984. Oxford: Oxford University Press.

Mettinger, T.
1979   The Veto on Images and the Aniconic God in Ancient Israel. In *Religious Symbols and Their Functions*, ed. H. Biezais, 15–29. Scripta Instituti Donnerians Aboensis, 10. Stockholm: Almqvist and Wiksell.

Meyers, C. L.
1976   *The Tabernacle Menorah: A Synthetic Study of a Symbol from the Biblical Cult.* American Schools of Oriental Research Dissertation Series, 2. Missoula, Mont.: Scholars Press.
1992a   Jachin and Boaz. In *Anchor Bible Dictionary*, ed. D. N. Freedman, 3:597–98. New York: Doubleday.
1992b   Lavers. In *Anchor Bible Dictionary*, ed. D. N. Freedman, 4:241–42. New York: Doubleday.
1992c   Sea, Molten. In *Anchor Bible Dictionary*, ed. D. N. Freedman, 5:1061–62. New York: Doubleday.
1992d   Temple, Jerusalem. In *Anchor Bible Dictionary*, ed. D. N. Freedman, 6:350–69. New York: Doubleday.

Ottosson, M.
1980   *Temples and Cult Places in Palestine.* Boreas, Uppsala Studies in Ancient Mediterranean and Near Eastern Civilizations 12. Uppsala: Uppsala University.

Parrot, A.
1958   *Mission Archéologique de Mari, Vol II. Le Palais: Peintures Murales.* Institut Français d'Archéologie de Beyrouth. Bibliothèque archéologique et historique, 59. Paris: Paul Geuthner.

Paul, S., and W. G. Dever, eds.
1973   *Biblical Archaeology*. Jerusalem: Keter.
Pfeiffer, R. H.
1922   Cherubim. *Journal of Biblical Literature* 41:249–50.
Porada, E.
1947   *Mesopotamian Art in Cylinder Seals of the Pierpont Morgan Library*. New York: Pierpont Morgan Library.
Schaeffer-Forrer, C. F.-A.
1983   *Corpus des Cylindres-Sceaux de Ras Shamra-Ugarit et d'Enkomi-Alasia*. Vol. 1. Éditions Recherche sur les Civilisations, 13. Paris: Association pour la Diffusion de la Pensée Française.
Scott, R. B. Y.
1939   The Pillars Jachin and Boaz. *Journal of Biblical Literature* 58:143–49.
Smith, M. S.
1988   Divine Form and Size in Ugaritic and Pre-exilic Israelite Religion. *Zeitschrift für die alttestamentliche Wissenschaft* 100:424–27.
1990   *The Early History of God: Yahweh and the Other Deities in Ancient Israel*. San Francisco: Harper and Row.
1992   The Psalms as a Book for Pilgrims. *Interpretation* 46:156–66.
Strange, J.
1985   The Idea of Afterlife in Ancient Israel: Some Remarks on the Iconography in Solomon's Temple. *Palestine Exploration Quarterly* 117:35–40.
Vollenweider, M.-L.
1967   *Catalogue Raisonné des Sceaux Cylindres et Intailles*. Vol. 1. Geneva: Musée d'art et d'histoire Genève.
Wright, G. E.
1941   Solomon's Temple Resurrected. *Biblical Archaeologist* 4:17–31.

3 | Archaeological Reflections on Amos's Targets

EDWARD F. CAMPBELL

Therefore because you trample on the poor
    and take from them levies of grain,
you have built houses of hewn stone,
    but you shall not live in them;
you have planted pleasant vineyards,
    but you shall not drink their wine.
For I know how many are your transgressions,
    and how great are your sins—
you who afflict the righteous,
    who take a bribe,
and push aside the needy in the gate.

                        (Amos 5:11–12, NRSV)

Alas for those who lie on beds of [inlaid] ivory,
    and lounge on their couches,
and eat lambs from the flock,
    and [fatted] calves from the stall. . . .

                        (Amos 6:4, NRSV augmented)

Hear this, you that trample on the needy,
    and bring to ruin the poor of the land,
saying, "When will the new moon [festival] be over
    so that we may sell grain;
and the sabbath [observance],
    so that we may offer wheat for sale?
We will make the ephah [dry measure] small
    and the shekel [counterweight] great,
    and practice deceit with false balances,
buying the poor for silver
    and the needy for a pair of sandals,
    and selling the sweepings of the wheat."

                        (Amos 8:4–6, NRSV augmented)

Hot words that burn the ears! Whose ears? To whom did the prophetic speaker address such critique?

Recent commentaries have usually gone in one of two directions in analyzing the composition of the Amos book, one seeing it as a rolling corpus beginning from Amos's eighth-century BCE career and accumulating updatings through the subsequent two centuries (e.g., Wolff 1977; Coote 1981), the other seeing it pretty much in its entirety as a product of the prophet and his own life span (e.g., Andersen and Freedman 1989; Paul 1991).

Whichever path is followed, the three passages quoted above, along with other strident critiques of those with power, are confidently assigned to Amos himself and dated to the mid–eighth century. They form a corpus to which Philip King's archaeological commentary (1988) has paid substantial attention. Composed in artistic judgment speech form (reason-plus-consequence), they certainly seem to fit the life of Samaria, capital city of the Northern Kingdom, in the time of Jeroboam II. Another passage pictures the wives of the ruling establishment as heifers of Bashan joining in the fruits of the high life gained by exploitation (4:1). All this we can place alongside the archaeological evidence of Samaria's ashlar citadel, its collection of fine ivory inlays, and the ostraca that catalogue shipments of luxury goods from the surrounding region to the capital. Surely Amos targets the capital.

But was Samaria Amos's only target? The problems addressed seem to be broadly societal. Indications of a wider audience come in Amos 4:1, which speaks not specifically of Samaria but of "Mount Samaria"—likely to be a regional reference. In 3:9 the "strongholds" of Ashdod and Egypt are to assemble on the mountains of Samaria to witness what will happen when Yahweh responds to the violations going on in Israel's "strongholds." This term (*'armĕnôt*) refers to forts, citadels, and fortifications, but in such a way as to make witnesses of those who populate them—those who live not just in the capital but also in surrounding, strategically located settlements. Amos addresses economic injustice and trade infractions, connecting some to home worship observances, others to practices at the "house of their God" (2:8)—at Bethel, Dan, or other worship centers. Amos speaks of judgments rendered in the gates—the locations where elders saw to the administration of community justice (e.g., Ruth 4 set in Bethlehem's "gate"). In short, he aims at a number of segments of the population at a variety of locations; his message, and even he himself, doubtless got around the countryside.

One neighbor of Samaria, 12 km (less than 8 miles) southeast by a direct road (Dorsey 1991:140–42), was the famous old city of Shechem. Shechem was in the eighth century at least a central market place, a candidate for Ze'ev Herzog's categories of "major administrative city" or "secondary administrative center," rather than his "provincial town" (1992:250–64). It was crucially sited at a major road junction. From Shechem, a road led through the Gerizim/Ebal Pass—a major security point in the central hill country—before dividing into main routes west to the coastal plain and northwest to Samaria. Another road led north through a narrow defile to Tirzah and the head of the Wadi Farᶜah, the major route to the Jordan Valley from the central hills. Shechem sat at the apex of a broad-armed, boomerang-shaped *sahl* of rather rich agricultural land spreading east and south; it looked out upon daughter towns and villages and military outposts in all directions surrounding its ample upland breadbasket (fig. 3-1; see Campbell 1992:95). Although there is much more we wish we knew about Building 5900 at Shechem, it was clearly a large granary (Currid 1989), making Shechem a likely candidate for administrative center of Solomon's first district of 1 Kings 4:8 (G. E. Wright 1967). Would not Amos's words to exploiters apply here as well? To what part of the population?

To get at this, I want to focus on the excavated dwellings of the eighth century in Shechem, the homes of the population who participated in the commonplace life of the times. Years ago, Roland de Vaux proposed that the house precincts in Tirzah (Tell el-Farᶜah North) Stratum II (specifically now Niveau VIId) displayed a discrepancy between wealth and poverty in light of which he invoked Amos 5:11, an interpretion many at the time thought naive (1967:377–78). But de Vaux's early effort at reconstructing social history should not be too quickly ignored.

At Shechem, coherent exposures of domestic occupation were studied in Fields VII and IX, both at the west center of town (fig. 3-2). Field VII lay at higher elevation and closer to the "hub" of life near the Northwest Gate. In both fields, remains of Stratum VII, securely dated to the period leading up to the Assyrian destruction of the city about 724 BCE, are well attested. One of the strongest pieces of evidence for the dating is the presence in the destruction debris of House 1727 (Field VII) of an exquisitely cut, early drilled-style Assyrian adorant seal (G. E. Wright 1965: Fig. 82:6), lost by a member of the invading Assyrian forces who sacked Samaria in 721.

As an archaeological context, House 1727 and its immediate surroundings relate effectively to Amos (cf. King 1988:61–64). It belongs to the familiar category of the four-room Israelite house (Shiloh 1970; Netzer 1992a). Is there anything about it that suggests it might be the home of those whom Amos targeted? G. Ernest Wright (1978:153) designates it a cheaply built house in comparison with other examples from Tirzah and Tell en-Nasbeh, but Amihai Mazar (1990:487) speculates it belonged (with others like it at Hazor and Tirzah) to "high officials, rich families, or landlords." It deserves a more detailed look, especially in light of ethnoarchaeological data collected in Iranian villages by P. J. Watson (1979) and C. Kramer (1979; 1982) and the study of family life and social conditions by Lawrence Stager (1985).

First about the preparations to site the house. Prior to its period of building, the terrain in Field VII, even though terraced, had sloped perceptibly from northwest to southeast. In Stratum IX, Shechem's ninth-century stratum, elevations on floors within houses here dropped down almost one meter from north to south. Even within a room, there was distinct declination. The whole Shechem mound is on the slopes of Mount Ebal. At no previous time at Shechem, from MB IIC to the eighth century, had a concerted effort been made to create level grades on which to construct domestic houses, though the elaborate filling and leveling for Shechem's Fortress Temple in the acropolis area are well known (G. E. Wright 1965:88–89).

The builders of House 1727 made the deliberate decision to level the ground between two old terrace walls before building, thereby destroying most of the evidence of Stratum VIII remains immediately below. They placed a retaining wall just off the southeast corner of where the house would sit, set deep into Stratum IX levels—it is designated "underpinning" on the plan (fig. 3-3). Against it they packed rocks and soil, probably from the Stratum VIII debris they were replacing.

They laid a leveling blanket of chocolate-brown soil under what would become Rooms 1, 2, and 6—the front half of the house. The result was a platform, consolidated and very nearly horizontal, with a slight uniform pitch to the east southeast. The platform neatly contains the house plus a narrow access path from the north along its east (front) wall.

Drainage involved the use of sumps. One lay just outside the front door to its south. It was 90 cm deep and 1.25 to 1.5 m in diameter, and was packed with sherds and pebbles. This leaching matrix was so loose we were able to excavate it with bare hands. No channeling was found beneath Room 1, so we suspect that a downspout or a "gargoyle" on the roof was positioned above the sump.

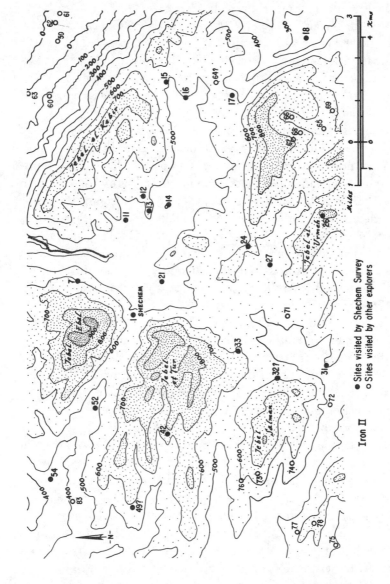

FIG. 3-1. Map of the Shechem region, showing surrounding sites where Iron II pottery has been found in surface survey. Dot-shading suggests relative altitude; note the open agricultural plain to east and south of the center market city.

FIG. 3-2. Aerial view of the Shechem tell; Field VII, site of House 1727, is left of center; Field IX, now back-filled, is represented by the earth hump near the orchard just right of upper center. Photo: Lee Ellenberger.

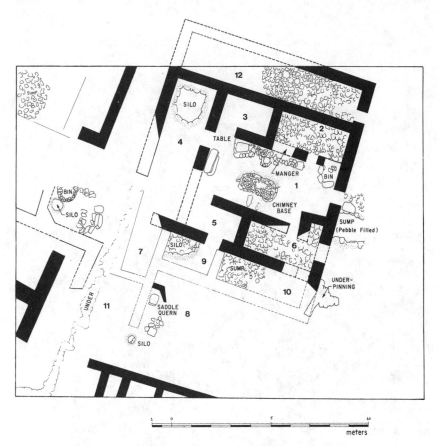

FIG. 3-3. Block plan of House 1727 and environs. Drawing by Kimberly Djerf.

Under Rooms 9 and 10, a drainage channel connected the "silo" in Room 9 with another sump in Room 10, and then ran toward the under-pinning wall at the southeast corner of the complex. Rooms 9 and 10 constituted an addition to the original design. Apparently the silo was first another sump, and the channel and sumps were part of the original drainage system; when Rooms 9 and 10 were added, the silo replaced the west sump and the other features went out of use.

With these elaborate preparations made, the builders constructed the house against the old terrace wall, which bowed slightly and had been refurbished repeatedly since the tenth century (Stratum X). They brought it to a height a meter or so above the level of the newly created platform, and produced another level platform behind it to the west. A passageway led out of Room 4, with steps giving access to the neighbors uphill. A facing (note the west wall of Room 7) was placed against the terrace wall at its south end, producing a straight line for the back wall.

The design the builders had in mind is comparable to forty or more homes known from archaeological remains. Rooms 1 through 6 constitute the core, 10.4 m by an average of 8 m—not a true rectangle— measured from the outside of the perimeter walls, yielding 83.2 m², to compare with measurements used by ethnographers in Iran. Its interior available space, deducting for the interior wall thicknesses, is about 65 m², a size that places it with the smaller of the four-room houses at Tell el-Farᶜah North (Chambon 1984:31–48, especially chart on p. 32).

Four-room houses consist of three parallel blocks of space with a long block across the ends of the three. As with our example, so with most, the two side parallel blocks and sometimes the end block are divided up into a variety of arrangements, resulting in five, six, or more rather small rooms. As usual, the central block is wider than the others; it is regularly interpreted as having been open to the sky, atrium style. Recently, however, that assumption has been widely challenged by interpreters who would roof the central room—and evidence from House 1727 is a major reason why.

Some things stand out about House 1727 at Shechem: the nature of the debris, and the variations from the standard form, especially in terms of augmentation to the plan and use of the central room. To elaborate:

1. Room 12 augments the standard design. It was cobbled throughout, although only the eastern two-thirds shows the cobbling preserved. (In the balk lying across the back part of this room cobbling shows in section.) The wall between Room 12 and Rooms 2, 3, and 4 is well preserved and has no doors through it. People living in the main house had to go out the front door to get into Room 12. Room 12 was part of the original design (cf. Holladay 1992:316). Though the east wall of the whole structure had tumbled eastward and is preserved in situ only at foundation level, it was laid as a continuous line, and it makes a bonded corner with the wall along the north of Room 12. Elevations on Room 12's cobbling correspond to those in the main house, and beneath it was the same chocolate-brown leveling material.

2. Rooms 7, 9, and 10 are a later addition. The walls separating 7 and 9, 9 and 10, abut the south wall of the main house, and the south wall of these rooms shows a different construction technique. Where all other

walls of the house are one rock thick, this wall is of two rows of rocks as preserved. There is an access from Room 5 to Room 9—whether punched through after the augmentation of the structure (less likely) or an original side door (more likely).

3. In the original design, residents could exit the house at its southwest corner into a yard, which filled all of spaces 7 through 11—a substantial 7 by 10 m of open area. South of this yard was sited another house, set down into Stratum IX remains in a huge shallow foundation excavation just at the south edge of Field VII—remains of parts of its walls appear on the plan. The residents of the two houses probably shared the yard, including the saddle quern and rubbing stone in a little circle of stones near House 1727, and the silo nearby. Judging from parallels elsewhere, and by ethnographic analogy to village arrangements in Iran, bread ovens and other food-processing installations would be located outside in this manner, and often would have been shared by the surrounding house-holds. Note, however, that a cooking pot and juglet were found crushed on the floor of Room 4 just against the (robbed-out) wall in its southeast corner. Some cooking was done on the ground floor, then, indoors. And on the floor of Room 4 near the silo was found an intact Cypro-Phoenician juglet of excellent design (G. E. Wright 1965: fig. 85); whether it contained some fine food product we cannot be sure.

4. Room 1 contains many features typical in four-room houses and other dwellings, along with some unique features. Typical: the wall between Rooms 1 and 2 is primarily defined by two large *nari* limestone pillars. The lowest blocks are preserved, standing about 50 cm high. Between the east pillar and the front wall of the house is a stone-lined circular basin projecting into the central room. Between the west pillar and the west wall of Room 2, a break in the cobbling and a thin wall define a small space John Holladay has proposed as a manger—or the location for a manger (1986:117–20). The thin wall runs on, then, as a low platform along the wall between Rooms 1 and 3, ending in a huge flat-topped rock, its top smoothed and worn—and with this we depart from the typical. Is it a built-in "counter-top" or chopping block? The adjacent platform has a jar stand with the base of a store jar in it. Bins and their like are typical in central rooms of four-room houses, but whatever this work-facility was, it is unparalleled so far as I can find.

Another unusual feature is the huge block of limestone near the back wall of Room 1, roughly shaped but not smoothed. It is propped in place by small stones. Also without parallel is the kidney-shaped stone-filled fire pit in the center of Room 1, 2 m long and 85 to 100 cm wide. Abundant evidence of smothered burn and of ash was on and around it, with quantities of what we posit was calcined lime, long since slaked and returned chemically to calcium carbonate.

On the assumption that House 1727 was a one-story house, Room 1 was presumably the main living room. A living room should have a warming hearth; Watson found one as a regular feature of homes in Hasanabad, Iran (1979:122, 124). But both her information and indications from Israelite sites suggest that a warming hearth would be small, 30 to 50 cm in diameter. The familiar basalt three-legged braziers were for this purpose (Jer. 36:23). So also were the tops of store jars, their rim and shoulder planted inverted in the floor; Shechem's Stratum IX complex in Field VII has an example.

The outsized fire pit in Room 1 is not a warming hearth, then, but almost certainly industrial; our working hypothesis has been that it was used to burn limestone to calcium oxide, quicklime (G. E. Wright 1978:153, who misused the term "slaking"). But this operation would require temperatures upwards of 900° centigrade. Even with Room 1 open to the sky, lime production there now seems an erroneous guess— although burning to lime was certainly an operation familiar to the times (Amos 2:1). No other explanation has commended itself.

As for the huge rock near the back wall, Ernest Wright proposed it was being shaped as ashlar, although no building elsewhere at Shechem used ashlar. A huge shaped block forms one course of the wall between Room 1 and Room 3 (fig. 3-4, center). A quartzite rubbing stone weighing 18.2 kg (40 lb) lay on the floor of Room 1; it may well have been used to shape the softer limestone. The family that lived in House 1727 may have worked both at shaping rock and at burning limestone to lime, in the central room of their ground floor.

In 1964, two years after its discovery, the expedition dismantled the fire pit and found immediately beneath it a *nari* vat, a flat limestone grooved platter, and a collecting jar (fig. 3-5). A nearly identical set of equipment had been found over the ruins of the East Gate in 1956 (G. E. Wright 1965: fig. 89). The platter is 90 cm in diameter, and the circular groove inside its perimeter channeled liquid through a spout into the collecting jar. The vat is oblong with interior diameters from 80 to 150 cm and is 55 cm deep. With the discovery of beam-press olive processing installations in houses at Ekron (Gitin and Dothan 1987:208–10) and Timnah/Tel Batash (Borowski 1987:117–26) belonging to the seventh

FIG. 3-4. Ruins of House 1727. Note fire pit, limestone block to its right, *nari* pillar-blocks flanking entrance to Room 2 in left center, and the shaped block in wall of Room 3, lower center. Photo: Lee Ellenberger.

century, we can properly conclude that this was an eighth-century precursor, representing a cottage industry (Mazar 1990:489–91); note a contemporary parallel from recent work at Hazor (Ben-Tor 1992:256).

All the industries evidenced in Room 1, with the probable exception of olive pressing, apparently transcend the needs of one family; they yielded a surplus and are pertinent to assessing the family's wealth and activity in commerce. Room 1 was work space, perhaps with more than one industry going on at a time, and with changes in industry over time.

Holladay (1992:312–16; 1990; 1982) has taken House 1727 as a case study to test the utility of ethnoarchaeological analogies from studies by Watson (1979) and Kramer (1979, 1982) of modern traditional villages in Iran. We can expect to find in homes some features belonging to the economic domain, some to the living domain. Part of the economic domain will have been for the care of animals, including much storage space for feed and straw; here will have been equipment for cottage industries; other spaces will have stored some of the family's food and fuel supplies. As for the living domain, it will need to have been sufficient in size for a family to sleep and eat, make clothing and store furnishings, and

FIG. 3-5. Olive press from beneath the fire pit in Room 1, the earlier industry in the economic domain of House 1727. Photo: Lee Ellenberger.

entertain guests. Ethnoarchaeological analogies suggest at least seven and more likely about ten square meters of living-domain space per family member.

If the ground floor was the economic domain, in figure 3-6 we see a proposal worked out by Holladay for how the rest of the space might have been used. Room 2 would stable two large animals (cows, donkeys), the bins serving as mangers. Cobbling is appropriate flooring for hoofed animals, and it allows liquid waste to percolate through and solid waste to be mucked out (Holladay 1986:133–44, 153–54). Holladay proposes Room 3 as a stall for a home-stalled calf. It should be noted that its doorway was blocked at some point during the use phase of the house, perhaps to make it into a pen where it had earlier served for storage. Other ground-floor rooms were used for storage, while Room 6 with its cobbling was probably another space for one or two hoofed animals. If the industrial activity required hot fires, as we have proposed, one of the rooms would have stored animal dung for fuel.

The stone-lined silo in Room 4 may have stored barley for animals or may have held the family's wheat stock. As for Room 12, its cobbled floor

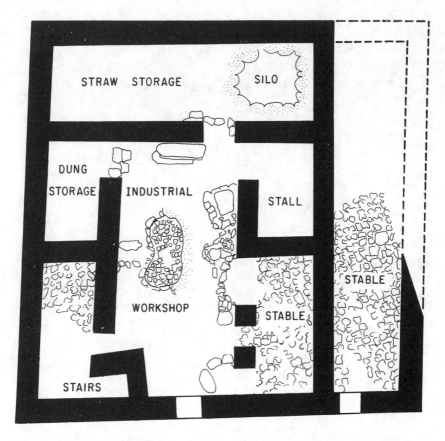

FIG. 3-6. Proposed uses of the ground floor of House 1727.

again suggests animal space—perhaps sheep and goats. The chocolate-brown fill beneath the east half of the house raises the question whether people knew it to be a good layering to let animal urine percolate through. Years after the excavation, we now wish we had subjected the layer to Holladay's proposed test for elevated phosphate levels (1986:154–56).

Room 6 may have held the access to the second floor, by ladder, or by stairs with a landing in the elbow in the northeast alcove; this must have been rather typical in four-room houses, though Hazor and other sites preserve instances where stairways run up the outside of the house.

What about the second floor? G. E. Wright (1965:161) proposed wall thicknesses on the ground floor of at least 60 to 80 cm, assuming thick mud plaster on the stone cores, and speculating that they were planned to be two cubits (89 cm) thick. But fragments of the wall plaster were recovered, and it would have added only about 5 cm to each face, yielding a total thickness of 50 to 55 cm. The load-bearing strength of the wall would, of course, have been in the rock core.

G. R. H. Wright in his invaluable study of Syro-Palestinian architecture has sought to assess the strength and quality of rubble walls as found in Israelite house construction, but he also indicates that we have not yet developed information about the capacity of walls to bear second floors in ancient construction (1985:292, 332–48, 396–408, and passim). Even the assumption that a two-stone-thick wall of, say, 80 cm thickness would bear weight better than a 45-cm, one-stone-thick wall is by no means to be taken for granted. In this connection, it should be said that observations made by de Vaux and A. Chambon about features of Houses 327 and 328 of Level VIId at Tell el-Farᶜah North, while pertinent to the care with which they were built and hence to the relative wealth of the owners, may speak more to local conditions confronting the builders than to whether they were sturdier or more capable of sustaining a second story than a structure like House 1727 (Chambon 1984:39–48; de Vaux 1967:377–78).

It is the destruction debris in House 1727 that establishes that houses of this kind had second floors. G. E. Wright (1965:161) describes the pairs of split logs serving as ceiling beams lying in Room 1. He proposes they slid to this position from over the side rooms onto the floor of the unroofed atrium, Room 1. The preserved pieces of log were found, though, in the center of Room 1, just to the east of the fire pit. They lay flat on the floor as though they had fallen from directly above; no brick debris lay beneath them. Above them were pieces of flooring of a noteworthy style of construction, 6 to 7 cm thick and of three layers, the lowest of whitish mud plaster with straw binder, the second of red clay with pebbles, the third of a white plaster flecked with calcite and polished smooth on its surface. (Geologist Reuben Bullard and I searched for sources of calcite near Shechem and found the nearest location on the summit of Mount Gerizim more than a mile away, so the creation of this "terrazzo" effect required effort and intention.)

Huge slabs of multilayered roofing landed in vertical orientation in Rooms 4, 5, and 9 (G. E. Wright 1965: fig. 80); adjacent were collapsed segments of mud-brick wall, next to the stone walls. It happens that nowhere in the house did roofing slabs lie on top of second-story flooring on top of ground-floor remains. Such stratification would clinch the reconstruction here proposed.

Apparently the entire house, except for Room 12, had a second story. The fire pit in Room 1 would have been in an enclosed room, vented through windows (Hosea 13:3) or possibly via a chimney, the only vestiges of which would be the two rows of stone between the fire pit and the south wall of Room 1. As for smoke, Watson observed at Hasanabad:

> Every Hasanabad living room is equipped with a hearth used for cooking, heat, and also for light if the family cannot afford a lantern or the necessary kerosene. . . . No special provision is made for the escape of smoke, so that all things and persons who remain for long in the room are permeated with it, and the roof beams and ceiling are well blackened. (Watson 1979:122)

If smoke and soot could be tolerated in the living room, it certainly could be in a work room, and there is an advantage: the result would be a warm second floor.

Holladay then takes the second floor as living domain (fig. 3-7). One pertinent piece of evidence snaps into focus: as many as a dozen clay loom weights were found in second-floor debris, indicating that the family loom was in one of the rooms upstairs. Assuming that upper walls of mud brick rode directly over ground-floor stone walls, this layout yields about 52.5 m² of covered living space, or, with the proposed third-floor "upper chamber," about 67 m². On Kramer's figure of 10 m² per person (see also Naroll 1962; LeBlanc 1971), that points to five, six, or seven family members; it would be seven to nine on the space requirement Watson calculated at Hasanabad (7 m²). We can speculate that one of the children married, and this was the occasion for adding rooms 7, 9, and 10, also with a second story. Megan Williams's reconstruction shown in figure 3-8 does not include the addition, but it does make Room 12 part of the original structure, and it adds the upper chamber. It proposes that the roof would have been strewn with branches and other debris to add to its protection. Note also that it places in the background the upper terrace with houses on it about a meter above the level of the platform on which House 1727 sits.

When destruction came, the east wall of the house and a mass of burned debris cascaded over the terrace wall at the east limit of the platform, carrying the terrace wall with it. In the debris was the Assyrian adorant seal—a hint that the Assyrian soldiers actually pulled the house down.

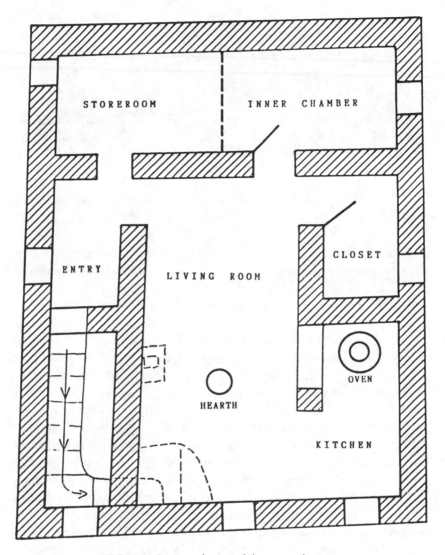

FIG. 3-7. Proposed uses of the second story.

Did the Assyrians select this part of town for destruction? The scraps of Stratum VII houses on the upper terrace just to the west show nothing like the same preservation of destruction debris, probably because the first Hellenistic builders (Stratum IV) leveled the terracing throughout all of Field VII. As a result they cleared to Stratum VII floor levels on the upper terrace, removing any remains of Strata VI and V that may have

5m

FIG. 3-8. Artist's reconstruction of House 1727, drawn by Megan Williams.

been there. Two isolated pockets of broken Stratum VII pottery on the upper terrace suggest that destruction was widespread on the terracing in this part of town.

On the other hand, in Field IX the end of Stratum VII shows no evidence of massive destruction. The structures there, which continue the layout of the preceding Stratum VIII buildings and show a phase of refurbishing within Stratum VII, were largely made of mud brick on skimpy stone foundations. Small humps of decaying mud brick show no evidence of fire that would have hardened them. Just at the north edge of the field is the corner of a stone-walled building that began its life in Stratum VIII and continued through to Stratum VI. This one structure looks to be as substantially built as House 1727, and it has a segment of flagstone flooring within its preserved elbow. But the debris with that building again does not show massive destruction. As to whether housing in Field IX had second floors, the evidence makes it doubtful. Mud brick, which is a stronger building material than we might think, is still inferior to stone; it is questionable that it could carry the weight of a second story unless the first-floor walls were made of kiln-fired brick rather than sun-baked—and we would then have more of it preserved. The small accumulation of debris in Field IX does not suggest two-story buildings.

It seems, then, that the Assyrians did demolish selectively. They may have chosen the houses that would yield better loot. Or they may have sought to punish and intimidate community leaders. This pattern of destruction is but one more of the indications that there was economic and social diversity at Shechem in the eighth century.

To summarize the evidence and our inferences:

1. House 1727 was sited on an elaborately prepared terrace and carefully founded on select materials; preparation was much finer than for the homes in Field IX.

2. Across an open yard from House 1727 was another house for which substantial preparation was made; this time a deep foundation trench was dug into earlier strata.

3. The large open yard meant even more space for the family or families living here, even what might be seen as recreational space.

4. The two-story construction of House 1727 permitted a large space for the economic domain. Its family lived beyond the level of subsistence agriculture, keeping many animals, storing quantities of grain, and carrying on industries that point toward surplus that could be traded.

5. The "terrazzo" flooring in House 1727 and the Cypro-Phoenician juglet are possible evidences of relative affluence. We do not have a wide range of artifacts or much of the building material in the Field IX buildings—they were not smothered by debris and preserved for us—so comparative judgment on that kind of indicator is admittedly hazardous.

6. Apparently the Assyrian army selected the region where House 1727 was for destruction and went about purposefully pulling this house down.

There does seem to be enough to go on here to posit that Shechem attests differentiation of lifestyle and wealth. Holladay (1992:316–17; 1990) risked a judgment about what disparities the attested houses might suggest, concluding that the range was not very great, and that social and economic egalitarianism was more nearly the condition among the peasant farmers who dwelt in these four-room houses. In an unpublished draft of his 1992 article he suggests that "the range of social inequality was probably closer to 'two or three times as rich' than to an order of magnitude (10 times richer)" (1990:22). But it should be remembered that the economy of the land was itself relatively close to marginality. As R. B. Coote has put it (1981:24–32), peasant farmers in an advanced agrarian society are always close to the edge of economic viability. To me it seems probable that the domestic housing evidence from Shechem as well as Tirzah, Hazor, and other such sites points to the reality a prophet like Amos faced. It was not just the significantly wealthy at the court at Samaria but also people who lived only relatively better than their neighbors who may have been tempted to take advantage of others, to cheat them in trading, to live too comfortably for the well-being of the community. The evidence of House 1727 at Shechem should be factored into our attempt to comprehend the conditions in the mid–eighth century that would call forth the invective of an Amos—to assess what goes into creating, or violating, a just and righteous society in monarchic Israel, and to sense what sends a herdsman and orchard farmer like an Amos from Tekoa to the loci of power, influence, and injustice.

WORKS CITED

Andersen, F. I., and D. N. Freedman
1989   *Amos: A New Translation with Introduction and Commentary*. Anchor Bible 24A. New York: Doubleday.
Ben-Tor, A.
1992   Notes and News: Tel Hazor, 1992. *Israel Exploration Journal* 42:154–260.
Borowski, O.
1987   *Agriculture in Iron Age Israel*. Winona Lake, Ind.: Eisenbrauns.
Campbell, E. F.
1992   *Shechem II, Portrait of a Hill Country Vale: The Shechem Regional Survey*. American Schools of Oriental Research Archaeological Reports. Atlanta: Scholars Press.
Chambon, A.
1984   *Tell el-Far'ah I: L'Âge du Fer*. Editions Recherche sur les Civilisations, no. 31. Paris: Association pour la Diffusion de la Pensée Française.
Coote, R. B.
1981   *Amos among the Prophets: Composition and Theology*. Philadelphia: Fortress.
Currid, J. D.
1989   A Note on the Function of Building 5900 at Shechem—Again. *Zeitschrift des deutschen Palästina-Vereins* 105:42–46.
Dorsey, D. A.
1991   *The Roads and Highways of Ancient Israel*. Baltimore: Johns Hopkins University Press.
Gitin, S., and T. Dothan
1987   The Rise and Fall of Ekron of the Philistines: Recent Excavations at an Urban Border Site. *Biblical Archaeologist* 50:197–222.
Herzog, Z.
1992   Settlement and Fortification Planning in the Iron Age. In *The Architecture of Ancient Israel from the Prehistoric to the Persian Periods: In Memory of Immanuel (Munya) Dunayevsky*, ed. A. Kempinski and R. Reich, 231–74. Jerusalem: Israel Exploration Society.

Holladay, J. S.

1982   The Palestinian House: A Case Example of the Use of Ethnographic Analogy in Archaeological Reconstruction. Unpublished manuscript, with kind permission of the author.

1986   The Stables of Ancient Israel: Functional Determinants of Stable Construction and the Interpretation of Pillared Buildings of the Palestinian Iron Age. In *The Archaeology of Jordan and Other Studies Presented to Siegfried H. Horn*, ed. L. T. Geraty and L. G. Herr, 103–65. Berrien Springs, Mich.: Andrews University.

1990   House, Israelite. Preprint version of Holladay 1992 (below), containing substantial additional detail. Unpublished manuscript, with kind permission of the author.

1992   House, Israelite. In *The Anchor Bible Dictionary*, ed. D. N. Freedman, 3:308–18. New York: Doubleday.

Hopkins, D. C.

1985   *The Highlands of Canaan: Agricultural Life in the Early Iron Age*. Sheffield: Almond.

King, P. J.

1988   *Amos, Hosea, Micah: An Archaeological Commentary*. Philadelphia: Westminster.

Kramer, C.

1979   An Archaeological View of a Contemporary Kurdish Village: Domestic Architecture, Household Size, and Wealth. In *Ethnoarchaeology: Implications of Ethnography for Archaeology*, ed. C. Kramer, 139–63. New York: Columbia University Press.

1982   *Village Ethnoarchaeology: Rural Iran in Archaeological Perspective*. New York: Academic Press.

LeBlanc, S.

1971   An Addition to Naroll's Suggested Floor Area and Settlement Population Relationship. *American Antiquity* 36:210–11.

Mazar, A.

1990   *Archaeology of the Land of the Bible*. New York: Doubleday.

Naroll, R.

1962   Floor Area and Settlement Population. *American Antiquity* 27:587–89.

Netzer, E.

1992a   Domestic Architecture in the Iron Age. In *The Architecture of Ancient Israel from the Prehistoric to the Persian Periods: In Memory of Immanuel (Munya) Dunayevsky*, ed. A. Kempinski and R. Reich, 193–201. Jerusalem: Israel Exploration Society.

1992b   Massive Structures: Processes in Construction and Deterioration. In *The Architecture of Ancient Israel from the Prehistoric to the Persian Periods: In Memory of Immanuel (Munya) Dunayevsky*, ed. A. Kempinski and R. Reich, 17–27. Jerusalem: Israel Exploration Society.

Paul, S.
1991   *Amos: A Commentary*. Hermeneia—A Critical and Historical Commentary on the Bible. Minneapolis: Fortress.

Reich, R.
1992   Building Materials and Architectural Elements in Ancient Israel. In *The Architecture of Ancient Israel from the Prehistoric to the Persian Periods: In Memory of Immanuel (Munya) Dunayevsky*, ed. A. Kempinski and R. Reich, 1–16. Jerusalem: Israel Exploration Society.

Shiloh, Y.
1970   The Four-Room House: Its Situation and Function in the Israelite City. *Israel Exploration Journal* 20:180–90.

Stager, L. E.
1985   The Archaeology of the Family in Ancient Israel. *Bulletin of the American Schools of Oriental Research* 260:1–35.

Vaux, R. de
1967   Tirzah. In *Archaeology and Old Testament Study*, ed. D. W. Thomas, 371–83. London: Oxford.

Watson, P. J.
1979   *Archaeological Ethnography in Western Iran*. Tucson: University of Arizona Press.

Wolff, H. W.
1977   *Joel and Amos*. Hermeneia—A Critical and Historical Commentary on the Bible. Philadelphia: Fortress.

Wright, G. E.
1965   *Shechem: The Biography of a Biblical City*. New York: McGraw-Hill.
1967   The Provinces of Solomon. *Eretz-Israel* 8:58*–68*.
1978   A Characteristic North Israelite House. In *Archaeology in the Levant: Essays for Kathleen Kenyon*, ed. R. Moorey and P. Parr, 149–54. Warminster, England: Aris and Phillips.

Wright, G. R. H.
1985   *Ancient Building in South Syria and Palestine*. 2 vols. Handbuch der Orientalistik 7.Abt.: Kunst und Archäologie. Leiden: E. J. Brill.

Yadin, Y.
1972   *Hazor: The Head of All Those Kingdoms*. The Schweich Lectures, 1970. London: Oxford University Press.

4 | Archaeology and the Messiah Oracles of Isaiah 9 and 11

DAN P. COLE

> For unto us a child is born . . . and the government shall be upon his shoulder.

Few words were to have as much importance in setting the direction for later Jewish messianic anticipation and for Christian proclamation as the oracles of the "messiah" in Isaiah 9:2–7 (Heb. 9:1–6) and 11:1–9.

Accumulating data from archaeological discoveries, beginning in the nineteenth century and continuing into most recent decades, have provided an increasingly strong argument for interpreting Isaiah's "messiah" oracles as initially focused on Hezekiah on the occasion of Jerusalem's deliverance from the Assyrian siege of 701 BCE. When the results of biblical analysis and the archaeological record are viewed together, the argument becomes even stronger.

THE ROYAL MESSIAH: A NEW THEME IN HEBREW PROPHECY

If the oracles in Isaiah 9 and 11 can be attributed to Isaiah of Jerusalem, they contain our earliest prophetic assertions that Israel's God, Yahweh, would deliver his people from oppression by means of a descendant of David ("a shoot from the stump of Jesse") on whom the "spirit of the LORD" would rest, who would establish a "kingdom of everlasting peace."[1]

The label "messiah" (literally, "anointed one") derives, of course, from the tradition in early Israel of anointing the newly acclaimed king's head with oil to symbolize the infusion of Yahweh's powerful "spirit." Isaiah does not invoke the term, but he alludes clearly to the process of divine anointment in both oracles when he asserts that "the zeal of Yahweh of hosts will do this" (Isa. 9:7) and "the spirit of Yahweh shall rest upon him" (Isa. 11:2).

The later biblical historians asserted that the ritual itself was initiated by Yahweh (1 Sam. 9:16; 10:1; 16:12–13). In actual practice, one must ask whether the ceremony may have originated not from within the religious community but from within the royal court, as a calculated device to provide religious legitimacy for the king (cf. 1 Kings 1:23–40). We do not have the first-person witness of a historical Samuel or Nathan to confirm the accounts or to tell us whether the early anointment ceremonies represented more than royal public relations pageantry.

When we turn to the earliest preserved prophetic collections, it is significant that neither Isaiah's prophetic predecessors nor Isaiah himself in his early oracles had held any positive thoughts for the kings who had been sitting on the thrones of Israel and Judah. Amos incurred the wrath of the northern king's priest at Bethel by declaring that "Jeroboam shall die by the sword" (Amos 7:11). Hosea asserted that the idea of kingship had never been approved by Israel's God: "They made kings, but not through me; they set up princes, but without my knowledge," and he went on to report Yahweh saying that "they shall cease for a little while from anointing kings and princes" (Hos. 8:4, 10; see also Hos. 7, especially vv 1, 5, and 13:10–11). Micah, Isaiah's contemporary, had dire prophecies for the rulers of both northern and southern kingdoms (Mic. 3:1–4, 9–12).[2]

Isaiah of Jerusalem stood solidly in this same tradition. His early oracles contain only grim words concerning Judah's rulers. Like Hosea, he forecasts an end of kings and a return to charismatic "judges" (Isa. 1:23, 26, 28).

Isaiah's early experiences with Judah's kings did not inspire religious admiration in him. In recalling his commissioning theophany, he places the death of King Uzziah (who died as a leper; see 2 Kings 15:5) in juxtaposition with his exalted vision of the Israelites' true king, Yahweh, seen "sitting upon a throne, high and lifted up" (6:1–2). In the following chapter, his encounter with the weak and vacillating King Ahaz leads to the threat that "the LORD will bring upon you and upon your people and upon your father's house such days as have not come since the day that Ephraim departed from Judah—the king of Assyria" (7:17).[3]

The question arising from the biblical text itself, therefore, is what led Isaiah to abandon this antimonarchical tradition and to envision a divinely sent deliverer of Israel in the form of a Davidic king.

CLUES FROM THE BIBLE

Without looking beyond the biblical texts, it could already be suggested that Isaiah's abrupt change of mind may have been inspired by the actions of Hezekiah. The biblical histories portrayed him as a devotee of Yahweh who enacted extensive religious reforms (2 Kgs. 18:3–6; 2 Chr. 29—31) and then—after attempts at appeasement had failed—as having courageously defied Sennacherib's demands for surrender when Assyrian forces besieged Jerusalem in 701 BCE (2 Kgs. 18:13—19:37; 2 Chr. 32:1–23).[4]

The siege apparently was abandoned suddenly and dramatically and was followed by a general retreat by Sennacherib from the region. We probably have an independent testimony to that dramatic reversal in the story recounted 250 years later to the Greek historian Herodotus by Egyptian priests. According to them, when Sennacherib was about to attack Egypt, "thousands of field-mice swarmed over them during the night, and ate their quivers, their bowstrings and the leather handles of their shields, so that on the following day, having no arms to fight with, they abandoned their positions and suffered severe losses during their retreat" (Herodotus 1972:185–86). On the basis of this account, some have suggested that Sennacherib's forces were struck by plague carried by rodents.

The later Deuteronomic historians understandably attributed the deliverance of Jerusalem to their God's direct intervention. "And that night the angel of the LORD went forth, and slew a hundred and eighty-five thousand in the camp of the Assyrians; and when men arose early in the morning, behold these were all dead bodies. Then Sennacherib king of Assyria departed, and went home, and dwelt at Nineveh" (2 Kgs. 19:35–36).

Isaiah lived through the trauma of the siege and the exhilaration of its sudden end. He already had been attuned to seeing Yahweh's hand at work in the Assyrians' victories (Isa. 7:17; 8:4–8; 10:5–6), after which he anticipated that Yahweh would also punish the Assyrian king for his pretensions and rapacious conduct (Isa. 10:5–15). Surely he would have attributed the sudden lifting of the enemy siege at Jerusalem to Yahweh's intervention, whatever its observable causes. It would not be a difficult step beyond that for him to have acclaimed Hezekiah as having been charismatically anointed to carry out Yahweh's plan to protect his people and his city.

Since early in the history of biblical criticism, some scholars have pointed to Hezekiah's stand against Sennacherib as the plausible occasion for Isaiah's exultant words in chapters 9 and 11. Most of them, however, have not taken advantage of the available archaeological data to advance their argument.

Other scholars have continued to look to different historical contexts for the origin of these messianic oracles. At one extreme are those who have seen the oracles as expressions of hope for rebuilding from the postexilic period (Gray 1912:165–68, 213–14; and note 1). At the other extreme is the recent commentator who postulates Hezekiah's father Ahaz as the focus of these oracles (Hayes and Irvine 1987:182).

Even among those who have seen Hezekiah reflected in Isaiah 9 and 11, many have preferred a date preceding the Sennacherib campaign. The clause "to us a child is born, to us a son is given" has suggested to some that the oracles were issued when Hezekiah was still an infant. Another common view has been that the oracles were composed for the occasion of Hezekiah's enthronement (Scott 1956:232, 247).

While opposing views of biblical scholars cannot be summarily dismissed, a growing body of archaeological data greatly strengthens the argument that it was the events of 701 BCE that inspired these earliest oracles concerning the Davidic messiah.

THE ARGUMENT FROM ARCHAEOLOGY

The archaeological evidence has come from four different quarters. Excavations in Assyria in the nineteenth century provided dramatic witness for the severity of Sennacherib's military operations in Palestine. During the twentieth century, diggings at Lachish and other sites in ancient Judah have documented the surprising extent of the devastation wrought by his forces. From Jerusalem has come information concerning the ambitious nature of Hezekiah's defensive measures. Finally, we should note the evidence from Egyptian coronation texts suggesting an origin for the imagery and structure of Isaiah's messianic oracles in the tradition of royal liturgy.

Sennacherib's Might Documented
in Assyria

The earliest evidence relevant to Hezekiah's confrontation with Sennacherib emerged from Austen Henry Layard's campaigns of 1846 to 1851 at Nineveh, Sennacherib's palace city. He found an exceptionally elaborate

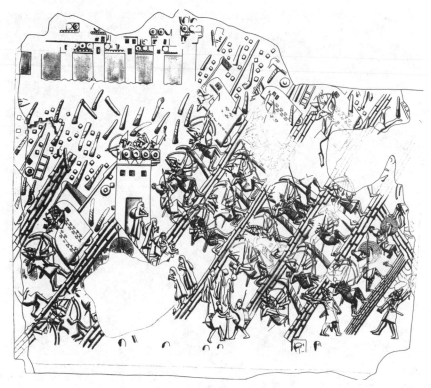

FIG. 4-1. Lachish under Assyrian siege, from the Nineveh Frieze, Panel III. Drawing by Judith Dekel (Ussishkin 1982:82).

and extensive palace complex, "seventy-one halls, chambers and passages, whose walls, almost without exception, had been paneled with slabs of sculptured alabaster recording the wars, the triumphs and the great deeds of the Assyrian king." In one centrally positioned room (perhaps an audience hall), he uncovered a dozen slabs that graphically depicted Sennacherib's methods of warfare being ferociously applied during the attack on Lachish, a major city of Judah.[5]

The twelve large orthostats composing this battle frieze, now in the British Museum, present a panoramic view of the besieged city—a strongly fortified one with defenders on the towers of two circuit walls. The slopes beneath the walls are crowded with Assyrian attackers in the various activities of a well-organized assault (fig. 4-1). Siege machines on wheels are being rolled up wooden roadways laid over a huge earthen siege ramp to pry loose wall stones at the corners of towers. Elsewhere on

FIG. 4-2. Sennacherib on his throne before Lachish, from the Nineveh Frieze, Panel VIII. The British Museum; photo by the author.

the rampways are ordered ranks of armored spearmen, archers, and sling-stone throwers. At the base of the slope soldiers are impaling prisoners on high poles within view of the city's defenders, while defeated citizens carrying their possessions file out of a portal beneath a tower.

Both the city and the ruler besieging it are clearly identified on the frieze itself (fig. 4-2). On a hill to the right of the battle a figure in Assyrian royal garb sits on an elaborately decorated portable throne. He is receiving a report from an Assyrian official while Judahite prisoners grovel in the background. Behind the king two eunuchs, standing in front of his personal tent, waft fans to cool his head. A cuneiform inscription above and to the left of the ruler's head was deciphered shortly after its discovery by another British scholar of the period, Colonel Henry Raw-linson. It reads: "Sennacherib, king of all, king of Assyria, sitting on his *nimedu*-throne while the spoil from the city of Lachish passed before him."

One can assume that Sennacherib's siege of Lachish was successful. He would not have decorated the walls of his palace with this scene if he could not point to it with pride. It is understandable that the biblical historians chose not to elaborate on this tragic episode. Indeed, the Nineveh frieze helps to explain the extreme sparseness of the biblical references to the Assyrian siege of Lachish. It is merely acknowledged in 2 Kings 18:13 (cf. 2 Chr. 32:9) that Sennacherib was at Lachish. A chapter later we are simply told that "the king had left Lachish" and was fighting against Libnah (2 Kgs. 19:8). Had his siege of Lachish failed, we could expect the biblical historians to have described the event in some detail.

Further documentation of Sennacherib's invasion of Judah has come from Assyria in three copies of the king's official annals, impressed on octagonal clay prisms about 40 cm (ca. 16 in) high.[6] The prism texts give a vivid description of the tribute Sennacherib extracted and the devastation he wrought on recalcitrant cities as his army swept down the Phoenician coast, through the Philistine plain, and into the territories of Moab, Edom, and Judah. Of his activities in Judah, Sennacherib declares:

> As to Hezekiah, the Jew, he did not submit to my yoke, I laid siege to 46 of his strong cities, walled forts and to the countless small villages in their vicinity, and conquered (them) by means of well-stamped (earth)-ramps, and battering-rams brought (thus) near (to the walls) (combined with) the attack by foot soldiers, (using) mines, breeches as well as sapper work. I drove out (of them) 200,150 people, young and old, male and female, horses, mules, donkeys, camels, big and small cattle beyond counting, and considered (them) booty. Himself I made a prisoner in Jerusalem, his royal residence, like a bird in a cage. I surrounded him with earthwork in order to molest those who were leaving his city's gate. (Oppenheim 1969:288)

Sennacherib goes on to claim that Hezekiah was overwhelmed by "the terror-inspiring splendor of my lordship" and asserts that Hezekiah presented him with much tribute, but it is noteworthy that he does not claim to have taken Jerusalem, and he acknowledges of the tribute that it was sent to him "later, to Nineveh."

Devastation of Judah's Cities

The Deuteronomic historians appear to corroborate the sweeping claim in Sennacherib's annals that he "laid siege to 46 of his strong cities . . . and conquered them," albeit in the briefest of acknowledgements: "In the fourteenth year of King Hezekiah, Sennacherib king of Assyria came up against all the fortified cities of Judah and took them" (2 Kgs. 18:13).

Excavations extending over the past century in the territory of ancient Judah have by now uncovered a significant body of data that strongly substantiate the testimony of Sennacherib and 2 Kings.

Most important have been excavations at the site of biblical Lachish. The 7.2 ha (18 acre) mound some 42 km (25 miles) southwest of Jerusalem, known in Arabic as Tell ed-Duweir, was initially excavated by British archaeologist James L. Starkey in 1932–38. It proved to have been a large, strongly fortified city in the Iron Age, strategically located to serve a key role in Judah's western defense network. But Starkey was unable to identify a destruction layer at Tell ed-Duweir to correlate with Sennacherib's well-documented attack. There clearly was a terminal Iron Age destruction (Level II) that could be associated by pottery typology with the Babylonian invasion by Nebuchadrezzar in 587/86 BCE (2 Kgs. 25:1–12). The building stratum immediately beneath that (Level III) also had experienced at least partial destruction, but the pottery of the two destruction layers seemed so similar that Starkey concluded Level III must have suffered its damage only a decade earlier, during Nebuchadrezzar's military campaign in Judah in 597 BCE (2 Kgs. 24:10–17). This seemed to leave no good candidate for a Lachish destruction at the end of the eighth century.

A new investigation of the site was begun in 1973 by David Ussishkin. Armed with comparative pottery data from more recent excavations in both Judah and northern Israel, he became convinced that the Level III destruction was much earlier than Starkey's 597 BCE dating and, indeed, the ceramic corpus from Level III fit the end of the eighth century comfortably.[7]

Moreover, he demonstrated that there was no Iron II destruction layer below Level III that could be assigned to Sennacherib's siege of 701 BCE (Ussishkin 1979, 1982).[8]

Ussishkin's excavations also confirmed the accuracy of details presented on the frieze, such as the citadel's many-towered city wall and supplementary outer defense wall and the location of the Assyrian earthen siege ramp to the right (east) of the main city gate as it would have been viewed from Sennacherib's camp. In 1983 he even uncovered a defensive counterramp inside the city wall opposite the Assyrian ramp (Ussishkin 1984).

As a result of Ussishkin's work at Lachish in clarifying the pottery typology for late eighth-century Judah, it can now be seen that most other excavated sites in Judah experienced a destruction at the end of the eighth century BCE. Moreover, some of these sites were not rebuilt during the remainder of Iron II. Tell es-Saba^c and Tel Halif are two examples of fortified cities of Judah excavated within the past two decades that were destroyed and abandoned at the end of the eighth century. Those few sites that were rebuilt, such as Tell Beit Mirsim and Tell Arad, tend to show evidence of a period of abandonment before they were rebuilt. Even Lachish's fortifications appear to have been left in ruins for some time before rebuilding (Ussishkin 1979:142). It now seems clear that Sennacherib's devastation of Judah was so extensive that the map of Judah in the early seventh century, following Sennacherib's incursions, needs to be redrawn to present a considerably diminished territory.

Hezekiah's Preparations
in Jerusalem

The information described above underscores how miraculous the escape of Jerusalem from its own siege must have seemed to those who lived through the experience.

Both the Deuteronomic historians and the later Chroniclers focus on the role that King Hezekiah played during that siege. Understandably, the official religious histories attribute his success to his religious faithfulness and his confidence in Israel's God to deliver his city and people. Both historical records, however, also make mention of measures that Hezekiah took to strengthen Jerusalem's defenses. The reference in 2 Kings 20:20 is very brief, hardly more than a footnote at the end of the account of Hezekiah's reign: "The rest of the deeds of Hezekiah, and all his might, and how he made the pool and the conduit and brought water into the city, are they not written in the Book of the Chronicles of the Kings of Judah?" The description in 2 Chronicles is somewhat fuller, adding that "he set to work resolutely and built up all the wall that was broken down, and raised towers upon it, and outside it he built another wall" (2 Chr. 32:2–5).

The accounts do not provide a clear location or description of these defensive projects, nor do they indicate whether or not Hezekiah undertook them before the threat of siege was upon him. Archaeological investigations, however, have uncovered evidence for both of these operations, and they prove to have been ambitious. It has become clear that Hezekiah must have begun his preparations for Jerusalem's defense some time before Sennacherib's arrival in the land.

The most dramatic element of Hezekiah's defense program to come to light has been the water tunnel, which scholars now attribute to Hezekiah. Hezekiah's Tunnel, as it is conventionally called, was actually first explored by Edward Robinson in 1838 (Robinson 1860), but the tunnel's proper date and identification were not understood until much later. At the time, Robinson had no way of knowing that the ancient location of the city of David had been on Ophel Hill above his head. In the nineteenth century that area lay outside and to the south of Jerusalem's medieval walls, which Robinson assumed marked the city limits of the early biblical period. He therefore had no reason to associate the tunnel he had explored with Hezekiah.

In 1880 an inscription was discovered carved into the wall of the tunnel near its southern exit. Hacked out of the wall, the inscription was later taken to the Istanbul Archaeological Museum, where it is today. The contents of the inscription suggested that it had been carved in commemoration of the tunnel's completion, and the paleography of its Old Hebrew script aided in the eventual proper dating of the project.

The next development came in the wake of Sir Flinders Petrie's excavations at Tell el-Hesi in 1890 and the beginnings he made there toward the establishment of a reliable pottery typology for Palestine. By 1910, several investigators had noted the concentrations of Iron Age and earlier potsherds on Ophel Hill, and attention became focused on that area as the site of early Jerusalem.[9]

Increasingly, scholars came to accept the conclusion that the tunnel system Robinson had first explored must be the "pool and the conduit" credited to Hezekiah in 2 Kings 20:20.

Hezekiah's tunnel remains the most ambitious by far of all the Iron Age water systems yet found. The tunnel was hewn for a distance of 533 m (1750 feet) through the bedrock beneath the Ophel Hill on which ancient Jerusalem stood in order to allow water from the Gihon Spring at the hill's eastern base to flow by gravity to a pool near the southern limits of the hill. Pick marks (as well as the contents of the inscription) confirm that the tunnel was cut by two teams starting from opposite ends and following curving routes to meet successfully deep within the heart of the hill (fig. 4-3). As they approached their intended rendezvous, only minor adjustments laterally were needed to bring the sections together.

Until that join was made, however, there must have been a heightening sense of tension within the city, especially if the project was being done under the threat of impending war. The inscription preserves the drama— and evident sense of relief—when that moment came:

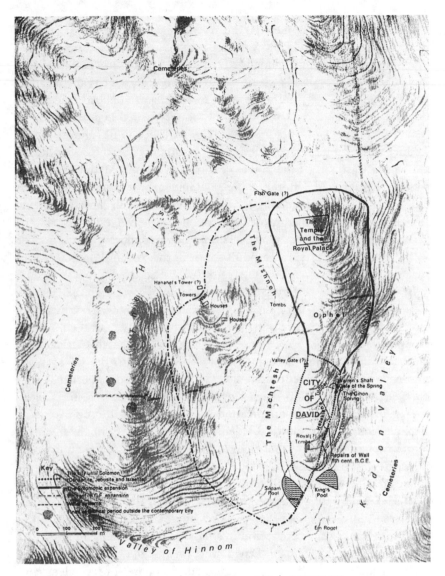

FIG. 4-3. Jerusalem in 701 BCE (Bahat 1983:13).

and while there were still three cubits to be cut through, [there was heard] the voice of a man calling to his fellow, for there was an overlap in the rock on the right [and on the left]. And when the tunnel was driven through, the quarrymen hewed (the rock), each man toward his fellow, axe against axe; and the water flowed from the spring toward the reservoir. (Albright 1969:321)

While Hezekiah's tunnel has been known for many years, another major element of Hezekiah's war preparations was detected only in the 1969–71 excavations by Nahman Avigad in the Jewish Quarter of the Old City. There he uncovered a section of a well-constructed city fortification wall 39 m long (128 ft) and some 7 m (23 ft) thick (so dubbed "the Broad Wall"), which could be dated from the pottery sealed beneath it to the final years of the eighth century BCE. The wall section lies almost 275 m (900 ft) west of the Temple Mount and is oriented northeast-southwest on the high ground of the ridge west of the Temple Mount. The wall must have connected with the Temple Mount at some point farther north and, to have been effective as a defensive wall, it then must have continued south beyond the exposed section along the ridge of the western hill to swing east at the Valley of Hinnom and connect with the earlier wall of the City of David at a point south of the Siloam Pool. This wall must have more than tripled the area of the walled city.[10]

Benjamin Mazar had already uncovered tombs west of the Temple Mount that remained in use until late in the eighth century, so it was clear that this area had remained outside the walls of the city until then. Avigad uncovered remains of some domestic houses in the Jewish Quarter that had been built during the eighth century, however, so the western hill must have begun to serve Jerusalem's expanding population, perhaps swollen after the fall of the Northern Kingdom of Israel to Assyria in 721 BCE.

Avigad found that the fortification wall cut directly through some of these previously built houses. Evidently a defensive wall for the area had not been planned initially, but then it was erected with sufficient urgency to sacrifice houses in its way (Avigad 1975:43–44).

Avigad concluded that this must be the other wall that the Chroniclers claim Hezekiah built "outside" the older walls of the city (2 Chr. 32:5). He furthermore suggested that the way houses were demolished in the path of the wall fit the description in a passage from Isaiah: "You saw that the breaches of the City of David were many, and you collected the waters of the lower pool, and you counted the houses of Jerusalem, and you *broke down the houses to fortify the wall.* You made a reservoir between the two walls for the water of the old pool" (Isa. 22:9–11; see Avigad 1980:56).

Certainly the water tunnel and the western wall were instrumental in Hezekiah's ability to withstand Sennacherib's siege. And certainly Hezekiah must have begun these defensive projects some time in advance of the enemy invasion. It is reasonable to suppose that the prophet Isaiah, who clearly saw divine protection at work in Jerusalem's deliverance, would have given Yahweh the credit for those defensive preparations.

Clues from
Egyptian Coronation Hymns

A number of scholars have suggested that Isaiah's messianic oracles in chapters 9 and 11 were structured as enthronement or coronation hymns celebrating the accession of Hezekiah—or some other king—to the throne (see, e.g., Crook 1949).

One further body of archaeological evidence is worth noting here which helps to validate this interpretation of the oracles. Over the years a number of Egyptian coronation hymns have been retrieved from several periods. They reveal patterns of content and imagery that can be found reflected in Isaiah's messianic oracles. To illustrate the similarities, it will suffice here to refer to two hymns that have been published in translation and are readily accessible to readers: the late-thirteenth-century BCE "Joy at the Accession of Mer-ne-Ptah" and the mid-twelfth-century "Joy at the Accession of Ramses IV" (Wilson 1969:378–79).

First of all, the Egyptian royal hymns typically describe the pharaoh as divinely "given" or "sent" by his father, the great god. "A lord—life, prosperity, health!—is given in all lands . . . the King of Upper and Lower Egypt" (Mer-ne-Ptah); "All the lands say to him: 'Gracious is the Horus upon the throne of his father Amon-Re, the god who sent him forth, the protector of the prince who carries off every land'" (Ramesses IV). Isaiah's words in 9:6, "to us a son is given," may draw upon this established theme in coronation liturgy.

The Egyptian hymns apply exalted titles to the pharaoh and describe his reign as eternal. Mer-ne-Ptah is described as "the lord of millions of years, great of kingship like Horus." Ramesses IV is greeted with the exclamation, "Thou ruler—life, prosperity, health!—thou art for eternity!" Isaiah says in 9:6–7, "His name will be called 'Wonderful Counselor, Mighty God, Everlasting Father, Prince of Peace.' Of the increase of his government and of peace there will be no end."

Egyptian royal theology provided a natural context for such exalted language. The pharaoh was asserted to be divinely incarnated and eternal. It is noteworthy that Isaiah employs similar imagery even though the subject of his oracle is clearly identified as a Davidic royal descendant— not a deity himself, but simply a charismatic human agent of the deity. The exalted titles in Isaiah 9:6, therefore, must be seen as applied not to the Davidic king but to the God whose powers are made manifest in him.[11]

The Egyptian hymns use superlative imagery also to extol the blessings that the new pharaoh brings to the land—typically peace, justice, and material prosperity. Of Mer-ne-Ptah's accession it is proclaimed: "Right has banished wrong. Evildoers have fallen (upon) their faces. All the rapacious are ignored. The water stands and is not dried up; the Nile lifts high. Days are long, nights have hours, and the moon comes normally." In other words, the new pharaoh has brought harmonious order both to society and to nature. The hymn to Ramesses IV echoes the same double theme:

> They who were fled have come (back) to their towns; they who were hidden have come forth (again).
> They who were hungry are sated and gay; they who were thirsty are drunken. . . .
> High Niles have come forth from their caverns, that they may refresh the hearts of the common people. . . .
> The ships, they rejoice upon the deep. They have no (need of) ropes, for they come to land with wind and oars.
>
> (Wilson 1969:378)

Isaiah proclaims the same dual theme: the Davidic king will establish perfect justice in the community while perfect peace will permeate nature. "With righteousness he shall judge the poor, and decide with equity for the meek of the earth. . . . The wolf shall dwell with the lamb, and the leopard lie down with the kid" (Isa. 11:4, 6).

It need not be suggested that Isaiah was directly acquainted with Egyptian royal litanies. It is more likely that the prophet was consciously echoing the literary style and content of earlier Israelite coronation hymns and that they, in turn, quite understandably had appropriated established forms of royal ritual.

By combining the archaeological evidence outlined above with a critical examination of the biblical texts, a compelling argument emerges that Isaiah's messianic oracles are, indeed, hymns celebrating the divinely installed king. They are most probably retrospective, however, presented not at Hezekiah's accession but after he had been on the throne for a number of years. The prophet has been inspired by the seemingly miraculous deliverance of 701 BCE to proclaim the king who could then be declared to have been divinely provided for this deliverance.

Like other prophets, Isaiah not only looked to the future, he also sought to interpret the true meaning of past events. Here he proclaims that it was Yahweh who had "given" Hezekiah to his people—who had placed his spirit upon this ruler years before in order to prepare for this moment of crisis.

NOTES

1. Some scholars have argued for a postexilic dating of these oracles because "the stump of Jesse" suggests that the kingdom of Judah had already been cut down (see Sandmel 1968:96) or because the joyous mood of these verses contrasts sharply with Isaiah's other oracles (see Ackroyd 1971:338, 340). But Isaiah 11:1 need only refer to a descendant from the "stock" of David's father, and the second argument weakens if we find an occasion within the life of the prophet to explain his change of mood.

2. The forecasts of restoration for the Davidic kingdom and throne in Micah 4—5 are almost certainly postexilic.

3. Isaiah 7:14, embedded in this oracle, was taken to be a messianic pronouncement in Christian tradition as early as Matthew 1:23, but the context in Isaiah makes clear that the child's birth is not miraculous and that he himself is not to be a leader. He is merely a time-sign similar to the one in Isaiah 8:1–4. "Immanuel" in this context must mean "God with us" for punishing destruction, as it certainly does in 8:8.

4. See also Isaiah 36—37, a variant of the account in 2 Kings. Whether Sennacherib mounted one expedition into Judah in 701 BCE or two campaigns in different years, as some have argued, does not affect this discussion.

5. Layard's accounts of his discoveries and drawings of the friezes were published within two years (Layard 1853a, b). An excellent modern summary is provided by Ussishkin (1982).

6. The earliest discovered copy, the Taylor Prism, is in the British Museum; another is in the Chicago Oriental Institute Museum, and a third is in the Israel Museum in Jerusalem.

7. A major development during the decades separating Starkey's work and Ussishkin's was the emerging awareness of differences between northern and southern pottery shapes during Iron II (see Amiran 1969:191–285), thus negating earlier arguments by Dame Kathleen Kenyon and others that the pottery from Tell ed-Duweir III differed too much from that of Samaria VI, destroyed in 721 BCE, to be dated only two decades later.

8. There had been earlier challenges to Starkey's date of 597 BCE for Tell ed-Duweir III, beginning with Olga Tufnell's official report on the Iron II pottery from the site (Tufnell 1953:55f, 340). Several scholars followed Tufnell's lead in arguing for a 701 BCE date for the stratum, most notably Yohanan Aharoni (1967:341–42; 1979:393, 395). But many others relinquished Starkey's later dating only after Ussishkin's excavations provided fresh, well-controlled data for all of the Iron II strata along with the dramatic siege ramp from Stratum III seemingly corroborating Sennacherib's frieze.

9. Excavations by Kathleen Kenyon in the late 1960s and Yigal Shiloh in the late 1970s would ultimately confirm that the "City of David" had indeed been located on Ophel Hill.

10. If the eighth-century wall extended even farther west, as a few scholars are suggesting (Bahat 1990:25, 29), that would simply make the fortification project even more impressive.

11. Isaiah twice elsewhere gave human children exalted names that did not describe the child but rather the activity of Israel's God to be accomplished within a given time of the child's life (Isa. 7:14; 8:1).

WORKS CITED

Ackroyd, P. R.
1971   The Book of Isaiah. *The Interpreter's One-Volume Commentary on the Bible*, ed. C. M. Laymon. New York and Nashville: Abingdon.

Aharoni, Y.
1967   *The Land of the Bible: A Historical Geography.* Philadelphia: Westminster Press.

Albright, W. F.
1969   Palestinian Inscriptions. In *Ancient Near Eastern Texts Relating to the Old Testament*, ed. J. B. Pritchard, 3d ed. with Supplement, 320–22. Princeton, N.J.: Princeton University Press.

Amiran, R.
1969   *Ancient Pottery of the Holy Land.* Jerusalem: Massada Press.

Avigad, N.
1975   Excavations in the Jewish Quarter of the Old City, 1969–1971. In *Jerusalem Revealed*, ed. Y. Yadin, 41–57. Jerusalem: Israel Exploration Society.

1980   *Discovering Jerusalem.* Nashville: Thomas Nelson.

Bahat, D.
1983   *Carta's Historical Atlas of Jerusalem.* Rev. ed. Jerusalem: Carta.
1990   *The Illustrated Atlas of Jerusalem.* New York: Simon and Schuster.

Crook, M.
1949   A Suggested Occasion for Isaiah 9:2–7 and 11:1–9. *Journal of Biblical Literature* 68:213–24.

Gray, G. B.
1912   *A Critical and Exegetical Commentary on the Book of Isaiah.* Vol. 1. Edinburgh: T. and T. Clark.

Hayes, J. H., and S. A. Irvine
1987   *Isaiah, the Eighth-Century Prophet: His Times and His Preaching.* New York and Nashville: Abingdon.

Herodotus
1972   *The Histories.* Rev. ed. Translated by A. Selincourt, from Greek. Baltimore: Penguin Books.

Layard, A. H.
1853a   *Discoveries in the Ruins of Nineveh and Babylon; with Travels in*

Armenia, Kurdistan and the Desert; Being the Result of a Second Expedition to Assyria. London.

1853b   *A Second Series of the Monuments of Nineveh; Including Bas-Reliefs from the Palace of Sennacherib and Bronzes from the Ruins of Nimrud. From Drawings Made on the Spot, During a Second Expedition to Assyria.* London.

Oppenheim, A. L.
1969   Babylonian and Assyrian Historical Texts. In *Ancient Near Eastern Texts Relating to the Old Testament*, ed. J. B. Pritchard, 3d ed. with Supplement, 265–317. Princeton, N.J.: Princeton University Press.

Robinson, E.
1860   *Biblical Researches in Palestine and in the Adjacent Regions.* Vol. 1, 2d ed. Boston: Crocker and Brewster.

Sandmel, S.
1968   *The Hebrew Scriptures: An Introduction to Their Literature and Religious Ideas.* New York: Alfred A. Knopf.

Scott, R. B. Y.
1956   The Book of Isaiah (Chapters 1—39). *The Interpreter's Bible*, vol. 5. New York: Abingdon.

Tufnell, O.
1953   *Lachish III (The Iron Age).* London: Oxford University Press.

Ussishkin, D.
1979   Answers at Lachish. *Biblical Archaeology Review* 5, no. 6:16–39.
1982   *The Conquest of Lachish by Sennacherib.* Tel Aviv: Tel Aviv University.
1984   Defensive Judean Counter-Ramp Found at Lachish in 1983 Season. *Biblical Archaeology Review* 10, no. 2:66–73.

Wilson, J. A.
1969   Egyptian Hymns and Prayers. In *Ancient Near Eastern Texts Relating to the Old Testament*, ed. J. B. Pritchard, 3d ed. with Supplement, 365–81. Princeton, N.J.: Princeton University Press.

5 | Gathered to His People: An Archaeological Illustration from Tell Dothan's Western Cemetery

ROBERT E. COOLEY
GARY D. PRATICO

Archaeological investigation at numerous sites throughout the Levant has yielded abundant data concerning burials and burial ritual (for the Late Bronze and Iron Ages, the periods of concern in this article, see Meyers 1970; Abercrombie 1979; Rahmani 1981; Gonen 1987; Bloch-Smith 1992). The nontextual data of archaeology are hardly sufficient, however, for an understanding of death and death ritual in this ancient context. The archaeological data must be viewed in light of the literary evidence, and here too the horizons of our knowledge have been expanded through discovery of pertinent epigraphic evidence, notably the Ugaritic texts among other sources (Lewis 1989; Tromp 1969; Healey 1977). Biblical references to death and mortuary practice appear lean by comparison (Bailey 1979; Bloch-Smith 1992). It is not the concern of this article to explore the theological and sociological inferences of mortuary practice but to present an important source of archaeological information, hitherto unpublished in technical detail, that will contribute to our understanding of death and burial ritual in the world of Canaanite-Hebrew culture.

Tomb 1 of Tell Dothan's western cemetery is one of the largest single-chambered cave burials of the Late Bronze and early Iron Ages to have been excavated in the Levant. The final publication of this burial chamber, with its rich funerary deposits, will provide a wealth of information for the inquiry noted above and also for numerous areas of research in biblical, archaeological, and ancient Near Eastern studies. In addition to announcing the Dothan Publications Project and briefly detailing the western cemetery in the context of the tell excavations, this study will provide an archaeological illustration for one of the biblical formulas indicating death and burial ritual and will highlight other areas of archaeological commentary on the biblical text.

70

FIG. 5-1. View of the Tell Dothan excavations during the 1960 season. Beyond the edge of the mound, the Dothan Valley stretches to the distant horizon.

TELL DOTHAN: DESCRIPTION, IDENTIFICATION, AND EXCAVATION

Description of the Site

Tell Dothan is located in the northern Samaria hills on the eastern side of the Dothan Valley, some 22 km north of Shechem and 10 km south of Jenin (fig. 5-1). The site dominates this plain, which has always been of strategic importance as the most easterly of the three main passes between the Sharon plain and the Jezreel valley through the mountainous ridge created by the northern Ephraimite hill country and the Carmel range (fig. 5-1). Rising approximately 60 m above the surrounding valley, Tell Dothan is a prominent mound that is composed of nearly 15 m of stratified remains on top of a natural hill some 45 m high. The site has a fairly flat top with steeply sloping sides. The summit comprises approximately 4 ha (10 acres), and the occupied area of the slopes includes another 6 ha (15 acres). Its area of occupation, therefore, consists of approximately 10 ha (25 acres). The eastern and southern slopes are today terraced with olive groves that are watered from a spring on the south side of the tell. This water source likely served the site in antiquity.

Identification

Tell Dothan has been identified with the biblical city of the same name, mentioned in Genesis 37 as the place where Joseph found his brothers in the course of their wanderings with the flocks of their father. According to the narrative, Joseph was sent by his father, Jacob, from the valley of Hebron to find his brothers in the region of Shechem but learned that they were tending the flocks in the area of Dothan. Thereafter, the narrative describes the intrigue that led to Joseph being taken to Egypt by a caravan of Ishmaelites (or Midianites) who were traveling to Egypt via Dothan from Gilead.

During the period of the monarchy, Dothan is described as a well-fortified city to which the Aramaean king sent emissaries in search of the prophet Elisha (2 Kgs. 6:13–14). It was in this context that Elisha's servant was encouraged by a vision of heavenly forces arrayed on a hill to the east of town. Other literary references include three notations in the book of Judith (3:9; 4:6; and 7:3) and one in the Onomasticon of Eusebius (76:13). Thutmose III records the taking of tribute from a place listed as Tutayana, identified by Gaston Maspero as biblical Dothan.

EXCAVATION HISTORY AND PUBLICATIONS

Dothan was excavated by Joseph Free (1911–1974) in nine seasons between 1953 and 1964. According to the excavator, the site yielded a nearly continuous occupational sequence in twenty-one levels, dating from the end of the Chalcolithic period through the Byzantine period with later occupation as late as the fourteenth century CE. Free published reports of his excavations only in popular articles and preliminary reports. Unfortunately these provide few technical details on the site's rich architectural traditions and artifact assemblages (Free 1953, 1954, 1955, 1956a, 1956b, 1958, 1959, 1960, 1962, 1975). Preliminary reports were prepared for the eighth (1962) and ninth (1964) seasons but they were never published.

The western cemetery, which consists of three tombs, was excavated over four seasons (1959, 1960, 1962, and 1964). Although Free was director of the Dothan Archaeological Project during these years, the tomb excavations were supervised by Robert E. Cooley. The publication phase of the project, which will begin with a volume on the western cemetery, is now under Cooley's direction.

Very little about this stratified tomb has been published to date. Apart from dictionary and encyclopedia articles, the most substantive studies are to be found in the preliminary reports (Free 1959:26–28; 1960:10–15) and in studies largely concerned with matters of interpretation (Cooley 1968, 1983).

EXCAVATION HIGHLIGHTS
ON THE TELL

Tell Dothan was investigated in six major areas of excavation designated (east to west) Areas T, B, A, D, L, and K. The western cemetery, which is the focus of this article, is located in Area K on the western end of the mound. As a context for the study of the western cemetery, selected highlights of the tell excavations will be briefly presented.

Area T is located on the eastern extremity of the tell's summit. It encompassed the highest part of the mound and that designated by Free as the "acropolis." Important among the discoveries was a medieval fortress-palace of the fourteenth century CE (Free 1956a:16–17; 1959:26). The excavated portion of the structure yielded a large open courtyard (10.5 m by 12.5 m) that was surrounded by twenty-five rooms, some with well-preserved jambs and sockets. The complex was thought to be con-siderably larger than that excavated within the confines of Area T. According to Free, the area also yielded ruins of the Iron Age, Hellenis-tic, and Roman periods.

Published data for Area B, just to the west of Area T and to the north of Area A, are exceptionally lean and consist only of a few observations related to remains of the Roman and Hellenistic periods. The excavation records and Free's unpublished ninth season report provide a few more details regarding occupation during the Roman, Byzantine, and medieval periods.

The central section of the tell's summit (Area A) was occupied by a Hellenistic settlement, dating to the third and second centuries BCE (Free 1954:15–16; 1955:3–5; 1956a:11). The records indicate that the archi-tectural remains for the Hellenistic settlement were lean, whereas the diagnostic pottery and artifacts were abundant. Beneath the Hellenistic occupation, substantial remains of an Iron Age settlement were uncov-ered. Notable among the architectural features of this earlier settlement was a section of a street (33.5 m long by 1.2 m wide) running southeast to northwest (Free 1955:6–7; 1956a:14–15 and fig. 2). "Wall Street" was bordered by well-preserved structures with walls that survived to a height of 2.15 m. Free discerned eight houses or rooms to the north of the street and seven to the south. The excavator noted that "Wall Street" lasted through several centuries of the Iron Age, but the rationale for his phasing of contiguous architecture is inscrutable.

Most notable among the Area D discoveries was a massive city fortification, the construction of which was dated to the beginning of the Early Bronze Age. This city wall was preserved to a height of 5 m with a projected original height of 7.5 m. Near the base of the wall was uncovered a large flight of stone steps, surviving to a maximum width of 4 m. Eighteen steps were preserved between the wall and the eroded edge of the mound. Free associated the stairway with the city fortification and dated it from the beginning of the Early Bronze Age through the Middle Bronze Age.

The largest of the areas of excavation was Area L, located on the western summit of the mound, contiguous with the eastern side of Area K and the western cemetery. The slope section of this area yielded substantial fortifications of the Early Bronze Age and, although few published details are available, the area also produced sections of the city's Middle and Late Bronze Age defenses. Further to the east in Area L, large sections of an Iron Age administrative building were uncovered (Free 1959:22; 1960:7–9). This building was excavated over the course of three seasons with substantial horizontal exposure.

It appears that several structures were uncovered in Area L (Free 1959:24; 1960:8) that were reminiscent of the so-called "open-court building," which has been regarded as a hallmark of Assyrian influence (Amiran and Dunayevsky 1958:25–32). The associated pottery was clearly in the Assyrian tradition of the eighth through seventh centuries BCE, consisting of palace-ware sherds and a complete palace-ware bowl.

TOMB 1 OF THE
WESTERN CEMETERY (AREA K)

Discovery

Toward the end of the 1959 season, the excavators uncovered a circular, stone-lined pit in Area K (on the western side of the tell) that diminished in size until it funneled into a square-cut shaft in the bedrock. About one meter down the shaft, a stone slab was uncovered, leaning against a vertical rock-cut doorway. Thus began the excavation of one of Tell Dothan's most significant discoveries, the so-called western cemetery (fig. 5-2).

The largest tomb of this cemetery (Tomb 1) was discovered four days before the conclusion of the 1959 season. During those four days, the team worked around the clock in eight-hour shifts in the hope of clearing the burial chamber. This objective was not realized. Approximately one meter of the tomb chamber was exposed, with removal of 52 ceramic vessels of the early Iron Age, including chalices, lamps, bowls, pyxides, and numerous other objects. Reluctantly, the tomb was sealed with reinforced concrete. No one imagined that nearly three thousand more vessels, 234 bronze objects, and several hundred burials awaited in the largest single-chambered tomb with the largest number of burial deposits to have been excavated in Levant up to that time (fig. 5-3).

Description

Tomb 1 consists of three architectural components: a vertical shaft, a stepped entryway, and the main tomb chamber in which were located eight crypts or loculi (fig. 5-3). Access to the stepped entryway and the main chamber was provided through a well-cut vertical shaft on the western side of the tomb (figs. 5-4, 5-5, 5-6). The chamber, therefore, has a west-east orientation. The shaft measures 1.75 m by 1 m wide and is 1.51 m deep. Of the seven steps that lead into the tomb chamber, three of the steps are located within the shaft. The shaft depth to the first step is 1.00 m; 1.32 m to the second step; 1.51 m to the third step. The remaining four steps are within the tomb chamber. The seventh step is 3.3 m below the uppermost level of the shaft. The doorway to the tomb chamber was blocked by a stone slab that measured 1.1 m high by 1 m wide (figs. 5-4, 5-5, 5-6).

The tomb chamber is irregularly shaped, although basically rectangular with rounded corners. At its largest extremities, the chamber measures 10.65 m west to east (Crypt H to the western wall of the shaft) and 6.9 m north to south (Crypt A to Crypt C). Excluding the crypts, the chamber walls measure 8.3 m west to east and 5 m north to south. The chamber contained eight crypts, of which six were cut into the rock (A, C, D, E, F, and H) and two were constructed at a later time (B in the northwestern corner of the tomb and G at the extreme eastern end). The two later crypts were created by constructing stone walls below Crypts C and H respectively. Crypt dimensions are as follows (see page 77):

FIG. 5-2. The area of Tell Dothan's western cemetery, located on the western edge of the mound (Area K). The collapsed ceiling of Tomb 1 is depicted in the lower half of the photograph. The vertical shaft is clearly visible on the other side of the modern doorway. Note also that portion of the stepped entryway that is within the tomb chamber, together with Crypts B (*right*) and A (*left*) on the northern and southern sides of the tomb chamber respectively. Tomb 2 is seen just to the west of Tomb 1 (*upper center*). Looking west.

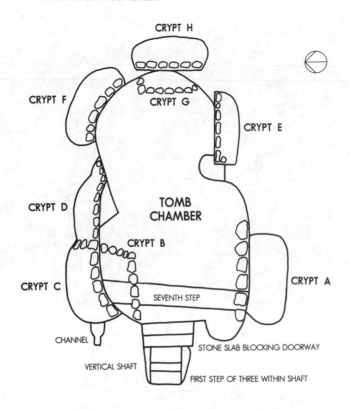

**TOMB 1 OF THE WESTERN CEMETERY
(AREA K)**

0   1m   2m   3m

BY IVAN S. CHOW, ARCHITECT, AFTER PLAN BY ROBERT E. COOLEY

FIG. 5-3. Plan of Tomb 1 of Tell Dothan's western cemetery.

A: 1.20 m by 2.80 m
B: 1.10 m by 2.30 m
C: 1.13 m by 2.60 m
D: 0.81 m by 2.25 m
E: 0.79 m by 2.25 m
F: 0.88 m by 2.30 m
G: 0.80 m by 2.20 m
H: 1.20 m by 2.20 m

FIG. 5-4. Detail of the view through the collapsed ceiling of Tomb 1, looking west. Crypt A is on the southern side of the tomb chamber. Crypts B and C are seen on the right, the northern side of the chamber.

The depth of the tomb chamber from the bedrock surface at the center to the collapsed ceiling is 5.50 m.

A small channel was discovered on the northwestern side of the tomb, directly above Crypt C. This channel created an opening from the outside of the tomb to the interior of one of the chamber niches. The opening was roughly square on the interior, measuring 60 cm by 60 cm, narrowing to roughly circular on the exterior with a diameter of 20 cm. Two large storage jars, each with a dipper juglet, were associated with this channel. Both were discovered on the outside of the tomb chamber, just below the channel entrance. This auxiliary opening, together with the associated pottery, obviously served a ritual function. Similar installations were discovered in the great tombs of Ugarit, dating to the fourteenth and thirteenth centuries BCE (Schaeffer 1939:50–51).

Tomb Stratification

Although atypical for multiple-burial tombs, Tomb 1 was clearly stratified. The uppermost level (Level 1) was completely sealed by the debris from the collapsed ceiling. Each of the five burial levels was clearly and completely separated from the others by a layer of limestone and/or

FIG. 5-5. Detail of the entrance to Tomb 1, photographed from within the tomb chamber and looking west. The meter stick is resting on the sixth step, the second step above the floor of the chamber. Four of the seven entryway steps are located within the tomb chamber; three are within the shaft. A portion of the vertical shaft is visible above the uppermost step.

FIG. 5-6. Detail of the western half of Tomb 1. The chamber floor occupies the lower third of the photograph. The modern doorway rests on the fourth step. Rock-hewn Crypts A and C are seen on the extreme southern (*left*) and northern (*right*) sides of the tomb chamber. Crypt B, a later construction, is located just below Crypt C.

earthen fill that varied in thickness from 5 to 40 cm. The earliest level of burials (Level 5) was separated from the bedrock floor of the tomb by a layer of limestone and earthen fill that was 40 cm thick.

Tomb Deposits

Pottery vessels constituted the largest class of burial deposits, numbering approximately three thousand pieces in the categories of lamps, bowls, jugs, dipper jugs, juglets, dipper juglets, pyxides, flasks, kraters, pots, strainer pots, jars, jar stands, storage jars, funnels, vases, stirrup cups, zoomorphic vessels, bilbils, kernos rings, chalices, cooking pots, pitchers, and bowl stands (fig. 5-7). It should be noted that these categories represent the vessel nomenclature of the Dothan field records. The final publication will refine the nomenclature of the vessel types (figs. 5-7a, 5-7b, 5-7c).

5-7a

5-7b

5-7c

FIG. 5-7. The concentration of vessels throughout the five levels of the tomb is illustrated by this sequence of three photographs from Level 1: Squares 2E, 2F, and 2G.

The following table provides numerical details, level by level, for those vessel types that are attested by more than ten examples. The tabulations are based on the numerical summaries recorded in the field reports.

TABLE 1

Vessel Types	Tomb Level 1	Tomb Level 2	Tomb Level 3	Tomb Level 4	Tomb Level 5	Total
Bowl	109	197	123	114	64	607
Lamp	115	163	108	116	76	578
Pyxis	173	196	129	52	17	567
Jug/Juglet	95	145	118	64	50	472
Pot	37	53	45	50	13	198
Chalice	25	33	31	24	6	119
Flask	15	12	14	11	5	57
Storage Jar	5	14	13	11	7	50
Krater	32	11	1	0	0	44
Stirrup Cup	1	3	8	9	0	21
Spouted Jug	4	2	2	3	0	11

Other vessel types, represented by less than ten examples, include: jar, funnel, vase, milkbowl, strainer, bilbil, cooking pot, incense burner, kernos ring, special lamp forms, and anthropomorphic vessels.

Several unique deposits are worthy of note: three seven-spouted lamps (Free 1960:14); a seven-spouted kernos ring; five zoomorphic vessels, each fashioned in the shape of a bull with sexual attributes clearly represented; a bronze lamp manufactured in identical form to its ceramic counterparts; and twenty-five scarabs. Imported Mycenaean and Cypriot wares are represented among the burial vessels. The tomb also yielded bronze weaponry (daggers, spearheads, and various projectiles), thirty-nine bronze bowls, and a complete faience bowl with painted lines on the bottom of the vessel. Other deposits included an alabaster chalice, basalt vessels, limestone platters, grinding stones, spindles, whorls, and jewelry (bracelets, necklaces, finger rings, toggle pins, beads, and pins). Two ivory pendants, fashioned in the shape of a mallet or hammer, were discovered on the chests of two skeletons. Very few remnants of the food offerings survived. These included olive pits, sheep bones, shellfish remains, and a fish vertebra.

Among the finds of Tomb 1 was an anthropomorphic lamp of unusual design (fig. 5-8). The lamp is wheelmade with sharply pinched spout. The form has a definite rim with the appearance of a slight base, though the body features of the applied figure may simply create the impression of a base. The lamp is buff-colored and of relatively poor manufacture (figs. 5-8a, 5-8b, 5-8c).

The applied human form extends from a point beyond the tip of the spout to the start of the slightly flaring rim. The figure's overall length is approximately 16 cm. The head extends 2 cm beyond the tip of the spout and is 3 cm wide by 4 cm high. Five clay globules, applied high on the forehead and extending ear to ear, create the impression of a coiffure or some type of head adornment. The skull terminates in a pointed ridge, 1 cm higher than the uppermost globule. The ears are created by elongated globules of clay. The nose is prominent, flaring slightly from the sloping forehead. The eyes were created by pushing excess clay upward, thereby forming a rounded depression. The lips consist of two thin lines of applied clay (1.3 cm wide by 0.7 cm thick). The arms (each 7.5 cm long) were fashioned with small coils of clay along the bottom fold of the pinched spout. The ends of the arms are splayed with no hands or fingers distinguishable. The legs are rather short in relation to the body, 5.5 to 6.0 cm long. Like the arms, the legs were created by the application of clay coils that were smoothed onto the bottom of the lamp. The feet are also splayed with no toe features discernible. The figure exhibits a bidirectional stance. The feet are molded in a left-to-right stance whereas the body and head are applied frontally. No gender characteristics are indicated, though the absence of breasts suggests that the figure is a male.

As expected in a tomb with multiple burials, the degree of disturbance made it extremely difficult to associate deposits with individual interments except for the burial in Crypt H. The deposits that were associated with this burial included seven pottery vessels and one clam shell. A dipper juglet and an oversize flask were placed at the head of the skeleton. A medium-sized bowl, rounded-bottom juglet, jug, pot, and a Cypriot bowl were placed at the feet. The clam shell was associated with this latter group. No personal adornments, implements, weapons, or ritual objects were included in the burial assemblage.

The following tables provide numerical specifics for selected artifact categories, according to distribution throughout the tomb's five levels.

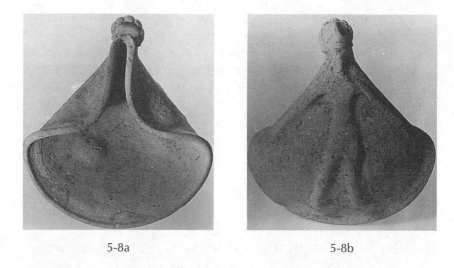

5-8a   5-8b

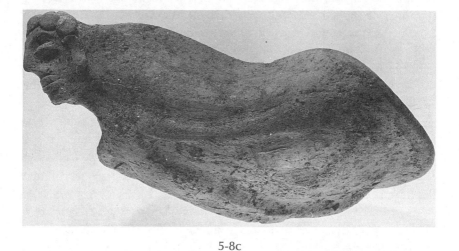

5-8c

FIG. 5-8. Three views of the figurine lamp (Reg. No. T1-2010-P1344): one view from the top and two from the bottom.

TABLE 2

Personal Ornaments	Tomb Level 1	Tomb Level 2	Tomb Level 3	Tomb Level 4	Tomb Level 5	Total
Bracelet	1	0	0	1	0	2
Ring	6	6	2	30	10	54
Earring	0	9	0	9	0	18
Gold Earring	0	0	0	0	1	1
Toggle Pin	0	0	0	3	1	4
Button	0	0	0	1	0	1
Ivory Pendant	1	1	0	0	0	2
Pin	3	0	0	9	0	12
TOTALS	11	16	2	53	12	94

TABLE 3

Weapons	Tomb Level 1	Tomb Level 2	Tomb Level 3	Tomb Level 4	Tomb Level 5	Total
Dagger	9	18	18	10	16	71
Projectile Point	2	0	1	1	0	4
Spear Point	2	7	5	3	2	19
TOTALS	13	25	24	14	18	94

TABLE 4

Amulets and Ritual Objects	Tomb Level 1	Tomb Level 2	Tomb Level 3	Tomb Level 4	Tomb Level 5	Total
Scarab	4	7	4	10	0	25
Kernos Ring	0	0	1	0	0	1
Zoomorphic Objects	2	2	1	0	0	5
TOTALS	6	9	6	10	0	31

Skeletal Remains

Although skulls were better preserved in Levels 3 through 5, the skeletal remains in all levels of this tomb were very fragmentary and in a state of complete disorder, often fused in limestone. The poorer state of preservation of the skeletal remains, especially the skulls, in Levels 1 and 2 may be explained by the damage incurred when the tomb ceiling collapsed. The five levels yielded a total of 204 skulls: 47 fragmentary skulls in Level 1; 57 fragmentary and 9 complete skulls in Level 2 (one infant skeleton was discovered); 22 fragmentary and 26 complete skulls in Level 3; 3 fragmentary and 30 complete skulls in Level 4; and, in Level 5, 3 fragmentary and 7 complete skulls. Based on these and other skeletal remains, it has been estimated that Tomb 1 contained between 250 and 300 burials.

Tomb Chronology

Based on the pottery and other material evidence, the following chronology is suggested for the five levels of this tomb:

Level 5   Late Bronze IIA (1400–1300 BCE). Remains of this earliest level were restricted to an area in the back of the tomb chamber.

Level 4   Late Bronze IIA (1400–1300 BCE). The chronology of this and the earliest level are established on the basis of both domestic and imported pottery (Cypriot and Mycenaean wares). Burials occupied the entire chamber in Level 4.

Level 3   Late Bronze IIB (1300–1200 BCE). The tomb was enlarged by the addition of crypts.

Level 2   This level contains a mixture of Late Bronze IIB and Early Iron I domestic pottery.

Level 1   Early Iron I (1200–1100 BCE). As noted above, diagnostic Iron I pottery was discovered in this latest level. No Iron II pottery was present. The shaft was widened from 0.90 m by 1.45 m to 1.25 m by 1.45 m with a depth of 1.00 m.

Although some chronological refinement may be proposed in the final publication of the western cemetery findings, Tomb 1 dates between the fourteenth and twelfth centuries BCE.

TOMB 1 IN THE CONTEXT
OF LATE BRONZE AGE BURIALS
IN CANAAN

Based on clearly prescribed burial characteristics, a recent study by Rivka Gonen discerns two distinct groups of Late Bronze Age burials in Canaan: pit burials for individual interment and cave burials for multiple interments (Gonen 1992). Both burial types are regarded as indigenous to Canaan, having been practiced since the beginning of the Middle Bronze Age. The study concludes with a presentation of eight foreign burial types that originated in different places and arrived in Canaan during different phases of the Late Bronze Age: bench burial caves, loculi burial caves, bilobate burial caves, open pits, structural chambers, and larnax, coffin, and jar burials. Tell Dothan's Tomb 1 clearly falls within the general category of cave burials for multiple interments and shares the specific characteristics of the loculi burial caves.

Unlike those burial sites in natural caves (such as Tell Jedur and Khirbet Rabud) or in reused Early or Middle Bronze Age burial sites (Tel Regev, Beth-shan, Gibeon, Jericho, Tell el-Farᶜah North, and certain ones at Gezer and Megiddo), Tell Dothan's Tomb 1 was a newly constructed burial site of the Late Bronze Age. It is interesting to note, however, that Tell Dothan's Tomb 3 was a nearby burial cave that was originally used as a cistern. As Gonen has correctly observed, a typology of Late Bronze Age tombs is impossible to establish at present and probably for the immediate future as well.

Like most multiple-burial caves of the Late Bronze Age, Tomb 1 was located outside of the settlement's fortifications on the western slopes of the mound. Other burial chambers located on the slopes of the mound are known from Megiddo, Lachish, Tell Jedur, Tell Beit Mirsim, and Beth-shemesh. While many settlements have only one associated burial cave, this tomb was part of a cemetery that consisted of three cave burials. Unfortunately, Tombs 2 and 3 were poorly preserved by comparison, though roughly contemporary (on the later side) with Tomb 1. Nevertheless, there is no clear tomb organization in the western cemetery, consistent with Gonen's observation that the positioning of Late Bronze Age burial caves in relation to associated settlements is irrelevant.

Again, consistent with the majority of Late Bronze Age cave burials, Tomb 1 was used for multiple interments with the well-known Middle Bronze II practice of removing old bones to the sides of the chamber in order to make room for new burials. This practice is well documented at Jericho, Megiddo, Beth-shan, and Gibeon. The number of interments in multiple-burial tombs varies from a handful, though this circumstance is relatively infrequent, to the numbers represented in Tell Dothan's largest burial chamber. The types and numbers of funerary objects detailed above are characteristic of the larger Late Bronze Age burial caves. Pottery vessels of various types, mostly local, represent the largest class of funerary deposits. Approximately 5 percent of the Tomb 1 assemblage is imported. This datum too is consistent with the typical multiple-burial cave of this period.

While Tomb 1 shares the general characteristics of cave burials for multiple interments, Gonen classifies this tomb among the categories of foreign burials, specifically caves with loculi burials (Gonen 1992:132–33). As is clear in figure 5-3, Tomb 1 had six rock-hewn and two constructed crypts or loculi. Similar tomb constructions that are roughly contemporary are known from Tell el-Ajjul (Petrie 1931:127, pl. 57, fig. 6; pl. 54), Lachish (Tufnell 1953: pl. 128; 1958:228, 240, 280–87), and Megiddo (Guy 1938:127, 129; pls. 41, 42, 140, 141). Though some would suggest a slightly earlier chronology, the typical tomb with loculi was introduced at the beginning of the Late Bronze Age. This burial design was obviously intended for individual burials but in the context of the group, often the family.

While noting that loculi burial caves in Canaan display hybrid features of Greek and Cypriot origin, Gonen finds the parallels closer to Cypriot models, where the design was common, beginning with the Early Cypriot period (Gonen 1992:24–25). She studies Tumulus Number 7 at Paleoskutela in the center of the Karpas Peninsula as representative of the Cypriot loculi burial cave (Sjoqvist 1940:Fig. 45:10; Gjerstad 1934:427–38). Although the number of burials in Tell Dothan's Tomb 1 is significantly larger, the architectural parallels between these two tomb contexts are striking.

OBSERVATIONS ON
MORTUARY PRACTICE IN TOMB 1

The following observations are advanced regarding the reconstruction of Tomb 1 burial ritual. Upon the death of a family member, the body was taken to the ancestral tomb that was located in the limestone escarpment on the western side of the settlement. The bones of earlier burials were unceremoniously swept to the sides of the chamber, thereby providing space for the new interment. The body was then placed on the floor of the chamber or on the debris of earlier burials, either in an extended or full-length position with no uniform orientation. No evidence for contracted positioning was discerned. Numerous burials were documented in which the skeletal remains were covered with the body sherds of large storage jars. Vessels, furnishings, and personal possessions were either placed around the circumference of the tomb or carefully arranged around the body. The deposits appear to represent a full complement of everyday articles that would provide the deceased with material needs for the afterlife and/or the journey thereto. Food and drink were included in the deposits and the presence of clay lamps in large numbers suggests the importance of light. Following interment, the doorway to the chamber was closed with the blocking stone and the shaft was filled with debris.

When a subsequent death in the family occurred and the tomb was to be used again, the debris in the shaft and then the blocking stone were removed and the corpse and its deposits were placed in the chamber. As before, the previous burials and deposits were brushed aside to make room for the new interment with its adornments.

Several inferences may be drawn from the study of tomb mortuary practice relating to such issues as the treatment of the body, the nature of the tomb as a temporary residence, and the significance of the burial deposits. The evidence suggests that there existed a contrast in attitude toward the corpse between the time of interment and after the decomposition of the flesh. At the time of burial, scrupulous care was exercised in the placement of the corpse and in the arrangement of the burial deposits. Once the body was transformed into a pile of bones, it was treated with little respect. It was normal practice to sweep aside the bones and deposits into a heap, oftentimes destroying both in the process in order to make room for subsequent burials. Apparently it was believed that the deceased was sentient and therefore needed sustenance as long as the flesh had not completely decomposed. With the decomposition of the flesh, however, the descendants could with impunity destroy or perhaps even remove certain of the burial deposits. The tomb was not considered as the permanent residence of the dead but as a temporary station on the way to the netherworld. There is no evidence that burial deposits were renewed periodically, nor were additional offerings placed in the tombs in the years that followed interment.

ARCHAEOLOGICAL ILLUSTRATIONS
FROM DOTHAN TOMB 1

Among the biblical formulas indicating death and the ritual of burial is the usage "gathered to his kin/ancestors" (Gen. 25:8, 17; 35:29; 49:29, 33; Num. 20:24; 31:2; Deut. 31:14; 32:50; 34:5; Judg. 2:10). Although various interpretations have been suggested and several nuances may be implied in the formula (Bloch-Smith 1992:110–12), this expression certainly evokes the image of the deceased being reunited with ancestors in the family tomb. Interpreting the formula in light of the archaeology of this burial chamber creates a much richer and more vivid understanding of the burial ritual and the biblical imagery. Another aspect of death and burial ritual that may be illumined by the material culture of Tell Dothan's Tomb 1 is the *marzēaḥ*, a long-lived and somewhat enigmatic institution of funerary practice mentioned in Amos 6:4–7 and Jeremiah 16:5–9 (see King 1988:137–61). Our understanding of this memorial meal, with its inordinate consumption of wine, will be enhanced by the details of burial ritual retrieved from Dothan Tomb 1.

WORKS CITED

Abercrombie, J. R.
1979   Palestinian Burial Practices from 1200 to 600 BCE. Ph.D. disserta-
               tion, University of Pennsylvania.
Albright, W. F.
1938   *The Excavation of Tell Beit Mirsim, II: The Bronze Age*. Annual of
               the American Schools of Oriental Research 17. Cambridge, Mass.:
               American Schools of Oriental Research.
Amiran, R.
1970   *Ancient Pottery of the Holy Land*. New Brunswick, N.J.: Rutgers
               University Press.
Amiran, R., and I. Dunayevsky
1958   The Assyrian Open-Court Building and Its Palestinian Deriva-
               tives. *Bulletin of the American Schools of Oriental Research*
               149:25–32.
Bailey, L. R.
1979   *Biblical Perspectives on Death*. Philadelphia: Fortress.
Bloch-Smith, E.
1992   *Judahite Burial Practices and Beliefs about the Dead*. Journal for the
               Study of the Old Testament Supplement Series, 123 and JSOT/
               ASOR Monograph Series, 7. Sheffield: Sheffield Academic Press.

Cooley, R. E.
1968   The Canaanite Burial Pattern in the Light of the Material
             Remains. Ph.D. dissertation, New York University.
1983   Gathered to His People: A Study of a Dothan Family Tomb. In
             *The Living and Active Word of God: Studies in Honor of Samuel J.
             Schultz*, ed. M. Inch and R. Youngblood, 47–58. Winona Lake,
             Ind.: Eisenbrauns.
Dajani, R. W.
1970   A Late Bronze-Iron Age Tomb Excavated at Sahab, 1968. *Annual
             of the Department of Antiquities of Jordan* 15:29–34.
Dornemann, R. H.
1983   *The Archaeology of the Transjordan in the Bronze and Iron Ages*. Mil-
             waukee, Wis.: Milwaukee Public Museum.
Dothan, T.
1979   *Excavations at the Cemetery of Deir el Balah*. Qedem 10. Jerusalem:
             Hebrew University.
Free, J. P.
1953   The First Season of Excavation at Dothan. *Bulletin of the American
             Schools of Oriental Research* 131:16–20.
1954   The Second Season at Dothan. *Bulletin of the American Schools of
             Oriental Research* 135:14–20.
1955   The Third Season at Dothan. *Bulletin of the American Schools of
             Oriental Research* 139:3–9.
1956a   The Fourth Season at Dothan. *Bulletin of the American Schools of
             Oriental Research* 143:11–17.
1956b   The Excavation of Dothan. *Biblical Archaeologist* 19:43–48.
1958   The Fifth Season at Dothan. *Bulletin of the American Schools of
             Oriental Research* 152:10–18.
1959   The Sixth Season at Dothan. *Bulletin of the American Schools of
             Oriental Research* 156:22–29.
1960   The Seventh Season at Dothan. *Bulletin of the American Schools of
             Oriental Research* 160:6–15.
1962   The Seventh Season at Dothan. *Annual of the Department of Antiq-
             uities of Jordan* 6–7:117–20.
1975   Dothan. In *The Zondervan Pictorial Bible Encyclopedia*, ed. M. C.
             Tenney, 157–60. Grand Rapids: Zondervan.
Gjerstad, E.
1934   *The Swedish Cyprus Expedition, I: Finds and Results of the Excavations
             in Cyprus 1927–1931*. Stockholm: Swedish Cyprus Expedition.
Gonen, R.
1987   Structural Tombs in Canaan in the Second Millennium B.C. In
             The Architecture of Ancient Israel, ed. H. Katzenstein, A. Kempinski,
             and R. Reich, 128–35. Jerusalem: Israel Exploration Society.
1992   *Burial Patterns and Cultural Diversity in Late Bronze Age Canaan.*

American Schools of Oriental Research Dissertation Series, 7.
Winona Lake, Ind.: Eisenbrauns.

Guy, P. L. O.
1938   *Megiddo Tombs*. Oriental Institute Publications 33. Chicago: University of Chicago Press.

Healey, J. F.
1977   Death, Underworld, and Afterlife in the Ugaritic Texts. Ph.D. dissertation, University of London.

King, P. J.
1988   *Amos, Hosea, Micah: An Archaeological Commentary*. Philadelphia: Westminster.

Lewis, T. J.
1989   *Cults of the Dead in Ancient Israel and Ugarit*. Harvard Semitic Museum Monographs, 39. Atlanta: Scholars Press.

Meyers, E. M.
1970   Secondary Burials in Palestine. *Biblical Archaeologist* 33:2–29.

Oren, E.
1973   *The Northern Cemetery at Beth Shan*. Leiden: E. J. Brill.

Petrie, W. M. F.
1931   *Ancient Gaza 1*. London: British School of Archaeology in Egypt.

Pritchard, J. B.
1963   *The Bronze Age Cemetery at Gibeon*. Philadelphia: University Museum.

1980   *The Cemetery at Tell es-Saʿidiyeh, Jordan*. University Museum Monograph 41. Philadelphia: University Museum.

Rahmani, L. Y.
1981   Ancient Jerusalem's Funerary Customs and Tombs: Part Two. *Biblical Archaeologist* 44:229–35.

Schaeffer, C. F. A.
1939   *The Cuneiform Texts of Ras Shamra-Ugarit*. London: Oxford University Press.

Sjoqvist, E.
1940   *Problems of the Late Cypriot Bronze Age*. Stockholm: Swedish Cyprus Expedition.

Stiebing, W. H., Jr.
1970   Burial Practices in Palestine during the Bronze Age. Ph.D. dissertation, University of Pennsylvania.

Tromp, N. J.
1969   *Primitive Conceptions of Death and the Nether World in the Old Testament*. Rome: Pontifical Biblical Institute.

Tufnell, O.
1953   *Lachish III: The Iron Age*. London: Oxford University Press.
1958   *Lachish IV: The Bronze Age*. London: Oxford University Press.

Ussishkin, D.
1975   Dothan. In *Encyclopedia of Archaeological Excavations in the Holy Land*, ed. M. Avi-Yonah, 1:337–39. Jerusalem: Israel Exploration Society.

6 | A Phoenician Inscription from Idalion: Some Old and New Texts Relating to Child Sacrifice

FRANK MOORE CROSS

A sherd inscribed in a semiformal Phoenician hand of the late fourth century BCE was found in the excavations at Idalion (figs. 6-1 and 6-2) in 1974.[1] It came from above the destruction debris of the citadel wall. The archaeological context of the find suggests, and the paleography of the text confirms, that it dates close to the time of the destruction of the citadel by the Ptolemaic forces in 312 BCE. The inscription is on a body sherd of a jar, perhaps an urn (see below), inscribed in alignment with the wheelmarks. This suggests that the inscription was made on a complete pot, subsequently broken, rather than on an ostracon. It reads:

] l bn rp [
] lt ṣmḥ [
š
n

I believe that the inscription can be plausibly reconstructed as follows:

1. [　]l bn rp[']　　　　1. [　]l son of Rapa[']
2. [ᶜ]lt ṣmḥ　　　　　2. [ho]locaust of a scion
3. š　　　　　　　　　3. Year
　　n　　　　　　　　　　50

In line 3, the *šin* and *nun* are ligatured, indeed written as a virtual monogram. Evidently we are dealing with an abbreviation of which the Phoenicians were fond. The *šin* is most easily interpreted as standing for *šatt*, "year." *Nun* should provide us the regnal year of a king of Idalion (and

FIG. 6-1. Photograph of the Idalion ostracon (Object No. 669).

FIG. 6-2. Drawing of the Idalion ostracon (Object No. 669).

Kition). Nevertheless, the appearance of a letter used as a number is surprising. Generally in Phoenician, as in Hebrew, numbers are written out or in inscriptions frequently recorded with a well-known set of arbitrary number symbols. In Greek, however, as early as the seventh century BCE, letters were in use for numbers. The early date of this system in Greek is clear from the fact that the letters *digamma* and *qoppa* are used in the number sequence. If we are correct then in our analysis, we have in this little text the earliest extant evidence of the borrowing of the Greek practice of using letters of the alphabet as numbers by Phoenician or West Semitic scribes. Fittingly, it appears in Cyprus where Greek, Cypriote Syllabic, and Phoenician scribal practices overlap and intertwine. In short, the ligatured *šin–nun* is to be read "year 50."

The sequence of the kings of Kition and Idalion beginning in the mid–fifth century is well known. Of these only one king reigned for fifty years, Pumayyaton, who reigned from about 362 to 312 BCE. His forty-seventh year is elsewhere recorded. The era of Citium followed the era of the kings of Kition beginning in 311 BCE. The fiftieth year of this era is too late for the script of the sherd. Its date from a paleographic point of view is circa 350–300. I believe the inscription provides the date of year 50 of Pumayyaton, 312 BCE, the year of the massive Ptolemaic destruction of the city.

There is now a considerable body of formal and cursive Phoenician that can be used to provide typological data for the dating of the Idalion inscription. Brian Peckham has dealt definitively with the formal scripts of Cyprus in the fourth century (1968:13–41 and pls. I–III) and with the cursive scripts of the sixth–fourth centuries BCE known at the date of his writing (1968: especially pls. I, X, and XI and the accompanying text). To the texts analyzed by Peckham must be added the cursive inscriptions from Shikmona from about 350 BCE (Cross 1968:226–33 and pl. 25); Ostracon 2070 from Elath from the early fourth century BCE (Glueck 1941:7–11, figs. 3–6; Naveh 1966:27–28); an early-fourth-century BCE text found at ᶜAkko (Dothan 1985:81–94 and pl. 13); and a group of ostraca of the fifth and fourth centuries BCE from the Temple of Eshmun near Sidon (Vanel 1967:45–95; 1969:345–64).

The script of the Idalion text is semiformal, that is, it stands somewhere between the formal script of Cyprus in the fourth century BCE and the extreme cursives of the mid– and late fourth century BCE known from Shikmona, the Cairo Papyrus (Aimé-Giron 1939: pl. I), and Bat Yam (Peckham 1966). *Lamed* (lines 1 and 2) is sharply ticked, a form that appears in the fifth century BCE in the formal and cursive character, for example, in the Cypriot tariffs (*Corpus inscriptionum semiticarum* 86 B and 86 A; Peckham 1968: pl. I). The type continues in the fourth-century BCE formal and cursive hands. The ligatured *bet-nun* (line 1) is found in the fifth-century BCE Elephantine ostraca, and later fourth-century BCE texts. The *bet* preserves a "head" and "tail," as in the Elath, Shikmona, and Cairo Papyrus scripts. The *nun* is a straight, elongated line, in contrast to the formal *nun* in line 3. Both forms are at home in the fourth century, one cursive, one formal (in origin). The *reš* is written in a cursive style known in both the fifth and fourth centuries. Formal and cursive *pe* is little differentiated in the scripts of this period, and is of little use in dating. *Taw* (line 2) with its very long and curving vertical and squarish right shoulder is semiformal, related to the *taw*s of Pumayyaton inscriptions. Its long curved vertical reminds one of the *taw*s of the Shikmona jars. *Ṣade* is drawn in a fashion close to that of the ᶜAkko Sherd. It is more formal than the cursive forms of the Elephantine Ostraca and made in a slightly different way (Lidzbarski 1912: nos. 21, 26, 34, 40, and 48). The *mem* too is more formal than the extreme cursive forms of the fourth century. It stands close to some of the forms in the ᶜAkko Sherd, and to some of the Elephantine forms (Lidzbarski 1912: nos. 4, 15c, 34c, 45, 51, and 52). The *ḥet*, while damaged, is a (late) fourth-century cursive type. Compare the forms of the Bat Yam Jar, the Cairo Papyrus, and the Mit Rahineh Ostracon (Aimé-Giron 1931: no. 1 and pl. I.1). The second stroke (counting from right to left) is vertical and long, a fourth-century characteristic. Perhaps the best letter for dating in the Idalion text is the *šin*. It is very broad and shallow, with a distinct tick downward at the right. It appears in the formal scripts of the texts of Milkyaton and Pumayyaton of Idalion, and in the cursive script of the Cairo Papyrus at the end of the fourth century BCE. It is not found in the ᶜAkko Sherd or in the texts from the Eshmun temple near Sidon. It is a form that develops in the mid–fourth century BCE.

The paleographical data assembled above establishes a date for the Idalion inscription between 350 and 300 BCE. Were it not for the archaeological context of the sherd, I should be inclined to date it to the mid–fourth century. However, the paleographical evidence fits easily into the assignment of the inscription to the fiftieth year of Pumayyaton, 312 BCE. Certainly it cannot be assigned to the fiftieth year of the era of Citium. Nor can it be dated before the fall of Idalion to the kings of Kition in the mid–fifth century BCE.

Line 1 of the sherd consists of a name, PN son of PN. Since line 2, as we shall see, is virtually complete, the names evidently were quite short. The first name may have been such a common name as ['Abi']ēl, [Bodbaᶜ]l, or the like. The patronymic is probably Rapa['] (Rapo') or Rapa['ēl] (Rapō'ēl).

The reconstruction of line 2 of the sherd is based on a neglected inscription on a funerary urn published by W. Spiegelberg (1904:89) and discussed briefly by M. Lidzbarski (1907:123–25). The urn comes from a necropolis in Memphis (Mit Rahineh). It is a typical Cypro-Phoenician store jar of the fifth century, also used for funerary remains.[2] The text is complete on the urn and reads:

ᶜlt ṣmḥ.

The Phoenician text is followed by an illegible demotic inscription.[3] We must ask first of all what the term ᶜlt in this context means. ᶜlt, unfortunately, is a homograph of several terms: a preposition meaning "on," a biform of ᶜl; a word for the cover of a sarcophagus; and notably, the term for a holocaust offering equivalent to Hebrew ᶜôlâ (Février 1955b:59–62; Ferron 1971:225–30). A key text is a Neopunic ex voto from Altiburus (Algeria) recording the sacrifices of the members of a funerary society (Donner and Röllig 1964–1966: no. 159). Line 8 reads:

'š ḥᶜl' k' ᶜlt 'w m[n]ḥt bmqdš.

This may be translated "who sacrificed here holocausts or meal offerings in the sanctuary."

Probably we are to translate ᶜlt similarly on an epitaph from Carthage (Ferron 1971; cf. Février 1955b:60):

(1) ᶜlt mgn m (2) qm 'lm mlt.

We read with J. Ferron, "Holocaust of Magon, curator of the god Mil[qar]t." The epitaph was found in a necropolis containing funerary urns. The term may also appear in an obscure passage in a text from Larnax tes Lapethou (line 13), where the term is juxtaposed with mnḥt (Donner and Röllig 1964–1966: no. 43; Honeyman 1941).

Biblical parallels are familiar. In 2 Kings 3:27 we read: "And he [the king of Moab] took his first-born son . . . and offered him up as a holocaust [*wayyaʿălēhû ʿōlâ*]." Jeremiah 19:5 reads: "And they built high places of Baal to burn their children in fire, holocausts to Baal [*ʿōlôt labbāʿal*]" (cf. Judg. 11:31). The same language is used of El's sacrifice of his firstborn (*monogenēs*) as a holocaust (*holokarpoi*) in Philo of Byblos (Attridge and Oden 1981:1.10.33).

The term *smḥ*, "sprout," "scion," is found elsewhere in Phoenician and Punic only in the sense of "offspring," "scion," or legitimate heir. This usage is well known in Hebrew. In Jeremiah 23:5 we read: "I [the Lord] will raise up unto David a legitimate scion [*ṣemaḥ ṣaddîq*]." And similarly in Jeremiah 33:15: "I will make to grow up a legitimate scion [*ṣemaḥ ṣĕdāqâ*] to David." In Zechariah 3:8 the Davidic prince is called "My servant *Ṣemaḥ* [Scion]," and again in 6:12 it is said of the Davidid, "Behold a man whose name is *Ṣemaḥ* [Scion]."

An inscription from Larnax tes Lapethou in Cyprus (Honeyman 1941; Donner and Röllig 1964–1966: no. 43) dating to the time of Ptolemy Philadelphus uses the term *ṣmḥ* in a most interesting way, applying it to Ptolemy Philadelphus, son of Ptolemy I, Soter: *ʿl ḥyy wʿl ḥy zrʿy ym md ym wlṣmḥ ṣdq wl'stw wl'dmy*, "for the sake of my life and for the life of my seed day by day, and for the legitimate scion and for his wives and his blood [relations]." The use of the term *ṣmḥ* applied to the (royal) heir here in Cyprus in Phoenician, in parallel with the identical use of the word in Hebrew, makes clear that we are dealing with a *terminus technicus*. The etymological meaning "sprout" is far in the background and the meaning "scion" in the sense of (legitimate) "heir" is in the foreground. Of interest too is the term *'dm*, literally "blood," Hebrew *dām*, in the sense of blood relations or kindred. This sense is familiar in the case of both Greek *haima* and Latin *sanguis*. The appearance of this form with prosthetic *'alep* is decisive in my opinion for the understanding of the sacrificial term *mlk 'dm*, which must mean a "sacrifice of a blood relation," namely of one's child (cf. Février 1953b; 1955a; *pace* Charlier 1953; Hoftijzer 1958; Mosca 1975:63–67).[4]

The term *ṣmḥ* also appears in two Neopunic inscriptions from Constantine (El Hofra) published by Février (1953a:161–71 and pls. 1–2; Donner and Röllig 1964–1966: nos. 162 and 163; Berthier and Charlier 1955: pl. 50 B–D). The first two lines of the first stele read:

(1) *l'y' 'dn ḥn bʿl 'dr bšrbl ḥmn*

(2) *bʿt tʿmt bṣmḥ tḥbt bš'rm.*

Put into older Punic orthography and translated, this would read:

lḥy' 'dn ḥn bᶜl ḥmn bᶜl 'dr bšrbᶜl bt tmt bṣmḥ ṭbt bš'rm

To Ḥayyo (the Living [God]), lord of grace, Baᶜl Ḥamon, awesome
lord: Bissirbaᶜl [has dedicated] a daughter without blemish, being a
goodly scion, his own flesh (and blood).

The readings *'dn ḥn*, *tᶜmt*, and *thbt* are new. The *ḥet* of *ḥn* is similar to
the *ḥet* of *ṣmḥ* and *thbt* in line 2. The lower part of the right stroke is not
clear in the photographs of the stele, but the traces conform to *ḥet*. The
nun is relatively short but almost identical with the *nun* of *'dn*. The readings
tᶜmt and *thbt* I regard as certain. The adjective *tᶜmt*, *tammat*, "perfect,"
"unblemished," appears elsewhere in Neopunic. In a text from Tripolita-
nia (Donner and Röllig 1964–1966: no. 121.l) is found the expression *dᶜt
htmt*, "perfect knowledge."[5] The *bet* of *thbt* is the more formal long-tailed
type, which interchanges dismayingly with the short cursive form in this
inscription. It appears also in the personal name *bšrbᶜl*. The word *thbt* is
probably a vulgar orthography for *ṭbt*, "good."[6] Less likely, it may be
taken as a t–preformative noun ("beloved one") from the root *ḥbb*, a root
that appears again in line 3 (*mḥbt*).

The formulaic expression *bš'ry/m* has been much discussed. Paul Mosca
(1975:85–116) has given a history of the discussion. My view has its own
nuances, although it is based in part on the analysis of J. G. Février
(1953a; 1953b; 1955a). The variety of spellings—*bš'ry*, (*mlk*) *bšr*, *bš'r*, *bšᶜr*,
bšrm, *bš'rm*, and *bšᶜrm*—suggests an analysis of the formula into three
elements: the preposition *b* plus *š'r* plus the third masculine singular suffix
–y (the older form) or *–m*. Further, the frequent use of *'alep* or *ᶜayin*
between the *šin* and *reš* suggests that there is a (lost) medial laryngeal in
the root preserved as historical spelling in these cases. So far we are with
Février. The sense of the preposition, however, is the key to the phrase's
meaning. I believe the *b–* to be the so-called *bet essentiae* ("*bet* of equivalence") or the closely related "*bet* of specification."[7] This usage is frequent
in Punic and Neopunic, especially in sacrificial terminology. In the
Marseilles Tariff (Donner and Röllig 1964–1966: no. 69) we find
the following specification of offerings:

b'lp, "[a sacrifice] consisting of an ox" (line 3)
bᶜgl, "[a sacrifice] consisting of a calf" (line 5)

bᶜz, "[a sacrifice] consisting of a he goat" (line 7)
b'mr, "[a sacrifice] consisting of a lamb" (line 9)
bgd', "[a sacrifice] consisting of a kid" (line 9) etc.

Compare the broken Carthage Tariff (Donner and Röllig 1964–1966: no. 74), which appears to have followed a similar pattern.

At Calama (Guelma) we find the repeated formula *zbḥ* PN *bmlk* or *nš'* PN *bmlk*, "to sacrifice So-and-so as a mulk offering." In an interesting pair of steles from Malta (Donner and Röllig 1964–1966: Nos. 61A and 61B), we find the following juxtaposed formulas:

nṣb mlk bᶜl 'š šm nḥm lbᶜl ḥmn
nṣb mlk 'mr 'š š[m 'r]š lbᶜl [ḥmn]

"Stele of a mulk-sacrifice consisting of an infant which Naḥum erected for Baᶜl Ḥamōn;"
"Stele of a mulk-sacrifice of a lamb which ['Ari]š [ere]cted for Baᶜl [Ḥamōn]."

This data concerning the extensive use of the preposition *b–* in Phoenician and Punic specifying what is sacrificed has led me to analyze the term *mlk bᶜl* as [*mulk bi-ᶜul*], "a mulk sacrifice consisting of an infant." The preposition specifies the victim in the tariffs. Below we shall see that in another text from Constantine (Donner and Röllig 1964–1966: No. 163; Février 1955a:166–71) we have the victim termed simply *ᶜūl*. Thus we have three types of mulk sacrifice, the *mlk 'mr* [*molchomor*] ("the mulk of a lamb"), the *mlk 'dm* ("the mulk of a blood relation [= one's child]"), and the *mlk bᶜl*, ("mulk of an infant").[8]

The formula *bš'ry/m* occurs only with *mlk 'dm*, with *mlk* (simply), or with zero. Put negatively, the formula never occurs with *mlk 'mr*. This conforms to my interpretation of its meaning as "(consisting of) his flesh (and blood)," that is, a human sacrifice, not a substituted lamb. It complements the use of the expression *bṣmḥ*, emphasizing that the sacrificed child is the flesh and blood of the one making the vow or the offering.[9] In view of reports that often slave or poor children were substituted for the children of nobles or the well-to-do, this emphasis on the kinship relationship of the child to the offerer is quite understandable (Diodorus Siculus 20.14.1–7, trans. Geer 1962:177–81). In line 4/5 of the first Constantine inscription cited above there is another passage of interest. It reads:

. . . l' btrbt šqlt,

". . . to him being a precious child." The term *tarbût* is familiar from the Rabbinic expression *trbwt rʿh*, "degenerate child." *Tarbût* is evidently another term for offspring. The adjective *šqlt* "precious, dear" is well attested in Punic (see Donner and Röllig 1964–1966: no. 121.1; cf. 126.5). Again we note the use of the preposition *b–* specifying the victim.

The first lines of the second stele from Constantine, in which we find the expression *bṣmḥ*, read and translate as follows:

(1) *'tm ṭšk' bntm ltt l'y' bʿl*
(2) *'bmṣbt bn' 'lm bdʿštrt*
(3) *ʿl trbt šqlt kbl l' bṣmḥ šʾrm*

Ṭaško' has fulfilled [his vow], with a whole heart, in giving to Hayyo' Baʿl—together with a stele of the shades [lit., "sons of God"]— Bodʿaštart, an infant, precious offspring, a gift to him consisting of a scion of his flesh [and blood].

There is one new reading in my transcription. The key word *ʿl*, [*ʿûl*], "infant," at the beginning of line 3 was misread by Février, who has been followed mechanically since. He read the first letter as *dalet* (*dl*), but the rounded head he identified as part of the *dalet* is in fact an *ʿayin*. On *trbt šqlt*, see above. Février transcribed the letters correctly, but missed the meaning of *šqlt*. Note again the use of *bet essentiae* with *ṣmḥ*.

In summary we are able to say that the urn inscriptions with the formula *ʿlt ṣmḥ*, "holocaust of a scion," record a sacrificial burning of the child of the offerer, with the term *ṣmḥ* used to stress the blood relationship of the victim to the offerer. In this case the sacrificial term *mulk* in use in Phoenician and Punic and the term *ʿlt* used in the Egyptian funerary inscription, at Idalion, and in the Bible are equivalents (see Delavault and Lemaire 1976).

Recently there have been attempts to revise the standard view of Punic tophets, and their grisly cult, by Sabatino Moscati and members of his school, who argue that the so-called tophets are merely children's cemeteries, for fetuses, newborn who died, and the young who perished by natural means (Moscati 1987:3–15; Benichou-Safar 1981, 1982; Fedele and Foster 1988; Simonetti 1983; cf. Stager 1980, 1982; Moscati 1965–1966). I am unconvinced by these efforts to absolve the Phoenicians and

Punic peoples from the practice of child sacrifice. It requires an extraordinarily hypercritical approach to the classical authors (conveniently collected in Mosca 1975:1–35, see also Day 1989:86–91) to discredit their unanimous testimony. Further, the biblical evidence for child sacrifice among the Israelites (and their neighbors), thanks to recent studies, has been put beyond doubt. Paul Mosca's treatment of the evidence is definitive (1975:117–284; see Day 1989; Heider 1985). It would be curious if the rite, rooted in the myths and legal traditions of El-Cronos, proved to have existed only in Israel.

The ideology of Phoenician and Punic child sacrifice is vividly reflected precisely in the texts that spell out the significance of the *molchomor*, the sacrifice of a lamb, as the vicarious substitute for a child. The Ngaous stele III reads as follows:[10]

1. Q(uod) B(onum) ET F(austum) F(actum) S(it) D(omino) S(ancto) S(aturno) S(acrum) M(agnum)
2. NOCTURNUM ANIMA PR[O]
3. ANIMA SANG(uine) PRO SANG(uine)
4. VITA PRO VITA PRO CON[CES]
5. SE SALUTE<M> EX VISO ET VOTO [SA]
6. CRUM REDDIDERUNT MOLC[HO]
7. MOR FELIX ET DIODORA L(ibentes)
8. ANIMO AGNUM PRO VIKA(rio).

1. Prosperity and salvation! To the holy lord Saturn a great
2. nocturnal sacrifice—breath for
3. breath, blood for blood
4. life for life for the salvation of Concessa
5. —on account of a vision and vow,
6. Felix and Diodora have offered a sacrifice, (namely) a
7. *molchomor*, with joyful
8. hearts, a lamb as a (vicarious) substitute.

If our reading and interpretation of the Idalion and Mit Rahineh urn inscriptions are correct, we are provided with evidence of the practice of child sacrifice among Phoenician populations of Egypt and Cyprus, and most likely the existence in these lands of tophets, precincts of child sacrifice. Tophets in Syria-Palestine have recently come to light, adding to the long list of precincts of child sacrifice found in the Punic cities of the West. The interpretation of the temple near Amman, with its masses of charred infant and children's bones, as housing a cult of child sacrifice seems to be sound (Hennesy 1966, 1970, 1985; *pace* Herr 1983a, 1983b). Tyre in its mainland quarter has produced what will probably prove to be a tophet that documents the practice of child sacrifice in the Phoenician mother city (Seeden 1991; Sader 1991, 1992).

I have argued that the brief inscription from Idalion records a holocaust of a child in the fiftieth year of Pumayyaton, the year of the Ptolemaic destruction of the city. Perhaps we shall be permitted to speculate that the sacrifice was one, perhaps one of many, in the crisis brought about by the overwhelming attack on the city. One remembers a vivid parallel in 2 Kings 3:26–27: "And [Mesha] the king of Moab saw that the battle was going against him and so he took seven hundred swordsmen to [attempt to] break through to the king of Edom, but could not. So he took his firstborn son, he who was meant to succeed him as king, and on the city wall offered him up as a holocaust [*wyᶜlhw ᶜlh*]."

NOTES

1. Reference to this ostracon (Object No. 669) is made in Stager and Walker (1989:466). Its full registration number is M 279-669. WSW 9/17 locus 001.1.11/17/1974.

2. The description and dating of the jar have been provided to me by Lawrence E. Stager.

3. Février (1955b:60) quotes Michel Malinine for an obscure reading of the demotic text, including a date formula "Year 9." An inquiry of the late George Hughes brought the response that the demotic was unintelligible. Whether the Phoenician and the demotic texts are related remains unclear.

4. The interpretation of the word '*dm* as "blood(-relation)" thus is not dependent on the statement of Augustine, *nam et punice edom, sanguis dicitur* (Cross 1974:78 n. 4), the basis of Février's argument and J. Hoftijzer's attack. In view of the term in the Larnax tes Lapethou inscription, however, it becomes clear that Augustine's *edom* is not to be analyzed as the article *e* + *dom*, but as the vocalization of the Phoenician word for blood, '*dm*.

5. Compare the causative (*yipᶜil*) verbal forms *ḥtm* and '*tm* (Donner and Röllig 1964–1966: Nos. 124.4 and 163.1).

6. On the use of *ḥet* in Neopunic orthography, see Menken 1981:72. On the confusion of *ṭet* and *taw* in Neopunic, see Friedrich and Röllig 1970:17, section 39.

7. See the discussions of Cyrus Gordon (1981), B. K. Waltke and M. O'Connor (1990:198, section 11.2.5e), and D. W. Baker (1987:190–91). I am not sure that a native speaker would have discerned the difference between these two uses of the preposition *b*–.

8. The etymology of the term *mulk* is not clear. There can be no doubt now that a divine epithet Mulk existed, probably taken from a specific (and popular) cult. J. Day (1989) most recently has collected the evidence. However, it is equally clear that the word *mulk* in Phoenician and Punic refers to a sacrifice. It may be that the sacrificial term is denominative from the divine epithet. Compare biblical ᶜ*štrt*, "fertility," *dgn* "grain," and *'šrh*, "stylized tree of life."

9. The use of *š'r*, Ugaritic *ṯi'r*, in the sense of flesh-and-blood kinship is well known. See, for example, the biblical expression *miššě'ēr běśārô mimmišpaḥtô*, "of the flesh of his own flesh of his family," that is, his close kindred (Lev. 25:49).

10. I have taken the readings of Mosca (1975:58) and have followed for the most part the translation of Day (1989:8 n. 23).

WORKS CITED

Aimé-Giron, N.
1931   *Textes araméens d'Égypte*. Cairo: Imprimerie de l'Institut Français d'Archéologie Orientale.
1939   Adversaria semitica I. *Bulletin de l'Institut français d'archéologie orientale* 38:1–18.
Amadasi Guzzo, M. G.
1986   *Scavi a Mozia: Le iscrizioni*. Collezione di Studi Fenici 22. Rome: Consiglio Nazionale delle Ricerche.
Attridge, H. W., and R. A. Oden, Jr., eds.
1981   *Philo of Byblos: The Phoenician History*. Catholic Biblical Quarterly Monograph Series, 9. Washington, D.C.: Catholic Biblical Association of America.
Baker, D. W.
1987   Leviticus 1–7 and the Punic Tariffs. *Zeitschrift für die alttestamentliche Wissenschaft* 99:188–97.
Benichou-Safar, H.
1981   À propos des ossements humains du tophet de Carthage. *Rivista di studi fenici* 9:5–9.
1982   *Les tombes puniques de Carthage: Topographie, structures, inscriptions, et rites funéraires*. Paris: Éditions du CNRS.
Berthier, A., and R. Charlier
1955   *Le sanctuaire punique d'El-Hofra à Constantine*. Paris: Arts et Métiers Graphiques (Gouvernment général de l'Algérie).
Brown, S.
1992   *Late Carthaginian Child Sacrifice and Sacrificial Monuments in Their Mediterranean Context*. Journal for the Study of the Old Testament Supplement Series/American Schools of Oriental Research Monograph Series, 3. Sheffield: JSOT Press.
Charlier, R.
1953   La nouvelle série de stèles punique de Constantine et la question des sacrifices dits "mochomor" en relation avec l'expression "BŠRM BTM." *Karthago* 4:1–48.

Cross, F. M.
1968   Jar Inscriptions from Shikmona. *Israel Exploration Journal* 18:226–33.
1974   Inscriptions from Idalion in Greek, Cypriot Syllabic, and Phoenician Scripts. In *American Expedition to Idalion, Cyprus: First Preliminary Report: Seasons of 1971 and 1972*, ed. L. E. Stager, A. M. Walker, and G. E. Wright, 77–81. Cambridge, Mass.: American Schools of Oriental Research.

Day, J.
1989   *Molech: A God of Human Sacrifice in the Old Testament.* University of Cambridge Oriental Publications, 41. Cambridge: Cambridge University Press.

Delavault, B., and A. Lemaire
1976   Une stèle "Molk" de Palestine: Dédié à Eshmoun? RÉS 367 reconsidéré. *Revue biblique* 83:569–83.

Donner, H., and W. Röllig
1964–1966   *Kanaanäische und aramäische Inschriften.* 3 vols. Wiesbaden: Harrassowitz.

Dothan, M.
1985   A Phoenician Inscription from ᶜAkko. *Israel Exploration Journal* 35:81–94.

Eissfeldt, O.
1935   *Molk als Opferbegriff im Punischen und das Ende des Gottes Moloch.* Beiträge zur Religionsgeschichte des Altertums, 3. Halle: Niemeyer.

Fedele, F., and G. V. Foster
1988   Tharros: Ovicaprini sacrificali e rituale del Tofet. *Rivista di studi fenici* 16:46.

Ferron, J.
1971   L'epitaph punique C.I.S. 5980. *Cahiers de Tunisie* 19:225–30.

Février, J. G.
1953a   Un sacrifice d'enfant chez les Numides. In *Mélanges Isidore Lévy*, 161–71. Annuaire de l'Institut de philologie et d'histoire orientales et slaves, 13.
1953b   Molchomor. *Revue d'histoire des religions* 143:8–18.
1955a   Le vocabulaire sacrificiel punique. *Journal asiatique* 243:49–63.
1955b   Sur le mot ᶜLT en phénicien et en punique. *Semitica* 5:59–62.

Friedrich, J., and W. Röllig
1970   *Phönizisch–punische Grammatik.* Analecta Orientalia, 46. Rome: Pontificium Institutum Biblicum.

Geer, R. M., trans.
1962   *Diodorus of Sicily. Books of History.* Loeb Classical Library. Cambridge, Mass.: Harvard University Press.

Glueck, N.
1941   Ostraca from Elath. *Bulletin of the American Schools of Oriental Research* 82:3–11.

Gordon, C.
1981   "In" of Predication or Equivalence. *Journal of Biblical Literature*
                100:612–13.
Heider, G. C.
1985   *The Cult of Molek: A Reassessment.* JSOT Supplement Series, 43.
                Sheffield: JSOT Press.
Hennesy, J. B.
1966   Excavation of a Late Bronze Temple at Amman. *Palestine Explora-*
                tion Quarterly 98:155–62.
1970   A Temple of Human Sacrifice at Amman. *Sydney University Gazette*
                2:20:307–9.
1985   Thirteenth-Century B.C. Temple of Human Sacrifice at Amman.
                Studia Phoenicia 3:85–104.
Herr, L. G.
1983*a*   The Amman Airport Structure and the Geopolitics of Ancient
                Transjordan. *Biblical Archaeologist* 46:223–29.
1983*b*   The Amman Airport Excavations, 1976. *Annual of the American*
                Schools of Oriental Research 48:1–31.
Hoftijzer, J.
1958   Eine Notiz zum punischen Kinderopfer. *Vetus Testamentum*
                8:288–92.
Honeyman, A. M.
1941   Observations on a Phoenician Inscription of Ptolemaic Date. *Jour-*
                nal of Egyptian Archaeology 26:57–67.
Lidzbarski, M.
1907   *Ephemeris für semitische Epigraphik.* 3 Band. Giessen: Alfred Töpel-
                mann.
1912   *Phönizische und aramäische Krugaufschriften aus Elephantine.* Berlin:
                Verlag der Königl. Akademie der Wissenschaft.
Menken, D.
1981   Neo-Punic Orthography. Ph.D. dissertation, Harvard University.
Mosca, P. G.
1975   Child Sacrifice in Canaanite and Israelite Religion: A Study in
                Mulk and Mlk. Ph. D. dissertation, Harvard University.
Moscati, S.
1965–1966   Il sacrificio dei fanciulli: Nuove scoperte su un celebre rito cart-
                aginese. *Rendiconti della Pontifica Accademia Romana di Archeologia*
                38:1–8.
1987   Il sacrificio punico dei fanciulli: Realtà o invenzione? *Problemi at-*
                tuali di scienza e di cultura. Accademia Nazionale dei Lincei 261:3–15.
Naveh, J.
1966   The Scripts of Two Ostraca from Elath. *Bulletin of the American*
                Schools of Oriental Research 183:27–30.
Peckham, J. B.
1966   An Inscribed Jar from Bat-Yam. *Israel Exploration Journal* 16:11–17.

1968   *The Development of the Late Phoenician Scripts.* Harvard Semitic Series, 20. Cambridge, Mass.: Harvard University Press.

Sader, H.
1991   Phoenician Stelae from Tyre. *Berytus* 39:101–26.
1992   Phoenician Stele from Tyre (continued). *Studi epigraphici e linguistici* 9:53–79.

Seeden, H.
1991   A Tophet in Tyre? *Berytus* 39:39–87.

Simonetti, A.
1983   Sacrifici umani e uccisioni rituali nel mondo fenicio-punico: Il contributo delle fonti letterarie. *Rivista di studi fenici* 11:91–111.

Spalinger, A. J.
1978   A Canaanite Ritual Found in Egyptian Reliefs. *The Society for the Study of Egyptian Antiquities Journal* 8:47–60.

Spiegelberg, W., trans.
1904   *Die demotischen Denkmäler: I. Die demotischen Inschriften.* Leipzig: Catalogue général des antiquités égyptiennes du Musée du Caire.

Stager, L. E.
1980   The Rite of Child Sacrifice at Carthage. In *New Light on Ancient Carthage,* ed. J. G. Pedley, 1–11. Ann Arbor: University of Michigan Press.
1982   A View from the Tophet. In *Phönizier im Westen,* ed. H. G. Niemeyer, 155–66. Madrider Beiträge 8. Mainz: Philipp von Zabern.

Stager, L. E., and A. M. Walker
1989   *American Expedition to Idalion, Cyprus 1973–1980.* Oriental Institute Communications, 24. Chicago: Oriental Institute of the University of Chicago.

Stager, L. E., and S. R. Wolff
1984   Child Sacrifice at Carthage: Religious Rite or Population Control? *Biblical Archaeology Review* 10:30–51.

Trebolle Barrera, J.
1987   La transcripción mlk = moloch: Historia del texto e historia de la lengua. *Aula Orientalis* 5.125–28.

Vanel, A.
1967   Six "ostraca" phéniciens trouvés au temple d'Echmoun, près de Saïda. *Bulletin du Musée de Beyrouth* 20:95.
1969   Le septième ostracon phénicien trouvé au temple d'Echmoun, près de Saïda. *Mélanges de l'Université Saint-Joseph* 45:345–64.

Waltke, B. K., and M. O'Connor
1990   *An Introduction to Biblical Hebrew Syntax.* Winona Lake, Ind.: Eisenbrauns.

7 | An Archaeological Commentary on Ezekiel 13

GRAHAM I. DAVIES

The idea of an "archaeological commentary" is Philip King's. But what is a commentary? One of the first Christian scholars to attempt an answer to this question was Jerome:

> [Jerome] defines the purpose of a commentary thus: "To explain what has been said by others and make clear in plain language what has been written obscurely" [*Apol.* 1:16]. And Scripture is full of obscurities [*Ep.* 105:5]. Hence the need for a reliable guide [*Ep.* 53:6]. Things in Scripture that seem perfectly plain often conceal all kinds of unexpected questions [*Comm. in Matt. (ad* 15:13)]. There are many people who profess to be able to resolve these questions, but few can really do so [*Comm. in Eccles. (ad* 1:8)]. Jerome himself does not claim to be in any way a "master" of scriptural interpretation: he is no more than a "partner" in study with others [*Ep.* 53:10]. But what he does claim is that he has read as many different authors as possible, that he has plucked from them as many "different flowers" as he can, and that he has distilled their essence for the benefit of his readers [*Ep.* 61:1]. (Sparks 1970:535)

Of course, a modern archaeological commentary will take its "flowers" not only from earlier commentaries, as Jerome did, but from the archaeological literature itself. But its aim is still "to explain" and "to make clear in plain language what has been written obscurely." It is not, primarily at least, to prove (or disprove) the historicity of the Bible. As such, to speak of an archaeological commentary corresponds well with the aim of those biblical scholars who continue to see the findings of archaeology and Near Eastern studies as having an important contribution to make to the understanding of the Bible alongside such disciplines as linguistic study, text-critical research, literary criticism in its varied senses, and theological reflection. An archaeological commentary in this sense will certainly not see itself as a rival to other kinds of commentary, but it will seek to identify those features in the biblical text (especially obscure ones) for which archaeological evidence can offer some clarification.

Just as an archaeological report will often begin with a general overview of the site, its topography, and its history, we shall first of all say something about the layout and contents of Ezekiel 13. The structure and main themes of the chapter are comparatively simple. Its outer boundaries are indicated by the repeated *Wortereignisformel* in 13:1 and 14:(1–)2, and internally a change of subject matter and the new introduction in 13:17 divide it clearly into two parts: verses 2–16 "against the prophets of Israel" and verses 17–23 against certain women who also "prophesy." Closer examination shows that these two parts of the chapter have been formulated in a very similar way. They both also make considerable use of phrases that recur often in Ezekiel to make further subdivisions. Each begins with an introductory call to the prophet (*bn 'dm*) and an indication of those to whom he is to prophesy (vv 2, 17 [with the first word of v 18, *w'mrt*]). An accusation follows, elaborating the preliminary identification of the addressees (vv 3–7, 18–19) and opening with the messenger formula and a declaration of woe (*hwy*). This is linked by the word "therefore" (*lkn*) and a further messenger formula to the announcement of judgment (vv 8–16, 20–23), which gives to each part of the chapter the classical pattern of the prophetic judgment speech (Westermann 1967). Within the announcements of judgment two formal features are notable. The accusations reappear, as not infrequently occurs elsewhere, and the announcements themselves involve a two-stage development that proceeds in an almost identical way in each case. They begin with a declaration that Yahweh is "against" the addressees, an announcement of direct divine intervention (vv 9, 20–21) and the recognition formula, "and you shall know that I am [the Lord] Yahweh." But then follows an elaboration of the earlier accusation, introduced by "Because" (*y'n*; in v 10 in the more emphatic form *y'n wby'n*), and a further announcement of judgment, which this time centers on the fate of those addressed (vv 14, 23). In each case the recognition formula recurs afterward.

This two-stage development of the announcement of judgment may well be a sign that in each part of the chapter we are dealing with material that has a complex literary history behind it. There are other indications that this is so, particularly in verses 2–16. We may in the first part of the chapter have what were originally two separate oracles of Ezekiel against other prophets, one directed against prophets in the exile (vv 2–9;

cf. v 9) and one against prophets still in Jerusalem (vv 10–16; cf. v 14). In the second part of the chapter this seems less likely to be the case, because verses 22–23 look too brief to have had an independent existence. It is possible that these verses represent an elaboration of verses 17–21, which was based on the formal model of verses 10–16, at the time when the two main parts of the chapter were joined together. It is notable that verses 22–23 pick up the language of verses 2–16 and also associate with it some themes from Ezekiel's wider message.

Whatever the earlier history of the material, the chapter has as it stands a clearly defined "diptych" structure. Its two panels are related not only by their parallel structure but also by the recurrence of the root *nb'*, "prophesy," and by the parallels in vocabulary between verses 6–9 and verse 23 that were noted above. Yet their themes are by no means the same. Verses 2–16 deal with a common theme of classical prophecy that is particularly frequent in Jeremiah, namely the confrontation of judgment prophecy with prophets who even in dire situations prophesied that all would be well. Ezekiel's critique (which is picked up again in 22:28–30) is notable not only for denying that these "salvation" prophets are speaking truly in the name of Yahweh but also for the criticism that they have failed to rebuke their contemporaries for their misdeeds and so provide a genuine defense against the judgment threatened by God (cf. Jer. 23:14, 22). They are in any case clearly prophets who addressed their oracles to the nation (or the exiled community) as a whole, and it is not without point that they are four times referred to as prophets of "[the house of] Israel" (vv 2, 4, 5, 16). Even if verse 16 is a later addition (so Zimmerli 1979:290), its reference to those "who prophesied concerning Jerusalem and saw visions of peace for it" gives an accurate identification of the prophet's opponents.

The "women who prophesy" who are attacked in verses 17–23—the avoidance of the term "prophetess" may well indicate their unofficial status, as W. Zimmerli thought (1979:296)—are by contrast clearly involved with individuals rather than with the nation as a whole. Their rituals are designed, according to verse 19, to affect the lives of different members of the community in different ways. In verse 22 their guilt is compounded by the fact that their aims are diametrically opposed to those of Yahweh, since they are directed against "the righteous" and support "the wicked." These terms may be being used in a quite general sense, as they are in Ezekiel 18 and the related passages 3:16–21 and 33:7–20, where language that is particularly close to the end of 13:22 is used. Then these women would be those who were hired for a pittance (v 19) to safeguard the unscrupulous from harm and to attack the enemies of such people by means of witchcraft. Alternatively, the terms "righteous" and "wicked" may be being used in a specifically judicial sense (as in Deut. 25:1 and 1 Kgs. 8:32), in which case these women were being hired to subvert the process of justice, like the priests and prophets in Micah 3:11 (cf. v 5) and the prophets in the MT of Ezekiel 22:25.

This essay will not be concerned with the use of archaeological evidence to reconstruct the wider historical and political background of Ezekiel's prophecy (on which see Malamat 1975, 1987; Smelik 1991:101–31). Rather will it seek to elucidate with some examples of archaeological evidence four points of detail in the *realia* referred to in chapter 13. In some cases a linguistic investigation will be a necessary preliminary to the archaeological discussion.

WALLS: DESTRUCTION AND REPAIR

Like other biblical writers, Ezekiel knew the power of a familiar image to convey, by comparison, the true meaning of a situation. His opening attack on the prophets who say that all will be well sets them in a scene that is as familiar to the modern archaeologist as it must have been to Ezekiel's audience:

> Your prophets have been like jackals among ruins, O Israel. You have not gone up into the breaches, or repaired a wall for the house of Israel, so that it might stand in battle on the day of the LORD. (13:4–5, NRSV)

Ruins and broken walls can be seen on most abandoned or excavated sites. Although Ezekiel does not here use the normal Hebrew word for a city wall (*ḥômâ*, as in 26:4, etc.), the context makes it clear that this is what he has in mind. He uses the less common word *gādēr* with its cognate verb ("repair" in NRSV). The word *gādēr* has a wide range of meaning, from a wall that surrounds a vineyard to keep out wild animals (Isa. 5:5; Ps. 80:13; cf. Num. 22:24) or a wall blocking a path (Hos. 2:8; cf. the verb in Job 19:8; Lam. 3:9) to a city wall (Mic. 7:11; cf. possibly Ezra 9:9). Particularly the reference to "battle" shows that a defense wall, that is, a city wall, is in mind here: that is why the "breaches" (or rather "breach": cf. 22:20 and Biblica Hebraica Stuttgartensia) need to be repaired. There is some archaeological evidence of such repairs from the later Israelite monarchy. At Lachish (Tell ed-Duweir) the Wellcome-Marston expedition directed by James L. Starkey (1932–38) found that a stone wall about 3.70 m wide attributed to Stratum II had been constructed on the ruins of the brick superstructure of the earlier wall of Strata IV–III (Tufnell 1953:87 with pl. 109). Further evidence of this wall has been uncovered by the Tel Aviv excavations directed by David Ussishkin in Area S on the west side of the mound (Ussishkin 1978:53–54) and in Area R in the southwest (Ussishkin 1983:146), and the chronology of the successive lines of fortification has been clarified to the satisfaction of most scholars. It now appears probable that the massive fortifications of Strata IV–III were destroyed following the Assyrian attack on the city under Sennacherib (Ussishkin 1977:28–60). It has always been agreed that the "city" of Stratum II represents the final stage of occupation during the Israelite monarchy, which was brought to an end shortly before 587/86 BCE, but the date of its construction remains uncertain. Ussishkin tentatively suggested the reign of Josiah, which is when Lachish is likely to have again come under Judahite control (1977:54). A similar situation exists at Beersheba (Tell es-Seba^c). The city of Stratum III was probably also a victim of Sennacherib's invasion in 701 BCE. Against the ruins of its casemate wall, on the inside, a retaining wall was subsequently built, consisting of alternate layers of small stones and soil (Aharoni 1973:11–12). This was the only structure attributed to Stratum I on the tell by the excavators, though they left open the possibility that there may have been a fortress, for example, in an area at the center of the tell that was not excavated. Again the date of these repairs to the fortifications is unclear, but the last generation or so of the monarchy again appears likely.[1]

"Breaches" in the narrower sense of a section of wall broken down in a siege, most likely by a battering ram (King 1988:73), ought also to be evident in excavated remains, though it may be doubted whether that is necessarily what the word used here by Ezekiel (*pereṣ*) means: in 2 Kings 14:13 the related verb is used for the demolition of a stretch of wall some 200 m in length (and cf. Neh. 1:3 with 2:13 and chap. 3). A different word was available to indicate the making of a "breach" as usually envisaged (*nibqa^c*: 2 Kgs. 25:4; Ezek. 30:16). Actual evidence of such breaches, still more of repairs, is in fact hard to identify in Iron Age Palestine. But the destruction of some of the eastern casemates at Hazor could well be due to enemy attack (such as that of Ben-hadad of Syria around 885 BCE, to which Yigael Yadin attributed the destruction layers under Stratum VIII [1972:143]). It is an obvious place for an attack, and there is no need to attribute the removal of the wall, as Yadin did (1972:141; 1975:198), simply to rebuilding operations when the enclosed area was enlarged in Stratum VIII. In the original report on the second season of excavation Yadin had himself noted that Casemates 137a and 150 had been destroyed by fire:

> In the southernmost room (Locus 150) only the foundations of the inner wall were found: the outer wall was razed to its foundations. The whole area here was covered by a thick layer of ashes. In the neighboring casemate too (Locus 137a), much destruction had been wrought; an entire section of the inner wall was missing, which was to be rebuilt and fundamentally altered in Stratum VIII.
>
> Perhaps this was the point at which the enemy broke into the city, and this may be the reason for the gross damage done to the Wall here. The spot is certainly suitable for a breakthrough in time of siege. (Yadin et al. 1960:5)

At Lachish, where the Assyrian reliefs from Sennacherib's palace show battering rams in action, it might have been anticipated that a breach would have been made in the city wall (so Eph'al 1984:66–69), but the excavations in the area of the Assyrian siege ramp (Area R) have shown that this did not occur there and it is likely that the attackers simply climbed over the wall when the defending forces had retreated (Ussishkin 1990:78). The mud-brick material of the wall as well as its thickness may have helped to withstand the attack (see Wright 1990:251).[2] A further defense line (on the counterramp) inside the city has been identified in the recent excavations, and this may be in a broad sense an example of "going up into the breach" (so Ussishkin 1990:71), though the latter term (*pereṣ*) normally implies damage to a wall. Evidence of a breach (and of repairs) was in fact found by the British expedition at two points in the lower Iron Age wall (the "revetment"), one where it joined the bastion on the north and the other about 100 m north on the west side of the mound (Tufnell 1953:91).

"THE REGISTER OF
THE HOUSE OF ISRAEL"

In verse 9 the exclusion of the salvation prophets from "the community [*sôd*] of my people" is reinforced by the statement that "they will not be enrolled in the register of the house of Israel." This implies that in the time of Ezekiel there was a list of the members of the Israelite community. The Hebrew word for "register" is the colorless kĕtāb, "writing," and it is used (elsewhere exclusively in literature of the Persian period or later) to refer to various kinds of documents. The closest parallel to the present occurrence is in the document purporting to list those who returned from exile with Zerubbabel, Jeshua, and others, which appears both in Ezra 2 and in Nehemiah 7. Toward the end of the list some families are included with a note to the effect that they could not prove their Israelite descent (Ezra 2:59–63 = Neh. 7:61–65). Among them are the members of three priestly families, of whom it is said:

> These looked for their entries in the genealogical records, but they were not found there, and so they were excluded from the priesthood as unclean. (Ezra 2:62 = Neh. 7:64)

The exact meaning of the words kĕtābām hammityaḥăśîm, translated "their entries in the genealogical records" above, is not certain (possibly there is an error in the MT), but the general sense is clear enough from the context and shows that kĕtāb refers either to a census list or to an individual entry in one. Presumably those exiles named earlier in Ezra 2/ Nehemiah 7 were able to locate their families in such a list, which must have been maintained in Babylonia. It is probable that Ezekiel too is referring, much earlier, to a list held among the exiles, since otherwise there would be no point in his adding "nor shall they enter the land of Israel." The prophets in question were therefore themselves presumably among the exiled community, like Ezekiel himself, and not in Jerusalem. But what of the "register" or "list" from which they were to be excluded? What antecedents did it have? The Priestly sections of the Pentateuch refer to the taking of a census twice in the wilderness (Num. 1—4; 26), but this presumably only indicates a desire to lay a firm foundation for later genealogies on the part of the Priestly authors in the sixth (or fifth) century BCE. There is probably more truth in the account of a census under David (2 Sam. 24), but the Chronicler's reference to a census of aliens under Solomon (2 Chr. 2:16) is too closely entwined with his apologetic treatment of the corvée to command much credence, and his other two references to a census, under Jehoshaphat (2 Chr. 17:14) and Uzziah (2 Chr. 26:11), are rendered questionable by the very large numbers of fighting men reported in them. In connection with these biblical passages, scholars generally refer to the evidence of census taking (tebibtum) at Mari, where its purpose seems to have been military conscription, taxation, and land distribution (Speiser 1958:17–25; Weinfeld 1991:293–98). But, as might be expected, the practice was more widespread. F. M. Fales mentions "numerous registers of male individuals according to their village of origin and to their social grouping, essentially for the supply of military contingents," in the archives of Alalakh IV and Ugarit (1992:882–83). Pride of place, however, must go to the so-called Assyrian Doomsday Book, which was published in 1901 by C. H. W. Johns from twenty-one tablets found at Nineveh (see Fales 1973 for a more up-to-date account). The opening of Tablet 1 is well preserved:

> Arnaba, son of Si'-nādin-aplu, a vineyard-keeper, his mother, total 2. Aḫabū, a vineyard-keeper, Sagibu his son, a youth, Ilu-abadi his son, of 4 spans, 2 women, total 5. 10,000 vines, 2 houses, 10 *imērē* of cultivable land of their own. Total of the area of Hanana in the city of Sarugi.

> Sîn-na'id(?), a vineyard-keeper, Nusku-ilayya, same occupation, Naš(u)ḫu-qatar his son, of 4 spans, 1 woman, 2 daughters, total 5. Aḫūnu, a vineyard-keeper, his mother, total 2. Total 3 vineyard-keepers, one weaned child, 2 women, 2 daughters, total 8. 15,000 vines, 6 *imērē* of cultivable land, 1 house. Total of the area of Maribatuari in the neighborhood of the city of Til-abnâ.

> (col. 1, lines 1–24: translation after Fales 1973:15–16)

The listing is thus by economic units, and the occupation of the head of each nuclear family is given. All family members are listed, but only the males are named. Details of the property held are given, with its location. To judge from other texts in this series, the name of the landowner whose tenants these farmers were would have been given in one of the damaged sections of the tablet. These documents come from the seventh century BCE and relate to the region around Harran in northern Mesopotamia.

It is also possible that some preexilic Hebrew inscriptions should be seen as deriving from a census of some kind. Lists of names are in fact quite numerous among the inscriptions, and they may be divided into several categories according to their form (I include only longer examples here; the reference given after each text is its number in Davies 1991):

1. Simple lists of names (Samaria C1012 [3.304], Tel ʿIra "Census" Ostracon [13.001])
2. Lists of names with patronymics (Lachish 1 [1.001], Lachish 31 [1.031], Arad 23 [2.023], Arad 27 [2.027], Arad 35 [2.035], Arad 39

[2.039; one name, at the end, lacks a patronymic], Arad 59 [2.059],
Khirbet el-Meshash Ostracon 1682/2 [32.003], Horvat Uza Ostracon B [37.002])
3. Lists in which some names have patronymics (Arad 58 [2.058],
Khirbet el-Meshash Ostracon 1543/1 [32.001])
4. List of names followed by a number (Arad 72 [2.072]; in Lachish 19
[1.019] the numbers seem unlikely to refer to people)
5. List of names, some with patronymics, followed by a number (Arad
38 [2.038])
6. Lists of names with patronymics followed by a place name (the
"Ophel Ostracon" from Jerusalem [4.101], Horvat Uza Ostracon A
[37.001; the list is preceded by a line of uncertain significance])
7. "Delivery notes," containing lists of names followed by quantities,
usually clearly of grain (Lachish 19 [1.019], Lachish 22 [1.022],
Arad 22 [2.022], Arad 31 [2.031], Arad 49 [2.049], Arad 76 [2.076],
Wadi Murabbaᶜat B [33.002])

Of these groups, group 7 certainly has nothing to do with a census: it
may relate to the issue of rations, contributions to an offering, or the
payment of taxes. This may also have been the setting of the lists with
numerals, groups 4 and 5, though the numbers involved could equally
well relate to persons in these cases. The remaining groups are simply
lists of names, except for 6, which includes in addition the name of a place
(of residence?) for each person. The function of these lists remains, for
the most part, unclear. They could be connected in some way with military organization. None is long enough to be an extract from a national
census. But they could be (or some of them could be) examples of the
"census returns" made in individual towns for incorporation in a larger
document. Some slender support for this view comes from the heading
mpqd, which has given the Tel ᶜIra "Census" Ostracon its name. The word
mipqād is used in 2 Samuel 24:9 of the census undertaken by David (and
similarly in the parallel account in 1 Chr. 21:5). But this is not its only
meaning in biblical Hebrew, and the consonants in the inscription could
have been vocalized in a different way, for example, mupqād, "appointed
overseer" (cf. 2 Kgs. 22:5, 9), referring perhaps to the first person on the
list.[3] Nevertheless, even if these lists have nothing to do with a formal
census, they bear witness to a practice of recording people's names (so far
as the evidence goes, only men's names) and sometimes their places of
origin, from which the compilation of a "register" such as that referred to

by Ezekiel early in the exile (probably before 586) was a natural development. The dates assigned to these inscriptions are evenly spread over the eighth, seventh, and sixth centuries BCE. While biblical texts such as 1 Chronicles 1—9 and Ezra 2 probably give the best idea of what Ezekiel's "register" looked like, these inscriptions help to show that already in preexilic times a beginning had been made on the compilation of lists of names in Israel.

THE PLASTERING OF WALLS

In verses 10–16 the prophet's diatribe again refers to walls in a metaphorical sense, but there are some important differences from verse 5 to note. Here the building of a wall is being carried out (by the people in this case), not neglected, and the prophets are criticized for what they are doing, not for what they fail to do. The "wall" in this case is no longer a city wall, but probably the wall of a building: this is the usual meaning of *qîr*, the word used in verses 12, 14, and 15. The hapax legomenon *ḥayis* in verse 10 is related to words in Mishnaic Hebrew and Aramaic that denote a screen or partition and even, in *Mishnah Šebiʿit* 3.8, a terrace- or dam-wall, through which water can flow. The prophets are compared to those who daub plaster (*twḥ*: the verb in vv 10–12, 14–15, also in 22:28; the cognate noun in 13:12) on the stones or bricks of a wall. This normal feature of house construction is clearly referred to in the law about "fungous infection" (REB) on the walls of a house (Lev. 14:33–53). Where infection is confirmed, the affected stones are to be replaced, the plaster throughout the house is to be scraped (or "cut," as MT has in two of the three instances), and new plaster is to be overlaid (vv 41–43). The use of *ʿāpār* here suggests that mud plaster is meant. Other biblical passages refer to the use of lime plaster (*śîd*, *gîrāʾ*), either as a facing for stones that are to be written on (Deut. 27:2, 5) or on the inner wall of the royal palace in Babylon (Dan. 5:5).

Archaeological evidence of this as of other aspects of wall construction is noted by G. R. H. Wright in his comprehensive guides to ancient architecture:

> From surviving evidence it is clear that mud brick walls were invariably plastered, either with mud or "lime" plaster. Traces of this plastering and regular replastering can be seen on many walls (cf. Megiddo II, p. 97). This plaster gives an acceptable finish to the aspect of the wall, but its basic purpose (on external wall faces) was not aspectual, fundamen-

tally it was to act as a preservative against damage to the wall face from driving and running damp, also a stiff coat of plaster on both faces increased the rigidity of the mud brick structure. (1985:420; cf. 1990:423–26 and Netzer 1992:23)

To the evidence cited from Megiddo, which relates to lime plaster on the internal walls of buildings from Strata XIX, XVII–XVI, XIII, and X, may be added the lime plaster on an exterior wall of a palace in Stratum VIII (Loud 1948:25) and the mud plaster, sometimes painted, in the Stratum VIIA palace (ibid., 29). At Lachish there is evidence of lime plaster on the brick city wall, the brick enclosure wall, the stone wall of Stratum II, and the stone outer "revetment," all of the Iron Age (Tufnell 1950:78–79; 1953:87, 89; Ussishkin 1978:47; 1983:142). Plaster is less often found adhering to rubble than to brick in excavations but, as Wright points out, it was a useful protection where mortar had been used between the stones, and mud plaster at least could easily be mistaken for normal debris in the course of excavation and so go unrecorded. He cites examples of lime plaster over rubble walls and steps from the so-called Solar Shrine at Lachish from the Hellenistic period (Tufnell 1953: pl. 24:3–4).

Sometimes lime plaster was overlaid on mud plaster. Three examples of this, which also show the use of straw as temper in mud plaster, may be cited. Wright illustrates the buildup of layers on the masonry of the Early Bronze Age Acropolis Temple at Ai and notes that the wall paintings at Kuntillet Ajrud were on a similar built-up surface: "either one or two coats of gesso were applied to the straw tempered mud plaster that covered all walls" (1985:421 [quoted from Beck 1982:63] and fig. 326). It is probable that the wall paintings referred to in Ezekiel 8:10 and 23:14–15 were (or were imagined as being) on similarly prepared surfaces. At Deir cAlla the plaster on which the Balaam text was inscribed in the early eighth century BCE has been carefully studied (Hoftijzer and van der Kooij 1976:23–24, 27–28). Lime plaster, tempered with straw and other organic material, was built up to a thickness of 7 mm on top of a layer of tempered clay plaster. The surface was smoothed with a brush, whose lines can still be seen, and with the fingers (handprints can also be seen in the repairs to plaster on the outer "revetment" at Lachish).

The evidence that we have surveyed, biblical and archaeological, should be sufficient to identify the *realia* referred to in Ezekiel 13:10–16 and to show that the numerous modern translators and commentators who see a reference to "whitewash" (German, *Tünche*) here are mistaken. Where a thin lime wash was used, it was a covering for a layer of mud plaster, not a direct application to stones or bricks (Wright 1985:421). The translation "whitewash" has become widespread in English-language biblical translations since 1950 (RSV, NEB, NIV, NRSV, REB), though it is not universal even at present: the Jerusalem Bible (except for 22:28) and the Jewish Publication Society translation both have "plaster," correctly (on the King James Version and the Revised Version, see below). No doubt an influence has been exercised by the *Lexicon* of Brown, Driver, and Briggs, which, following Gesenius-Buhl, gives "whitewash" as the meaning of *tāpēl* in Ezekiel 13. But the only justification given for this rendering is a comparison of the root *tpl* II to *tāpal*, for which, however, it gives the meanings "smear, plaster, stick, glue" (cf. the cognates that it cites), with no reference to "whitewash" specifically. The origin of this error is a matter for further research, but the most likely explanation is that an image that is used elsewhere in the Bible (cf. Matt. 23:27; Acts 23:3) and has become part of modern English parlance seemed appropriate to Ezekiel's overall meaning, and as a result architectural accuracy was sacrificed.

Older renderings of the word *tāpēl* are also of interest, which is in part architectural. The early versions gave three different types of interpretation. The Septuagint and Peshitta read the Hebrew consonants as *tippōl*, third singular feminine imperfect Qal of *nāpal*, and translated "[the wall] shall fall." This is certainly an error, because the words for "wall" used here are masculine,[4] and the later Greek versions "correct" it to the meaning that similar words have elsewhere, though in different ways. Thus Aquila and Symmachus render *tāpēl* by words meaning "unsalted" or "unseasoned" (cf. *tāpēl* in Job 6:6), while Theodotion gives "foolishly" (cf. *tiplā* in Job 1:22; 24:12). Theodotion's view has a recent advocate (Propp 1990), and it can claim support from the fact that in two other passages these same Hebrew words are used with specific reference to prophecy that is regarded as false (Jer. 23:13; Lam. 2:14). The force of these parallels is increased by the fact that they are both likely to be closely contemporary with Ezekiel, and indeed Jeremiah 23 is a chapter with which Ezekiel 13 has other points of contact in addition to the common overall theme (cf. v 7 with Jer. 23:21, v 10a with Jer. 23:13b, and v 22 with Jer. 23:22). The third type of interpretation is represented by the Targum and the Vulgate, and it relates *tāpēl* directly to the comparison with building operations. The Targum has "with plain clay that is not mixed with straw" in verses 10–11 and 22:28 (in vv 14–15 it gives the interpretation "prophesied false prophecy in it"), and the Vulgate has "with mud unmixed with straw" in verse 10 and "with untempered mud" in the other verses. The same understanding of *tāpēl* is attributed to the mysterious "Hebrew" in 22:28 (cf. Ziegler 1952:191 and, on the "Hebrew," Field 1875:lxxv–lxxvii), and it was adopted (from the Vulgate and the medieval Jewish commentators) by the King James Version ("untempered morter"), whence it found its way into the Revised Version. As we have already seen, archaeological evidence shows that it was common practice to add straw to mud and lime plaster, to prevent cracks in the plaster as it dried (see Wright 1985:352; Reich 1992:5). In other words, according to this interpretation the other prophets are like builders who do not do their job properly and make the plaster coating useless as protection against coming storms. Such an understanding of *tāpēl* might have been based on actual knowledge of the word's usage or on an intelligent reading of the context, but in Jerome's case at least we know that it was neither of these. He tells us in his commentary on this passage of Ezekiel that he derived his translation from Symmachus and that Aquila gave the same meaning in different words (Migne, *Patrologia Latina* 25:112c–113a). It may well be the case that this tradition of interpretation was simply making explicit what Symmachus (less likely Aquila) had intended: when his version of the whole passage was read, the "unseasoned stuff" used in the daubing would naturally have been understood to indicate something lacking in the plaster. Even so, his choice of such a rendering makes it unlikely that he was basing his interpretation on a common use of *tāpēl* as a builder's term: if he were, he would surely have chosen a more appropriate Greek expression.

The modern view of the meaning of *tāpēl* relies, even where the mistranslation "whitewash" appears, on an association with the root *tpl*, assuming an interchange of *taw* and *ṭet*. Although not common, this interchange does occur in Hebrew (cf. *tᶜh* [as in Jer. 23:13] and *ṭᶜh* [in Ezek. 13:10] = "err"), and although biblical Hebrew only exhibits instances of the verb *tāpal* in a figurative sense, this clearly presupposes the literal sense "plaster," which occurs in later texts. On this understanding of *tāpēl* the prophets who are being attacked are not compared to unskillful builders but to those who follow standard building practice. The sense will then be that by their reassuring oracles they are improving appearances and, perhaps, offering temporary protection to the people and their leaders despite their extortionate behavior (cf. 22:27–29), but that none of them will be able to stand up to the catastrophe that is imminent. Because of the uncertainty over the meaning of *tāpēl* in this passage, the exact point of Ezekiel's comparison must remain in doubt, but a knowledge of ancient building practice at least helps to clarify the possibilities for interpretation that exist.

"BANDS" AND "VEILS"

In the closing verses of Ezekiel 13 the prophet turns his attention to magic practices whose details remain obscure. Two key terms are kĕsātôt and mispāḥôt, which occur only in this passage (vv 18, 20, 21). The kĕsātôt are "sewn" on the arms, while the mispāḥôt are made "on the head of every height"(?), which has been understood to mean "on the heads of persons of every height" (so, e.g., NRSV). Both are to be "torn off," according to verses 20–21. The kĕsātôt are generally taken to be "bands" and the mispāḥôt, with less justification, are identified as "veils." The magical associations of these objects have been recognized since antiquity: the "Hebrew" version and Ephraem Syrus saw the kĕsātôt as amulets (Cooke 1936:145), while the Targum's rendering "a dark patch" probably also points in the direction of magic. For mispāḥôt the Targum has patkômārîn, the same word it uses for the brightly colored coverings of the bāmôt in 16:16.

In modern times archaeological discoveries and texts from Babylonia in particular have shed further light on what might be involved: G. A. Cooke cited Hellenistic figurines from Tell Sandahannah (Mareshah) in Palestine with wire twisted around their arms or ankles (1936:145–46, with reference to Bliss and Macalister 1902:154–55 [cf. pl. 85])[5] and a magical text from Babylonia that speaks of white and black wool being bound to a person or to someone's bed (on such texts see further Oppenheim 1964:226, 285 and Scurlock 1992:464–68). Perhaps the most important discovery, which was made by J. Herrmann (1924:81), is that both words can be related to Akkadian verbs, kasû and sapāḥu, which mean respectively "to bind" and "to loose" (or better "to annul"). Herrmann also drew attention to texts in which these verbs were used in a specifically magical sense (1924:86; for some references see von Soden 1965–81:455 [kasû G-stem, 1c; D-stem, 2b], 1024–25 [sapāḥu D-stem, 5]). This indicates that, whatever the objects referred to were, their function was to act as "binders" and "loosers" in a magical sense, in other words as means of attack and defense in sorcery. This fits well with the context in Ezekiel, which speaks of the preservation of life as well as its destruction (v 19; cf. v 22). Such an explanation of these unfamiliar terms most likely implies that women of Jerusalem ("the daughters of your people," v 17) had adopted the language and practices of Babylonian magic and were making a scant living by using them in a way that raised a fundamental challenge to Ezekiel's attempts at moral reform (18:30–32). The reference to "all wrists" in verse 18, even if we allow for some exaggeration, suggests that these practices had become popular and widespread among the exiled Jewish community.

NOTES

1. A further example may be the building of a thin wall 2 m inside the southern wall of the fort at Arad in Stratum VII/VI. But the excavators could only say that "it must be assumed" that the southern wall of Stratum VIII had been damaged in 701 (Herzog et al. 1984:22). The recent discussion of the chronology of Arad by D. Ussishkin (1988:15–54) would place the addition of this wall sometime between 701 and 586.

2. H. Weippert suggested that the counterramp built inside the city was meant to prevent a breach in the wall (1988:611). This is plausible, since it supported the wall across the whole area where the Assyrian attack was concentrated.

3. The proposal of Y. Garfinkel (1987) that *mpqd* means "guard" assumes its precise equivalence to *mšmr*. The evidence he reviews points rather to the meaning "[special] unit."

4. The only exception in the whole Bible is in verse 14b here, but the sudden transition from masculine to feminine endings must mean that the first clause of verse 14b is of a separate origin and probably did not refer to a wall at all, but to the city of Jerusalem (cf. v 16).

5. The interpretation of the figurines as magical is strengthened by the discovery in the same excavations of numerous Greek magical inscriptions (Bliss and Macalister 1902:158–87). The Hellenistic figurine from Samaria, also mentioned by G. A. Cooke, has no wire on it and is therefore not relevant to the present issue.

WORKS CITED

Aharoni, Y.
1973   *Beersheba I, Excavations at Tel Beer-sheba, 1969–1971 Seasons*. Tel Aviv: Institute of Archaeology, Tel Aviv University.
Beck, P.
1982   The Drawings from Ḥorvat Teiman (Kuntillet ᶜAjrud). *Tel Aviv* 9:3–68.
Bliss, F. J., and R. A. S. Macalister
1902   *Excavations in Palestine during the Years 1898–1900*. London: Palestine Exploration Fund.

Cooke, G. A.
1936   *A Critical and Exegetical Commentary on the Book of Ezekiel.* International Critical Commentary. Edinburgh: T. and T. Clark.

Davies, G. I.
1991   *Ancient Hebrew Inscriptions: Corpus and Concordance.* Cambridge: Cambridge University Press.

Eph'al, I.
1984   The Assyrian Siege Ramp at Lachish: Military and Lexical Aspects. *Tel Aviv* 11:60–70.

Fales, F. M.
1973   *Censimenti e catasti di epoca neo-assira.* Studi economici e tecnologici 2. Roma: Istituto per l'Oriente.
1992   Census: Ancient Near East. In *The Anchor Bible Dictionary*, ed. D. N. Freedman, 1:882–83. New York: Doubleday.

Field, F.
1875   *Origenis Hexaplorum Quae Supersunt.* Oxford: Clarendon.

Garfinkel, Y.
1987   The Meaning of the Word MPQD in the Tel ʿIra Ostracon. *Palestine Exploration Quarterly* 119:19–23.

Herrmann, J.
1924   *Ezechiel.* Kommentar zum Alten Testament. Leipzig: A. Deichert.

Herzog, Z.; M. Aharoni; A. F. Rainey; and S. Moshkovitz
1984   The Israelite Fortress at Arad. *Bulletin of the American Schools of Oriental Research* 254:1–34.

Hoftijzer, J., and G. van der Kooij
1976   *Aramaic Texts from Deir ʿAlla.* Documenta et Monumenta Orientis Antiqui 19. Leiden: E. J. Brill.

Johns, C. H. W.
1901   *The Assyrian Doomsday Book or Liber Censualis.* Assyriologische Bibliothek 17. Leipzig: J. C. Hinrichs.

King, P. J.
1988   *Amos, Hosea, Micah: An Archaeological Commentary.* Philadelphia: Westminster.

Loud, G.
1948   *Megiddo II, Seasons of 1935–39.* Oriental Institute Publications 62. Chicago: University of Chicago Press.

Malamat, A.
1975   The Twilight of Judah in the Egyptian-Babylonian Maelstrom. *Supplement to Vetus Testamentum* 28:123–45.
1987   The Last Years of the Kingdom of Judah. In *Archaeology and Biblical Interpretation* (D. Glenn Rose Volume), ed. L. G. Perdue, 287–314. Atlanta: John Knox.

Netzer, E.
1992   Massive Structures: Processes in Construction and Destruction. In *The Architecture of Ancient Israel from the Prehistoric to the Persian*

Periods, ed. A. Kempinski and R. Reich, 17–27. Jerusalem: Israel Exploration Society.

Oppenheim, A. L.
1964   *Ancient Mesopotamia*. Chicago: University of Chicago Press.

Propp, W. H.
1990   The Meaning of *Tāpel* in Ezekiel. *Zeitschrift für die alttestamentliche Wissenschaft* 102:404–8.

Reich, R.
1992   Building Materials and Architectural Elements in Ancient Israel. In *The Architecture of Ancient Israel from the Prehistoric to the Persian Periods*, ed. A. Kempinski and R. Reich, 1–16. Jerusalem: Israel Exploration Society.

Reisner, G. A.; C. S. Fisher; and D. F. Lyon
1924   *Harvard Excavations at Samaria*. Cambridge, Mass.: Harvard University Press.

Scurlock, J. A.
1992   Magic: Ancient Near East. In *The Anchor Bible Dictionary*, ed. D. N. Freedman, 4:464–68. Garden City, N.Y.: Doubleday.

Smelik, K. A. D.
1991   *Writings from Ancient Israel: A Handbook of Historical and Religious Documents*. Translated by G. I. Davies, from Dutch. 1984. Edinburgh: T. and T. Clark.

von Soden, W.
1965–1981   *Akkadisches Handwörterbuch*. Wiesbaden: Harrassowitz.

Sparks, H. F. D.
1970   Jerome as Biblical Scholar. In *The Cambridge History of the Bible*, ed. P. R. Ackroyd and C. F. Evans, 1.510–41. Cambridge: Cambridge University Press.

Speiser, E. A.
1958   Census and Ritual Expiation in Mari and Israel. *Bulletin of the American Schools of Oriental Research* 149:17–25.

Tufnell, O.
1950   Excavations at Tell ed-Duweir, Palestine, Directed by the Late J. L. Starkey, 1932–1938: Some Results and Reflections. *Palestine Exploration Quarterly* 82:65–91.

1953   *Lachish III: The Iron Age*. London: Oxford University Press.

Ussishkin, D.
1977   The Destruction of Lachish by Sennacherib and the Dating of the Royal Judaean Storage Jars. *Tel Aviv* 4:28–60.

1978   Excavations at Tel Lachish 1973–1977: Preliminary Report. *Tel Aviv* 5:1–97.

1983   Excavations at Tel Lachish 1978–1983: Second Preliminary Report. *Tel Aviv* 10:97–185.

1988   The Date of the Judaean Shrine at Arad. *Israel Exploration Journal* 38:142–57.

1990   The Assyrian Attack on Lachish: The Archaeological Evidence
                from the Southwest Corner of the Site. *Tel Aviv* 17:53–86.

Weinfeld, M.
1991   The Census in Mari, in Ancient Israel, and in Ancient Rome. In
                Storia e tradizioni di Israele: Scritti in Honore di J. Alberto Soggin, ed.
                D. Garrone and F. Israel, 293–98. Brescia: Paideia.

Weippert, H.
1988   *Palästina in vorhellenistischer Zeit.* Handbuch der Archäologie,
                Vorderasien II/1. Munich: C. H. Beck.

Westermann, C.
1967   *Basic Forms of Prophetic Speech.* Translated by H. C. White, from
                German. 1964. Philadelphia: Westminster.

Wright, G. R. H.
1985   *Ancient Building in South Syria and Palestine.* Handbuch der Orien-
                talistik 7.1.2.B.3. Leiden: E. J. Brill.
1990   *Ancient Building in Cyprus.* Handbuch der Orientalistik 7.1.2.B.8.
                Leiden: E. J. Brill.

Yadin, Y.
1972   *Hazor: The Head of All Those Kingdoms.* The Schweich Lectures for
                1970. London: British Academy.
1975   *Hazor: The Rediscovery of a Great Citadel of the Bible.* London:
                Weidenfeld and Nicolson.

Yadin, Y.; Y. Aharoni; R. Amiran; T. Dothan; I. Dunayevsky; and J. Perrot
1960   *Hazor II: An Account of the Second Season of Excavations, 1956.*
                Jerusalem: Magnes Press.

Ziegler, J.
1952   *Ezechiel.* Septuaginta, vol. 16/1. Göttingen: Vandenhoeck and Rup-
                precht.

Zimmerli, W.
1979   *Ezekiel,* vol. 1. Hermeneia. Translated by R. E. Clements, from
                German. 1969. Philadelphia: Fortress.

8 | Khirbet Qumran Revisited

PHILIP R. DAVIES

In an earlier study of the archaeology of Qumran (Davies 1988),[1] I realized I had been as much in the wrong as all the other scholars who had accepted Roland de Vaux's data and deductions without adequate reflection (see Davies 1982). The many problems and queries arising from the excavations of the site and their subsequent interpretation have since been caught up in the current debate about the origin of the Qumran scrolls themselves. The occasion of this volume provides an opportunity to review developments in our understanding of Khirbet Qumran over the past five years. My remarks fall into two parts: a reflection on the role of Khirbet Qumran and its archaeology in the ongoing debate about the origin of the Dead Sea Scrolls, and then some indications of the perspectives that further investigation of the site might adopt in the future.

ARCHAEOLOGY AND THE DEAD SEA SCROLLS: SO FAR

The proximity of Khirbet Qumran to the scroll caves was not initially the main factor leading to its excavation. The ruin had at first been noticed but then discounted, as a Roman fort, by those archaeologists hunting for scrolls caves. Cave 1 is in any event some 1.5 km distant from the ruins. It was the account of Pliny the Elder (*Natural History* 5.17.73), written in the last quarter of the first century CE locating a colony of Essenes on the Dead Sea shore, probably between En-gedi and Jericho (the text of *Natural History* on this point is not entirely unambiguous; see Milik 1959:44–45; Vermes and Goodman 1989:3 n. 19), that seems first of all to have convinced de Vaux to excavate this site in the hope of uncovering the

126

place from which the scrolls came. The scrolls of Cave 1 furnished the most extensive and plausible description of a Jewish community with somewhat unorthodox (as it then seemed) beliefs and practices, and with the aid of Josephus and Philo, sufficient parallels between their Essenes and the *yaḥad* of the *Community Rule* (known as 1QS) were drawn to identify them as the authors of the scrolls as well. With the subsequent discovery of Caves 4, 5, and 6 in or beside the actual Qumran marl plateau, some kind of link between the scrolls recovered from there and the site appeared to be confirmed.

The evidence for the "Essene hypothesis" was enhanced by the interpretation of the ruins of Qumran and was powerful enough to secure for it within Qumran scholarship the status of an assured result for over two decades. Earlier suggestions denying links between the ruins and the caves were obliterated: the scrolls were, as F. M. Cross (1958) put it, "the ancient library of Qumran." Indeed, the Essene identification, if less secure than previously, remains popular and will undoubtedly persist until or unless the current textbooks are replaced. Among scholars at the forefront of Qumran research, however, there are many, perhaps a majority, who now doubt the Essene identification. How has the reign of this fairly plausible and well-entrenched theory come to give way to skepticism and dispute? And what are the implications of this attitude for our understanding of the site itself?

Doubts about the Essene theory did not come about directly as a result of any revaluation of the archaeological data. It must be appreciated that from the beginning of the new field of Dead Sea Scrolls scholarship, archaeology contributed little to the elucidation of the scrolls themselves, which say little or nothing about the location, politics, economics, and daily routine of the communities they describe. The situation was rather the reverse: the community revealed in the Cave 1 scrolls (i.e., the *Community Rule*, in which the group referred to itself as the *yaḥad*) explained—rather, imposed itself on—the ruins: dining room, writing room, bathing pools, kitchens, and council room were discovered for the monastic Essenes. There was little or no evaluation of the site outside the context provided by the scrolls, and accordingly its capacity to generate a critique of the prevailing hypothesis deriving from the scrolls was extremely limited.

It was therefore by means of literary and historical analysis that the "Essene hypothesis" was dislodged from its preeminent position. The publication of the *Temple Scroll* by Yigael Yadin (1977–83) played an important role in this, though Yadin himself was not aware of it at the time. Yadin's very full, rapidly completed edition and commentary was marred by his insistence that this work was a product of "the sect," meaning the *yaḥad*. Other commentators moved toward the opposite conclusion (e.g., Levine 1978; Schiffman 1980; see in reply Yadin 1980). The contents of this longest of the Qumran nonbiblical manuscripts were generally regarded as unexpected and problematic. Apart from a solar-based calendar, the Temple Scroll did not really rehearse the "sectarian" theology in which the Cave 1 manuscripts had been so rich: no eschatology, no dualism, no community organization or principles. Nor did it share the distinctive vocabulary of the *yaḥad*. Instead, it comprised a detailed collation of biblical and biblically derived legislation about the Temple and other legal matters that could have been of no immediate practical relevance to the "sect" as conceived by scholarship up to that point. The concerns of this text suggested a highly modified if not quite different profile of its authors. Dates for its composition varied widely: the Achaemenid period and the time of Herod the Great were both suggested (see Brooke 1989). Was it, then, a "sectarian document" (as the issue was put by both Yadin [1980] and Schiffman [1980])? If so, this "sect" was not the *yaḥad* one had become used to; if not sectarian, what was it doing in Qumran Cave 11? The problem opened up by the *Temple Scroll* was widened further by the argument, initiated by H. Stegemann (1971) and elaborated in Davies (1983), that the *Damascus Document* (known as CD) and the *Community Rule* (1QS) did not describe the same community. According to this new analysis of the *Damascus Document*, there had been a prehistory to the formation of the *yaḥad*, one which, moreover, had also involved living in settlements (called "camps"). There were thus several communities described in the Dead Sea Scrolls. The *Temple Scroll* had extensive links with one of these, that of CD, and indeed with the book of *Jubilees* also, but not with the *yaḥad*, the definitive "Qumran sect" (see Davies 1989 and VanderKam 1989). The view of the Qumran Essene sect as having migrated directly to Qumran in opposition to what they saw as an illegitimate high priesthood was being seriously questioned, and a more complicated history of formation was replacing it. Obviously, there were to be implications for the role of Qumran itself in this revised reconstruction.

Finally, two more or less simultaneous developments in the late 1980s brought consensus entirely to an end by proposing even more radical revisions to the accepted view. One came from outside the scholarly establishment, the other from its very core. The former was the single-handed and sustained assault by Norman Golb (1985, 1989) on the theory that the scrolls came from Qumran at all. He revived the older suggestion by K. H. Rengstorf (1960) that they were the contents of Jerusalem libraries placed there during the 60s CE for safekeeping in the face of the advancing Romans. These scrolls, as Golb argued, did not come from any one sect or group, but from a wide spectrum of Jewish sources, and reflected the diversity of Jewish belief and practice at the time of their composition. The site of Qumran itself reverted, in Golb's view, to what it had been thought to be before the manuscripts came to light, and indeed, what in de Vaux's opinion it had become after its evacuation by the Essenes—a fort.

The second development came about through quite different mechanisms. For several years the existence of a text of a so-called letter from the Teacher of Righteousness had been announced by John Strugnell, to whose responsibility these particular manuscript fragments had fallen. Since only the smallest scraps were leaked (Qimron and Strugnell 1985), and the text itself, though almost entirely reconstructed since the late 1950s and its publication continuously promised, remained unpublished (and still remains so, at least by its official editors), only Strugnell and his coeditor Elisha Qimron could discuss this text. But this entirely unacceptable policy was circumvented when the mysterious text, called 4QMMT (= 4QMiqṣat Maʿasê ha-Torâ), began to circulate in an unauthorized draft. As a result, debate about its significance expanded beyond the circle of official editors with access to the fragments. The ensuing debate, though deprecated by the official editors, nevertheless had to be acknowledged, and a number of specialists were invited to inspect the text and give their comments on its contents. The view strongly emerged from this circle that the authors of 4QMMT were a hitherto unknown group of Sadducees. The official hypothesis underwent a dramatic and sudden change, and the Essenes were usurped by another and even more mysterious group. The reasons for the new identification, based on this text plus a very few others were, and are, tenuous and contradictory. Those texts which had once suggested Essene identification, such as 1QS, were now being simply relegated to a less significant position in the debate.

This reason for this *volte-face* may be summarized as follows. 4QMMT contains a list of points of law (principally on purity) in which the writer(s) and addressee(s) disagree. The opinions asserted by the authors of the text against their addressees are identified as Sadducean on the basis of a very few halakhic positions that correspond to those attributed to "Sadducees" (if that is what *ṣaddûqîm* means) in rabbinic literature. But since these "Sadducees" of MMT disagree fundamentally with the Sadducees known to us from Josephus and the New Testament (the Qumran "Sadducees" believe in angels and afterlife and remain distant from the Temple), these are held to be a sectarian Sadducee group. As a result of this classification, both agreement and disagreement with "Sadducee" features known from elsewhere can be equally explained. The most vociferous exponent of this view has been Lawrence Schiffman (1989, 1990). But whether or not the "Sadducee" hypothesis is coherent, it does seem from the cumulative evidence of the *Damascus Document*, the *Temple Scroll*, and 4QMMT that halakhic disagreement, probably centering on the liturgical calendar and on certain purity laws, provides the most likely explanation for the origin of some or all of the groups behind the Qumran literature.

But how do these new perspectives and questions—the possibility of no connection between the scrolls and the site, the notion of more than one "Qumran community," the "Sadducee" theory—affect our interpretation of the site of Khirbet Qumran? Obviously, they do so in varying respects. On Golb's theory, for instance, there is no "Qumran community"; on my own suggestion, there could be more than one possible "Qumran community." Those who favor the "Sadducee" identification have jettisoned the best evidence for a link between the scrolls and the site—the evidence from the classical authors about Essenes—and offer us instead a community about which we know nothing except what is inferred from a few scrolls; thus, connections between this group and whatever kind of settlement they may or may not have had are somewhat ethereal.

In the light of so much uncertainty over the proper setting of the scrolls themselves, it is wise for those interested in the archaeology of the site to set aside theories about communities, of whatever identity, and focus instead on the archaeological data and arguments: the environment, the architecture, and the artifacts. Reappraisal of the interpretation bequeathed by de Vaux had in any case been manifesting itself while controversy about the scrolls was brewing, and the unsatisfactory nature of much of the original work was becoming more widely acknowledged. As we have seen, Golb promoted the theory that the site had been a military establishment. Other possibilities also emerged. Already in 1986, work had begun on the editing and publishing of de Vaux's final report on

Khirbet Qumran from his notes. The École Biblique brought in Robert and Pauline Donceel to accomplish this. According to Pauline Donceel, in a television documentary produced by "Nova" and shown in the United States in late 1991, the ruins of Qumran might be the remains of a villa; more recently she has proposed that the site may have been a commercial installation dedicated to the production of balsam or other cosmetic substances ("Horizon," BBC Television, March 22, 1993).

It may surprise nonarchaeologists to learn that such dramatic differences of interpretation are possible. Archaeologists themselves will be less surprised; faith in what is widely seen by outsiders as purely a science is touching but often misplaced. The difficulty of interpreting finds is notorious and literary materials are often a necessary recourse. As our knowledge of ancient Palestinian architecture and settlement history improves, it becomes easier to identify certain structures and complexes, and reliance upon literature and imagination (or literary imagination) recedes. Even so, Khirbet Qumran remains a difficult case. The challenge to interpret the site independently of the contents of the scrolls is nevertheless one that needs to be met, and the dispute over the identity and origins of the scrolls has at least been helpful in promoting this realization.

REAPPRAISAL

I wish in this short essay to draw attention to a number of factors that may play a role in the reappraisal that has just begun to occur and that may become a major topic in the coming years. I shall comment on two aspects of Qumran: the topography, which is well known and often remarked, though, in my view, often poorly assessed; and the environment, namely the western shore of the Dead Sea, which affords a number of valuable sites for comparison.

Topography

Obviously the first point to note with respect to the site is its proximity to caves (see de Vaux 1973: pl. 40). Within 3.5 km of the site lie forty caves so far discovered that, according to de Vaux, bear traces of human habitation. Of these, eleven lie within 500 m, and one more between 500 m and 1 km. Six of these caves were, again according to de Vaux, "not utilized by the Qumran community." Of the eleven manuscript caves, numbers 4–10 lie very close to Qumran, while 1 and 2 are about 1 km north, and 3 and

11 are 1 km farther north. There is no one theory that can satisfactorily account for this distribution, nor for the difference in the mode of preservation of the manuscripts between, say, Cave 1, where they were wrapped in linen and jars, and Cave 4, where they were apparently not protected at all. While some caves with major deposits lie a considerable distance from the site, it is reasonable to think that the large deposit in Cave 4 could only have been made with the knowledge or connivance of inhabitants of Qumran, but whether the site was occupied at the actual moment of deposit is not proven, and even if it were, it does not necessarily follow that the inhabitants wrote, kept, or hid them themselves. There is another peculiarity to be noted. Access to Cave 4 was only possible initially via an entrance in the plateau wall, until the excavators cut an access from the surface. Why was this artificial cave constructed in this manner, so difficult of access from the ruins? Since there were plenty of natural caves nearby, it could hardly have been created for manuscript storage. Moreover, according to de Vaux, there is no sign of habitation by the "Qumran community" in this cave. It is possible that the considerable erosion that has taken place over two thousand years has removed traces of an earlier entrance from above (and possibly also removed traces of other structures, too, especially on the western, "industrial" side of the settlement), but this is doubtful and leaves the opening in the rockface unexplained. It is more probable that this cave was made deliberately difficult of access, and if so, surely not for the purpose of storing scrolls. (It could not have been suddenly created in an emergency.) There are for this purpose less conspicuous natural caves reasonably nearby. If Qumran were a religious settlement at some time, the cave might have been a place of confinement for disciplinary offenses, and on the "Essene community" theory this seems to me to be the most plausible suggestion.

But, as the above comments are intended to show, the relationship between caves and ruins raises too many problems and possibilities for one to remain entirely satisfied with the explanation that the scrolls were written at Qumran and either stored here in the form of individual libraries, or concealed at one particular moment in the expectation of unwelcome visitors. Those explanations arose directly from the conclusion that Qumran was an (or *the*) Essene settlement and that these scrolls were Essene scrolls. But since this theory is now being questioned on many sides, the relationship between site and caves can and needs to be reopened to other equally or more attractive possibilities, of which there are a good many.

Another problematic feature of the site is its water system. Khirbet Qumran affords a modest supply of seasonal rainwater from rainfall on the plateau itself which, as in the Iron II settlement, can be drained into a cistern. More rainwater can be collected from the nearby Wadi Qumran, in which case the gathering requires considerable effort if enough is to be sufficient for more than a handful of persons. An aqueduct (including a tunnel) and six large rectangular cisterns were added to the single Iron II round cistern. Such a system is of itself extremely modest when compared with many other contemporary systems. But the engineering is not the issue. The real problem is that little more than 2 km south, ᶜAin Feshkha offers a convenient and copious water supply. If one accepts, with de Vaux, that the inhabitants of Qumran also occupied ᶜAin Feshkha, it becomes difficult to explain why this settlement was constructed at all. It seems to me more logical that the inhabitants of Qumran did not also occupy ᶜAin Feshkha, and hence had no access to its water supply. But whatever the case, the water system at Qumran can hardly have been constructed for ritual washing, unless the inhabitants walked some way beyond the site to fetch drinking water. Neither is it likely that this hard-won water was used to wash out a refectory floor, as has also been maintained (de Vaux 1973:26; Davies 1982:48).

Of more relevance to understanding the original function of this site may be its strategic location: on a marl plateau difficult of access and affording clear visibility over much of the Dead Sea and its western coastal plain. This feature, along with the presence of a tower among the structures, has suggested to some scholars that the settlement was built as a military installation. There are no other signs of fortification, and the walls are less robust than such an interpretation ideally requires, but it may be that the Iron II structure (with or without a tower) was a fortress, since it appeared to conform to an established design (see Hoglund 1992:181–82). That the site was used for military purposes at some time may be very likely, but this secondary usage does not explain its primary construction. The tower may have provided some minimal element of defense, but the tower was a common feature of several kinds of ancient architecture, from agricultural settlements (including vineyards; see Isa. 5:2) to temples, and it is more likely to have served merely as a watchtower. The buttressing that is so evident is probably secondary, either for strengthening the structure or enhancing its military usefulness. In either case, the implication is that originally the tower was not strongly built. Nevertheless, it is possible to accept that the strategic location of the site was a major factor in its occupation, without concluding that it was constructed, at least in the Greco-Roman period, as a military or quasi-military installation.

The importance of cemeteries is well established in determining ethnic, racial, or religious affiliation. In the case of Qumran, cemeteries have their own particular significance. De Vaux claimed to have found three, the main one situated to the east of the plateau, the others to the north and south. The main cemetery lay only 50 m to the east of the settlement and contained over a thousand tombs, mostly of males laid in very careful order. The corpses were arranged (with one exception) in a north-south orientation; twenty-six of these were excavated. The cemetery extends farther east over lower hills, and here four of six excavated skeletons were female, and another one that of a child. Of the other two cemeteries, one to the north contains over a dozen tombs, similar to those in the main cemetery: two were excavated, of which one was female, the other male. In the cemetery to the south, four of some thirty tombs were excavated, one of a woman, three of children (de Vaux 1973:58). The contents of these cemeteries have been claimed to show the peculiar religious character of the nearby "Qumran community." But that theory is at best consistent with only part of the evidence. The existence of burials of women and children remains a puzzle on the theory that the Qumran community was all male, and in any case the separate burial grounds and different manners of burial suggest more than one group of inhabitants here, perhaps at different times. Again, the "community" theory does not give an adequate explanation of the tombs.

One could instance other features of the site that need to be reassessed independently of scroll-derived theories. For example, do over a thousand items of pottery stacked in one room indicate a community pantry or a warehouse? My intention at this point, however, is not to multiply such instances of problematic data, but simply to show that once the theory of a "Qumran community" is recognized as being merely a theory, or abandoned as a consensus, the results of the excavation invite reconsideration independently of that theory. If this is done, the site emerges as both fascinating and problematic. The indications of purpose and use are varying, with many problematic features, and the task of deducing—from the archaeological indications alone—who occupied the site and what they did is an intriguing problem.

Environment

On the supposition that a group of sectarian Jews fleeing from persecution by the authorities took refuge in a spiritual and literal "wilderness," their putative place of settlement can be regarded as unique, custom-built for a purpose that no other settlement served. What other Jewish "monasteries" exist for comparison, in any case? It is scarcely a traditional Jewish building type. Accordingly, the layout of Qumran has been explained from the assumed needs of such a group, perhaps with some help from the analogy of Christian monasteries. Rather than presuppose uniqueness, however, a sounder approach is to start out by looking for comparable settlements, and by considering the ecology of the area for clues to the reason for the foundation of such a complex. The environment is clearly dominated by the Dead Sea, and other contemporary settlements along its western shores are the most obvious for comparison. A number of nearby sites in the Buqêcah, behind the cliff face, were surveyed by Cross and J. T. Milik (1956), who reached the conclusion that a series of small settlements, probably for agricultural purposes, had been established in Iron Age II, of which Khirbet Qumran was one. cAin Feshkha, the only other Greco-Roman settlement considered, was taken to be part of the same complex, with some evidence of agricultural and industrial character, though its main industrial installation remained unexplained. De Vaux's initial suggestion of a tannery (scroll production still dominated the approach) was later withdrawn with no alternative offered (de Vaux 1973:78–83; Poole and Reid 1961). But the lack of adequate natural water provision at Qumran makes the theory of a Qumran-Feshkha complex more problematic. To this consideration can be added the industrial complex on the western side of the Qumran plateau, which presumably used much of the water gathered in the cisterns there. Why carry out industrial processes at all at Qumran, when cAin Feshkha offered a much more convenient site?

Other sites have subsequently been excavated in this region. In 1971 P. Bar-Adon reported on a site at cAin el-Ghuweir, 15 km south of Qumran, which he suggested was another settlement of the "Judean desert sect." Like cAin Feshkha (but not Qumran), it is watered by a spring, and, like Qumran, it seems to have been first occupied in Iron II before being resettled, somewhat later than Qumran, in the Roman period. It comprised a large hall, a kitchen, and two smaller rooms. Bar-Adon also found four pillar bases (pillar bases were also found at Qumran; see Allegro

1959:175, pl. 160, for the photograph, and 180, pl. 167, for a plastered pillar). About 800 m to the north was a cemetery with the graves oriented (with a single exception) north-south, as in the main Qumran cemetery, with the same manner of interment, including the piling of a cairn of stones over the grave. According to Bar-Adon, skeletons from both Qumran and ᶜAin el-Ghuweir exhibited colored stains, whether from dye or diet. Bar-Adon is convinced that ᶜAin el-Ghuweir was a "secondary settlement" of the Qumran sect. But here the graves contained both male and female skeletons.

Apart from their location close to the Dead Sea shore, the cemetery is the only clear connection between the two sites of ᶜAin el-Ghuweir and Qumran. The pottery at ᶜAin el-Ghuweir, as Bar-Adon observes, is certainly similar to that at Qumran—but similar pottery to that at Qumran has also been found in Jericho and Jerusalem. ᶜAin el-Ghuweir gives evidence of having been destroyed twice, but there is no particular reason to link these destructions with any at Qumran and Feshkha. Overall, Bar-Adon's interpretation of the site at ᶜAin el-Ghuweir as a religious center reads more into the site than the data warrant and is highly dependent on the interpretation of Qumran as a religious sectarian settlement. Nevertheless, the question of a relationship of some kind between ᶜAin el-Ghuweir, ᶜAin Feshkha, and Qumran must remain, regardless of the presence or otherwise of religious communities, and the similar manner of interment at least suggests habitation by groups of a similar culture. As far as economic activity is concerned, Bar-Adon suggests that the inhabitants supported themselves by "livestock breeding and the cultivation of medicinal and perfumery herbs and orchards. Also important was the sale of salt and other minerals which were extracted from the Dead Sea" (Bar-Adon 1977[1971]:20). He adds that ᶜAin Feshkha, Qumran, and En-gedi provided similar "processing plants" for mineral extraction, though in the case of ᶜAin el-Ghuweir the evidence is not fully presented.

En-gedi is the most important site on the west shore of the Dead Sea. Tel Goren lies by the oasis of En-gedi and was occupied during late Iron II (Stratum V), the Persian period (IV), the Hasmonean period (III), the early Roman period (II), and the Roman-Byzantine (I). Stratum IV yielded domestic architecture, Stratum II a fortified complex, apparently a Hasmonean citadel. The citadel of Stratum II included a tower and nearby a courtyard with rooms to the north and west and ovens along the southern courtyard wall (Mazar, Dothan, and Dunayevsky 1966). En-gedi was, of course, most illustrious for its dates and balsam trees, and the structures and artifacts of Stratum V strongly suggest that perfume processing took place here then, as presumably throughout the whole period of its occupation.

Finally, we should mention ᶜAin Boqeq, on the southwestern shore of the Dead Sea, also situated near an oasis. Here the earliest phase of occupation is probably Herodian. The main structure is 20 m square with a central courtyard and was identified by the excavators as a "factory" (Gichon 1970, 1976), though it underwent changes of occupation. The rooms were plastered (including plastered benches), with ovens, and one room had a sloping plastered floor. The castellum, of the same size as the factory, indicates military occupation, and an aqueduct 1 km long carried water from the spring to square cisterns by the oasis. Evidence of field enclosures and terraces was also found. The likely purpose of the industrial installation was the production of cosmetics and perfume.

Some comparisons and contrasts can now be drawn between the five sites along the western Dead Sea shore: Qumran, ᶜAin Feshkha, ᶜAin el-Ghuweir, En-gedi, and ᶜAin Boqeq.

1. All except Qumran were built at or near springs, though ᶜAin Boqeq also had an aqueduct and at ᶜAin Feshkha water was taken from the spring into artificially constructed pools. The construction of the elaborate water system at Qumran is therefore exceptional.

2. All were occupied during the Roman period, but ᶜAin Boqeq and En-gedi showed, even during a relatively short period, evidence of successive occupation, often with buildings adapted for different use. ᶜAin el-Ghuweir was apparently burned at least twice in its relatively short occupation. If such a pattern is typical of settlements in this area, we ought to reassess the conclusion that Qumran was continuously occupied (or with only a single break) by the same group for two hundred years.

3. All, including Qumran, show clear evidence of industrial use, which in some cases certainly, and in other cases very probably, was connected with perfume manufacture.

4. All share various features, such as a tower, manner of burial, ovens, cisterns, plastered rooms, sloping floors. There is no single site that resembles Qumran in more than a few particulars, but both Qumran and En-gedi show a mixture of industrial and military architecture (if the Qumran tower is to be thus explained). Altogether the common features are quite numerous.

5. The sites show evidence of military occupation (as opposed to architecture) at some time. This is not surprising during a period in which several wars were fought in this area. In this connection we could refer to the presence at Masada of manuscripts of the same kind as Qumran (e.g., the *Songs of the Sabbath Sacrifice*; see Newsom and Yadin 1984).

A superficial comparison of these sites shows sufficient similarities to justify our approaching the site of Khirbet Qumran in the context of western Dead Sea shore settlements, and in particular the economic basis of this region generally, which seems to have been a mixture of agriculture and industry, both in minerals and perfumes. In this connection, mention needs to be made of the discovery of a jar, possibly containing balsam oil, from a cave near Qumran (Patrich and Arubas 1989). The cave in question lies 2.8 km north of Qumran, quite close to Qumran Cave 3, the most northerly of the manuscript caves. The vessel is dated to the Herodian period and contains a plant oil that is no longer recognized (the balsam has been extinct for fifteen hundred years). Recent excitement has been caused by this find, though such a single discovery, and at some distance from Qumran, is not necessarily a clue to the purpose of the industrial structures there. In view of the economic production of the region, such a find is not surprising, but it reinforces the need to reconsider Qumran as a possible site for the production of this or similar products.

CONCLUSIONS

In advance of the publication of work by R. and P. Donceel, it may be premature to deliver a verdict on the interpretation of the remains at Khirbet Qumran, and I have not attempted to do so. But there can be little doubt that reconsideration of the site of Qumran will continue to take place, and, whatever verdicts may result, some provisional suggestions are already possible. It is clear that Qumran shares some features with other nearby sites, together with some unusual features (manuscripts, water supply). It is also clear that the patent evidence of successive occupancy at Qumran may need to be reevaluated. De Vaux's own reconstructed history allowed for Essenes and Roman soldiers as the only inhabitants. But he also identified a break in occupation between Ib and II, and had no reason to suggest that the occupants of phase II were the same as those of Ib, except, as he put it, that "the buildings were used for the same purpose," which is logically economical but archaeologically naive, since we have little evidence of how the buildings were used throughout its habitation. Thus, if Qumran were at some point occupied by a group who also hid the scrolls, this group does not need to have been there during the 150 or more years of its Greco-Roman age occupation. The evidence of the cemeteries certainly suggests the possibility of multiple occupancy, and discovery of manuscripts from the same collection at Masada opens the way to suggesting an occupation, however fleeting, by Zealots during the war of 66–73. Similarly, or perhaps consequently, the four different interpretations—monastery, fortress, villa, perfume factory—that have been offered to date are not necessarily all contradictory; more than one may be true, either successively or even in combination. Finally, if we have evidence of successive occupation for different purposes and by different groups, the question will then be, Which, if any, of these phases of occupation is to be associated with the placing of the scrolls in the caves?

In the light of the factors I have sketched above—that the site of Qumran turns out to have a more complicated history than previously thought and one more closely connected with its regional economy— there will be two benefits. The lesser benefit is that the site will continue to offer a possible link with the scrolls, and thus continue to afford scholars of the scrolls ample scope for speculation, deduction, and disagreement. Otherwise, if insufficient evidence links the site to a religious community, the majority of scholars working on the Dead Sea Scrolls will abandon interest in the site itself, no doubt with great reluctance. The larger benefit will be that archaeology, including the archaeology of the whole area of the western Dead Sea shore, can play an important role in the study of the Dead Sea Scrolls. Perhaps the most fundamental question raised by this whole discussion is how far the religious beliefs of a community (whether real or reconstructed) can be even theoretically isolated from economic questions, as if religious ideas do not arise from or interact with other cultural features. In the exploration of such interaction the entire discipline of biblical studies has a great deal of research yet to do.

NOTE

1. Originally a paper delivered at the SBL International Meeting in Sheffield in 1987 at the invitation of Philip King. This chapter was completed before the appearance of two important publications, which I have not been able to incorpo-

rate into the text: *Die Essener, Qumran, Johannes der Täufer und Jesu* by H. Stegemann (Freiburg-im-Breisgau: Herder/Spektrum, 1993) and *The Dead Sea Scrolls
Today* by J. C. VanderKam (Grand Rapids: Eerdmans, 1994).

WORKS CITED

Allegro, J.
1959   *The People of the Dead Sea Scrolls.* London: Routledge and Kegan
               Paul.
Bar-Adon, P.
1971   Another Settlement of the Judean Desert Sect at cEn el-Ghuweir
               on the Shores of the Dead Sea. *Eretz-Israel* 10:72–89 (Hebrew) =
               Bulletin of the American Schools of Oriental Research 227:1–25 (1977).
Brooke, G. J., ed.
1989   *Temple Scroll Studies.* Journal for the Study of the Pseudepigrapha
               Supplements, 7. Sheffield: JSOT Press.
Cross, F. M.
1958   *The Ancient Library of Qumran and Modern Biblical Studies.* Lon-
               don: Duckworth. Rev. ed., Garden City, N.Y.: Doubleday, 1961.
Cross, F. M., and J. T. Milik
1956   Explorations in the Judaean Buqêcah. *Bulletin of the American
               Schools of Oriental Research* 142:5–17.
Davies, P. R.
1982   *Qumran.* Cities of the Biblical World. Guildford, Surrey: Lutter-
               worth Press.
1983   *The Damascus Covenant: An Interpretation of the Damascus Docu-
               ment.* Journal for the Study of the Old Testament Supplement
               Series, 25. Sheffield: JSOT Press.
1988   How Not to Do Archaeology: The Story of Qumran. *Biblical
               Archaeologist* 203–7.
1989   The Temple Scroll and the Damascus Document. In *Temple Scroll
               Studies*, ed. G. J. Brooke, 201–10. Journal for the Study of the
               Pseudepigrapha Supplements, 7. Sheffield: JSOT Press.
Gichon, M.
1970   Chronique archéologique: cEn Boqeq. *Revue biblique* 77:579–80.
1976   cEn Boqeq. In *Encyclopedia of Archaeological Excavations in the Holy
               Land*, ed. M. Avi-Yonah, 2:365–70. London: Oxford University
               Press, and Jerusalem: Massada Press.
Golb, N.
1985   Who Hid the Dead Sea Scrolls? *Biblical Archaeologist* 48:68–82.
1989   The Dead Sea Scrolls: A New Perspective. *The American Scholar*
               59:177–207.
Hoglund, K. G.
1992   *Achaemenid Imperial Administration in Syria-Palestine and the Mis-
               sions of Ezra and Nehemiah.* Society of Biblical Literature Disserta-
               tion Series 125. Atlanta: Scholars Press.

Levine, B. A.
1978   The Temple Scroll: Aspects of Its Historical Provenance and Literary Character. *Bulletin of the American Schools of Oriental Research* 232:5–23.

Mazar, B.; T. Dothan; and I. Dunayevsky
1966   En-Gedi: The First and Second Seasons of Excavations. *ʿAtiqot* (English Series) 5.

Milik, J. T.
1959   *Ten Years of Discovery in the Wilderness of Judaea*. Translated by J. Strugnell, from French. 1957. London: SCM Press.

Newsom, C., and Y. Yadin
1984   The Masada Fragment of the Songs of the Sabbath Sacrifice. *Israel Exploration Journal* 34:77–88.

Patrich, J., and B. Arubas
1989   A Juglet Containing Balsam Oil(?) from a Cave near Qumran. *Israel Exploration Journal* 39:43–59.

Poole, J. B., and R. Reed
1961   The "Tannery" at ʿAin Feshkha. *Palestine Exploration Quarterly* 93:27–36.

Qimron, E., and J. Strugnell
1985   An Unpublished Halakhic Letter from Qumran. In *Biblical Archaeology Today*, ed. J. Amitai, 400–407. Jerusalem: Israel Exploration Society = *Israel Museum Journal* 4:9–12.

Rengstorf, K. H.
1960   *Khirbet Qumran und der Bibliothek vom Toten Meer*. Studia Delitzschiana 5. Münster: Institutum Delitzschianum.

Schiffman, L. H.
1980   The Temple Scroll in Literary and Philological Perspective. In *Approaches to Ancient Judaism* II, ed. W. S. Green, 143–58. Brown Judaic Studies 9. Chico, Calif.: Scholars Press.

1989   The Temple Scroll and the Systems of Jewish Law of the Second Temple Period. In *Temple Scroll Studies*, ed. G. J. Brooke, 239–55. Journal for the Study of the Pseudepigrapha Supplements, 7. Sheffield: JSOT Press.

1990   The New Halakhic Letter (4QMMT) and the Origins of the Dead Sea Sect. *Biblical Archaeologist* 52:64–73.

Stegemann, H.
1971   *Die Entstehung der Qumrangemeinde*. Bonn: privately published.

VanderKam, J. C.
1989   The Temple Scroll and the Book of Jubilees. In *Temple Scroll Studies*, ed. G. J. Brooke, 211–36. Journal for the Study of the Pseudepigrapha Supplements, 7. Sheffield: JSOT Press.

Vaux, R. de
1973   *Archaeology and the Dead Sea Scrolls*. Oxford: Oxford University Press.

Vermes, G., and M. D. Goodman
1989   *The Essenes according to the Classical Sources*. Sheffield: JSOT Press.
Yadin, Y.
1977-83   *The Temple Scroll*. 3 vols. Jerusalem: Israel Exploration Society.
1980   Is the Temple Scroll a Sectarian Document? In *Humanizing America's Iconic Book*, ed. G. M. Tucker and G. A. Knight, 153–69. Chico, Calif.: Scholars Press.

9 | The Silence of the Text: An Archaeological Commentary on 2 Kings 23

WILLIAM G. DEVER

In *The First Historians: The Hebrew Bible and History*, Baruch Halpern observes: "Rightly or wrongly, denying the historicity of Hezekiah's or Josiah's reform has been a reliable cottage industry" (1988:26). Norbert Lohfink previously posed the issue succinctly:

> It remains an open question what kind of historical and sociological reality stands behind the Deuteronomic phenomenon. Was there actually a "movement"? Or are we concerned with "literature," behind which stand only a few individuals, be they writers, theologians, or government officials? (1987:459)

Lohfink then proceeded to raise the explicit question whether the account of the Josianic reform in 2 Kings 23 could be construed as a reliable source for the history of Israelite religion. He had stated, however, at the outset of his analysis that "archaeology and epigraphy are not of much further help" (1987:459). As a consequence, Lohfink's study becomes mired in minute, internal analysis of the text, without yielding any firmer historical conclusions than innumerable previous studies had. As a recent survey of scholarly interpretations of 2 Kings 23 points out:

> If laid end to end, the scholarly pages written about Josiah's reform might well reach to the moon. Much has been written, because interpreters long have realized that in Josiah's reform lies the key to Deuteronomy, and in Deuteronomy lies the key to much of the Old Testament. (Lowery 1990:190)

It is the contention of this chapter that the skepticism or indecisiveness of most biblical scholars regarding the historicity of 2 Kings 23 is unwarranted, and further that recent archaeological data provide for the first time a credible historical-cultural context for this notoriously enigmatic passage in the Hebrew Bible. It would seem obvious, given the increasing attention being paid to archaeology and the ancient Israelite cult in recent years, that someone would have surveyed the rich archaeological data that now illuminate almost every single aspect of the reforms attributed to Josiah. Yet most commentators—even those as recent and as comprehensive as R. H. Lowery—ignore the archaeological data altogether.

PROLEGOMENON: TEXT AND ARTIFACT

More than simple neglect is involved in biblical scholars' typical exclusion of archaeological evidence in discussing 2 Kings 23, or any other aspect of the Israelite cult. The most benign explanation of the omission would be that most historians of ancient Israel have been trained not as historians but as philologians, and thus have been quite naturally preoccupied with analysis of the texts, which do indeed pose sufficient problems in themselves. There is, however, a rather naive historiographical presupposition here, namely that the biblical texts alone, properly understood, will yield an adequate history. At best, this leads to what G. Garbini (1988:7) and others have rightly characterized as simply paraphrasing the Bible. At worst, biblical scholars have formed an unconscious (?) alignment with the theological biases of the orthodox nationalist, minority parties that shaped the literary tradition in the Hebrew Bible in its final form in the postexilic period (Garbini's "state of psychological subjection"; 1988:174). But philology plus theology does not equal history, as Halpern has shown in his brilliant exposé of historiographic models in biblical scholarship (Halpern 1988:3–35). And since it is becoming increasingly clear that an understanding of the development of Israelite religion is dependent upon working out the larger history of the entity we call Israel, modern scholarship is at an impasse. The crucial question, now widely acknowledged, is: How to write an adequate history of Israel? The recent works of T. L. Thompson (1992) and G. W. Ahlström (1993), far from representing the breakthrough that they claim, only prove how serious the dilemma is.

At a deeper level, text-based histories of Israel and of Israelite religion have exacerbated the problem. Since Gunkel and the advent of form criticism, it has been commonplace to state that the biblical texts will yield the kernel of historical truth that they are presumed to contain, but only if they can be located in an appropriate (i.e., original) *Sitz im Leben*.

But in practice, the task has been reduced to that of recovering merely a *Sitz im Literatur*. Of course, the Hebrew Bible is literature. But literature is not life, at least not "real life"; it is, rather, the product of the literate imagination, and therefore more fiction than history (although by that account no less true in some sense). It is only archaeological evidence—Albright's *realia*—that can help to balance the picture derived from texts, by providing external data that have not been subjected to the same editorial process as texts, and therefore in principle constitute a more objective witness to events in the past.[1]

Most biblical scholars, however, biased as they are toward texts, have tended to follow Martin Noth in ignoring or denigrating archaeological data as "mute" (Noth 1960:47–48; Herrmann 1975:36 n. 25; Rendtorff 1983:2; Miller 1976:40–48; 1987; Rösel 1992:74—all using the terms "mute" [*stumm*], "silent," "dumb"). The obvious point is that artifacts are no more mute than texts: for the student who does not know Hebrew, the Hebrew Bible will appear to be mute. In the same way, if the biblical scholar does not know the language of archaeology, or does not consult the specialist who does know, the material culture record will remain silent (see Knauf 1991:26). Yet archaeology today can be eloquent, and, as several of us have argued, archaeological evidence can even take precedence over texts in history writing. That is especially true in writing a history of Israelite religion, although no recent work has done justice to the full potential of archaeology today.[2]

A final stricture in this connection is even more serious than neglect or negative assessments of archaeological data: the actual bias against cult that is evident in many works, especially those of Christian scholars. Elsewhere I have suggested that the fault may be due to the influence of the typically Protestant doctrine of *sola scriptura*, which tends to favor the written and spoken word, that is, theology, at the expense of religious practice or ritual, and regards overly rational formulations as more normative than emotional or psychological expressions of belief. This elitist approach to Israelite religion, typically male and clerical, may be characterized in terms of a verbal versus visceral gestalt, and it has many shortcomings (Dever, forthcoming c). A refreshing alternative is seen in several recent works on popular or family religion (see definitions below), some of them utilizing much more of the newer archaeological evidence on actual religious practice—several, not surprisingly, by women writers.

What is needed in my opinion is a phenomenological or functionalist approach to religion and cult in ancient Israel, using archaeological data to illuminate the biblical texts. Until then, it is the text—not archaeology—that will remain silent, or at least ambiguous. That is certainly true of intransigent texts like 2 Kings 23. Instead of embarking upon yet more futile quests for a *Hebraica veritas*, let us seek behind the present text of the Bible (all we shall ever have) a more fundamental *archeologica veritas*, a notion of how it really was in the past. We may never know precisely, but this venture will likely be more fruitful than continually manipulating texts that by now have yielded all the history they contain.

DESCRIPTIONS OF
THE CULT IN 2 KINGS 23:
FACT OR FICTION?

Much of the critical discussion of 2 Kings 23 over the past century has revolved around the question of whether or not the Deuteronomistic account of Josiah's sweeping religious reforms, edited into its present form in the exilic period, is propaganda. One's suspicions that the litany of Josiah's successful reform measures in 2 Kings 23 may be simply a literary convention are strengthened by looking at the parallel passages in 2 Kings 18:4 regarding Hezekiah and in 2 Kings 21:1–9 regarding Manasseh. We have virtually the same list—*bāmôt, maṣṣēbôt,* "asherim," the "host of heaven," child sacrifice, magic, etc.—all typifying, of course, precisely the overriding *Tendenz* (one might say obsession) of the later Deuteronomistic historians.

Let us admit at the outset that the *Sitz im Literatur* of 2 Kings 23 is propaganda. But what of the *Sitz im Leben*, in real life? The point often missed is that the very force of the polemic against popular cults in the Deuteronomistic history, projected back into the seventh century BCE, is the best argument that they existed at that time—and continued later. Thus far, however, our argument for the historicity of 2 Kings 23 is based on a common-sense application of form-critical methods to the text alone. Is there any external evidence for the cults that Josiah is said to have suppressed? There is indeed, in the archaeological data. Yet the most recent survey of scholarship (Lowery 1990) reveals that this is a rich lode that virtually no one has mined.

Let us begin with the texts themselves. An initial examination of all the references to what I shall call popular cults in 2 Kings 23 allows us to group their principal features conveniently into several general categories.

Unauthorized priests
Bāmôt and *maṣṣēbôt*
Veneration of the goddess Asherah and her cult-symbol the "asherah"
Proscribed altars and incense offerings
Horse-and-chariot imagery, connected with solar and astral deities
Temple prostitution
Child sacrifice
Magic
Tombs and burial practices

Further analysis shows that these aspects of popular cults can be distributed into three locales: the Jerusalem Temple itself; the immediate vicinity of the Temple and elsewhere in Jerusalem; and the countryside. Thus, in the Temple the point of contention in the Josianic story was the presence of "vessels" for Baal and Asherah; of "vestments" (or "tent-shrines") for Asherah; of shrines/sanctuaries for "male prostitutes," *'ăšērîm* or asherah symbols, and representations of horses and chariots. Elsewhere in Jerusalem, the attack on cults focuses on *bāmôt*, *maṣṣēbôt*, incense altars, *'ăšērîm*, child sacrifice, and tombs and rites for the dead. In other cities and in the rural areas, the references are to *bāmôt* and *băttê-bāmôt* (often in city gates and dedicated to foreign gods such as Chemosh and Milcom); local, unauthorized priests eating unleavened bread; local altars, sometimes for burning incense to Baal; and offerings to the "host of heaven."

Although the above references to popular cults are relatively straightforward in the Hebrew text of 2 Kings 23 (apart from a few difficulties; see below), commentators seem curiously reluctant to take these references seriously. Are scholars simply unaware of recent archaeological data? Or is there some hidden theological or other ideological presumption at work, such as that the cult of ancient Judah could not have been that corrupt compared to an idealized pure Yahwism? Whatever the reasons for the neglect, the fact is that every one of the above aspects of the "popular cults" mentioned in 2 Kings 23 can now be illuminated by archaeological discoveries, and in some detail.

Unauthorized Priests

As is well known, the Deuteronomistic tradition regards only the Jerusalem or Aaronide priesthood as legitimate. Nevertheless, among the seventh–sixth century BCE ostraca at Arad, where there is a flourishing tripartite temple (see below), there are references to local individuals, no doubt priests, who bear the names of priestly families known from biblical texts (Meremoth, Pashur, and the "sons of Korah"; note also Ostracon 18, mentioning a *bēt YHWH*, probably not Jerusalem but the Arad temple, contra Yohanan Aharoni). Furthermore, two shallow offering plates, found at the base of the altar in the outer court, are incised with the letters *qōp kāp*, probably an abbreviation for *qodeš kohănîm*, "set apart for the priests" (Aharoni 1981:35–38, 115–17; Herzog et al. 1984:12–22; Ussishkin 1988:155). At Dan, a fine bronze scepter was certainly used by local priests in the ninth–eighth century BCE sanctuary there (Biran 1989:29). The above evidence underlines the concern of the Deuteronomistic historians to discredit all but the Jerusalem priesthood: these were rivals.

Bāmôt and Maṣṣēbôt

Much ink has been spilled trying to identify the mysterious *bāmâ* on textual grounds. The archaeological picture, however, is sufficiently clear to enable us to use the evidence to illuminate many biblical texts in more detail (although it was already clear that *bāmôt* were simply raised platforms or outdoor shrines, often associated with Asherah symbols like trees or wooden poles, standing stones, and altars). A full-fledged ninth–eighth-century BCE sanctuary at Tēl Dan, the northern capital, provides us with an excellent example of what an Israelite *bāmâ* probably looked like. The central installation, a massive stone platform approached by steps, no doubt a large outdoor altar, may in fact be the very *bēt-bāmôt* referred to in 2 Kings 12:31 (probably not an example of a "house on a highplace," but rather a "shrine on a highplace"; see Biran 1980, 1986, 1989). An earlier Israelite cult place, the twelfth-century BCE "Bull Shrine" in the tribal territory of Manasseh, a hilltop sanctuary with an altar and a standing-stone, can also be plausibly construed as a *bāmâ* (Mazar 1982). Fragments of terra-cotta stands may illuminate the reference in 2 Kings 23:5 to "burning incense on the highplaces." Finally, a series of eighth–seventh-century BCE hilltop tumuli west of Jerusalem may well be connected with both *bāmôt* and funerary rites (see below, and see Holladay 1987:260–61). The congruence between these (and other) actual archaeological discoveries and biblical descriptions of *bāmôt* is adequate, in my opinion, to support the identification of the two, whatever etymological difficulties may remain.

We now know a number of Iron Age *maṣṣēbôt*, which are simply commemorative standing-stones erected in cult places. Most instructive is the example of a *maṣṣēbâ* at tenth-century BCE Tell el-Farᶜah North, the biblical capital city of Tirzah, which is actually located in the gate plaza (2 Kgs. 23:8; see Chambon 1984: pl. 8). Note also the contemporary *maṣṣēbâ* in the tenth-century BCE "Cultic Structure" at Taanach (Lapp 1967:19–20). We have already mentioned the *maṣṣēbâ* at the Iron I "Bull Site." Finally, there is a *maṣṣēbâ* at the center of the rear wall of the inner chamber (the biblical *dĕbîr*) of the ninth–seventh-century BCE temple at Arad (Herzog et al. 1984:7). It may be noteworthy that at two of the three sites listed above, *maṣṣēbôt* are associated with *bāmôt*, just as they are in 2 Kings 23.

Veneration of Asherah

Until recently, biblical scholars had followed the redactors of the biblical text, as well as nearly all later Jewish and Christian commentators, in downplaying the more than forty occurrences in the Hebrew Bible of the term *'ăšerâ* in its various forms, as though *'ăšerâ* referred merely to a tree, wooden pole, or some other symbol, not to the deity herself. This remained true despite the obvious fact that in at least half a dozen or so passages in the Hebrew Bible the term must refer not merely to a symbol of the goddess, but to Asherah the great Mother Goddess of Canaan herself (including 2 Kgs. 23:4, 7), well known from the Ugaritic texts as the consort of El. Today, all that has changed, largely as a result of archaeological discoveries. These include especially the eighth-century BCE Hebrew texts from Khirbet el-Qôm and Kuntillet Ajrud mentioning Asherah as an agent of blessing alongside Yahweh as his consort. Several recent studies now acknowledge the pervasiveness of the cult of Asherah in ancient Israel, from the period of the judges until the end of the monarchy and even into the exilic period—and in official Yahwist circles, as well as in the popular cults.[3] It is no surprise that 2 Kings 23 refers to "vessels made for Asherah" (v 4) and women "weaving vestments [?] for Asherah" (v 7). In neither case can we interpret these as references to the cult symbol or the like. In the first instance, *'ăšerâ* is in parallelism with Baal; if Baal is a deity, so is Asherah. The occurrence of the definite article is almost certainly a Deuteronomic addition, at a later period when there was evidently a great deal of confusion as to who/what the now prohibited and largely forgotten *'ăšerâ* actually was.

This suggestion is strengthened by the fact that in the second reference to *'ăšerâ* (v 7) the present Hebrew text is corrupt or at least confused, and it obviously was so already by the third century BCE, when the LXX translation was made. The MT has *'ŏrĕgôt bāttîm*, the women "wove houses/temples"—an impossibility, unless one takes *bāttîm* periphrastically to mean "tent-shrines." The LXX, however, reads *chettiein*, and the Lucianic (Lagarde) text has *stolas*, both of which mean "garment," "tunic," and may presuppose Hebrew *kotnôt*, "tunic," "priestly garment" (from which the RSV derives "vestments," emending *bāttim* to *baddîm*, "white linen"). Some targums have *mĕkôlîn*, "curtains"; Qimhi, perhaps combining several versions, reads "curtain enclosures" (see Cogan and Tadmor 1988:286). Which is the superior text? Is it the LXX, in which case one might argue that "vestments" were being woven for a wooden or metal image of the goddess (as one sees clothed images of the Virgin in Roman Catholic churches)? Or is it the MT, in which case woven tent shrines—perhaps in the ancient (and modern) Near Eastern desert tradition—were being erected as pavilions for Asherah in the Temple precincts (alongside the *bāttîm* of the "consecrated ones" in the same verse)? As for weaving in Temple precincts, it may be significant that the eighth-century BCE shrine at Kuntillet Ajrud produced more than one hundred examples of linen and woolen textiles, very similar to those mentioned in biblical passages describing priestly vestments (Meshel 1978a, b; Stager and Wolff 1981:98). The very persistence of the symbols and imagery of Asherah attests to her real power, namely her existence in the consciousness of the majority of ordinary folk in ancient Israel and Judah. As Susan Ackerman trenchantly observes: "In the ancient Near East the idol was the god" (1992:65; see Keel and Uehlinger 1992:203).

To be sure, in verse 6 a cult symbol of the goddess, rather than Asherah, is implied, something that could be brought out from the Temple, burned, and pounded into dust—here probably a wooden image. Not surprisingly, archaeology has not managed to recover any such wooden *'ăšerim* from the Iron Age, because of lack of preservation. In some passages (as 2 Kgs. 21:7), the image of the *'ăšerâ* appears to have been made of metal (*pesel*, "graven image"), probably iron or bronze, but these have not been recovered either by archaeology.

I would argue, however, that the hundreds of ninth- to sixth-century BCE terra-cotta *dea nutrix* figurines (as Albright dubbed them) should be understood as representations of the Mother Goddess—manifestations, to bring the reality of the goddess and her power closer to hand. Certainly these are not mourner figurines, like their Late Bronze Age predecessors; nor are they merely toys or the like. These figurines portray the great Mother Goddess of Canaan, primarily as a nursing mother; that is, in one of her primary roles, that of ensuring the successful rearing of infants and children. The figurines must, therefore, be associated with Asherah, virtually the only Canaanite fertility goddess still known in the Iron Age in Israel. Anat and Astarte are rarely mentioned in the Hebrew Bible, apparently having coalesced with Asherah, who was undoubtedly assimilated into early Israel from Late Bronze Age Canaan, along with her consort El (later, however, identified with Baal so as to discredit her).

Despite our inability to be certain of the above identification, increasing numbers of scholars are coming to this common-sense realization, which I have long held (see Holland 1977; Dever 1987:226; forthcoming c; Winter 1983:95–199; Schroer 1987:260–81; Holladay 1987:276–78; Bird 1990, 1992; Beck 1990; Bloch-Smith 1992:94–100; Keel and Uehlinger 1992:380–86). If we are right, these common figurines are miniatures of life-sized images of Asherah that once existed throughout ancient Israel and Judah.

There are estimated to be more than three thousand of the terra-cotta figurines, found everywhere, but particularly in domestic contexts and also in tombs (Holladay 1987:272–80), where they attest to family religion (see below). A mold for mass producing these figurines, however, found in the tenth-century BCE "Cultic Structure" at Taanach, suggests that they could also be presented as votives, or used as tokens of sympathetic magic (see below), at shrines (Lapp 1967:24). The larger examples of Asherah, either in wood or metal, may all have been destroyed, as the Deuteronomistic history claims. And the biblical writers, who as far as we can tell from the terminology never explicitly mention the miniatures, probably tried to suppress them as well, although by chance many have survived. In any case, it was the perceived actual existence of Asherah, no doubt in many circles regarded as the consort of Yahweh, that gave these images their awesome power. Thus Josiah would naturally have attempted to purge such images from the Temple in Jerusalem, as well as destroying the numerous examples in the countryside. He was foiled, however, by what we now call the formation processes of the archaeological record, and also by the persistence of the "popular" cults that were devoted at least in part to Asherah, the ancient Mother Goddess of Canaan (see further Dever 1984; Oden 1976).

Proscribed Altars and
Incense Offerings

Large altars are now known at many twelfth- to sixth-century BCE archaeological sites, including the Bull Site (Mazar 1982); Dan (Biran 1986:179–87); Arad (above); and Kuntillet Ajrud (benches, which certainly served as altars for offerings, as in Late Bronze Age temples; Meshel 1978a, 1978b, 1979). At Dan several shovels were found adjacent to the stone altar in the *liškâ* (or biblical "shrine") adjacent to the high place, presumably for burnt animal offerings, as in the biblical descriptions (Biran 1986:181–83). At Arad, preliminary reports indicated burned animal bones around the large altar in the outer court as well as an oily organic substance on top of the small stone altars at the entrance to the inner sanctum. Unfortunately, inadequate excavation methods and incomplete publication prevent us from being more specific (Herzog et al. 1984:11–15; see Ussishkin 1988; Holladay 1987:256, 257).

The complaint in 2 Kings 23:5 and 8 about altars and incense burning clearly has to do with local altars that violated the Deuteronomistic attempt at centralization of worship. As for incense burning, it was an accepted part of Israelite worship according to the Deuteronomistic and Priestly sources, and indeed it is attested archaeologically. In addition to the Arad evidence noted above, we have dozens of small stone horned altars from tenth- to sixth-century BCE Israelite and Judahite sites, which were presumably used for incense burning (among other offerings; see Gitin 1992; and, on incense, Haran 1978:236–38).

Horse-and-Rider Imagery;
Solar and Astral Deities

The reference in verse 11 to horses and chariots of the sun has sometimes been thought problematic. The allusion to solar and astral worship, however, is clear (see Taylor 1989; Smith 1990:116; Ackerman 1992:79–99). It was possibly of Phoenician or Neo-Assyrian origin, but equally likely to have had a continuous local ancestry going back to Canaanite origins in the Late Bronze Age.

The horse and chariot may have a similar pedigree. Miniature terracotta chariot models—usually drawn by horses or oxen and driven by a deity (or a pair of deities)—are well known from Syria throughout the second millennium BCE. They are also attested in Palestine by fragments (wheels, etc.) from the Middle Bronze Age and possibly later. In the Iron Age, however, we have preserved for us only the horse figurines, although these are fairly common in eighth- to sixth-century BCE archaeological contexts (Holladay 1987:265; Bloch-Smith 1992:101–2; see Keel and Uehlinger 1992:392–95).

References in verses 4 and 5 to "the sun, the moon, the planets, and all the host of heaven" clearly imply that solar and astral deities were commonly venerated (see above). Archaeological evidence of such cults, however, would not be likely to survive, except in figurative art, and Israelite art is generally thought to have been nonexistent, except perhaps for the ninth–seventh-century BCE ivories and seals.

Several members of the Freiburg school have recently challenged the above assumptions, such as Urs Winter (1983), Silvia Schroer (1987), and particularly Othmar Keel, culminating in his *Göttinnen, Götter, und Gottessymbole: Neue Erkenntnisse zur Religionsgeschichte Kanaans und Israels aufgrund bislang unerschlossener ikonographischer Quellen* (1992; with C. Uehlinger). Keel's earlier works brought together a surprising array of genuinely Israelite and comparative artistic motifs, especially on hundreds of seals and seal impressions. Keel and Uehlinger (1992:322–69), building largely on seals—many of them with horses, bearing sun disks on their heads, or with winged sun disks—argue that by the seventh century BCE Judahite religion was heavily influenced by Phoenician, Aramaean, and Neo-Assyrian solar and astral cults. One might recall even earlier evidence, as seen for instance in the winged sun disk carried on the back of a bullock on the tenth-century BCE Taanach stand (Hestrin 1987a; Dever 1984:28; Taylor 1989); the moon crescent and stars of the Pleiades on the tenth-century *naos*, or house temple (probably of Asherah), at Tell el-Farʿah North (Chambon 1984:66; see Dever 1990:153–54); or several tenth–eighth-century BCE female figurines that are sometimes interpreted as holding a sun disk (Beck 1990).

Temple Prostitution

The interpretation of *qĕdēšîm* in verse 7 as male prostitutes may be open to question. Usage of the feminine form in such passages as Deuteronomy 23:16, 17 and Hosea 4:14 in parallel with *zônâ*, "prostitute," may suggest a sexual function. The remaining passages, however (as 1 Kgs. 14; 24; 15:12; 22:47; Job 36:14), simply associate the term with *ʾăšerîm*, idols, and other "abominations." It is worth recalling that the consonantal text can be read simply as "consecrated ones," that is, temple functionaries, those dedicated to temple service, both male and female. Furthermore, we now have actual archaeological evidence of the use of the term *qodeš* for inani-

mate cult objects, such as kraters, platters, and store jars in eighth–
seventh-century BCE cultic contexts at Arad, Beer-sheba, and Tel Miqne/
Ekron (Aharoni 1975:107; Herzog et al. 1984:12–15; Gitin 1990:41). The
common notion of cultic prostitution, which seems to derive from somewhat dubious interpretations of the Ugaritic evidence, or else from out-
dated views of the Scandinavian-British "myth and ritual school," may be
mistaken (Smith 1990:28 n. 14 and references there). The "woman-
at-the-window" motif on the ninth–eighth-century BCE ivories is sometimes taken to represent a temple prostitute, but I think that these scenes
are rather to be connected with the female deity who stands in the door
or peers out of the window of the terra-cotta *naos*, or household temple
model, of which we now have numerous Iron Age examples (see above;
one from Idalion, in Cyprus, has the deity at the window; see Schroer
1987:519). It must be admitted, however, that ritual prostitution would
not have been out of keeping with the overall picture of what we know of
the cult of Asherah, given her fertility associations. In any case, we have
no direct archaeological witness of cultic prostitution in the Iron Age in
Israel or Judah.

It may be significant that the Iron Age Asherah figurines (above) are
decidedly chaste in comparison with the typical Late Bronze Age fertility
plaques. Full frontal nudity and exaggerated sexual features are replaced
by a completely stylized lower body (the pillar base), and only the breasts
are prominently modeled. This may suggest that the more overtly sexual
aspects of the Canaanite fertility cults were de-emphasized in later Israel,
so that Asherah was now more mother than consort. But this is largely
speculative.

Child Sacrifice

A number of studies have explored the limited textual evidence for child
sacrifice in ancient Israel (Smith 1990:132–38; Ackerman 1992:117–43
and references there). There is no direct archaeological evidence, however, nor should we expect any to be preserved—unless, of course, child
sacrifice had been practiced on a scale large enough to compare with the
well-known Phoenician Topheth at Carthage, where hundreds of crema-
tion urns of children and dedicatory stelae have been excavated (Brown
1991). Archaeologically, all we can say is that 2 Kings 23:10 locates the
Topheth in the Valley of Hinnom, south and southwest of the Dung Gate
(see Jer. 7:31–32; 19:6), which later tradition still remembered as a place
of death, desolation, and abomination (Hebr. *gê'-hinnōm* = Gk. *geenna*;

Lat. *Gehenna*, "hell"). No systematic excavations have ever been carried out in most of the Hinnom valley, so the archaeological record is thus far silent. A few Iron Age tombs excavated south of the Jaffa Gate simply confirm the fact that areas outside the city walls were traditionally used for burials (see below).

Magic

A number of passages in the Bible reveal that a component of popular cults, going back at least to the period of the judges, was magic in various forms. This included consulting diviners or astrologers for omens, sorcerers for casting spells, mediums for inquiring of the dead, and so on (Kuemmerlin-McLean 1992). In the Deuteronomistic tradition, these practices were, of course, proscribed, but there is no reason to suppose that they were rare in ancient Israel and Judah. On the contrary, once again the strong polemic against magic in 2 Kings 23:24 (and also in regard to the reigns of Hezekiah and Manasseh; 2 Kgs. 17:17; 21:5) indicates how widespread it actually was.

The technical terms used by the biblical writers and editors are somewhat vague and ambiguous (perhaps deliberately so), and thus they do not give us much information on actual paraphernalia of the type that might be recovered by archaeology. Nevertheless, there are classes of ninth- to sixth-century BCE archaeological artifacts, generally overlooked in this connection, that could be adduced as evidence of magic. First, the *dea nutrix*, or Asherah/Mother Goddess, figurines discussed above are symbols. And these symbols can only have possessed the awesome power that made them popular if people believed that they worked—that is, that they were talismans that successfully identified the devotee with the deity through sympathetic magic. In addition to this evidence, Iron Age tombs have produced significant quantities of other artifacts that clearly were thought to have had magical powers, not only for the dead but also for the living. These include Egyptian-style figurines of Bes, an apotropaic deity who was very popular throughout the Levant in the Iron Age (Dever 1984:25–26); faience Eye-of-Horus plaques, obviously to ward off the evil eye; and other types of seals (see above), charms, and amulets. A class of terra-cotta models, including beds, thrones, and shrines, surely represents something other than toys, and probably denotes again some form of sympathetic magic. Another group of objects includes many types of so-called "trick vessels" (*kernoi*). These are bowls that are hollow-rimmed and allow one to pour out a liquid through one of the typically hollow animal heads attached to the rim. No up-to-date study exists, but it seems that these *kernoi* originated in Cyprus, were brought to Palestine with the Sea Peoples, and continued in use there until the eighth century BCE or so. The *kernoi* are sometimes regarded simply as libation vessels, but the intricate nature of their pouring function suggests to me that they could indeed have been trick vessels, perhaps designed to give an omen, depending on how they were manipulated. Belonging to another category of magical items are *astragali*, or knucklebones, which are not only recovered in small numbers from Iron Age tombs, but occur in a hoard of 140 found in the tenth-century BCE "Cultic Structure" at Taanach, alongside an assemblage of other demonstrably cultic items (Lapp 1969:45–57; see Stager and Wolff 1981:98). These *astragali*, like second/first-millennium BCE Chinese scapulimancy bones, were probably used in divination rites. Another indication of magic is the well-carved "hand of Fatima" on the eighth-century BCE Khirbet el-Qôm inscription, possibly our earliest example of this well-known good luck charm. Finally, the seventh-century BCE Ketef Hinnom silver amulet, with the words of the Priestly Blessing in Numbers 6:22–24 (Barkay 1986), clearly shows that by then even sacred texts could be used magically.

Also under the category of magic we must include several Iron II tomb inscriptions (below), even though these are not usually considered as involving magic. The seventh–sixth-century BCE Khirbet Beit Lei inscription (Naveh 1963) includes not only a formula of praise and blessing but pictographic representations of praying figures. Both the well-known eighth-century BCE Khirbet el-Qôm inscription (No. 3) and several of the contemporary Kuntillet Ajrud inscriptions include such blessing formulas as "May X be blessed by Yahweh and his Asherah." Uttered by the living, such formulas may be considered simply a part of everyday speech, but I would suggest that when they were written on the walls of a sanctuary or a tomb, they inevitably took on a certain magical significance. I would argue the same for the abecedaries at Kuntillet Ajrud (and elsewhere), which were executed not only as writing exercises but could also be highly symbolic acts.[4] There are other tomb inscriptions, like Avigad's "Royal Steward Inscription," which reads in part, "Cursed be the man who will open this" (Avigad 1953). Surely these curses were thought to influence the living in ways that could only be described as magic. They secured beneficial behavior through the operation of invisible powers that could be symbolically invoked.

Finally, the drawings on the plastered walls and on several large store jars at Kuntillet Ajrud have been considered merely as graffiti, but in my view they are nothing of the sort. There was very little such casual art in the ancient world; nearly all of what we have, even in the minor traditions, is charged with meaning, whether we can always decipher that meaning or not. The Ajrud drawings include a tree of life, lions that probably relate to Asherah the "Lion Lady," the familiar cow suckling her calf, processional scenes, two Bes figures, and an enthroned, half-nude female figure that I have interpreted as Asherah, going with the textual reference to "Yahweh and his Asherah" just above (Dever 1984). Some scholars have minimized the significance of the motifs or have even denied that Ajrud is in part a cult site. Others, however, have rightly seen that here at last we have, through archaeological discoveries, an evocative glimpse of the popular cults that the religious establishment and the latest redactors of the biblical texts sought to obscure or to suppress entirely (see Miller, Hanson, and McBride 1987:59, 118–20, 143–49, in addition to Dever 1987 in the same volume; Ackerman 1992:66). Since religion is not only theology and belief but also practice, then the supposedly superstitious practices at Kuntillet Ajrud and other sites are as genuinely a part of ancient Israelite religion as the idealized portrait in much of the Bible—more so, I would argue.

Tombs and Burial Practices

The references in 2 Kings 23:16–20 to tombs on the hills surrounding Jerusalem, some of them impressive above-ground monuments, are easily confirmed. Archaeological investigations have brought to light many such tombs from the eighth to the sixth century BCE, not only to the east in the Silwan (Siloam) cliffs, but to the west, and to the north of the Damascus Gate. Some of the Silwan tombs are indeed monumental sepulchers, including one bearing the name of "[Sheban]iah, who is over the house" (Avigad 1953; see Isa. 22:16, perhaps this very royal steward).

Elizabeth Bloch-Smith's recent *Judahite Burial Practices and Beliefs about the Dead* has surveyed the material so thoroughly that little further comment is needed. While we know of the monumental rock-hewn tombs referred to in 2 Kings 23:16–17, the graves of the common people (v 6) were no doubt simple pit graves and have gone undetected archaeologically. Finally, given the evidence, the looting of tombs and the burning of the bones on the altar (v 16) remain enigmatic, apart from the obvious intent to defile altars that were regarded as illegitimate. All we can say is that many eighth- to sixth-century BCE tombs in Jerusalem were visible, and thus vulnerable to robbing or desecration. Perhaps this can be seen simply as an instance of Josiah's attempt to blot out the very memory of noble families who had supported Manasseh, whose reign (2 Kgs. 21:1–9) represented all the abominations against which Josiah stood. It is interesting that, after making inquiries about the visible tomb of "the man of God who came from Judah," Josiah spared his tomb (and that of another prophet from Samaria; vv 16–18).

TOWARD A DEFINITION
OF POPULAR RELIGION IN
ANCIENT ISRAEL

The preceding discussion has shown that all nine aspects of the Judahite cult that Josiah is presumed in 2 Kings 23 to have reformed can be documented in more or less detail by recent archaeological discoveries. Does that prove the historicity of the passage? Perhaps not, nor is that the purpose of archaeology. I would argue, however, that such archaeological convergence with the text, read on the basis of an appropriate form-critical analysis, does offer a certain kind of corroboration. If nothing else, such external data tip the scales of the balance of probability with which the historian must always work. Beyond that, such a convergence of artifact and text has important, perhaps critical, implications for our understanding of the actual nature of religious belief and practice in ancient Israel, as I shall suggest in summing up.

Elsewhere (Dever 1987:210–22; see Dever forthcoming a, b, c, d) I have pointed out that nearly all histories of ancient Israelite religion are deficient because they are almost exclusively text-based and thus tend to ignore the sort of rich archaeological data adduced above (and much more). Several recent studies, however, have begun to grapple with the problem by focusing on various aspects of popular religion. Thus Susan Ackerman states at the outset of her seminal 1992 work on religion in the sixth century BCE: "The program that is called for here is a rewriting of the history of the religion of Israel so as to take popular religion fairly into account" (1992:2; her "non-Deuteronomistic, non-priestly, non-prophetic" religion, p. 1). That is just what I had called for in an earlier programmatic essay on archaeology and cult (Dever 1983).

In 1987, Holladay made a significant start by attempting to define nonconformist or distributed worship over against established or state-centralized worship, on strictly archaeological grounds. Other essays in the same volume, *Ancient Israelite Religion* (Miller, Hanson, and McBride 1987), marked a similar, though far less systematic, revival of interest in popular religion.

Subsequently, several scholars began to take up the challenge of popular religion, including especially Carol Meyers (1988, 1991) and Phyllis Bird (1990, 1991). For Meyers, the key is to explore the neglected role of women in ancient Israelite religion by analyzing the household mode of production, together with its archaeological correlates in little-excavated domestic areas, and thus to characterize the religion of what I would call "hearth and home." Bird turns away from major communal acts of worship to consider "visits to local shrines, pilgrimages, and individual acts of piety and dedication related to particular needs . . . favored by women and better suited to the general rhythms and the exigencies of their lives" (1991:102–3; presumably women's concerns focus more than men's on conception, childbirth, and the rearing of children).

Such studies offset the all-too-prevalent biases of male commentators (see above), and they certainly help to balance the picture. But I would caution against setting up a false dichotomy that presumes that men operated only in the realm of public religion (which became, of course, the orthodox, Deuteronomistic version), while women were restricted to private or domestic religion (or mere superstition, in the view of the literary tradition). Jeremiah 7:18 describes a family ritual—probably typical, despite the prophetic and Deuteronomistic prohibition—in which children gathered wood, fathers kindled the fire, and mothers "made cakes for the Queen of Heaven" (on the latter, see Ackerman 1992:5–35).

The latest works are Mark Smith's *The Early History of God: Yahweh and the Other Deities in Ancient Israel* (1990) and especially Rainer Albertz's magisterial two-volume *Religionsgeschichte Israels in alttestamentlicher Zeit* (1992; see also 1978). Smith's work, in my view, is the first full-scale treatment of Israelite religion in English that attempts to take popular religion seriously, but even this work is based largely on texts (including virtually all the nonbiblical material), rather than including archaeological discoveries. Albertz gives even more attention to popular religion, distinguishing between (1) state/national (*Volk*) religion; (2) local religion (*Ortsreligion*); and (3) family religion. The latter equals my "popular religion"—avoiding "folk" because of the possible confusion with *Volk*, which in German connotes "people" in the sense of "national," rather than "popular" as in English. Nevertheless popular religion may be somewhat misleading, since we do not actually know how widespread or popular this alternate vision of Israelite religion (i.e., of Yahwism itself) actually was. Did it appeal only to "the uneducated, the lower classes, the rustics, the unsophisticated," as Ackerman (1992:1) phrases the question? Or was such popular religion, far from being an aberrant minority version of official Yahwism, the actual religion of Israel—the norm, rather than the late Deuteronomistic version? Here, then, is the crucial question: What is normative in religion? Who decides, and why?

Whatever the case, I suggest as a working definition of popular religion, for both archaeologists and biblical scholars, the following. "Popular religion" is an alternate, nonorthodox, nonconformist mode of religious expression. It is noninstitutional, lying outside priestly control or state sponsorship. Because it is nonauthoritarian, popular religion is inclusive rather than exclusive; it appeals especially to minorities and to the disenfranchised (in the case of ancient Israel, most women); in both belief and practice it tends to be eclectic and syncretistic. Popular religion focuses more on individual piety and informal practice than on elaborate public ritual, more on cult than on intellectual formulations (i.e., theology). By definition, popular religion is less literate (not by that token any less complex or sophisticated) and thus may be inclined to leave behind more traces in the archaeological record than in the literary record, more ostraca and graffiti than classical texts, more cult and other symbolic paraphernalia than scripture. Nevertheless, despite these apparent dichotomies, popular religion overlaps significantly with official religion, if only by sheer force of numbers of practitioners; it often sees itself as equally legitimate; and it attempts to secure the same benefits as all religion, namely the individual's sense of integration with nature and society, of health and prosperity, of ultimate well-being.

The major elements of popular religion in ancient Israel, as we can gather both from substrata of the biblical text and archaeology, probably included: frequenting *bāmôt* and other local shrines; the making of images; veneration of *'ăšerim* (whether sacred trees or iconographic images) and the worship of Asherah the Great Lady herself; rituals having to do with childbirth and children; pilgrimages and saints' festivals; *marzēaḥ* feasts; various funerary rites, such as libations for the dead; baking cakes for the "Queen of Heaven" (probably Astarte); wailing over Tammuz; various aspects of solar and astral worship; divination and sorcery; and perhaps child sacrifice. These and other elements of folk religion are often assumed to have characterized the religion of hearth and home, and thus to have been almost the exclusive province of women. That assumption, typically made by male scholars, inevitably carries with it a note of conde-scension. After all, women in ancient Israel were largely illiterate and marginalized; they played an insignificant role in the socio-political pro-cesses that shaped Israelite life and institutions.

CONCLUSION

The popular cult revealed in 2 Kings 23 and now corroborated by archae-ological evidence, where it has been acknowledged at all by scholars, has usually been regarded as foreign (i.e., Canaanite), syncretistic, heterodox, or pagan—almost always with the presumption (often unstated, even unconscious) that such popular religion is the antithesis of an original Mosaic monotheism or pure Yahwism, and therefore less authentic (read "less to my liking").[5]

It is time that such sophistry be set aside, if we are ever to comprehend the religion of ancient Israel and Judah in all its variety and vitality. Religion is not merely what clerics and theologians (or biblical scholars) think people should have believed and done in the name of religion but what the majority actually did. I have shown that the silence of 2 Kings 23, when amplified by archaeological data, may reveal what the actual religious situation was in seventh-century BCE Judah. Whether or not the Josianic reform was successful is not a matter to be decided here;[6] nor can we justify alignment with the Deuteronomistic view of Yahwism on the grounds that it was this version of the tradition that was vindicated by history (whose history?).

One may choose whether or not to accept the biblical writers' and editors' opinion of what the purported events of ancient Israel's history meant, but the archaeologist or historian must guard against reading mod-ern notions of any kind back into either the textual or the archaeological record. The past was always more complex, more intractable than we think; let it speak for itself, if possible.

NOTES

1. See Dever 1990, forthcoming b, c, d; Thompson 1987:25–28; and the several essays in Edelman 1991. Add now, more from the perspective of art history, Winter 1983; Schroer 1987; Keel and Uehlinger 1992. These recent works con-tain bibliography to a much larger literature on the problems of relating texts to artifacts in the study of Israelite history and religion—a study that in my opinion is just beginning.

2. As discussed below, Smith's (1990) treatment of deities makes a significant beginning, but Albertz's (1992) synthesis comes closest by far to what I envision a history of Israelite religion to be. Yet even Albertz (1992:1, 307–37) deals only with the general literary-historical setting of what he calls the struggle between "official syncretism and poly-yahwism," between "private syncretism and internal religious pluralism." See further Dever 1983, 1987:209–22; and see also references in note 1 above.

3. The bibliography is now extensive, but for Khirbet el-Qôm see Dever 1970, 1984; Zevit 1984; Hadley 1987; Keel and Uehlinger 1992:199–317. For Kuntillet Ajrud, see Meshel 1978a, 1978b, 1979; Beck 1982; Dever 1984; Smith 1990:85–88; Keel and Uehlinger 1992:199–317. Several essays in Miller, Hanson, and McBride 1987 discuss both these inscriptions, as well as acknowledging their crucial significance, including those of P. D. Miller, M. D. Coogan, P. K. McCarter, and J. H. Tigay. On the cult of Asherah, add Winter 1983; Dever 1984; Hestrin 1987a, 1987b; Olyan 1988; Smith 1990:80–114; and Hadley, forthcoming.

4. Abecedaries are so common, and tend to occur in such singular contexts (i.e., ʿIzbet Sarteh, Kuntillet Ajrud [three incomplete examples]), that they can scarcely all be regarded as simply "schoolboy's exercises." Equally unacceptable is the notion of André Lemaire (oral communication) that the abecedaries at Kuntillet Ajrud show that this was not a "cult site" but a "scribal school." See also Lemaire 1981.

5. See further Smith 1990:145–46, 154–57; Ackerman 1992:1–2, 215–17; Bloch-Smith 1992:150. I have used such terms as "Canaanite," "syncretism," even "pagan" (Dever 1984:31, 1987:236). But the confusion, or lack of precision, is partly semantic. By "Canaanite," I do not imply that those features of Israelite religion "borrowed" from Late Bronze Age Canaan were not then regarded as authentically "Israelite"; I mean only that they were later and in that sense derivative. If "syncretistic" means "combining differing beliefs in religious belief and practice" (as commonly held), then ancient Israel's religion was indeed syncretistic. Finally, it should be recalled that "pagan" does not necessarily imply a value judgment (certainly not in my view); the word derives from Latin *pagus*, "country," and referred originally to peasants in the countryside, who were slow to convert to Christianity. The "popular religion" discussed here was precisely "pagan," i.e., the rural religion of most of Israel and Judah in the monarchy.

6. Kenyon (1971:120) had tentatively connected her well-known cache of hundreds of broken seventh-century BCE figurines from Cave 1 in Jerusalem with the Josianic reforms, a tantalizing suggestion that unfortunately cannot be confirmed. Herzog et al. (1984:22–26), following Aharoni, attributed the destruction of the Stratum VIII temple and the new plan of Stratum VII to the reforms of Josiah, but the few reports on pottery of Strata VIII–VII that have been published (1984: Figs. 22, 24) are not decisive; see further the skepticism of Holladay (1987:257); Ussishkin (1988:155–56). The demise of the supposed "horned-altar temple" at Beer-sheba was attributed by the excavators (Herzog, Rainey, and Moshkovitz 1977:53–58) to Stratum III and was thought to have been due to a destruction by Hezekiah, but Yadin (1976) argued for a Stratum II assignment and thought the

destruction due to Josiah. Again, precise historical correlations are unfortunately impossible. Finally, Avriham Eitan's excavation of a late-seventh-century BCE fortress-sanctuary at Vered Jericho, although published only preliminarily, offers tantalizing hints of a deliberate destruction, i.e., decommissioning; see Shanks 1986. In any case, Susan Ackerman (1992) has demonstrated amply that the popular cults still prevailed in the sixth century BCE (and undoubtedly even later).

WORKS CITED

Ackerman, S.
1992   *Under Every Green Tree: Popular Religion in Sixth-Century Judah.* Harvard Semitic Monographs, 46. Atlanta: Scholars Press.
Aharoni, Y.
1968   Arad: Its Inscriptions and Temple. *Biblical Archaeologist* 31:1–32.
1975   Beersheba, Tel. In *Encyclopedia of Archaeological Excavations in the Holy Land*, ed. M. Avi-Yonah, 1:160–68. Jerusalem: Israel Exploration Society and Massada Press.
1981   *Arad Inscriptions.* Jerusalem: Israel Exploration Society.
Ahlström, G.
1993   *A History of Ancient Palestine from the Paleolithic Period to Alexander's Conquest.* Sheffield: Almond Press.
Albertz, R.
1978   *Personliche Frömmigheit und offiziele Religion.* Stuttgart: Calwer Verlag.
1992   *Religionsgeschichte Israels in alttestamentlicher Zeit: Erster und zweiter Teilband.* Göttingen: Vandenhoeck and Ruprecht.
Alpert-Nakhai, B.
forthcoming   *Religion in Canaan and Israel: An Archaeological Perspective.*
Avigad, N.
1953   The Epitaph of a Royal Steward from Siloam Village. *Israel Exploration Journal* 3:137–52.
Barkay, G.
1986   *Ketef Hinnom: A Treasure Facing Jerusalem's Walls.* Israel Museum Catalog 274. Jerusalem: Israel Museum.
Beck, P.
1982   The Drawings from Horvat Teiman (Kuntillet ʿAjrud). *Tel Aviv* 9:3–68.
1990   A Figurine from Tel ʿIra. *Eretz-Israel* 21:87–93 (Hebrew).
Biran, A.
1980   Tel Dan Five Years Later. *Biblical Archaeologist* 43:168–82.
1986   The Dancer from Dan, the Empty Tomb, and the Altar Room. *Israel Exploration Journal* 36:168–78.
1989   Prize Find: Tel Dan Scepter Head—Belonging to Priest or King? *Biblical Archaeology Review* 15, no. 1:29–31.
Bird, P.
1990   Gender and Religious Definition: The Case of Ancient Israel. *Harvard Divinity Bulletin* 20:12–13, 19, 20.

1991   Israelite Religion and the Faith of Israel's Daughters. In *The Bible and the Politics of Exegesis: Essays in Honor of Norman Gottwald on His Sixty-fifth Birthday*, ed. D. Jobling, P. L. Day, and G. T. Sheppard, 97–108. Cleveland: Pilgrim.

Bloch-Smith, E.
1992   *Judahite Burial Practices and Beliefs about the Dead.* Journal for the Study of the Old Testament Supplement Series 123 and JSOT/ ASOR Monogram Series 7. Sheffield: Sheffield Academic Press.

Brown, S.
1991   *Late Carthaginian Child Sacrifice and Sacrificial Monuments in Their Mediterranean Context.* Sheffield: JSOT Press.

Chambon, A.
1984   *Tell el-Far^cah I: L'âge du Fer.* Paris: Éditions Recherche sur les Civilisations.

Cogan, M., and H. Tadmor, eds.
1988   *II Kings.* Anchor Bible. New York: Doubleday.

Dever, W. G.
1970   Iron Age Epigraphic Material from the Area of Khirbet el-Kom. *Hebrew Union College Annual* 40–41:139–204.

1983   Material Remains and the Cult in Ancient Israel: An Essay in Archaeological Systematics. In *The Word of the Lord Shall Go Forth: Essays in Honor of David Noel Freedman in Celebration of His Sixtieth Birthday*, ed. C. L. Meyers and M. O'Connor, 571–87. Philadelphia: American Schools of Oriental Research.

1984   Asherah, Consort of Yahweh? New Evidence from Kuntillet ^cAjrûd. *Bulletin of the American Schools of Oriental Research* 255:29–37.

1987   The Contribution of Archaeology to the Study of Canaanite and Israelite Religion. In *Ancient Religion: Essays in Honor of Frank Moore Cross*, ed. P. D. Miller, P. D. Hanson, and S. D. McBride, 209–47. Philadelphia: Fortress.

1990   *Recent Archaeological Discoveries and Biblical Research.* Seattle: University of Washington Press.

forthcoming a Asherah Abscondita: The Changing Fortunes of the Great Mother in Ancient Israel, Judaism, and Christianity. Forthcoming in *Conceptions and Cultic Roles of Female Deities in Ancient Israel and Canaan*, ed. W. G. Dever and S. Ackerman.

forthcoming b From Chiefdom to State: A Critique of State Formation Processes in Ancient Israel. Forthcoming in *Nuove fondazioni nel Vicino Oriente antico*, ed. S. Mazzoni.

forthcoming c Ancient Israelite Religion: How to Reconcile the Differing Textual and Archaeological Portraits? Forthcoming in *YHWH unter den Göttinnen und Götten des Alten Orients*, ed. W. Dietrich and M. Klopfenstein.

forthcoming d Archaeology, Texts, and History-Writing: Toward an Epistemology. Forthcoming in *Uncovering Ancient Stones: Essays in Memory of H. Neil Richardson*, ed. L. Hopfe. Winona Lake: Eisenbrauns.

Edelman, D. V., ed.
1991   *The Fabric of History: Text, Artifact, and Israel's Past.* Journal
            for the Study of the Old Testament Supplement Series 127.
            Sheffield: Almond Press.
Garbini, G.
1988   *History and Ideology in Ancient Israel.* New York: Crossroad.
Gitin, S.
1990   Ekron of the Philistines, Part II: Olive-Oil Suppliers to the World.
            Biblical Archaeology Review 16, no. 2:32–41.
1992   New Incense Altars from Ekron: Context, Typology, and Func-
            tion. *Eretz-Israel* 23:43*–49*.
Hadley, J. M.
1987   The Khirbet el-Qôm Inscription. *Vetus Testamentum* 37:50–62.
forthcoming *Yahweh's Asherah in the Light of Recent Discoveries.*
Halpern, B.
1988   *The First Historians: The Hebrew Bible and History.* New York:
            Harper and Row.
Haran, M.
1978   *Temples and Temple Service in Ancient Israel.* Oxford: Oxford Uni-
            versity Press.
Herrmann, S.
1975   *A History of Israel in Old Testament Times.* Philadelphia: Fortress.
Herzog, Z.; M. Aharoni; A. F. Rainey; and S. Moshkovitz
1984   The Israelite Fortress at Arad. *Bulletin of the American Schools of
            Oriental Research* 254:1–34.
Herzog, Z.; A. F. Rainey; and S. Moshkovitz
1977   The Stratigraphy at Beer-sheba and the Location of the Sanctu-
            ary. *Bulletin of the American Schools of Oriental Research* 225:49–58.
Hestrin, R.
1987a   The Lachish Ewer and the Asherah. *Israel Exploration Journal*
            37:212–23.
1987b   The Cult Stand from Taᶜanach and Its Religious Background. In
            Phoenicia and the East Mediterranean in the First Millennium B.C., ed.
            E. Lipiński, 61–77. Studia Phoenicia, 5. Louvain: Uitgeverij Peeters.
Holladay, J. S.
1987   Religion in Israel under the Monarchy: An Explicitly Archaeolog-
            ical Approach. In *Ancient Israelite Religion: Essays in Honor of Frank
            Moore Cross*, ed. P. D. Miller, P. D. Hanson, and S. D. McBride,
            249–99. Philadelphia: Fortress.
Holland, T. A.
1977   A Study of Palestinian Iron Age Baked Clay Figurines, with Spe-
            cial Reference to Jerusalem: Cave 1. *Levant* 19:121–55.
Keel, O., and C. Uehlinger
1992   *Göttinnen, Götter, und Gottessymbole: Neue Erkenntnisse zur Religions-
            geschichte Kanaans und Israels aufgrund bislang unerschlossener ikono-
            graphischer Quellen.* Freiburg: Herder.

Kenyon, K. M.
1971   *Royal Cities of the Old Testament*. New York: Schocken Books.
Knauf, E. A.
1991   From History to Interpretation. In *The Fabric of History: Text,
               Artifact, and Israel's Past*, ed. D. V. Edelman, 26–64. Sheffield:
               Almond Press.
Kuemmerlin-McLean, J.
1992   Magic: Old Testament. In *Anchor Bible Dictionary*, ed. D. N. Freed-
               man, 4:468–71. New York: Doubleday.
Lapp, P. W.
1967   The 1966 Excavation at Tell Ta^cannek. *Bulletin of the American
               Schools of Oriental Research* 185:2–39.
1969   The 1968 Excavations at Tell Ta^cannek. *Bulletin of the American
               Schools of Oriental Research* 195:2–49.
Lemaire, A.
1981   *Les écoles et la formation de la Bible dans l'ancien Israël*. Göttingen:
               Vandenhoeck and Ruprecht.
Lemche, N. P.
1985   *Early Israel: Anthropological and Historical Studies on the Israelite
               Society before the Monarchy*. Leiden: E. J. Brill.
Lohfink, N.
1987   The Cult Reform of Josiah of Judah: 2 Kings 22–23 as a Source
               for the History of Israelite Religion. In *Ancient Israelite Religion:
               Essays in Honor of Frank Moore Cross*, ed. P. D. Miller, P. D. Hanson,
               and S. D. McBride, 459–75. Philadelphia: Fortress.
Lowery, R. H.
1990   *The Reforming Kings: Cults and Society in First Temple Judah*. Shef-
               field: Almond Press.
Mazar, A.
1980   *Excavations at Tell Qasile, Part One. The Philistine Sanctuary: Archi-
               tecture and Cult Objects*. Qedem 12. Jerusalem: Institute of Archae-
               ology, Hebrew University.
1982   The "Bull Site"—An Iron Age I Open Cult Place. *Bulletin of the
               American Schools of Oriental Research* 247:27–42.
Meshel, Z.
1978a   *Kuntillet ^cAjrud: A Religious Centre from the Time of the Judaean
               Monarchy on the Border of Sinai*. Israel Museum Catalog 175. Jeru-
               salem: The Israel Museum (no pagination).
1978b   Kuntillet ^cAjrud—An Israelite Religious Center in Northern Sinai.
               Expedition 20:50–54.
1979   Did Yahweh Have a Consort? The New Religious Inscriptions
               from the Sinai. *Biblical Archaeology Review* 5, no. 2:24–35.
Meyers, C. L.
1988   *Discovering Eve: Ancient Israelite Women in Context*. New York:
               Oxford University Press.
1991   "To Her Mother's House": Considering a Counterpart to the

Israelite *Bêt 'āb*. In *The Bible and the Politics of Exegesis*, ed. D. Jobling, P. L. Day, and G. T. Sheppard, 39–51. Cleveland: Pilgrim.

Miller, J. M.
1976   *The Old Testament and the Historian*. Philadelphia: Fortress.
1987   Old Testament History and Archaeology. *Biblical Archaeologist* 49:51-62.

Miller, P. D.; P. D. Hanson; and S. D. McBride, eds.
1987   *Ancient Israelite Religion: Essays in Honor of Frank Moore Cross*. Philadelphia: Fortress.

Naveh, J.
1963   Old Hebrew Inscriptions in a Burial Cave. *Israel Exploration Journal* 13:235–56.

Negbi, O.
1976   *Canaanite Gods in Metal: An Archaeological Study of Ancient Syro-Palestinian Figurines*. Tel Aviv: Institute of Archaeology, Tel Aviv University.

Noth, M.
1960   *The History of Israel*. New York: Harper and Row.

Oden, R.
1976   The Persistence of Canaanite Religion. *Biblical Archaeologist* 39:31–36.

Olyan, S.
1988   *Asherah and the Cult of Yahweh in Israel*. Atlanta: Scholars Press.

Rendtorff, R.
1983   *The Old Testament: An Introduction*. Philadelphia: Fortress.

Rösel, H. N.
1992   *Israel in Kanaan: Zum Problem der Entstehung Israels*. Beiträge zur Erforschung des Alten Testaments und des antiken Judentums II. New York: Peter Lang.

Schroer, S.
1987   *In Israel gab es Bilder: Nachrechten von darstellender Kunst im Alten Testament*. Göttingen. Vandenhoeck and Ruprecht.

Shanks, H.
1986   *BAR* Interview with Avraham Eitan. *Biblical Archaeology Review* 12, no. 4:30–38.

Smith, M. S.
1990   *The Early History of God: Yahweh and the Other Deities in Ancient Israel*. New York: Harper and Row.

Stager, L. E., and S. R. Wolff
1981   Production and Commerce in Temple Courtyards: An Olive Press in the Sacred Precinct at Tel Dan. *Bulletin of the American Schools of Oriental Research* 243:95–102.

Taylor, J. G.
1989   Yahweh and Asherah at Tenth-Century Taanach. *Newsletter for Ugaritic Studies* 37/38:16–18.

Thompson, T. L.
1987   *The Origin Tradition of Ancient Israel I: The Literary Formation of Genesis and Exodus 1—23.* Sheffield: Almond Press.
1992   *Early History of the Israelite People from the Written and Archaeological Sources.* Leiden: E. J. Brill.
Tigay, J. H.
1986   *You Shall Have No Other Gods before Me: Israelite Religion in the Light of Hebrew Inscriptions.* Atlanta: Scholars Press.
Ussishkin, D.
1988   The Date of the Judaean Shrine at Arad. *Israel Exploration Journal* 38:142–57.
Winter, U.
1983   *Frau und Götten: Exegetische und ikonographische Studien zum weiblichen Gottesbild im Alten Israel und in dessen Umwelt.* Göttingen: Vandenhoeck and Ruprecht.
Yadin, Y.
1976   Beersheba: The High Place Destroyed by King Josiah. *Bulletin of the American Schools of Oriental Research* 222:1–17.
Zevit, Z.
1984   The Khirbet el-Qôm Inscription Mentioning a Goddess. *Bulletin of the American Schools of Oriental Research* 255:33–41.

10 | The Archaeology of the Days of Manasseh

ISRAEL FINKELSTEIN

The biblical account of King Manasseh's reign is laconic and its historical value questionable (Ben-Zvi 1991, forthcoming; Schniedewind 1991). Moreover, all scholars agree today that it is dominated by the negative approach of the Deuteronomistic historian to this monarch. Reference to Manasseh in the Assyrian records (Gane, forthcoming) are also too brief to allow a comprehensive historical reconstruction. Scholars (e.g., Halpern 1991) have therefore turned to archaeology to shed light on the days of this king who ruled for over half a century; his reign spanned one of the most crucial periods in the history of Judah, after the devastation of the kingdom by Sennacherib and before the days of the celebrated reformer Josiah. (For several possibilities for the exact years between 699 and 640 BCE, see, e.g., Hayes and Hooker 1988:109–11; Hughes 1990:223; Na'aman 1986; Thiele 1983:176).

But it is also difficult to pinpoint Manasseh archaeologically, as it is virtually impossible to refer to the archaeology of the days of any Judahite or Israelite king, with very few possible exceptions, to be specified below. Although the pottery of the late Iron II, that is the late eighth to early sixth century BCE, is known better than the pottery of any other phase of the Bronze and Iron Ages in Palestine, it has not yet reached the stage of accurate dating to a specific generation.

THE PROBLEM

The main reason for this unfortunate situation is that in order to date pottery assemblages in an accurate way we need to uncover indisputable destruction layers that can safely be assigned to a particular historical event mentioned in the Bible or in other ancient Near Eastern sources. The identification of such destruction layers in the field is a very treacherous task, to say nothing of the historicity, and thus reliability, of some of the biblical sources. For the specific geographical and chronological frameworks discussed here—the territory of the Judahite state in the late Iron II—we possess only two events, for which we obtain this combination of unambiguous archaeological destruction layer and reliable historical source: the first is Sennacherib's campaign in 701 BCE and the second is the destruction of Judah by Nebuchadrezzar in 587/6 BCE. All other cases, such as the suggested second campaign of Sennacherib, or the Babylonian campaign in the year 597 BCE, cannot be supported archaeologically (in the case of the latter), or should be dismissed historically (in the case of the former; Na'aman 1979:77; Kitchen 1986:552–53; Yurco 1991 contra Shea 1985).

To add to the frustration, most of the geographically and chronologically relevant sites have not supplied the desired information even for these two events. Two examples follow. (1) The destruction of Stratum II at Beer-sheba was assigned by the excavator to Sennacherib's campaign (Aharoni and Aharoni 1976), but Na'aman (1979:75) attributed it to an earlier Assyrian campaign. There are two explanations for this dispute: the site is not mentioned in the relevant Assyrian sources, and for either chronological or regional reasons, its pottery assemblage is not completely identical to that of Stratum III at Lachish, the key site for the study of the late-eighth-century pottery. (2) The compact stratigraphy of Arad in the late Iron II, with destruction layers assigned to Sennacherib (Stratum VIII), Pharaoh Neco or the first Babylonian campaign (VII), and the Babylonians or Edomites (VI) (Aharoni 1981; Herzog et al. 1984) has been challenged by Yigael Yadin (1979:219–22), David Ussishkin (1988), Amihai Mazar and Ehud Netzer (1986), Orna Zimhoni (1985:84–87), and others.

Surprising as it sounds, the entire pottery chronology of Judah in the late Iron II is based on a single site, Lachish. First, the renowned relief from Nineveh leaves no doubt that the city was indeed devastated by Sennacherib. Second, the biblical reference to Azekah and Lachish as being the last strongholds to withstand the Babylonian assault (Jer. 34:7), and the Lachish Ostracon Number 4, which seems to be related to these events, give clear evidence that the site was annihilated by the Babylonians in 587/6. No less important, Lachish was properly excavated by both James Starkey and his colleagues in the 1930s and Ussishkin and his team in recent years. It yielded rich finds in clear, undisputed stratigraphic contexts (Ussishkin 1978, 1983). Lachish is therefore the key site for the study of the archaeology of Judah in late Iron II.

The British excavators of Lachish assigned two strata, III and II, to late Iron II. There has been a consensus that the Stratum II destruction should be dated to the Babylonian conquest of 587/6 BCE, but the dating of Stratum III was disputed, even among the excavators. Starkey dated its destruction to the first Babylonian campaign in 597 BCE. But Olga Tufnell, who published the Lachish finds, maintained that it was destroyed by Sennacherib. Because of its crucial importance for the dating of other late Iron II assemblages in Judah, this issue became one of the hottest debates in Palestinian archaeology. W. F. Albright, G. E. Wright, K. M. Kenyon, P. W. Lapp, F. M. Cross, and J. A. Holladay supported Starkey's opinion, while Y. Aharoni, B. Mazar, and A. Rainey endorsed Tufnell's view (for summary and references see Ussishkin 1977:31–33). The renewed excavations by David Ussishkin have confirmed Tufnell's judgment beyond any doubt: Stratum III was indeed destroyed by Sennacherib (Ussishkin 1977, 1982).

Comparing late Iron II assemblages exposed in other Judahite sites to the two rich, different, and well-dated pottery assemblages of Strata III and II at Lachish, Yohanan and Miriam Aharoni (1976) were able to distinguish two stratigraphic-chronological horizons in the eighth and seventh centuries BCE: first, sites that were destroyed by Sennacherib, that is, by Sennacherib's or another Assyrian campaign of the late eighth century BCE; and second, sites destroyed by the Babylonians or in the course of other events related to the Babylonian campaigns, such as the suggested Edomite assault on the southern border of the monarchy (e.g., Herzog et al. 1984:29; Beit-Arieh 1988).

The reign of Manasseh falls between these two horizons. Since Manasseh was a loyal vassal of Assyria (Evans 1980; Nelson 1983; Machinist 1992:74), there were no great destructions in Judah during his reign. Therefore, we do not have even a single stratum firmly dated to his time. I. Beit-Arieh (1985:25) has argued that the major construction effort in the fortified Negeb town of Tel ʿIra was undertaken in the first half of the seventh century BCE, that is, in the days of Manasseh. His suggestion has been based on both stratigraphic and typological observations: two construction phases were discerned in a storage building and casemate rooms uncovered at the site, with some possible typological differences between the assemblage found in the early phase and that retrieved from the final destruction of the site. But since the pottery of Tel ʿIra was not analyzed quantitatively, it is doubtful whether this crucial issue will be resolved even when the finds are fully published.

Future studies of additional late Iron II pottery assemblages will shed light on this perplexing problem only if carried out with advanced quantitative methods capable of tracing the gradual change of the ceramic repertoire between the Lachish III and Lachish II horizons. A good example is the case of Tel ʿEton in the southeastern Shephelah. Two strata were unearthed in a sounding in this large mound (Ayalon 1985). Their pottery was found to be very similar and both were dated to the late ninth-eighth century BCE (Zimhoni 1985). The earlier stratum was the more violently destroyed (by Sennacherib?). Since the limited number of sherds allowed only a partial quantitative study, it was impossible to trace minute differences between the two assemblages and thus the precise dates of the two destructions remained elusive.

It goes without saying that these difficulties in pinpointing early-seventh-century strata make every effort to deal with the material culture of the period very problematic (e.g., Halpern 1991). Therefore, I will be able to outline only general settlement, demographic, and cultural trends in Judah between 701 and 586. Bearing in mind that the days of Manasseh come right after Sennacherib's campaign, even this less than complete and less than desired information should be of much value.

SETTLEMENT AND DEMOGRAPHIC TRANSFORMATIONS

The settlement patterns will be described according to the biblical division of the territory of Judah into four geographical units: Shephelah, Har (hill country = the Judean hills), Negeb (the Beer-sheba valley), and Midbar (the Judean desert). Two points should be made at the outset: First, the dating of eighth- and late-seventh/early-sixth-century sites is based on comparison to the assemblages of Lachish Strata III and II. Second, survey material is very different from rich excavated assemblages. The precise dating of sites that yielded only a few Iron II sherds is often dubious.

The Shephelah

Yehuda Dagan has been conducting a comprehensive survey in the Shephelah in the past fifteen years. The results of his survey (Dagan 1992) illustrate the dramatic devastation of the Shephelah by Sennacherib. The region reached a settlement and demographic peak in the second half of the eighth century BCE, with 276 sites so far recorded that yielded Lachish III pottery types. According to my estimate (based on Dagan's data, but somewhat lower than his calculations), these sites occupied a total built-up area of about 250 ha (ca. 617 acres). The settlement system of the eighth century was virtually annihilated by Sennacherib. Only thirty-eight late-seventh- to early-sixth-century BCE settlements have been recorded, with a total built-up area of about 80 ha. Most of these sites are concentrated in the eastern part of the Shephelah. Hence, about 85 percent of the settlements of the Shephelah in the eighth century had not been reoccupied in the last phase of the Iron II. The total built-up area decreased by about 70 percent. According to Dagan, the main decrease in the Shephelah was in unwalled villages and farmhouses, rather than in the central tells; most of the latter were occupied in the late seventh century, although many of them were probably destroyed by Sennacherib and then rebuilt; this can be clarified only by meticulous excavations.

It is interesting to compare these data to the results of a recent survey around the valley of Aijalon. This area borders on the Judahite Shephelah, but it was apparently outside the territory of eighth-century Judah. Alon Shavit has recently conducted a full-coverage survey in this region (Shavit 1992). He found scores of small, unwalled seventh-century farmhouses, which must reflect conditions of reasonable security. The situation here is therefore opposite that of the Judahite Shephelah immediately to the south; an explanation must be sought in the different political conditions that prevailed in the two regions in the seventh century. In Philistia, too, settlement flourished in the seventh century BCE, as attested by results of excavations and surveys alike (see summary in Finkelstein 1992). The prosperity of Philistia should be attributed to economic advantages under Assyrian domination, especially for the gateway communities of the Arabian trade (see below).

The survey evidence on the devastation of the Judahite Shephelah is supported by the results of excavations in most of the major mounds in the eastern part of the region. Lachish was apparently abandoned after the destruction of Stratum III. In Stratum II, in the second half of the seventh century, the city was rebuilt, but the palace remained in ruins and the rest of the site was only sparsely settled (Ussishkin 1977:51; 1983:133). Tell Beit Mirsim and Beth-shemesh were destroyed at the end of the eighth century BCE and were not resettled in the last phase of Iron II

(Aharoni and Aharoni 1976). The only site in the Shephelah that grew in size in the seventh century BCE is Tel Miqne, which is located in the western part of the region, bordering on the coastal plain (Gitin 1989:23). I will return to this interesting anomaly, but for the present we should note that the history of this site in late Iron II was shaped by forces that dominated the coastal plain rather than the highlands.

The Judean Hills

Data on the settlement and demographic patterns in the Judean hill country south of Jerusalem have been collected by M. Kochavi (1972) and by Avi Ofer, who carried out a comprehensive archaeological survey in the region. According to Ofer's estimates (1994), the eighth century marks the settlement peak in this region. He assigned 122 sites to that time (including sites that were surveyed in the past and later rechecked), with their aggregate built-up area estimated at 85 ha. Ofer assigned 113 sites to the seventh–sixth century BCE, with the total built-up area dropping to about 60 ha, a decrease of about 30 percent. According to Ofer, the southern part of the region suffered more than other parts of the Judean hill country.

But solid evidence from excavations in the region seems to contradict Ofer's notion of a population decrease in the seventh century. First, Tell en-Nasbeh and Gibeon were not only inhabited at that time but may even have reached their peak occupation. Ramat Rahel also reached its settlement peak in the seventh century. Gabriel Barkay's recent excavations at the site revealed a full-scale settlement in addition to the palace uncovered by Yohanan Aharoni (Barkay, oral communication). Second, unlike the Shephelah, all major excavated sites in the Judean highlands were occupied in both the eighth and the seventh centuries BCE (e.g., Beth-zur and Khirbet Rabud). Third, a group of forts found around Jerusalem, including the one at Tell el-Ful, were established during the seventh century (Barkay 1985). Fourth, a system of farmhouses was built in the seventh century around Jerusalem (Meitlis 1989) and to the south, near Bethlehem (Amit 1991). Fifth, the Judahite population spread at that time to the nearby arid zones, to both the Judean desert and the Negeb (see below). It is unlikely that this expansion of rural settlement was accompanied by decrease in the total number of sites and a drop in population.

There are two possible explanations for what seems to be Ofer's misinterpretation of the survey material. First, the dating of the seventh-century

BCE pottery in Judah is usually based on three pottery types, easily missed at small sites that yield a limited quantity of sherds. If these types are absent, the rest of the assemblage may look like that of the eighth century. Second, in many of the Judahite sites, the late Iron II stratum was exposed to erosion (see Kochavi 1974 for the case of Khirbet Rabud), and as a result part of the last settlement had apparently been washed away.

I therefore assume that the seventh-century occupation in the Judean hills south of Jerusalem was no less dense than in the eighth century. Farmhouses and small settlements that have recently been surveyed and excavated in the region may even hint at a settlement and demographic growth at the late Iron II. Accordingly, I would take the 85 built-up ha of the eighth century as a minimum number for late Iron II.

The teams that conducted a full-coverage survey in the hill country between Jerusalem and Ramallah (Feldstein et al. 1993; Dinur and Feig 1993) did not distinguish between eighth-century and late-seventh- to early-sixth-century BCE sites. Altogether, about 100 Iron II sites have been recorded there, with a total built-up area of about 90 ha. These numbers include the main mounds, such as Gibeon and Tell en-Nasbeh. About 10 ha should be added for sites west of Jerusalem not included in this survey. The Bible hints that the area north of Jerusalem was desolated by an Assyrian campaign, probably Sennacherib's (Na'aman 1979:69), but the archaeological evidence seems to indicate that it soon recovered.

The question of the size of Jerusalem in Iron II has been bitterly debated. The prevailing view relates the great expansion of the city to the torrent of refugees that inflated the city in the period following the destruction of the northern monarchy and Sennacherib's campaign in the Judahite Shephelah (Broshi 1974; but see Barkay 1985, where he argues that the expansion of Jerusalem to the western hill started in the ninth to eighth centuries). In the late eighth century the city had not yet reached its maximal area, though it is reasonable to assume that the expansion out of the City of David was already underway. At the end of Iron II the city extended to an area of about 60 ha (90–100 ha, according to Barkay 1985).

The Judean Desert

Permanent eighth-century BCE sites have not been recorded in the Judean desert (with the possible exception of En-Gedi; see Mazar, Dothan, and Dunayevsky 1966; 53–58, figs. 29–33). All late Iron II sites found in the region date to the seventh/early sixth centuries BCE. These are: En-Gedi

(Mazar, Dothan, and Dunayevsky 1966:17–38), the Buqêᶜah sites (Stager 1975), the farmhouse at Vered Jericho (Eitan 1983), sites along the western coast of the Dead Sea (Bar-Adon 1989) and Horvat Shilha east of Ramallah (Mazar, Amit, and Ilan 1984).

The Negeb

In the Judahite Negeb (the Beer-sheba valley) the number of sites grew in the seventh century far beyond previous periods. Beer-sheba was abandoned (Aharoni and Aharoni 1976), but new sites were established at Tel Masos (Fritz and Kempinski 1983), Horvat Uza (Beit-Arieh and Cresson 1991), Horvat Radom (Beit-Arieh 1991), Tel ᶜIra (Beit-Arieh 1985), and Aroer (Biran and Cohen 1981). Altogether, five sites were occupied in the eighth century, with a total built-up area of about 4 ha. In the seventh-early sixth century there were seven sites with a total built-up area of almost 10 ha. These data relate to excavated sites. Recent surveys (Govrin 1991) and my preliminary impression in visits to several unchecked sites in the region indicate that when fully surveyed, the Beer-sheba valley will yield more seventh–early-sixth-century sites.

DISCUSSION

To summarize, the total built-up area of the eighth-century sites in Judah can be estimated at about 470 ha. Employing a density coefficient of 250 people per built-up hectare yields a population of approximately 120,000 people (slightly more than estimated by Broshi and Finkelstein 1992, due to a better knowledge of the settlement pattern of the Shephelah). In order to estimate the population of Judah in the first half of the seventh century BCE, one should deduct the Shephelah and calculate the population of Jerusalem according to its maximal size (that is, ca. 60 ha). The total built-up area of the late seventh century BCE can accordingly be estimated at about 255 built-up hectares, with a population of roughly 65,000 people.

Thus, there were four drastic demographic alterations in the Judahite state in the early seventh century, that is, in the days of Manasseh:

1. The Shephelah was lost. The calamity that Sennacherib's campaign inflicted on Judah is best demonstrated by the fact that in the eighth century BCE, the Shephelah had over 50 percent of the built-up area and hence population of the Judahite state. As Dagan

(1992) has rightly observed, these data should reopen the discussion on the number of Judahite deportees claimed by Sennacherib.

2. Almost all the population of the Judahite state now lived in the hill country.

3. The proportion of the population of Jerusalem to the total population changed from about 6 percent to about 23 percent in the late seventh century. In the early seventh century, before Judah expanded again to the Shephelah, the demographic share of the capital was even higher.

4. Settlement expanded into the arid zones to the east and south of the Judean hills. All sedentary sites of the Judean desert were established at that time, and the Beer-sheba valley witnessed a significant growth in both number of sites and total built-up area.

The sudden expansion into the marginal areas requires explanation. Until Sennacherib's campaign, the economy of the Judahite kingdom was well balanced by the different ecological niches of its territory: horticulture in the hill country and possibly also in the Shephelah, dry farming in the Shephelah and the eastern and southern flanks of the central range, and animal husbandry in the Judean desert and the south. The Assyrian campaigns wrought a great catastrophe on the Judahite state: the Shephelah was handed over to the Philistine city-states, and a torrent of refugees poured into Judah from vanquished Israel and from the destroyed districts of the Shephelah (Broshi 1974). Judah lost its rich cereal-producing lands in the west, and in addition, heavy tax was imposed by the Assyrian authorities. Demographic pressure drove part of the population to the marginal areas of the kingdom, which compensated for the lost dry-farming lands of the Shephelah. The Beer-sheba valley alone could produce over five thousand tons of grain per year (Herzog 1990), while the basic needs of its population can be estimated at no more than 5 percent of this amount. The Beer-sheba valley, if organized to assure maximum exploitation in good years and efficient storage in dry years, could therefore supply around one-quarter of the overall grain needs of Judah. The evidence from the region, both archaeological (the forts of Arad and Khirbet ʿUza) and epigraphic (the Arad ostraca; Aharoni 1981), attests to the existence of sophisticated administration. It is therefore reasonable, even necessary, to assume that the expansion into the marginal regions began immediately after Sennacherib's campaign, that is, in the beginning of the seventh century, rather than in the second half.

In other words, since the expansion into the arid regions was a matter of survival, we can safely argue, though we cannot prove it, that it took place in the days of Manasseh (For a similar dating from a different perspective, see Na'aman 1987; see also Tatum 1991).

The loss of the Shephelah and the expansion into the Judean desert and the Negeb forced Manasseh to reorganize the Judahite state (2 Chr. 33:15; for different views on the historicity of this text see, e.g., McKay 1973:24–27; Eph°al 1979:282; Williamson 1982:394; Miller and Hayes 1986:374–76; Rainey 1993). This task demanded sophisticated administration, especially for the efficient management of agriculture of the arid areas—the distribution of commodities and storing of large quantity of surplus grain in good years—and of the horticulture products of the highlands (see below). Supporting this hypothesis is the dramatic growth in the seventh century of seals and seal impressions found in Judah. Under Josiah, Judah took the first opportunity to reclaim at least some of the important territories of the Shephelah. This renewed westward expansion is attested in the town lists of Joshua 15.

The expansion of Manasseh into the Beer-sheba valley had another economic advantage, that of participating in the thriving trade in the south (Finkelstein 1992; also Halpern 1991:62). This move could not have been undertaken without the approval of the Assyrians, who had solid interests in the Arabian trade and thus in the northern termini of the desert roads, and who dominated the region from their centers in the southern coastal plain. The seventh-century Arabian trade is attested in both the Assyrian records and in the archaeological finds of the vast areas from Tell el-Kheleifeh and Edom in the south to Judah and the Mediterranean coast in the north.

Tiglath-pileser III counted Gaza "as a custom-house of Assyria," that is, he set his officials there to collect duties from the harbor. Sargon II declared that he had opened the border of Egypt to trade, mingled Assyrians and Egyptians, and encouraged mutual trade (Borger 1984:382).

Assyrian forts and/or administrative centers have been uncovered at Tell Abu-Salima on the Sinai coast (Reich 1984), Tell Jemmeh (Van Beek 1983), Tel Sera (Oren 1978:1060–62), and Tel Haror (Oren et al. 1991:13–18). A fortified site, with remains of storehouses, has recently been excavated on the coast south of Gaza (Oren et al. 1986). It yielded Phoenician, Cypro-Phoenician, Cypriot, Greek, and Egyptian pottery. The southern lands, from the coastal plain through the Beer-sheba–Arad basin to the Edomite highlands, experienced an unprecedented demographic prosperity in the seventh century. Noteworthy among the seventh-century sites of the Beer-sheba valley is the building excavated near the wells of Tel Masos, defined by the excavators as a road station (Fritz and Kempinski 1983:123–37, 233). The faunal assemblage from Tell Jemmeh is significant to the topic under discussion. Camels were very poorly represented until the seventh century BCE, when their number increased dramatically. Osteological studies by P. Wapnish (1981, 1984) indicated that the Tell Jemmeh camels were probably used in caravan trade.

South Arabian and Hijazi inscriptions found at Tell Jemmeh (Van Beek 1983:19), Tell el-Kheleifeh (Sass 1991:35–36), and Ghrareh in Edom (Knauf 1988) supply evidence for connections with Arabia at that time (for the literary evidence, see Elat 1990). Three ostraca with South Arabian script were uncovered in the City of David in Jerusalem, two of them in the early-sixth-century destruction level. They were carved on Judahite vessels and therefore probably attest an Arabian population living in Judah (Shiloh 1987). Nahman Avigad (1975:71) reported a seventh-century Hebrew seal, which in his opinion carries a South Arabian name. In this connection it is worth noting J. McKay's (1973:23–24) assumption that King Manasseh of Judah married an Arabian woman, possibly in order to strengthen his commercial interests in the south.

The rich archaeological finds from the vast area between Edom in the south to Philistia in the north indicate that Assyrians, Arabians, Phoenicians, Edomites, and possibly Judahites were involved in this thriving commercial activity (Finkelstein 1992). This economic prosperity provides another clue for the date of the Judahite expansion into the Beer-sheba valley. It is difficult to imagine that this was the sole region in the south to be sparsely settled in the first half of the seventh century BCE. The eclectic nature of the religion of Judah at the time of Manasseh (McKay 1973:20–27; Cogan 1974:72–88) should be evaluated on the background of the cultural *koine* in the region in the seventh century BCE (Rainey 1993).

Another economic phenomenon that should be mentioned here is the Tel Miqne (Ekron) olive oil production center (Eitam and Shomroni 1987), dated by Seymour Gitin (1989) to the seventh century, with peak operation in the first half of that century. As mentioned above, the occupational history of Tel Miqne in the late Iron II period is the opposite of that of the eastern Shephelah: Tel Miqne was a relatively small settlement in the eighth century BCE, the peak period of activity in the Judahite Shephelah. It flourished when the eastern Shephelah was desolated (first half of the seventh century) and declined with the partial recovery of that region in the late seventh century. Gitin (1989:49) rightly observed that the orchards that supplied the olives to the Tel Miqne industry must have been located in the hill country (contra Eitam and Shomroni 1987:48–49), while the main distribution centers were on the coast to the west. Indeed, the Shephelah has never been a prominent olive-growing region: varied data on the agricultural patterns of premodern Palestine indicate that it had relatively few olive orchards (Hütteroth and Abdulfattah 1977; Government of Palestine 1942/43, 1945). But proximity to the coastal ports and to the main highways of the country could make it a convenient location for olive oil production and distribution (Eitam and Shomroni 1987:49).

In the eighth century BCE there were several oil-production centers in Judah, in both the highlands and the Shephelah (Eitam 1987). Sennacherib's campaign altered the economic and political systems in the region: the Judahite centers in the eastern Shephelah were destroyed and Judah was forced to ship its produce to a new center in the western Shephelah, close to the gateway communities of the coast. Under the Assyrian domination, Tel Miqne emerged as the main olive oil production and distribution center in the south. (See also Tel Batash—Kelm and Mazar 1987—though it is not clear whether its industry already operated in the early seventh century.) It was fed by the orchards of the Judean and Samaritan hills; it is reasonable to suggest that a large part of Judah's tribute to Assyria was paid in kind, in the form of olives sent to this center. It is not surprising, therefore, that the decline of Assyrian power in the later seventh century BCE and the reclamation of the eastern Shephelah by Josiah brought about the degeneration of the Miqne industry.

CONCLUSIONS

Manasseh's realpolitik in his relations with Assyria (Evans 1980; Nelson 1983) enabled him to profit from the geopolitical conditions of the early seventh century BCE. It is reasonable to assume that, despite the tribute that had to be paid to Assyria, Judah under Manasseh started an economic revival (Nielsen 1967; Halpern 1991), mainly because of its activity in the south, in the Beer-sheba sector of the Arabian trade routes. It is conceivable that the Assyrians encouraged this revival, in order to maintain the economic strength of the Judahite buffer state. It is worth noting in this connection that a text reporting tribute given by south Levantine states to

Esarhaddon or Ashurbanipal indicates that Judah's tribute was smaller than that paid by Ammon and Moab (Gane, forthcoming).

Some scholars have argued that in the days of Manasseh Judah also reclaimed the lost territories of the Shephelah (Evans 1980; Åhlström 1982; Halpern 1991). The archaeological data seem to contradict this. Both excavations and surveys indicate that the partial recovery of the Shephelah took place in the "Lachish II" period, that is, in the late seventh century BCE (for the historical background, see Rainey 1987). Archaeology also supports the dating of the list of Judahite towns in Joshua 15 to the late seventh century BCE (for the latest discussion of this list, see Na'aman 1991). The prosperity of Tel Miqne in the early seventh century and its decline in the late seventh century also point in this direction.

Thus, in the later days of Hezekiah and in the reign of Manasseh, Judah went through a painful transformation from a relatively large state with a varied economic system to a small community, in fact not much more than a city-state, with a large capital and a small but densely settled countryside. But the days of Manasseh also show the first signs of economic and political recovery.

WORKS CITED

Aharoni, Y.
1981   *Arad Inscriptions*. Jerusalem: Israel Exploration Society.
Aharoni, Y., and M. Aharoni
1976   The Stratification of Judahite Sites in the Eighth and Seventh
            Centuries B.C.E. *Bulletin of the American Schools of Oriental Research*
            224:73–90.
Åhlström, G. W.
1982   *Royal Administration and National Religion in Ancient Palestine.*
            Leiden: E. J. Brill.
Amit, D.
1991   Farmsteads in Northern Judaea (Betar Area), Survey. *Explorations
            and Surveys in Israel* 10:147–48.
Avigad, N.
1975   New Names on Hebrew Seals. *Eretz-Israel* 12:66–71 (Hebrew).
Ayalon, E.
1985   Trial Excavation of Two Iron Age Strata at Tel ᶜEton. *Tel Aviv*
            12:54–62.
Bar-Adon, P.
1989   Excavations in the Judean Desert. *Atiqot* 9:1–88 (Hebrew).

Barkay, G.
1985   Northern and Western Jerusalem in the End of the Iron Age.
            Ph.D. dissertation, Tel Aviv University (Hebrew).
Beit-Arieh, I.
1985   Tel ᶜIra—A Fortified City of the Kingdom of Judah. *Qadmoniot*
            18(69–70):17–25 (Hebrew).
1988   New Light on the Edomites. *Biblical Archaeology Review* 14, no.
            2:28–41.
1991   A Small Frontier Citadel at Horvat Radum in the Judean Negev.
            Qadmoniot 24(95–96):86–89.
Beit-Arieh, I., and B. Cresson
1991   Horvat ᶜUza, A Fortified Outpost on the Eastern Negev Border.
            Biblical Archaeologist 54:126–35.
Ben-Zvi, E.
1991   The Account of the Reign of Manasseh in II Reg 21:1–18 and the
            Redactional History of the Book of Kings. *Zeitschrift für die alttes-
            tamentliche Wissenschaft* 103:355–74.
forthcoming Reconstructing the Historical Manassic Judah. In *Judah in the
            Late Iron Age*, ed. D. V. Edelman. Chicago.
Biran, A., and R. Cohen
1981   Aroer in the Negev. *Eretz-Israel* 15:250–73 (Hebrew).
Borger, R.
1984   Historische Texte in akkadischer Sprache. In *Texte aus der Umwelt
            des Alten Testaments I*, ed. R. Borger, W. Hint and W. H. Römer,
            354–410. Gütersloh: Verlagshaus Gerd Mohn.
Broshi, M.
1974   The Expansion of Jerusalem in the Reigns of Hezekiah and
            Manasseh. *Israel Exploration Journal* 24:21–26.
Broshi, M., and I. Finkelstein
1992   The Population of Palestine in Iron Age II. *Bulletin of the Ameri-
            can Schools of Oriental Research* 287:47–60.
Cogan, M.
1974   *Imperialism and Religion: Assyria, Judah and Israel in the Eighth and
            Seventh Centuries B.C.E.* Missoula, Mont.: Scholars Press.
Dagan, Y.
1992   The Shephelah during the Period of the Monarchy in Light of
            Archaeological Excavations and Surveys. M.A. thesis, Tel Aviv
            University (Hebrew).
Eitam, D.
1987   Olive-Oil Production during the Biblical Period. In *Olive Oil in
            Antiquity*, ed. M. Heltzer and D. Eitam, 16–36. Haifa: University
            of Haifa.
Eitam, D., and A. Shomroni
1987   Research on the Oil Industry during the Iron Age at Tel Miqne: A
            Preliminary Report. In *Olive Oil in Antiquity*, ed. M. Heltzer and
            D. Eitam, 37–56. Haifa: University of Haifa.

Eitan, A.
1983   Vered Yeriho. *Explorations and Surveys in Israel* 2:106–7.
Elat, M.
1990   International Trade in Palestine under the Assyrian Domination.
             In *Commerce in Palestine throughout the Ages*, ed. B. Kedar, T. Dot-
             han, and S. Safrai, 67–88. Jerusalem: Yad Ben-Zvi (Hebrew).
Eph^cal, I.
1979   Assyrian Domination in Palestine. In *The World History of the Jew-
             ish People: The Age of the Monarchies, Political History*, ed. A. Mala-
             mat, 276–89. Jerusalem: Massada Press.
Evans, C. D.
1980   Judah's Foreign Policy from Hezekiah to Josiah. In *Scripture in
             Context: Essays on the Comparative Method*, ed. C. D. Evans, W. W.
             Hallo, and J. B. White, 157–78. Pittsburgh: Pickwick Press.
Feldstein, A.; Y. Kamaisky; G. Kidron; N. Hanin; and D. Eitam
1993   Ramallah and el-Bireh and Ein Kerem (map). In *Archaeological
             Survey of the Hill Country of Benjamin*, ed. I. Finkelstein and Y.
             Magen, 133–264. Jerusalem: Israel Antiquities Authority (He-
             brew).
Finkelstein, I.
1992   Horvat Qitmit and the Southern Trade in the Late Iron Age II.
             Zeitschrift des deutschen Palästina-Vereins 108:156–70.
Fritz, V., and A. Kempinski
1983   *Ergebnisse der Ausgrabungen auf der Hirbet el-Msas (Tel Masos) 1972–
             1975.* Wiesbaden: Otto Harrassowitz.
Gane, R.
forthcoming   The Role of Assyria in the Ancient Near East during the Reign
             of Manasseh. In *Judah in the Late Iron Age*, ed. D. V. Edelman.
             Chicago.
Gitin, S.
1989   Tel Miqne-Ekron: A Type Site for the Inner Coastal Plain in the
             Iron Age II Period. In *Recent Excavations in Israel: Studies in Iron
             Age Archaeology*, ed. S. Gitin and W. G. Dever. Annual of the
             American Schools of Oriental Research 49:23–58.
Government of Palestine
1942/43   *Census of Olive Oil Production Office of Statistics.* Special Bulletin 8.
             Jerusalem.
1945   *Village Statistics.* Jerusalem.
Govrin, Y.
1991   *Archaeological Survey of Israel: Map of Nahal Yattir (139).* Jerusalem:
             Israel Antiquities Authority.
Halpern, B.
1991   Jerusalem and the Lineages in the Seventh Century BCE: Kinship
             and the Rise of Individual Moral Liability. In *Law and Ideology in
             Monarchic Israel*, ed. B. Halpern and D. W. Hobson, 11–107. Shef-
             field: JSOT Press.

Hayes, J. H., and P. K. Hooker
1988   *A New Chronology for the Kings of Israel and Judah*. Atlanta: John
            Knox.
Herzog, Z.
1990   From Nomadism to Monarchy in the Beer-sheba Valley. In *From
            Nomadism to Monarchy: Archaeological and Historical Aspects of
            Early Israel*, ed. N. Na'aman and I. Finkelstein, 215–41. Jerusalem:
            Israel Exploration Society (Hebrew).
Herzog, Z.; M. Aharoni; A. F. Rainey; and S. Moshkovitz
1984   The Israelite Fortress at Arad. *Bulletin of the American Schools of
            Oriental Research* 254:1–34.
Hughes, J.
1990   *Secrets of the Times*. Sheffield: JSOT Press.
Hütteroth, W.-D., and K. Abdulfattah
1977   *Historical Geography of Palestine, Transjordan, and Southern Syria in
            the Late Sixteenth Century*. Nurnberg: Frankischen Geographis-
            chen Gesellschaft.
Kelm, G. L., and A. Mazar
1987   7th Century B.C.E. Oil Presses at Tel Batash, Biblical Timna. In
            Olive Oil in Antiquity, ed. M. Heltzer and D. Eitam, 121–25. Haifa:
            University of Haifa.
Kitchen, K. A.
1986   *The Third Intermediate Period in Egypt*. Warminster: Aris and
            Phillips.
Knauf, E. A.
1988   A Thamudic Seal Impression. *Levant* 20:98–99.
Kochavi, M.
1972   The Land of Judah. In *Judaea, Samaria, and the Golan: Archaeolog-
            ical Survey, 1967–1968*, ed. M. Kochavi, 19–89. Jerusalem: Carta
            (Hebrew).
1974   Khirbet Rabud = Debir. *Tel Aviv* 1:2–33.
Machinist, P.
1992   Palestine, Administration of: Assyrian and Babylonian Adminis-
            tration. *Anchor Bible Dictionary*, ed. D. N. Freedman, 5:69–81.
            New York: Doubleday.
Mazar, A.; D. Amit; and Z. Ilan
1984   The "Border Road" between Michmash and Jericho and Excava-
            tions at Horvat Shilhah. *Eretz-Israel* 17:236–50 (Hebrew).
Mazar, A., and E. Netzer
1986   On the Israelite Fortress of Arad. *Bulletin of the American Schools of
            Oriental Research* 263:87–91.
Mazar, B.; T. Dothan; and I. Dunayevsky
1966   En-Gedi: The First and Second Seasons of Excavations, 1961–
            1962. *Atiqot* 5.
McKay, J.
1973   *Religion in Judah under the Assyrians*. Studies in Biblical Theology
            Second Series 26. London: SCM Press.

Meitlis, Y.
1989   Rural Settlement in the Vicinity of Jerusalem in the End of the
              Iron Age. M.A. thesis. Hebrew University, Jerusalem (Hebrew).
Miller, J. M., and J. H. Hayes
1986   *A History of Ancient Israel and Judah*. Philadelphia: Westminster.
Na'aman, N.
1979   Sennacherib's Campaign to Judah and the Date of the LMLK
              Stamps. *Vetus Testamentum* 29:61–86.
1986   Historical and Chronological Notes on the Kingdoms of Israel
              and Judah in the Eighth Century BCE. *Vetus Testamentum* 36:71–
              92.
1987   The Negev in the Last Century of the Kingdom of Judah. *Cathe-
              dra* 42:3–15 (Hebrew).
1991   The Kingdom of Judah under Josiah. *Tel Aviv* 18:3–71.
Nelson, R.
1983   Realpolitik in Judah (687–609 B.C.E.). In *Scripture in Context II:
              More Essays on the Comparative Method*, ed. W. W. Hallo, J. C.
              Moyer, and L. G. Perdue, 177–89. Winona Lake, Ind.: Eisen-
              brauns.
Nielsen, E.
1967   Political Conditions and Cultural Developments in Israel and
              Judah during the Reign of Manasseh. In *Fourth World Congress of
              Jewish Studies*, 103–6. Jerusalem: Union of Jewish Studies.
Ofer, A.
1994   "All the Hill Country of Judah": From a Settlement Fringe to a
              Prosperous Monarchy. In *From Nomadism to Monarchy: Archaeolog-
              ical and Historical Aspects of Early Israel*, ed. I. Finkelstein and N.
              Na'aman, 92–121. Jerusalem: Israel Exploration Society.
Oren, E.
1978   Esh-Sharica, Tell (Tel Serac). In *Encyclopedia of Archaeological Exca-
              vations in the Holy Land*, ed. M. Avi-Yonah and E. Stern, 4:1059–
              69. Jerusalem: Israel Exploration Society and Massada Press.
Oren, E.; N. Fleming; S. Kornberg; R. Feinstein; and P. Nahshoni
1986   A Phoenician Emporium on the Border of Egypt. *Qadmoniot*
              19(75–76):83–91 (Hebrew).
Oren, E.; Y. Yekutieli; P. Nahshoni; and R. Feinstein
1991   Tel Haror—After Six Seasons. *Qadmoniot* 24(93–94):2–19
              (Hebrew).
Rainey, A. F.
1987   Arad in the Latter Days of the Judean Monarchy. *Cathedra* 42:16–
              25 (Hebrew).
1993   Manasseh, King of Judah in the Whirlpool of the Seventh Century
              B.C.E. In *kinatūtu ša dārâti* (*Tel Aviv* Occasional Publication 1), ed.
              A. F. Rainey, 147–64. Tel Aviv: Tel Aviv University.
Reich, R.
1984   The Identification of the "Sealed Karu of Egypt." *Israel Explora-
              tion Journal* 34:32–38.

Sass, B.
1991   *Studia Alphabetica: On the Origin and Early History of the Northwest Semitic, South Semitic and Greek Alphabets.* Orbis Biblicus et Orientalis 102. Freiburg. Universitätsverlag Freiburg.

Schniedewind, W. M.
1991   The Source Citations of Manasseh: King Manasseh in History and Homily. *Vetus Testamentum* 41:450–61.

Shavit, A.
1992   The Ayalon Valley and Its Vicinity during the Bronze and Iron Ages. M.A. thesis, Tel Aviv University (Hebrew).

Shea, W. H.
1985   Sennacherib's Second Palestinian Campaign. *Journal of Biblical Literature* 104:410–18.

Shiloh, Y.
1987   South Arabian Inscriptions from the City of David, Jerusalem. *Palestine Exploration Quarterly* 119:9–18.

Stager, L. E.
1975   Ancient Agriculture in the Judaean Desert: A Case Study of the Buqêᶜah Valley. Ph.D. dissertation, Harvard University.

Tatum, L.
1991   King Manasseh and the Royal Fortress at Horvat ᶜUza. *Biblical Archaeologist* 54:136–45.

Thiele, R. E.
1983   *The Mysterious Numbers of the Hebrew Kings.* Grand Rapids: Zondervan.

Ussishkin, D.
1977   The Destruction of Lachish by Sennacherib and the Dating of the Royal Judean Storage Jars. *Tel Aviv* 4:28–60.
1978   Excavations at Tel Lachish, 1973–1977, Preliminary Report. *Tel Aviv* 5(1).
1982   *The Conquest of Lachish by Sennacherib.* Tel Aviv: Tel Aviv University.
1983   Excavations at Tel Lachish, 1978–1983: Second Preliminary Report. *Tel Aviv* 10(2).
1988   The Date of the Judaean Shrine at Arad. *Israel Exploration Journal* 38:142–57.

Van Beek, G. W.
1983   Digging Up Tell Jemmeh. *Archaeology* 36:12–19.

Wapnish, P.
1981   Camel Caravans and Camel Pastoralists at Tell Jemmeh. *Journal of the Ancient Near Eastern Society of Columbia University* 13:101–21.
1984   The Dromedary and Bactrian Camel in Levantine Historical Settings: The Evidence from Tell Jemmeh. In *Animals and Archaeology 3, Early Herders and Their Flocks,* ed. J. Clutton-Brock and C. Grigson, 171–200. British Archaeological Reports International Series 202. Oxford: British Archaeological Reports.

Williamson, H. G. M.
1982   *1 and 2 Chronicles.* Grand Rapids: Eerdmans.

Yadin, Y.
1979   The Archaeological Sources for the Period of the Monarchy. In
            The World History of the Jewish People: The Age of the Monarchies.
            Culture and Society, ed. A. Malamat, 187–235. Jerusalem: Massada
            Press.
Yurco, F. J.
1991   The Shabaka-Shebitku Coregency and the Supposed Second
            Campaign of Sennacherib against Judah: A Critical Assessment.
            Journal of Biblical Literature 110:35–45.
Zimhoni, O.
1985   The Iron Age Pottery of Tel ʿEton and Its Relation to the Lach-
            ish, Tell Beit Mirsim, and Arad Assemblages. *Tel Aviv* 12:63–90.

11 | Amos's Earthquake and Israelite Prophecy

DAVID NOEL FREEDMAN
ANDREW WELCH

THE EARTHQUAKE
AND THE PROPHET AMOS

Archaeology

This chapter does not constitute a comprehensive investigation of Israelite Iron Age sites for earthquake evidence; consider it rather a plea for one. The earthquake of Amos 1:1 is established in the archaeological record. Yigael Yadin and coauthors (1960:24) provided the first solid evidence, in Stratum VI at Hazor: walls were bent or cracked, or simply fallen in courses. They recorded anecdotal opinions of geologists, who confirmed that the pattern is consistent with earthquake damage and surmised that Hazor was "some distance" from the epicenter (p. 26). William Dever has made the most recent summary of evidence for the earthquake. He finds clear signs of earthquake damage (split walls and fallen courses, as at Hazor) at Gezer in the collapse of the "Outer Wall" (1992:28–30). Philip King (1988:21) notes Yohanan Aharoni's conjecture that Beer-sheba Stratum III shows earthquake destruction. Dever (1992:35) lists Lachish Stratum IV and Deir ʿAlla as sites for which earthquakes are a plausible explanation of observed destruction. Among other sites, Ashdod and Bethel are good candidates for earthquake evidence. All these examples can be dated to the first half of the eighth century BCE, consistent with Amos 1:1.

Concerning Jerusalem, J. A. Soggin identifies the earthquake with "a landslide involving part of the Mount of Olives with the temporary obstruction of the Kidron valley, giving rise to the short depression which separates the Mount of Olives from Mount Scopus" (1987:25). This hypothesis relies on the accuracy of Josephus's account of Uzziah's leprosy (*Antiquities of the Jews* 9.222–27). Josephus conflates Amos 1:1, Zechariah 14:5, and 2 Chronicles 26:16–21 to make the earthquake, Uzziah's sacerdotal transgression, and his leprosy's onset coincide. Of the earthquake, Josephus writes:

> But while he spoke, a great tremor shook the earth, . . . the temple was riven, . . . while before the city at a place called Eroge half of the western hill was broken off and rolled four stades till it stopped at the eastern hill and obstructed the roads and the royal gardens. (Marcus 1966:119)

This account, though unsupported archaeologically, is important because it forms the model for later rabbinic discussion of the earthquake (Shalem 1949).

The earthquake's severity obviously cannot be reconstructed (nor can we even be certain that the archaeological evidence reflects only one earthquake). Yet we can note the geographical range of sites, from Hazor in the north to Lachish or Beer-sheba in the south. We can also note the profound impression it made on biblical and postbiblical writers. J. Milgrom (1964:179) quotes N. Shalem's reasoning that since the available evidence suggests a homogeneous distribution through time of earthquakes in Israel, including severe earthquakes, "the Uzzianic quake must have been of unparalleled violence." At the very least, as Zechariah 14:5 shows, the earthquake "in the days of Uzziah" was strong enough to become paradigmatic of massive catastrophe. A modern example would be the San Francisco earthquake of 1906, which, though eclipsed on the Richter scale by other earthquakes, remains a colloquial standard of comparison.

Theophany

Because earthquakes were associated with theophany, the earthquake of Amos 1:1 made a powerful impression for theological as well as seismological reasons. The earliest biblical example occurs in Judges 5:4, where Yahweh's ascent from Edom is accompanied by earthquake (*'ereṣ rāʿāšâ*). Similarly, in 2 Samuel 22:8 (= Ps. 18:7), earthquake is part of Yahweh's manifestation, as are lightning (v 15), thunder (v 14), and wind (v 11). At Sinai, earthquake appears with smoke and fire (Exod. 19:18) when Yahweh manifests himself. Among other instances (e.g., Pss. 29; 46), Elijah's experience on Mount Carmel (1 Kgs. 19:11–12) demonstrates conclusively that an earthquake is quintessentially theophanic: Yahweh fails to appear in the trio of phenomena—wind, earthquake, fire—as expected. In all these cases, earthquake is linked to thunder as part of Yahweh's portrayal as storm god, the Divine Warrior (a portrayal with pre-Israelite antecedents; see discussion in Cross 1973:147–76). And even when a complete theophany is lacking, its characteristic language persists, as in Amos 1:2 (Cross 1973:174–77; Wolff 1977:118). Thus the assimilation of earthquake-in-storm to earthquake per se as theophany is easily made. Common sense suggests that only Yahweh can make the earth move.

THE EARTHQUAKE IN AMOS

The earthquake of Amos 1:1 has a profound effect on both the book of Amos and subsequent Israelite prophecy. The notation in Amos 1:1 is unique in prophetic annals. Evidently the redactor felt it important enough to make it a part of the book's formal superscription. Was the redactor simply dating Amos's ministry precisely? Perhaps. But the nature of Amos's oracles (and perhaps Amos's career) suggests more than chronological concern.

Amos's oracles announce judgment (e.g., 1:2—2:16) and the day of Yahweh (5:18–20). Fire is the dominant image in Amos (1:4, 7, 10, 12, 14; 2:2, 5; 5:6; 7:4), but the prophet also uses earthquake language to proclaim Yahweh's judgment. Both fire and earthquake, of course, are integral to the storm god theophany already discussed, and on a purely physical level, fire often results from earthquake (on fire, see Andersen and Freedman 1989:194, 239–40). Earthquake is most prominent in 9:1–5 (where the root $r\dot{s}$ occurs), but it can also plausibly be inferred in 3:13–15 (Yahweh's direct action to destroy [hpk] Bethel and royal palaces); 4:11 (Israel to be overthrown [hpk] like Sodom and Gomorrah); 6:11 (Yahweh will smash [hkh] all of Israel's houses); 8:8 (the land will rise and fall like the Nile [on all these passages, see Andersen and Freedman 1989]). While Yahweh brings fire upon Israel and foreign nations alike, Yahweh reserves earthquake exclusively for Israel.

The implicit claim of 1:1, then, is that a direct connection exists between Amos's prophecy (particularly 9:1) and a devastating earthquake two years later. In short, Amos predicted the earthquake. This connection does not depend on whether Amos 9:1 is authentic (before the fact). What matters is that for the editor of Amos's oracles, the earthquake confirms Amos's message (Paul 1991:36). The earthquake shows that Amos was a true prophet, because his message of Yahweh's judgment is followed by Yahweh's definitive action. This conclusion does not depend on a particular reconstruction of Amos's life. Certainly Amos's words survived, if only orally, until the earthquake, whether Amos was alive or dead at the time of the catastrophe. The earthquake might have been the catalyst for a written collection of Amos's oracles, or perhaps simply their dissemination. In either case, the earthquake is essential to Amos's validation as a prophet of Yahweh. Moreover, it was enough for the editor (and those who preserved Amos's memory and message) that the earthquake happened within at most two years of Amos's prophecy.

The argument here is that given the test of true prophecy (Deut. 18:18; see below), the credibility of the prophet depended on proof that the prophecy was made before the predicted event came to pass, and that the prediction was framed so that prophecy and event coincided. To meet such a test, on which the fate of the nation as well as the life of the prophet might depend (as in Jeremiah 28), oral tradition alone could not suffice. Only a written record, confirmed by witnesses, could produce the required evidence. Only in this way could true prophets be distinguished from false, and the right decisions be made by the body politic. While we have very little data for eighth-century prophetic practice, there is enough to imply that writing was a necessary if limited component (Isa. 8:16–20). By the seventh and sixth centuries we find prophets deeply engaged in literary prophecy: writing down predictions and checking them against events. Small wonder that Jeremiah is almost always accompanied by his shadow, the scribe Baruch, or that Ezekiel faithfully records and carefully dates and edits his own book of oracles.

PROPHETIC VALIDATION

The time frame for testing prophecy as prediction by its realization in historical event was a matter of serious interest in preexilic and exilic Israel and Judah. The necessary link between prophecy and fulfillment is affirmed explicitly in Deut. 18:15–22, especially 21–22 (cf. Jer. 28:9):

> And if you say in your heart, "How will we know the word that Yahweh has not spoken?" As for the prophet who speaks in the name of Yahweh, and the word does not occur and does not come to pass, that is the word that Yahweh has not spoken.

The negative side of the equation of word and deed is exemplified by the impatience of the people even with true prophets, who were perceived as hedging their predictions or unduly extending the time for their prophecy's fulfillment. We can observe this impatience in the sharp exchanges between people and prophet recorded in Ezekiel 12:21–28. The people's skepticism and disillusionment are cited in proverbial form. Yahweh, through the prophet, responds with divine assurances that from now on he will speed the process; fulfillment will follow prediction within a very short time:

> And the word of Yahweh came to me, as follows: "Son of man, Behold the house of Israel are saying,
> 'The vision that he envisions is for many days,
> and for distant times he is prophesying.'
> Therefore say to them, 'Thus has said my Lord Yahweh: "There will be no further delay regarding all my words. When I speak a word, then it shall be done."'" Oracle of my Lord Yahweh!

Ezekiel provides another example of the difficulties growing from a gap between oracle and fulfillment. In the midst of a long complex of oracles concerning Tyre, Ezekiel predicts that it will fall to Nebuchadrezzar (26:7). According to reliable reports by Josephus (*Antiquities of the Jews* 12.1; *Contra Apionem* 1.21), Nebuchadrezzar II attacked and besieged the city in 585 BCE. Ezekiel's initial prediction is dated to the eleventh or twelfth year of the exile (Cooke 1936:288), probably early in 585 BCE. Josephus says that the siege was not a success and that after thirteen years the Babylonians withdrew. Ezekiel himself ultimately gave up on this particular prophecy and added a comment in the twenty-seventh year of the exile, about 571 BCE. The time frame for the original prediction would have been perhaps two or three years, as sieges rarely extended much longer (cf. the sieges of Samaria from 724 to 722 BCE, and Jerusalem from 589 to 587/86). In this case, the Babylonian monarch persevered, although after a while it could have been little more than a holding operation, and then finally withdrew. The prophet waited a little longer to record the failure of the prediction, but does so forthrightly, with an interesting qualification:

> So it happened in the twenty-seventh year of the first month, on the first of the month, that the word of Yahweh came to me as follows: "Son of man, Nebuchadrezzar, the king of Babylon, made his army work with great effort against Tyre. Every head was made bald, and every shoulder was rubbed sore, but there was no payment for him or for his army from Tyre for all the labor they labored against it." Therefore thus has said my Lord Yahweh, "Behold, I am giving to Nebuchadrezzar, the king of Babylon, the land of Egypt; and he will carry off

its multitude [or its wealth] and despoil its spoils and plunder its plunder, and that will be payment for his army; his accomplishment for
which he labored, I have given to him the land of Egypt, which they
have done for me." Oracle of my Lord Yahweh. (Ezek. 29:17–20)

Although the original prophecy failed, it belonged to a larger plan,
centered on Nebuchadrezzar, to make him the preeminent figure in the
whole of the ancient world. While Ezekiel does not say that the original
prophecy was wrong, he concedes that the prediction failed. By the time
he wrote down the correction, the time allotted for fulfillment had long
since run out. While this would appear to be a clear case of false prophecy
in light of Deuteronomy 18:21–22, the prophet himself doubtless thought
differently.

Ezekiel could have argued that the prophet's role is to hear Yahweh's
word and then transmit it to the appropriate audience, generally the
people as a whole. The outcome is entirely in Yahweh's hands, however,
and may on occasion diverge significantly from the oracle entrusted to
the prophet. In dramatic cases the very force of words of admonition,
warning, and prediction may alter the outcome. Jeremiah makes this very
argument concerning Micah's preaching to Hezekiah and Judah in the
eighth century (Jer. 26:16–19). In other words, the prophet reports Yahweh's word, but the results are the responsibility of Yahweh, or of Yahweh
and his people's interaction.

In Ezekiel's oracles on Tyre, no reasons are given for the prophecy's
failure, not even a change in divine intention. The failure is left at the
human level: the Babylonians simply could not capture Tyre. Ezekiel
asserts, however, that Yahweh's basic plan has not changed, and since Tyre
is not defeatable, Yahweh will give Nebuchadrezzar Egypt. The Babylonian Chronicle records an invasion of Egypt in 568/7 but is silent about
its outcome. The very absence of further information may indicate that
the second prophecy also did not come to pass, but by then the prophet
or his editor(s) may no longer have been on the scene. No doubt such
failed prophecies, vague prophecies, or undated prophecies (such as eschatological projections) contributed to the skepticism about prophecy
noted in Ezekiel 12.

Isaiah takes the unusual step of using the birth and growth of children,
his own and others, to indicate the time frame for a prophetic prediction.
Immanuel (Isa. 7:14) will signify Aram and Israel's destruction. The *terminus ad quem* for this destruction is the child's arrival at the age of discre-
tion (i.e., his ability to distinguish right from wrong [7:15–16]), perhaps

four or five years, perhaps later, but certainly by adolescence. The time allotted for fulfillment is much shorter in the case of Isaiah's second son, Maher-shalal-hash-baz, "Spoil speeds, booty hastens." The fate of the two nations invading Judah will be settled before this child is old enough to cry, "My father and my mother" (Isa. 8:1–4, especially v 4), no doubt within two years at most.

Pursuing the matter of prophetic time frame, we come to the dramatic confrontation between the prophets Hananiah and Jeremiah (Jeremiah 28), dated to the fifth month of the fourth year of Zedekiah (perhaps July/August 594 BCE). With Jeremiah present, Hananiah prophesies:

> Thus has said Yahweh of hosts, the God of Israel, as follows: "I have broken the yoke of the king of Babylon. *Within two years* I will restore to this place all the vessels [= utensils] of the house of Yahweh, which Nebuchadrezzar, the king of Babylon, took from this place and brought them to Babylon. And Jeconiah, the son of Jehoiakim the king of Judah, and the whole captivity of Judah, the ones who came to Babylon, I will restore to this place, oracle of Yahweh, because I will break the yoke of the king of Babylon." (Jer. 28:2–4, italics added)

Jeremiah responds with disbelief to Hananiah's prediction, chiefly because he had received the opposite message from Yahweh, namely that the captivity would last long, with the sacred vessels remaining in Babylon. It is important to note that the prophets did not disagree on the substance of the message: the exiles would return and they would bring the Temple's utensils with them (28:6). They differ radically only with respect to the time of the return. Hananiah chose the immediate future, a two-year time limit (by now commonly accepted?), while Jeremiah had a much more distant time in mind, seventy years (25:11–12; 29:10), which would correspond to the normative life span in that society (Ps. 90:10). After Jeremiah shoulders a yoke to symbolize his oracle and Hananiah breaks it, Hananiah repeats his two-year prediction:

> Thus has said Yahweh, "Accordingly, I will break the yoke of Nebuchadnezzar, the king of Babylon, *within two years*, from upon the neck of all the nations. . . ." (Jer. 28:11, italics added)

We note in passing that this oracle could be expected to be popular among its hearers, both because it offered enthusiastic encouragement to their fondest hopes, and because it set a strict time limit for its fulfillment.

Jeremiah's message, on the contrary, was both very pessimistic about the near future and almost open-ended about the date of the return.

Seventy years is a long time. Jeremiah was saying in effect that there would be no good news for Judah in the lifetime of anyone now living, including Jeremiah. He would be dead before he knew whether his prophecy came true. The same charge leveled by the people against Ezekiel could have been said of Jeremiah (Ezek. 12:27): "The visions he sees are for many days, and concerning times far off he prophesies." In short, Hananiah has at least as good a claim as Jeremiah to the mantle of authentic prophet of Yahweh.

Jeremiah fights back, however, with a new, clear, time-limited message, directed at Hananiah himself:

> "Listen here Hananiah, Yahweh has not sent you, and as for you, you have made this people trust in a lie. Therefore, thus has said Yahweh: 'Behold I am going to dispatch you from off the face of the earth. This year, you will die, because you spoke apostasy to Yahweh.'" And Hananiah the prophet died in that year, in the seventh month. (Jer. 28:15–17)

The biographer, presumably Baruch, added the last sentence to confirm Jeremiah's predictive powers and to underscore the awful fate of those who pretended to be prophets but were not.

The inference we draw from these episodes is that prophecy often, if not generally, was linked with specific historical circumstances, and either explicitly or by implication was time-bound. One of the more common periods within which prophecy was supposed to come true was two years. We might also infer that unless otherwise specified, two years (*šĕnātayim*) would be the normal expectation for the fulfillment of historical predictions. It is stipulated in some instances and implied in others, whether referring to the fall of nations or city-states, the return of exiles, or the death of a prophet. We may even speculate that the reference to "two years" in Amos 1:1 derives from an oracle of the prophet himself.

Whether *šĕnātayim* goes back to Amos or not, the event of the earthquake within the two-year period definitely made the prophecy effective. Had the earthquake been delayed for several years, or had it been less powerful or widespread, Amos's oracle's impact and the corresponding validation of his message and ministry would have been severely diminished. Living along so many fault lines, including one of the major fault lines of the world (Shalem 1949:22–30), people experienced earthquakes with some frequency; anyone could predict an earthquake in the relatively near future (ten to fifteen years) with confidence. What is required, therefore, for a putative prophet is precision in dating and accuracy with regard

to place and structures (i.e., we must infer from the biblical and archaeological evidence that Amos's earthquake wreaked catastrophic damage in
both nations, specifically including their respective major shrines at Bethel
and Jerusalem), and a good approximation of its magnitude. This Amos
achieved.

THE EARTHQUAKE'S EFFECT ON
ISRAELITE PROPHECY

The importance of Amos's authentication for the history of Israelite
prophecy cannot be overstated. Before Amos, Israelite prophecy followed
the model of Elijah and Elisha, which featured wonder-working, direct
transmission of prophetic mantle, and (in Elisha's case) groups of prophets,
the *běnê hannĕbi'îm*. Amos stands outside the Elijah/Elisha tradition. First,
he explicitly denies being a *ben nābî'* (7:14); he is completely outside any
organization claiming prophetic authority. Second, he is definitely not a
wonder-worker; the authenticity of his message from Yahweh is not revealed until two years later. Whatever his status in his hometown of
Tekoa (Willoughby 1992:203–5), in the northern kingdom Amos is surely, in R. W. Wilson's typology, a peripheral prophet (Wilson 1980:266–
70).

Amos stands outside another model, those prophets devoted to (and
supported by) the royal house in 1 Kings 22. Though Amos shares some
features with the peripheral prophet Micaiah, he has no responsibility to
or status with the king, nor even any access to him. Amos the outsider,
the upstart, has just one outstanding prophetic achievement: Yahweh had
revealed to him the earthquake. This was enough to legitimate a prophet
otherwise without credentials.

Amos's legitimacy allowed others to adopt Amos's message as their
own, including earthquake imagery. Isaiah incorporates it into his vision
of the day of Yahweh (2:10–21). Not only people, but everything tall—
trees, mountains, towers, ships—will be brought low (Milgrom 1964:178–
82). Isaiah returns to earthquake imagery in 13:13; 24:18–20; 29:6; and
perhaps 9:18 (Milgrom 1964:167, n. 2). Isaiah 5:25 appears to be a direct
reference to the quake in Uzziah's day. And Isaiah 6:4 may reflect Amos
9:1. Obviously Isaiah could appeal to the people's experience of the earthquake to bolster his own message. Yahweh's judgment was not a hypo-
thetical construct.

From Isaiah forward, the earthquake theme becomes a staple of prophetic language (Hag. 2:6–7; Jer. 4:23–26; Ezek. 38:17–20; Nah. 1:5; Joel 4:16 [//Amos 1:2]; Zech. 14:5). In these later passages it is difficult to determine the extent to which the prophet employs the earthquake theme metaphorically. In most cases, the earthquake is, as in Judges 5, a sign of Yahweh's presence in power. All these prophets bear witness to the power of the memory of the earthquake "in the days of Uzziah." The convergence and coincidence of the earthquake's time, place, and magnitude with Amos's prediction combined to make an indelible impression on the prophetic community and its audience, and thus instigated the corpus of prophetic literature in the Hebrew Bible. It literally began with a Big Bang!

WORKS CITED

Andersen, F. I., and D. N. Freedman
1989   *Amos: A New Translation with Introduction and Commentary*. Anchor
                Bible 24A. New York: Doubleday.
Cooke, G. A.
1936   *The Book of Ezekiel, Vol. 2*. International Critical Commentary.
                New York: Charles Scribner's Sons.
Cross, F. M.
1973   *Canaanite Myth and Hebrew Epic: Essays in the History of the Religion
                of Israel*. Cambridge: Harvard University Press.
Dever, W. G.
1992   A Case-Study in Biblical Archaeology: The Earthquake of *Ca.* 760
                BCE. *Eretz-Israel* 23:27–35.
King, P. J.
1988   *Amos, Hosea, Micah—An Archaeological Commentary*. Philadelphia:
                Westminster.
Marcus, R., trans.
1966   Josephus. *Jewish Antiquities*. Loeb Classical Library. Cambridge:
                Harvard University Press.
Milgrom, J.
1964   Did Isaiah Prophesy during the Reign of Uzziah? *Vetus Testamen-
                tum* 14:164–82.
Paul, S. M.
1991   *Amos*. Hermeneia Series. Minneapolis: Fortress.
Shalem, N.
1949   The Earthquakes in Jerusalem. *Jerusalem* 2:22–60 (Hebrew).
Soggin, J. A.
1987   *The Prophet Amos*. London: SCM Press.

Willoughby, B. E.
1992   Amos. In *Anchor Bible Dictionary*, ed. D. N. Freedman, 1:203–11.
                New York: Doubleday.
Wilson, R. W.
1980   *Prophecy and Society in Ancient Israel*. Philadelphia: Fortress.
Wolff, H. W.
1977   *Joel and Amos*. Hermeneia Series. Philadelphia: Fortress.
Yadin, Y.; Y. Aharoni; R. Amiran; T. Dothan; I. Dunayevsky; and J. Perrot
1960   *Hazor II: An Account of the Second Season of Excavations, 1956.*
                Jerusalem: Magnes.

12 | Alalakh Studies and the Bible: Obstacle or Contribution?

RICHARD S. HESS

Ancient Near Eastern studies have presented whole worlds of culture and history that have found ready use among biblical scholars in quest of a means to contextualize the Hebrew texts among surrounding peoples. Such studies naturally raise questions about the legitimacy of comparative methods and the extent to which they can demonstrate any viable conclusions. The purpose of this chapter is to consider examples of the comparative method as scholars have applied it to a particular cuneiform archive and to consider the legitimacy of their comparisons with the biblical texts. I propose to approach this question by using the following procedure. I will identify Alalakh as a sample cuneiform culture that scholars have discussed in terms of its relevance to biblical studies. I will review some of the applications to biblical studies that authors have suggested. I will then consider several specific comparisons, their evaluation in later discussions, and what can be known from the Alalakh texts. Special attention will be given to the Ḫapiru and to the ḫupšu. These terms have been the subject of linguistic and of sociological studies. Both have been compared with similar terms used in other cuneiform cultures of the second millennium BCE and in the Hebrew Bible. Present research suggests weaknesses in some of the traditional comparisons and certain distinctive elements in the appearance of these terms at Alalakh.

The Levant of the second millennium BCE has proven fruitful in the excavation of archives. The discovery of the Amarna correspondence in the nineteenth century and its subsequent publication uncovered a wealth of information regarding the language of Canaan before the appearance of Israel, as well as the social world of Late Bronze Age Canaan. Although discovered in Egypt, most of the Amarna texts proved to have originated in the administrative and population centers of the Levant. The texts from Ugarit have proven of unusual interest in addressing questions regarding the religious and mythological world in which early Israel developed. The Mari archives have provided examples of an early-second-millennium society of West Semitic peoples whose onomastic, prophetic, and social traditions have found application to the Hebrew Bible. More recently, archives from the site of ancient Emar have been published. Their initial study has revealed further rituals of West Semitic religious practice as well as some specific points of comparison with biblical customs related to marriage and property.

Of particular interest here is the site of Tell Atchana, identified with Alalakh. Lying on the heavily populated and fertile Amuq plain beside the Orontes River, this site commanded trade routes from the east, toward Aleppo and on to the Euphrates Valley, and from the west, toward the seacoast and the eastern Mediterranean commercial world (Woolley 1953:19–20). It also lay on important ways north to the land of the Hittites and south to Damascus and the Jordan Valley. This ideal location led Sir Leonard Woolley to choose it as the site for his excavation, which proposed to examine the cultural influences from the west and from the east and their effects upon one another. The seventeen levels unearthed at the site date from about 3100 BCE until about 1200 BCE. As is well known, Levels VII and IV excited the most interest because they yielded hundreds of cuneiform texts whose study has served to reconstruct the society. The texts are cited in this chapter under the standard abbreviation AT (Alalakh Text).

At Level VII Woolley found structures that he identified as a palace, a temple, and a city gate. The period covered the reigns of three kings and is dated subsequent to the Mari texts, at the end of the eighteenth century. Frescoes decorated the palace rooms. Most of the tablets that can be dated come from the reign of Yarim-Lim. Some were found in rooms of the palace that were identified by Woolley as "magazines" (Woolley 1955:91–106). Others were uncovered on the floor of the temple archive room (Woolley 1955:59–65). Yarim-Lim's rule probably saw the expansion of the buildings and the fortifications. A fire destroyed the city, which was known to its inhabitants as Alalakh.

A second cuneiform archive was discovered in Level IV of Woolley's excavation, dated one or two centuries after that of Level VII. More tablets than those of Level VII were found here in the royal palace (Woolley 1955:110–31). In addition, an important inscription was found on a broken statue of Idrimi, which had been buried in a room in the annex of a temple from the latest level of Alalakh, destroyed around 1200 BCE. The inscription identifies the figure as Idrimi and relates his life. It is an adventure story about a prince who flees the kingdom when his father is murdered. He lives in Emar and then in Ammia in Canaan for seven years. Upon his return, Idrimi reestablishes his rule and extends it with an expedition into Hittite territory. He records his building activities in Alalakh, including a palace that is probably to be identified with the structure of thirty-three rooms found on the site. Idrimi reigns thirty years before causing the inscription to be written and passing rulership to his son.

GENERAL COMPARISONS

The contribution of the studies of the texts from Alalakh to our understanding of the Bible was summarized in 1958 by Matitiahu Tsevat and, with further comparisons, in 1967 by the original publisher of those texts, Donald Wiseman. These scholars collected comparisons, both conceptual and linguistic. Wiseman divided them into three groups: politics, economic and social conditions, and culture and religion.

The political parallels come from two sources, treaty texts and related documents and the Idrimi inscription. An international treaty from Level VII (AT 1; see Na'aman 1980) along with several other texts (AT 52–58; see Kienast 1980) record the exchange of a city or towns and villages. This may be compared with Solomon's gift of twenty towns to Hiram of Tyre (1 Kgs. 11:11; see Fensham 1960). As with David's public statement identifying Solomon as his heir (1 Kgs. 1:17, 20, 30–36), so Yarim-Lim attempted to reduce sibling rivalry for his power by publicly naming his heir (AT 6). The extradition of fugitives, common enough in ancient Near Eastern treaties and mentioned in Level IV treaties at Alalakh (AT 2 and 3; see Reiner 1969:531–32), is comparable to the diplomacy that lay behind Shimei's search for fugitive slaves in Philistine territory (1 Kgs. 2:39–40). In AT 2 this extradition was accomplished by elders of the city, as in Deuteronomy 23:15–16 (Wiseman 1982:23).

The story of David's rise to kingship has been compared with the Idrimi inscription and its account (Oppenheim 1955). Both share a "free-flowing narrative style" (Wiseman 1967:122), include flight to maternal relatives (1 Sam. 22:3–4; 2 Sam. 13:37), inquiries to the deity before attempting to regain rulership (2 Sam. 2:1–4; 5:1, 3), and the use of spoils of war to build a temple. E. L. Greenstein and D. Marcus (1976:76–77) add the story of Jephthah in Judges 11 to the comparisons between David and Idrimi. In addition to the flight, they suggest that all three narratives include the recognition by kinsmen, the act of others joining the exiled hero, and the recognition of the hero as their leader. Albright (1950:20; see also Oppenheim 1955) observed parallels with the Joseph story, especially in the occurrence of seven-year periods, its emphasis on divination, and its reconciliation of brothers.

Some of the political comparisons, such as the exchange of territories and towns and the extradition of fugitives, could occur elsewhere in the ancient Near East. However, the story of Idrimi is special. A comparison outside the Bible has been made with the Apology of Hattusilis (Dietrich and Loretz 1981:255), which itself has been compared with the story of David's rise to kingship (Wolf 1967). As others have observed, there seems to be a narrative tradition that is common to the Levantine world and appears as early as the second millennium BCE. The literary theme of the outcast hero who gains his place as leader of a people and who then succeeds in battle is a distinctive feature of these comparisons. It has its origin and development in biographical literature. On the basis of present evidence, this style of literature, which becomes so popular in Semitic and Western cultures, makes its first appearance at Alalakh.

The cuneiform texts dealing with economic and social conditions include terms used to express particular types and classes of individuals. There were the "stand-ins" or pledges (*manzazānūtu* and *mazzazānu*) who owed the king money and rendered service as a means of paying interest on a loan (AT 18–28, 36, 41, 43, 44, 47, 49; see Klengel 1963; Eichler 1973:63–78; Zeeb 1991:428–29), which may be compared to dwelling in the house of the king as in Psalms 23:6; 27:4. As at Mari, so in Old Babylonian Alalakh Level VII, the mention of the Hittites and their capital, Hattusa, in the first half of the second millennium has been compared with their appearance in Genesis 23 (AT 456.44; see Wiseman 1958:125). Although the term *mištannu*, "equivalent," in AT 3 has been used to translate *mišneh* in Deuteronomy 15:18 and Jeremiah 16:18 (Tsevat 1958:125–26; Wiseman 1982:24), recent arguments have called this comparison into question with the observations that the word is originally Indo-Aryan (Mayrhofer 1965) and that the traditional meaning, "double," which appears elsewhere in the Hebrew Bible, also makes sense here (Lindenberger 1991).

The appearance of *darārum* in the Old Babylonian texts from Level VII (AT 29.11; 30.9; 31.9; 38.10; 42.6) has been used for comparison with the biblical concept of *dĕrôr*, "release," during the year of Jubilee, as suggested in Leviticus 25:10–15, where the land is to lie fallow and the debtors are to regain their patrimony. Although there has been discussion as to whether there is a relationship between the Mesopotamian *mīšarum* and the Jubilee and as to whether the biblical custom is premonarchic (Lewy 1958:29*–30*; Weinfeld 1972:153) or postexilic (Lemche 1979; Westbrook 1991:44–55), the use of *dĕrôr* in this context and in the prophets (Isa. 61:1; Jer. 34:8, 15, 17; Ezek. 46:17) is distinct from the usage of its cognate at Alalakh. At Alalakh it occurs normally in a formula describing a debt that cannot be changed: *ú-ul us-sa-ab ú-ul id-dá-ra-ar*, "it cannot increase [through interest] nor can it decrease" (Zeeb 1991:426–27). In Leviticus 25 it describes the return of the land to its original owners (vv 10–15) and the return to their freedom of those sold into debt servitude (vv 39–42; see C. J. H. Wright 1990:123–28, 249–58). The occurrences of *dĕrôr* in Jeremiah and Ezekiel repeat these two usages. The context of Isaiah 61:1 suggests an additional aspect, the release of prisoners (North 1978). An Akkadian cognate of *darārum* is *andurārum*. This appears in another Old Babylonian text, AT 65. The contract describes a *kinattu*, a household servant, who is purchased. This person cannot go free during an *andurārum* (lines 6–7): *i-na an-da-ra-ri-im ú-ul i-na-an-da-ar*, "At a general release, she may not be released." This type of contract may account for the Levitical law. It was designed to guarantee that citizens of Israel should not be able to bind themselves or their families to permanent servitude. Such a usage of *andurāru(m)* occurs in all periods of Akkadian.

Family customs included the practice in which the bridegroom sought from the father permission to marry his daughter (AT 17.4–6; Gen. 34:12; see Finkelstein 1969:546) by bringing a betrothal gift (*nidnu*; Hebrew *mattān*). Two contracts specify that seven years of barrenness in the first wife were necessary before the husband was allowed a second wife (AT 93 and 94, though 94 is fragmentary). This invites a comparison with Jacob and the seven additional years he served before marriage to Rachel (Gen. 29:18, 27). The additional inheritance of the firstborn son could be legally transferred to a figure other than the biological firstborn (AT 92.15–19; see Mendelsohn 1941, 1959). Known at Ugarit and Nuzi, this custom may also apply to Abram's adoption of Eliezer (Gen. 15:2–3) and to Jacob's choices of Joseph instead of Reuben (Gen. 48:14, 22; 49:3–4) and of Ephraim instead of Manasseh (Gen. 48:13–14).

The inheritance of family estates by daughters, known from Numbers

27:1–11, Deuteronomy 25:5–10, Joshua 17:3–4, and Job 42:15, is also found in second-millennium BCE cuneiform texts from sites such as Nuzi and Emar (see Ben-Barak 1980; Huehnergard 1985; Paradise 1980, 1987). The example from Alalakh, Level VII text AT 7, actually describes a daughter's inheritance along with a son's, as Ben-Barak (1980:28–31) observes. The closest cuneiform comparisons with the biblical texts are not found at Alalakh. Texts from Nuzi and especially Emar have provided closer parallels with the biblical examples of inheritance by daughters.

As in the case of Ahab and Naboth (1 Kings 21), royal confiscation of the property of an executed criminal was known at Alalakh (AT 17; see Finkelstein 1969:546; Westbrook 1991:123). A Level VII text describes grabbing the hem of a garment as an act of submission (AT 456.45–57). To this Wiseman compares the opposite act by David of cutting the hem of Saul's garment (1 Sam. 24:3–4).

Many of the comparisons made here are of the sort that could be found elsewhere in the ancient Near East. Some have been noted in texts from Nuzi and Ugarit. What is significant at all these sites is not so much the presence of a single comparison, such as may also be found in some of the first-millennium BCE sources, but rather the large number of societal comparisons. When these are taken together, their cumulative weight argues for a similar milieu for much of the biblical material.

In religious matters, Wiseman also identifies an oath similar to the Hebrew "God do so to you and more also if . . ." (e.g., 1 Sam. 3:17). It occurs as "So [be done to me] if I take back what I have given you" (AT 456.40–46). Of special interest is how the chief goddess, to whom the temple was dedicated, claimed the king of Alalakh as her special posses-sion (AT 2 seal et passim; see Reiner 1969:531–32), with an expression (*sikiltu*) similar to that used by Israel's deity to describe a relationship with Israel (*sĕgullâ*; e.g., Exod. 19:5). This expression, used of a deity to de-scribe a special relation with a mortal, occurs frequently and almost ex-clusively at Alalakh (Seux 1967:261–62). Scholars have observed this usage in two other occurrences (CAD vol. 15, p. 245) that are both Middle Babylonian. Thus all the evidence suggests that this expression is characteristic of the second millennium BCE.

Finally, it is significant to observe the comparisons made between Genesis 15 and Old Babylonian Alalakh Text 456. The Bible describes how Abram requests an assurance of the divine promise of land. He is instructed to place before God several animals, most of which Abram cuts in two. (He kills the birds but does not divide their bodies.) As part of God's demonstration of assurance, he provides Abram with a verbal promise and then proceeds to move between the carcasses. Wiseman's publication of AT 456 provided another text in which someone kills an animal, in this case a lamb, while making a promise (see Wiseman 1958; Draffkorn 1959). M. Weinfeld (1970; 1972:74–75, 102) identified both texts as land grants. D. J. McCarthy (1978:86–87) compared the Alalakh text to Hittite treaties, although he observed that no other treaty text involves the cutting of a sheep's throat. Instead of a comparison with Genesis 15, he suggests that the act of cutting an animal's throat forms the background for the Hebrew and the West Semitic practice of describing the making of a covenant with the phrase, "to cut [krt] a covenant."

J. Van Seters (1975:100–103) has explicitly rejected the Alalakh comparison with Genesis 15, suggesting that the biblical text has closer associations with Jeremiah 34:18–20 and with the Aramaic Sefire I treaty. But this is not apparent from an examination of the relevant texts. I will consider only one aspect here (for more on this, see Hess 1993). Both the Sefire I text (IA.39–40; see Fitzmyer 1967:14–15) and the Jeremiah 34 passage describe substitutionary rites (see also Neo-Assyrian examples; Parpola and Watanabe 1988:9, 58), that is, the animals that are killed and their method of killing are illustrations of what will happen to the party of the treaty who does not keep its promise. On the other hand, neither Genesis 15 nor AT 456 is explicit that a substitution is involved. Instead, the killing of the animals symbolizes the solemnity of the oath and the guarantee of the life of the participants as support for the oath. Unlike the first-millennium rituals, no substitution is involved in which the particular type of slaughtering of the animal becomes the type of death to be suffered by one who forfeits the agreement. Thus Genesis 15 stands closer to the Alalakh ritual than it does to Jeremiah 34 or to the first-millennium Sefire treaty.

SPECIFIC ISSUES
OF INTERPRETATION

The following discussion will focus on two items of comparison that invite further study: the identification of the biblical Hebrews with the Ḫapiru and the occurrence of the latter at Alalakh, and the ḫupšu and their relation to the Hebrew ḥopšî.

The Ḫapiru

The issue of the identification and nature of the Ḫapiru (= ʿapiru), a group mentioned in numerous texts throughout the ancient Near East of the second millennium BCE has provoked a great deal of discussion (for summaries, see Bottéro 1954; Greenberg 1955; Loretz 1984; Lemche 1992). The absence of any clear means of establishing a linguistic identification between this group and the Hebrews (Rainey 1989:571) means that no historical identification can be made with certainty, however similar their place in society may be in various texts (Na'aman 1986).

The occurrences of Ḫapiru in the Amarna texts are often used as evidence for their banditlike nature, in which they are in revolt against established authority, an "enemy of the crown" (Moran 1987:212). However true this may be in the Amarna texts, their occurrences at Level IV Alalakh reveal a different aspect (see Greenberg 1955:20–22). Most of the citations indicate a certain integration of the Ḫapiru into the society. Here they are often indicated by the logographic signs SA.GAZ, as is true in the Amarna texts and elsewhere in the ancient Near East. AT 180–183 provide lists and totals of Ḫapiru forces, with an indication of the towns from which they come. Sometimes additional information is provided. This includes a variety of occupations (see Redford 1992:195). For example, a *túl-pí-ya* is described as a priest, LÚ SANGA *iš-[ḫa-ra]* (AT 180.20). A *ma-zi-ya* is a diviner, LÚ *bá-a-ru* (AT 182.16). Another individual is a mayor, LÚ *ḫa-za-an-nu* (AT 182.13), and another is a slave, ÌR (AT 182.14). Whatever the origins of the peoples on these lists, they are under the direction of the military leadership of Alalakh at the time of the composition of these texts. As Ḫapiru soldiers who carry weapons and form the military conscripts from particular towns (see AT 180.1, ERÍN.MEŠ LÚ.SA.GAZ EN.GIŠ.TUKUL.MEŠ URU GN), these figures are best understood as defenders, not enemies, of the crown. Their occupations indicate a variety of social strata. Like other groups in the society, they are associated with land or property, É (AT 183.5; 198.48; cf. AT 226 and the occurrence of LÚ SA.GAZ in the broken text of A 84/27, line 5, in Dietrich and Loretz 1969b:103), as well as sheep, UDU.Ú.ḪÁ (AT 350).

Two additional attestations of Ḫapiru at Alalakh have been suggested. They appear to reflect the military or warlike nature of the Ḫapiru in that society. One was found at the end of a Level VII text as part of a year-date, "year when Irkabtum, the king, made peace with Šemuba and with the Ḫapiru forces," MU *Ir-kab-tum* LUGAL ᴵ*Še-mu-ba ù* ERÍN.MEŠ *ḫa-aḫ-bi-ru iš-li-mu* (AT 58.28–30). Now the second sign of *ḫa-aḫ-bi-ru* was suggested to be an erasure or an attempt to write a long vowel as an *'alep* sign (Greenberg 1955:20, using Wiseman's translations and notes). If

Ḫapiru forces appear in this text, it is possible that they could be rendered as nothing more specific than "the enemy forces." The syllabic spelling of Ḫapiru has been questioned in this text, however; although such a spelling occurs two or three times in a fragmentary tablet (AT 164.4, 5, and perhaps 7), it is as ḫa-pí-ri, never as ḫa-aḫ-bi-ru. Further, these other appearances are in a Level IV text. There is no other attestation of Ḫapiru at Alalakh Level VII. Finally, M. Dietrich and O. Loretz (1969b:119 n. 29), followed by B. Kienast (1980:58), have proposed an alternative reading, KI.GA.RU, as a result of their collation. Thus AT 58 should not be considered in discussions of the Ḫapiru.

The second occurrence appears in the Idrimi inscription. When Idrimi flees to Canaan, he lives for seven years "in the land of the Ḫapiru forces," a-na li-bi ERÍN.MEŠ. LÚ. SA.GAZ (line 27; see Dietrich and Loretz 1981:204, 214). While there, he learns arts of divination. The Ḫapiru may be understood as enemies of the established order in Alalakh. If Idrimi wished to hide from his own personal enemies, the "enemy territory" of the Ḫapiru might appear as a good place to do it, even as David is recorded as having fled to the Philistines. But this parallel may be drawn too quickly. The land of the Ḫapiru could be nothing more than a country far enough away from Aleppo for Idrimi to find a safe haven there. This makes Idrimi's flight and return closer to that of Jephthah in Judges 11, as noted by Greenstein and Marcus (1976:76–77). Jephthah flees to the land of Tob, understood not as enemy territory in the story but simply as a place away from his home. Likewise, Idrimi may have settled among the Ḫapiru simply because they were away from the danger he sensed in his homeland. If so, this tells us nothing about the disposition of these Ḫapiru in relation to Aleppo. Thus the text may imply that the Ḫapiru are an enemy of the crown, but such is not a necessary conclusion from the evidence. However, this evidence does support that from the Level IV lists where the Ḫapiru have military associations.

Notice should also be made of several hundred fragments that are probably from Level IV of Alalakh but have not been published (Hess 1992). In these, references to Ḫapiru have been identified in at least three fragments. It is always spelled logographically, as SA.GAZ. One text is a letter in which LÚ.MEŠ.SA.GAZ are mentioned in context with na-ak-ru, "foe," "enemy." Unfortunately, the left side of the tablet is missing, which makes further identification difficult. Another fragment gives only the name but without a context. A final fragment appears to be similar to AT 180–184, mentioned above. It refers to SA.GAZ in a military context.

Thus these fragments reinforce our understanding of the military context of the Ḫapiru. It continues to be impossible to state with certainty that any of the Ḫapiru mentioned in the Alalakh texts are enemies of the established authority.

The *Ḫupšu*

The Alalakh *ḫupšu* (AT 186, 187, 202, 211; see Dietrich and Loretz 1969b:97–99, 104–6; 1969c:43–45), who could own houses or live as tenants (Mendelsohn 1955), have been compared with the Hebrew *ḥopšî*, as freeborn individuals exempt from certain royal taxes (see Exod. 21:5; 1 Sam. 17:25) and enjoying a status higher than a slave but of a lower class (see the summary in C. J. H. Wright 1990:256–57). Attempts to equate Alalakh and Amarna *ḫupšu* with Hebrew *ḥopšî* have always been supplemented by Ugaritic *ḫp/ḫt*. Recent studies, however, have challenged this comparison. The occurrences in the Bible are not entirely consistent. Although the legal texts (Exod. 21:2–6, 26–27; Lev. 19:20; Deut. 15:12–13, 18; see also Jer. 34:9–16) attest a usage that describes the freedom of a slave, and although this is supported by occurrences elsewhere (Job 3:19 and possibly Isa. 58:6), the usage is different in other passages. Psalm 88:6 relates *ḥopšî* to the dead and their graves. Although some might suggest death as a liberation (Loretz 1977:255–57), this interpretation is not universally agreed upon (Lohfink 1986:116). More controversial are the occurrences of this term in 1 Samuel 17:25 and a possible usage of a different form in 2 Kings 15:5 (= 2 Chr. 26:21).

The occurrence in 1 Samuel 17:25 involves Saul's promise of "freedom" for anyone who will engage in battle with Goliath. Since this is presumably intended to encourage warriors, it is not freedom from slavery that is implied. Instead, freedom from taxation or service of some sort is assumed. This has been compared to the sort of freedom that the *ḫp/ḫt* at Ugarit and the *ḫupšu* at Alalakh and Amarna enjoy. However, as CAD (vol. 6, p. 241) observes, these terms are normally applied to the lower classes, not to the higher ones. This is not the situation in 1 Samuel 17:25. In this verse, the implication is one of upper-class figures who are to be given *ḥopšî*. Instead, as Anson Rainey (1975:104; see Loretz 1977:167, n. 29; McCarter 1980:304) observes, Akkadian *zaki* and Ugaritic *brr* are closer semantic parallels. He identifies the former as a *nisbe* adjective similar to Hebrew *ḥopšî*, with the same semantic range, from slaves who are freed from slavery to figures from higher classes who are freed from royal service.

The occurrence of *bêt hahopšît* in 2 Kings 15:5 (= 2 Chr. 26:21) has been related to Hebrew *hopšî* and to Ugaritic *bt ḫptt* (D. P. Wright 1987:144, n. 25). It describes the residence of "leprous" King Azariah. Attempts have been made to understand this as "house of freedom," whether literally (see the summary in Loretz 1976:131) or euphemistically (de Moor 1987:66, n. 304). However, the absence of semantic equivalence between the Hebrew and Ugarit/Alalakh/Amarna equivalents implies that no certainty can be assigned to the meaning of this expression at present (Cogan and Tadmor 1988:165–67).

As already suggested, the identification of the *ḫupšu* at Alalakh has depended on analysis of the appearance of the same term at Ugarit and Byblos (via the Amarna texts), as well as from Middle Assyrian sources. N. P. Lemche's sociological analysis and critique of Norman Gottwald's study (Lemche 1976; 1985:167, 193–94; Gottwald 1979:480–84) produced a definition of the *ḫupšu* as clients, bound by specific contractual terms to work the land for a certain number of years. This suggests a dependent status. To this hypothesis, however, it is necessary to add the evidence from the Alalakh census lists as studied and summarized by Dietrich and Loretz (1969a, 1969b). Of special interest are the occupations that they cull from the census lists (1969a:87). These include an artisan who works with reeds, a leather worker, a weaver, a doctor, a potter, a diviner (A.ZU), shepherds, breeders of fowl, a smith, a groom, and a slave. Although a variety of occupations are represented, there is no indication of individuals in positions of political or priestly power. Thus the evidence at Alalakh agrees with that of its neighbors regarding the social status of *ḫupšu*, unlike that of the Ḥapiru.

CONCLUSION

This study has shown the wide-ranging sorts of comparisons that have been drawn between the Alalakh texts, other contemporary Akkadian texts from West Semitic cultures, and the Bible. Many of the general comparisons are found to apply in all three categories. However, some, such as Akkadian *mištannu* and Hebrew *mišneh*, illustrate how further research can qualify earlier suggestions. Akkadian *darārum* and Hebrew *děrôr* also lack similar usages, though this in part may be due to their different contexts. Such a view is supported by the cognate *andurārum*, which seems to have a similar usage as *děrôr* in a similar context regarding the release of slaves.

Among the specific issues discussed, the use of the term "Ḫapiru" is different at Alalakh from the references to the Hebrews in the Bible. It is also distinct from the use of the same term at Ugarit and in the Amarna correspondence. The evidence of the *ḫupšu* at Alalakh provides possible similarities with some occurrences of *ḫopšî* in the Hebrew Bible, but others are not similar. Instead, the semantic range of the Hebrew term is closer to other Ugaritic and Akkadian terms. Unlike Alalakh Ḫapiru, Alalakh *ḫupšu* have a similar social status as those designated by the term at Ugarit and also in the Amarna correspondence from Byblos.

If there is a conclusion to be drawn, it is that the comparative method must be evaluated on a case-by-case basis. It is not possible to generalize. Each new collation and reading of the Alalakh texts can provide further controls on the existing comparisons and the conclusions drawn from them, and thus new insights into the West Semitic world in which the Hebrew Bible and its traditions were born and shaped. Renewed interest in the Alalakh texts may yield fruitful discussion and debate regarding specific comparisons and their value, as has existed for some time with such texts as those from Nuzi and from Ugarit (see, e.g., Selman 1980; Craigie 1981; Eichler 1989).

WORKS CITED

Albright, W. F.
1950   Some Important Recent Discoveries: Alphabetic Origins and the
                Idrimi Statue. *Bulletin of the American Schools of Oriental Research*
                118:11–20.
Ben-Barak, Z.
1980   Inheritance by Daughters in the Ancient Near East. *Journal of
                Semitic Studies* 25:22–33.
Bottéro, J.
1954   *Le problème des Habiru à la 4e rencontre assyriologique internationale.*
                Cahiers de la Société asiatique 12. Paris: Imprimerie Nationale.
Chicago Assyrian Dictionary
1956–   *The Assyrian Dictionary of the Oriental Institute of the University of
                Chicago.* Chicago: Oriental Institute, and Glückstadt: J. J. Augustin.
Cogan, M., and H. Tadmor
1988   *II Kings: A New Translation and Commentary.* Anchor Bible 11.
                Garden City, N.Y.: Doubleday.
Craigie, P. C.
1981   Ugarit and the Bible: Progress and Regress in Fifty Years of Liter-
                ary Study. In *Ugarit in Retrospect: Fifty Years of Ugarit and Ugaritic,*
                ed. G. D. Young, 99–111. Winona Lake, Ind.: Eisenbrauns.

de Moor, J.
1987   *An Anthology of Religious Texts from Ugarit.* Nisaba 16. Leiden: E. J. Brill.

Dietrich, M., and O. Loretz
1969a   Die soziale Struktur von Alalaḫ und Ugarit (II): Die sozialen Gruppen *ḫupše-namê, ḫaniaḫḫe-ekû, eḫele-šūzubu* und *marjanne* nach Texten aus Alalaḫ IV. *Welt des Orients* 5:57–93.
1969b   Die soziale Struktur von Alalaḫ und Ugarit (IV): Die É=*bītu*-Listen aus Alalaḫ IV als Quelle für die Erforschung der gesellschaftlichen Schichtung von Alalaḫ im 15. Jh. v. Chr. *Zeitschrift für Assyriologie*, n.f., 60:88–123.
1969c   Die soziale Struktur von Alalaḫ und Ugarit (V): Die Weingärten des Gebietes von Alalaḫ im 15. Jahrhundert. *Ugarit-Forschungen* 1:37–64.
1981   Die Inschrift der Statue des Königs Idrimi von Alalaḫ. *Ugarit-Forschungen* 13:201–68 (plus Nachträge).

Draffkorn, A.
1959   Was King Abba-AN of Yamḫad a Vizier for the King of Ḫattuša? *Journal of Cuneiform Studies* 13:94–97.

Eichler, B. L.
1973   *Indenture at Nuzi: The Personal Tidennūtu Contract and Its Mesopotamian Analogues.* New Haven, Conn.: Yale University Press.
1989   Nuzi and the Bible: A Retrospective. In *DUMU-E₂-DUB-BA-A: Studies in Honor of Åke W. Sjöberg,* ed. H. Behrens, D. Loding, and M. T. Roth, 107–19. Occasional Publications of the Samuel Noah Kramer Fund 11. Philadelphia: University Museum.

Finkelstein, J. J.
1969   Documents from the Practice of Law. In *Ancient Near Eastern Texts Relating to the Old Testament,* ed. J. B. Pritchard, 542–47. 3d ed. with Supplement. Princeton, N.J.: Princeton University Press.

Fitzmyer, J. A.
1967   *The Aramaic Inscriptions of Sefîre.* Biblica et Orientalia 19. Rome: Pontifical Biblical Institute.

Fensham, F. C.
1960   The Treaty between Solomon and Hiram and the Alalakh Tablets. *Journal of Biblical Literature* 79:59–60.

Gottwald, N. K.
1979   *The Tribes of Yahweh: A Sociology of the Religion of Liberated Israel, 1250–1050 B.C.E.* Maryknoll, N.Y.: Orbis.

Greenberg, M.
1955   *The Hab/piru.* American Oriental Series 39. New Haven, Conn.: American Oriental Society.

Greenstein, E. L., and D. Marcus
1976   The Akkadian Inscription of Idrimi. *Journal of the Ancient Near Eastern Society of Columbia University* 8:59–96.

Hess, R. S.
1988   A Preliminary List of the Published Alalakh Texts. *Ugarit-Forschungen* 20:69–87.
1992   Observations on Some Unpublished Alalakh Texts, Probably from Level IV. *Ugarit-Forschungen* 24:113–15.
1993   The Slaughter of the Animals in Genesis 15: Genesis 15:8–21 and Its Ancient Near Eastern Context. In *He Swore an Oath: Biblical Themes from Genesis 12–50*, ed. R. S. Hess, P. E. Satterwaite, and G. J. Wenham, 55–65. Cambridge: Tyndale House.

Huehnergard, J.
1985   Biblical Notes on Some New Akkadian Texts from Emar (Syria). *Catholic Biblical Quarterly* 47:428–34.

Kienast, B.
1980   Die altbabylonischen Kaufurkunden aus Alalaḫ. *Welt des Orients* 11:35–63.

Klengel, H.
1963   Zur Sklaverei in Alalaḫ. *Acta Antiqua* 11:1–15.

Lemche, N. P.
1976   The Manumission of Slaves—The Fallow Year—The Sabbatical Year—The Jobel Year. *Vetus Testamentum* 26:38–59.
1979   *Andurārum* and *Mišarum*: Comments on the Problem of Social Edicts and Their Application in the Ancient Near East. *Journal of Near Eastern Studies* 38:11–22.
1985   *Early Israel: Anthropological and Historical Studies on the Israelite Society before the Monarchy.* Supplements to Vetus Testamentum 37. Leiden: E. J. Brill.
1992   Ḫabiru, Ḫapiru. In *Anchor Bible Dictionary*, ed. D. N. Freedman, 3:6–10. Garden City, N.Y.: Doubleday.

Lewy, J.
1958   The Biblical Institution of *Děrôr* in the Light of Akkadian Documents. *Eretz-Israel* 5:21*–31*.

Lindenberger, J. M.
1991   How Much for a Hebrew Slave? The Meaning of *Mišneh* in Deut. 15:18. *Journal of Biblical Literature* 110:479–82.

Lohfink, N.
1986   *ḥopšî.* In *Theological Dictionary of the Old Testament*, ed. G. J. Botterweck and H. Ringgren, 5:114–18. Translated by D. E. Green, from German. Grand Rapids: Wm. B. Eerdmans.

Loretz, O.
1976   Ugaritisch—Hebräisch *ḤB/PṬ, BT ḤPTṮ—ḤPŠJ, BJT ḤḤPŠJ/ WT. Ugarit-Forschungen* 8:129–31.
1977   Die Hebräischen Termini *ḤPŠJ* "Freigelassen, Freigelassener" und *ḤPŠH* "Freilassung." *Ugarit-Forschungen* 9:163–67.
1984   *Habiru-Hebräer: Eine sozio-linguistische Studie über die Herkunft des Gentiliziums ʿibrî vom Appellativum ḫabiru.* Beiheft zur Zeitschrift

für die alttestamentliche Wissenschaft 160. Berlin: Walter de Gruyter.

McCarter, P. K., Jr.
1980   I Samuel: A New Translation with Introduction and Commentary. Anchor Bible 8. Garden City, N.Y.: Doubleday.

McCarthy, D. J.
1978   Treaty and Covenant. Analecta Biblica 21A. Rome: Pontifical Biblical Institute.

Mayrhofer, M.
1965   Ein arisch-hurritischer Rechtsausdruck in Alalaḫ? Orientalia, n.s., 34:336–37.

Mendelsohn, I.
1941   The Canaanite Term for "Free Proletarian." Bulletin of the American Schools of Oriental Research 83:36–39.
1955   New Light on the Ḫupšu. Bulletin of the American Schools of Oriental Research 139:9–11.
1959   On the Preferential Status of the Eldest Son. Bulletin of the American Schools of Oriental Research 156:38–40.

Moran, W. L.
1987   Join the ᶜApiru or Become One? In "Working with No Data": Semitic and Egyptian Studies Presented to Thomas O. Lambdin, ed. D. M. Golomb, 209–12. Winona Lake, Ind.: Eisenbrauns.

Na'aman, N.
1980   The Ishtar Temple at Alalakh. Journal of Near Eastern Studies 39:209–14.
1986   Ḫabiru and Hebrews: The Transfer of a Social Term to the Literary Sphere. Journal of Near Eastern Studies 45:271–88.

North, R.
1978   Dĕrôr. In Theological Dictionary of the Old Testament, ed. G. J. Botterweck and H. Ringgren, 3:265–69. Translated by J. T. Willis, G. W. Bromiley, and D. E. Green, from German. Grand Rapids: Wm. B. Eerdmans.

Oppenheim, A. L.
1955   Review of The Statue of Idri-mi, by S. Smith. Journal of Near Eastern Studies 14:199–200.

Paradise, J.
1980   A Daughter and Her Father's Property at Nuzi. Journal of Cuneiform Studies 32:189–207.
1987   Daughters as "Sons" at Nuzi. In Studies on the Civilization and Culture of Nuzi and the Hurrians, Volume 2: General Studies and Excavations at Nuzi, ed. D. I. Owen and M. A. Morrison, 203–13. Winona Lake, Ind.: Eisenbrauns.

Parpola, S., and K. Watanabe
1988   Neo-Assyrian Treaties and Loyalty Oaths. State Archives of Assyria 2. Helsinki: University Press.

Rainey, A. F.
1975   Institutions: Family, Civil, and Military. In *Ras Shamra Parallels: The Texts from Ugarit and the Hebrew Bible, Volume II*, ed. L. R. Fisher, 69–107. Rome: Pontifical Biblical Institute.
1989   Review of *Les lettres d'el-Amarna: Correspondance diplomatique du pharaon*, by W. Moran. *Biblica* 70:566–72.
Redford, D. B.
1992   *Egypt, Canaan, and Israel in Ancient Times*. Princeton, N.J.: Princeton University Press.
Reiner, E.
1969   Akkadian Treaties from Syria and Assyria. In *Ancient Near Eastern Texts Relating to the Old Testament*, ed. J. B. Pritchard, 531–41. 3d ed. with Supplement. Princeton, N.J.: Princeton University Press.
Selman, M. J.
1980   Comparative Customs and the Patriarchal Narratives. In *Essays on the Patriarchal Narratives*, ed. A. R. Millard and D. J. Wiseman, 91–139. Leicester: Inter-Varsity.
Seux, M.-J.
1967   *Épithètes royales Akkadiennes et Sumériennes*. Paris: Letouzey et Ané.
Smith, S.
1949   *The Statue of Idri-mi*. Occasional Publications of the British Institute of Archaeology at Ankara 1. London: British Institute of Archaeology at Ankara.
Tsevat, M.
1958   Alalakhiana. *Hebrew Union College Annual* 29:109–43.
Van Seters, J.
1975   *Abraham in History and Tradition*. New Haven, Conn.: Yale University Press.
1992   *Prologue to History: The Yahwist as Historian in Genesis*. Louisville, Ky.: Westminster/John Knox.
Weinfeld, M.
1970   The Covenant of Grant in the Old Testament and in the Ancient Near East. *Journal of the American Oriental Society* 90:184–203.
1972   *Deuteronomy and the Deuteronomic School*. Oxford: Clarendon.
Westbrook, R.
1991   *Property and Family in Biblical Law*. Journal for the Study of the Old Testament Supplement, 113. Sheffield: JSOT Press.
Wiseman, D. J.
1953   *The Alalakh Tablets*. Occasional Publications of the British Institute of Archaeology at Ankara 2. London: British Institute of Archaeology at Ankara.
1958   Abban and Alalah. *Journal of Cuneiform Studies* 12: 124–29.
1967   Alalakh. In *Archaeology and Old Testament Study: Jubilee Volume of the Society for Old Testament Study 1917–1967*, ed. D. W. Thomas, 118–35. Oxford: Clarendon.

1982   Alalah. In *New Bible Dictionary*, ed. J. D. Douglas, 23–24. 2d ed.
                Leicester: Inter-Varsity.

Wolf, H. M.

1967   The *Apology of Ḫattušiliš* Compared with Other Political Self-
                Justifications of the Ancient Near East. Ph.D. dissertation, Bran-
                deis University.

Woolley, C. L.

1953   *A Forgotten Kingdom, Being a Record of the Results Obtained from the
                Excavation of Two Mounds, Atchana and Al Mina, in the Turkish
                Hatay.* London: Penguin Books.

1955   *Alalakh. An Account of the Excavations at Tell Atchana in the Hatay,
                1937–1949.* Reports of the Research Committee of the Society of
                Antiquaries of London 18. London: Society of Antiquaries.

Wright, C. J. H.

1990   *God's People in God's Land: Family, Land, and Property in the Old
                Testament.* Grand Rapids: Wm. B. Eerdmans, and Exeter: Pater-
                noster.

Wright, D. P.

1987   *The Disposal of Impurity: Elimination Rites in the Bible and in Hittite
                and Mesopotamian Literature.* Society of Biblical Literature Disser-
                tation Series 101. Atlanta: Scholars Press.

Zeeb, F.

1991   Studien zu den altbabylonischen Texten aus Alalaḫ. *Ugarit-
                Forschungen* 23:405–38.

1992   Studien zu den altbabylonische Texten aus Alalaḫ II: Pfandur-
                kunden. *Ugarit-Forschungen* 24:447–80.

13 | "Who Is This That Comes from Edom?"

NANCY LAPP

"Who is this that comes from Edom?" (Isa. 63:1). "Behold [my sword] descends for judgment upon Edom, upon the people I have doomed" (Isa. 34:5). "Remember, O Lord, against the Edomites, the day of Jerusalem" (Ps. 137:7). Why this harsh judgment on Edom? Why is Edom used by postexilic prophets and poets to symbolize every enemy and all evil? What was Edom doing when the prophets spoke, or what had been its history, that it should be scorned so?

EDOM

Although its history is still largely unknown, biblical and archaeological research has thrown some light on Edom and the kingdoms of Transjordan. From the biblical stories alone we think of conquering kings who stopped Moses in his march through Jordan, of David devastating a threatening nation, and then of Edom reviving to take terrible revenge, which the people of Judah and the prophets never forgot, so that Edom came to symbolize the most evil of enemies deserving judgment and the wrath of Yahweh.

Literary criticism of the Genesis narratives, the Deuteronomic history, and the ancestry of Esau and the Edomite king list (Genesis 36) has shown that these passages derive from the period of the Israelite monarchy, probably not before the eighth century BCE (for a summary of the evidence see Bartlett 1992:288–89). Prior to the time of David, political boundaries were minimal and organization was hardly more than tribal. From the reign of David onward possible historical references become more credible.

Archaeological surveys in Edom indicate some occupation, probably thinly spread agricultural settlements, but no Iron I site or even early Iron II town in Edom has yet been excavated. According to 2 Samuel 8:13–14, David slew eighteen thousand Edomites in the Valley of Salt, put garrisons in Edom, and made the Edomites his servants. It is probable that David wanted to dominate the land east of the Wadi Arabah in order to have full control over the route to the Gulf of Aqaba and its ports.

Although in subsequent decades the nationalism of the surrounding states probably stimulated Edom's self-consciousness, it took some time for the Edomites to recover from David's conquests. In the mid–ninth century BCE, in the reign of Jehoram, Edom was able to revolt against Judah and set up a king of its own (2 Kgs. 8:20). Judah did not easily give up control, though, and at the beginning of the eighth century Amaziah attacked Edom (2 Kgs. 14:7). Uzziah was able to rebuild Elath (2 Kgs. 14:22), and it was not until the beginning of Ahaz's reign, the latter half of the eighth century, that Edom drove Judah from Elath (2 Kgs. 16:6). From then on control of trade passing through the Gulf of Aqaba was in Edom's hands. Edom's rebellion took on great proportions in Judah's collective memory as time passed, and Edom's efforts to become a nation would call down the wrath of the prophets.

Undoubtedly Edom became a vassal of Assyria along with Judah after 732 BCE, and perhaps even before this Edom was paying tribute (Bartlett 1989:124). Apparently the stability brought by the occupation of Assyria allowed Edom to prosper. Archaeologists have found little evidence of established kingdoms or even towns before the late eighth century.

The Iron Age sites that have been excavated all indicate settlements of varying kinds from the eighth century BCE to the end of the sixth century, but they give little evidence of prior occupation. In his excavation of Tell el-Kheleifeh, near the northern shore of the Gulf of Aqaba, between 1938 and 1940, Nelson Glueck identified six major periods of occupation, which he dated between Iron I and the Persian period; he identified the site with Ezion-geber (Pratico 1985:1). A final report was never completed, however, so in recent years Gary Pratico has undertaken a comprehensive reappraisal of the excavations from the records and finds available. He has distinguished two architectural phases, the earlier casemate fortifications and the later offset-inset wall settlement. It is impossible to date the earlier phase from the stratigraphic and ceramic evidence, but the later phase dates between the eighth and the early sixth century BCE (Pratico 1985:26).

The excavations of C. M. Bennett and the British School of Archaeology at Umm el-Biyara, Tawilan, and Buseirah in the central mountain range of Edom all show significant building operations between the late eighth century BCE and the early sixth, with major occupation in the seventh century. Although the towns, particularly Buseirah, which became the Edomite capital (biblical Bozrah), were undoubtedly growing and developing throughout the eighth century BCE, it was during Edom's vassaldom to Assyria that their prosperity reached its height.

Recent surveys indicate a similar situation throughout Edom (Weippert 1982; MacDonald 1982a, 1982b, 1992; Hart and Falkner 1985; Hart 1987; Jobling 1985). Architectural remains and more concentrated occupation appear only during later Iron II, the eighth through sixth centuries. The evidence of late Iron II smelting, especially at Feinan and Khirbet en-Nahas, should also be mentioned.

Soundings and excavations west of the Arabah in the Negeb, where "Edomite" pottery has been found in late Iron II contexts, indicate extended influence at this time. Most of this pottery is recognized as Edomite because of its painted designs (see below). This ceramic evidence, along with a number of ostraca and seals with Edomite inscriptions that are dated to late Iron II, suggests the expansion of Edom or at least the presence of an Edomite element in the region between Beersheba and the southern end of the Dead Sea. If some of the wilderness narratives in their present form are no earlier than the seventh or sixth century BCE, the Edomite presence may help explain the Israelites' stop at Kadesh-barnea and their route to the Promised Land (see Bartlett 1992:292).

Occupation at some sites in Edom continued after the fall of Jerusalem in 587/86 BCE (Tawilan: Bennett 1984:19; Kheleifeh: Pratico 1985:27), but there is little archaeological evidence of the strength required to have been a participant in the destruction wrought in Judah. The extent of Edomite control and settlement west of the Arabah in the Negeb during the sixth century BCE and Edom's part in the destruction of Jerusalem is debated among scholars. Psalm 137:7 and Obadiah strongly suggest that Edom was allied with the Babylonians at the gates of Jerusalem. But these passages, as well as the story in 1 Esdras 4:41–46, may reflect a later time when the Babylonians were no longer a threat and the Idumaeans—Edomites who had settled in southern Judah—were indeed in the land (Bartlett 1989:153–57). J. R. Bartlett cites Jeremiah 40:11, which relates that Edom had given refuge to Jews fleeing from the Babylonians, as the most reliable evidence for Edom's part in the events of 587/86 BCE (1992:292).

Thus recent historical and archaeological research indicates an Edom that prospered as a national entity only in the latter part of the Iron Age, and this during a time when it was subservient to a larger power. But the collective memory of Judah's enemy to the east and south is reflected in the biblical record. Edom becomes in effect a designation for the quintessential enemy of Judah (Cresson 1972:137). In loosening its ties from Judah, perhaps retaliating for its years of bondage to Judah, Edom left a residue of fierceness, bitterness, and even blame among the inhabitants of Judah.

Much still remains to be discovered about the Edomites and their political and social power. With few inscriptions and contemporaneous sources, and a biblical record characterized by intense emotions and symbolic representation, the history of the Edomites as a people remains to be uncovered. Each excavation revealing Iron Age material, such as recent investigations at Feifa, makes a contribution.

THE SOUNDING AT FEIFA

In the final season (1990–91) of the present series of excavations of the Expedition to the Dead Sea Plain, in addition to excavating in the Early Bronze cemetery that stretched to the east, the walled site of Feifa was investigated (fig. 13-1). The most recent surveys (MacDonald et al. 1987) suggested that the visible structures belonged to the Iron Age or Roman period. It was hoped that a small sounding could date the encompassing wall and determine the nature of the town settlement.

An area was chosen near the southeast corner of the town wall. The Roman and even Byzantine occupation seemed to be concentrated toward the west, where there are the remnants of a tower; on the east, earlier occupation might be fairly near the surface. Two-meter-wide areas were excavated to varying levels from 3 m west of the wall to 4 m east of it.

The principal feature in the two-meter-wide trench was the perimeter town wall, plastered on the exterior. Rock tumble along with mud-brick debris was present everywhere on the surface and to a depth of about 1.25 m. The surface layers contained Iron II pottery and a few Roman and Byzantine sherds. The latest pottery in the brick and sandy layers below, some silt layers outside the wall, and bricky material inside the town wall, was Iron II. At about 1.60 m below the surface, fairly flat levels

FIG. 13-1. Surface of the perimeter wall that can be traced around the Feifa,
mound; east face of the wall looking south.

that contained a few diagnostic Iron II sherds were reached on both sides of the town wall. There is little doubt that the wall was constructed during the Iron Age, probably in the seventh century BCE.[1]

The Pottery

Although the area excavated was small, about forty diagnostic Iron II sherds make it possible to give a tentative date to the Iron Age occupation and the town wall. These sherds show strong affinity to the other excavated and surveyed Iron II sites of Edom, especially Kheleifeh, Buseirah, Tawilan, and Umm el-Biyara. These sites have been dated by inscriptions and parallel material to primarily the seventh and early sixth centuries BCE.

The latest pottery in the fill against the Feifa city wall as well as in the debris or occupational layers against it, and the bedded sand and debris layers on which it sat, belonged to Iron II. However, since the area excavated was very small and was relatively sterile of artifacts, the diagnostic material is limited. Many of the sherds are fragmentary. Fortunately there is enough to characterize the occupation, particularly if we supplement the Iron II loci with the Iron II material that came from the surface clearance. Several pottery types are of particular significance chronologically and make a contribution to the Edomite corpus, so they will be discussed here.

First it should be noted that no sherds of painted wares, which were so important in first characterizing Edomite pottery (Glueck 1935:124–37), were found in the Feifa sounding. Besides that found at Kheleifeh (Glueck 1967), painted Edomite pottery has been found in quantities at Buseirah (Bennett 1974: figs. 15, 16; 1975: figs. 5–8), Tawilan (Bennett 1984: figs. 3, 4), and Ghrareh (Hart 1988: fig. 9). In more extensive excavation at Feifa undoubtedly some painted pottery would come to light, but Feifa could well follow the pattern of the Negeb sites to the west where the painted pottery was found in "minimal" quantities (Mazar 1985:264), sites such as Tell Malhata (Kohavi 1967:273; 1977:772), Tel ʿIra (Beit-Arieh 1981:244), Horvat Qitmit (Beit-Arieh 1985:202), and Aroer (Biran and Cohen 1976:139).[2]

Assyrian Bowls

A few fragmentary sherds, several from one small bowl (fig. 13-2:1–2), have the form and higher quality ware of the type known as "Assyrian," found at many Palestinian as well as Transjordanian sites of the seventh

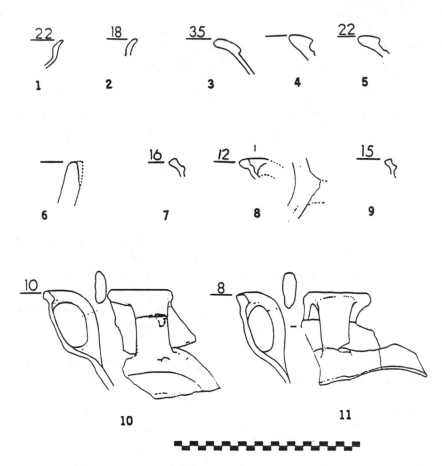

FIG. 13-2. Significant Iron II sherds from Feifa.

and sixth centuries BCE. (For many examples, see Lugenbeal and Sauer 1972:42–43.) The Feifa bowl is undoubtedly locally made, like similar bowls from other southern Jordan sites. Note especially two bowls of thin ware from the sounding at Ghrareh (Hart 1987: fig. 9:5, 6), a small bowl from Buseirah (Bennett 1975: fig. 7:9), and several from Umm el-Biyara (Bennett 1966: figs. 2:10, 4:6 et passim). Sometimes these bowls have handles, and at Buseirah and Tawilan there are painted examples (Bennett 1975: fig. 5:8, 9, 11; 1984: fig. 3:841). At Tell el-Kheleifeh "Assyrian" bowls in local imitation were ubiquitous, forming the second largest group after the "Negebite" wares (Pratico 1985:25, fig. 15:2–6).

Holemouth Kraters

Rims (fig. 13-2:3–5) are all from good Iron II loci in the levels against the perimeter wall or in the fill beneath. They are all fragmentary with little of the neck or side of the vessel attached. The rims are comparable to those of the common Iron II holemouth jar from southern Palestine, but it is more likely that they are examples of what has been called the "holemouth krater," a popular Transjordanian vessel. Two rims were found by Walter Rast and R. T. Schaub at Feifa during their survey in 1973 (1974: fig. 9:255, 256); the first has part of the body and handle stubs attached, indicating the form of the vessel. It is possible that some of the handles found in the Feifa sounding came from these kraters.

Complete or fairly complete "holemouth" or "inverted-rim" kraters, some with two or four handles, are included in reports from the excavated late Iron II sites in southern Jordan: Tell el-Kheleifeh (Pratico 1985:fig. 15:1), Umm el-Biyara (Bennett 1966: fig. 2:7), and Buseirah (Oakeshott 1978: pls. 24:12–16, 25:1–6, 26:1–5). Elsewhere in southern Jordan rims were found on the surveys in Edom (Hart and Falkner 1985: fig. 1:19–21), and at Sela (Hart 1986:14). In central Jordan very similar rims to those from Feifa are included in reports from Heshbon (Lugenbeal and Sauer 1972:333–75; note Sauer's parallels, pp. 50–51) and Dibon (Tushingham 1972: fig. 1:41–45; Winnett and Reed 1964: fig. 74:7, 8, 75:18). To be noted are the many kraters, with two, four, or no handles, and some with rather elaborate painted designs, from the Mount Nebo tombs (Saller 1966: figs. 24, 26, 27, 35, 36). From an early expedition to Balu ͨah some rims were reported similar to those from Feifa (Crowfoot 1934: pl. 2, figs. 1:1, 2; 2:1), but a different "holemouth" rim belonged to a large two-handled pithos (pl. 3).

Cooking Pots

Figure 13-2:6 is the one sherd from the sounding that may be of the distinctive "Negeb" ware. This ware is crude, handmade, medium baked, dark reddish brown, and wet-smoothed (Glueck 1971:45). It was first found in the Negeb (Woolley and Lawrence 1914–15:67), and Glueck distinguished it in his surveys in the Wadi Arabah, the Negeb, and even Sinai, and especially in his excavations at Tell el-Kheleifeh (Glueck 1971: figs. 2–7; Pratico 1985: figs. 12–13). More recently it has been found at numerous fortresses and sites throughout the Negeb (Cohen 1979:75–77; Pratico 1985:23). In Jordan, in addition to Tell el-Kheleifeh, a few specimens have been found at the Edomite sites of Buseirah (Bennett 1975:

fig. 6:8, 12), Tawilan (Bennett 1984: fig. 3:791; Oakeshott 1978: pl. 44:8), and Baᶜja III (Lindner and Farajat 1987: fig. 4:8). The ware is still not closely dated, since besides the late Iron II sites it has also appeared at some tenth-century Negeb fortresses, and perhaps even earlier (Lapp 1976:27; Cohen 1979:77; Pratico 1985:23).

The most usual form in "Negeb" ware is a straight-sided vessel with a plain rounded rim and flat base, generally used as a cooking pot (Pratico 1985:23, fig. 12:1–5). The Feifa sherd is very fragmentary and even broken at the rim, but it could well be from this type of vessel.

Two fragmentary cooking pot rims of typical late Iron II type came from good Iron II loci (fig. 13-2:7–8) and another came from a surface locus (fig. 13-2:9). Figure 13-2:8 has a handle attachment at the rim. This is a common Palestinian form, but is also popular in Transjordan and is found at all the excavated southern Jordanian sites. The closest parallels are from Tell el-Kheleifeh (Pratico 1985: fig. 14:2), Tawilan (Bennett 1984: fig. 5:797 especially), Umm el-Biyara (Bennett 1966:8), Buseirah (Bennett 1974: fig. 15:10; Oakeshott 1978: pl. 26:6–11), and Ghrareh (Hart 1987: fig. 9:7). At Kheleifeh the handles often have stamp impressions in a script dated to the late seventh or early sixth century BCE (Pratico 1985:24).

Jugs

The most common rim form and probably the most helpful chronologically comes from a jug that is now known in southern Transjordan. In two cases at Feifa it was possible to join rims with the jug handle (fig. 13-2:10–11). The rim is sometimes described as "rectangular." It is thickened and slightly grooved on the outside, rather similar in form to the typical late Iron II cooking pot. From the rim it forms a rather straight, only slightly outsloping neck. The flattened handle goes from the rim to the shoulder. Although this form is occasionally drawn with two handles, probably it usually, if not always, had only one (see below). Among the small collection of diagnostic sherds excavated during the sounding, there were twelve of these rim sherds belonging to different vessels. They were from the Iron II loci as well as plentiful in the surface material.

A whole jug of this type is reported from Tell el-Kheleifeh (Pratico 1985: fig. 14:4). A Feifa base fragment could be from this jug type. This was the most common "jar" form at Kheleifeh, and most examples have a *qaws ᶜanal* stamp on the handle (Pratico 1985:24; Glueck 1969:51).[3] A good parallel to this jug form is reported from Umm el-Biyara (Bennett

1966: fig. 2:11); it is drawn with two handles, but whether both were present may be questioned. Other rim sherds are probably from similar jugs (figs. 3:5, 9; 4:2–4, 9). Others come from Buseirah (Oakeshott 1978: pl. 37:2–8), and Tawilan (Oakeshott 1978: pl. 50:6–8). From the Feifa survey several sherds are published (Rast and Schaub 1974:257–59; also somewhat similar are 252 and 253 with a handle). Others found on surveys or small soundings in southern Jordan include Ghrareh (Hart 1987: fig. 9:8), Baᶜja III (Lindner and Farajat 1987: figs. 5:13, 6:2, 4, 5), Sela (Hart 1986: fig. 2:9), es-Sadeh (Lindner et al. 1988: fig. 8:6, 11), and Site 34 (east side of the Wadi Fidan) from Burton MacDonald's survey of the southern Ghor and northeast Arabah (MacDonald 1992: pl. 19:9–10).

Dating

Although so far none of the decorative wares (with paint, perforations, dentilations, or protrusions) or compartment lamps, which are typical of some Edomite sites,[4] have been identified at Feifa, there is no doubt that the wheel-made Feifa pottery is closely related to that of Tell el-Kheleifeh, as well as Buseirah, Umm el-Biyara, and Tawilan. A ceramic relationship can also be seen with the small surveys and soundings that have been made in southern Transjordan or "Edom."

The pottery types we have discussed are of particular importance: rectangular grooved-rim jug, thus far a unique but common form in southern Jordan; the "holemouth" krater, a Transjordanian form but widely known in central Transjordan as well as the south; the Assyrian bowls along with their local imitations; and the typical late Iron II cooking pots also widely known in Palestine.

The Iron II occupation at Tell el-Kheleifeh to which the parallel jugs, kraters, and cooking pots belong is closely dated to the seventh and sixth centuries BCE by the *qaws ᶜanal* seal impressions (the name of a known Edomite king) that often appear on their handles (Glueck 1967:8; 1969:51; Pratico 1985:24). The Umm el-Biyara occupation is also dated by a royal seal impression reading "Qos-Gabri, King of Edom," another Edomite king mentioned in seventh-century Assyrian inscriptions (Bennett 1966:399–400; Bienkowski 1990:91–92). The final pottery reports or stratigraphical studies for Tawilan and Buseirah have not yet appeared, but there does not seem to be any evidence for heavy occupation before the late eighth century, though their occupation may have continued into the Persian period (Bienkowski 1990:101, 103).

The parallel kraters, cooking pots, and jugs from good Iron II loci and further sherds from the surface material date the Feifa material to the seventh and early sixth centuries BCE, and the pottery from the stratified layers dates the construction of the wall around the site to the seventh century BCE.

CONCLUSION

This small sounding provides evidence for the first known Edomite settlement in the southern Ghor. Feifa is located on the Arabah road leading south to Kheleifeh (Bartlett 1989:230, Map 1), and the finds from the small sounding show the closest links to Tell el-Kheleifeh near the shore of the Gulf of Aqaba. There are also important links with the larger Edomite towns in the eastern highlands. Further excavation should reveal more about trade and communication in Edomite times, as well as about the political and social situation of Edom and its relation to Judah.

We can only surmise at this point that the claim Edom made to independence from the Judahite monarchy and the prosperity it knew in the eighth through the sixth centuries contributed to the symbolic use by the postexilic prophets; it was the enemy nation deserving of Yahweh's wrath and a sign of universal judgment to come. The fierceness and determination of Edom's rebellion against Judah, followed by the success Edom experienced under Assyrian rule while Judah rebelled and suffered, and perhaps Edom's standing aside as Jerusalem was destroyed, were magnified in the minds of prophet and poet: The Lord's judgment would fall upon Edom.

NOTES

1. In surface debris as well as in the Iron II levels occasional Early Bronze sherds appeared. Below the town wall and at that depth east of the wall, several disturbed EB IA tombs appeared, similar to those in the large cemetery to the east of the Feifa town site. Some of the Early Bronze sherds seem to be from domestic pottery, so there may well have been a small Early Bronze I settlement in the area.

2. Because the records of pottery, particularly the plain wares, from most of the Negev sites remain unpublished, little can be used in the comparative pottery study below.

3. Pratico did not recognize or have available all the parallels, particularly of southern Jordan, now known for this form (1985:24). It is probably not necessary to draw upon Palestinian vessels for form or body profile. Mazar also does not have the parallels for this form as well as others (1985:256).

4. For decorated wares, see above. For compartment lamps at Kheleifeh, see Glueck 1969:59, fig. 3:17–24; at Buseirah, see Bennett 1974:14:2–4; 1975: fig. 7:3, 8.

WORKS CITED

Bartlett, J. R.
1989   *Edom and the Edomites.* Journal for the Study of the Old Testament Supplement Series, 77. Sheffield: JSOT Press.
1992   Edom. In *Anchor Bible Dictionary,* ed. D. N. Freedman, 2:287–95. Garden City, N.Y.: Doubleday.
Beit-Arieh, I.
1981   Tel ᶜIra, 1980. *Israel Exploration Journal* 31:243–45.
1985   H. Qitmit. *Israel Exploration Journal* 35:201–2.
Bennett, C. M.
1966   Fouilles d'Umm el Biyara: Rapport Préliminaire. *Revue biblique* 73:372–403.
1974   Excavations at Buseirah, Southern Jordan, 1972: Preliminary Report. *Levant* 6:1–24.
1975   Excavations at Buseirah, Southern Jordan, 1973: Third Preliminary Report. *Levant* 7:1–9.
1984   Excavations at Tawilan in Southern Jordan, 1982. *Levant* 16:1–23.
Bienkowski, P.
1990   Umm el-Biyara, Tawilan, and Buseirah in Retrospect. *Levant* 22:91–109.
Biran, A., and R. Cohen
1976   Aroer, 1976. *Israel Exploration Journal* 26:139–40.
Cohen, R.
1979   The Iron Age Fortresses in the Central Negev. *Bulletin of the American Schools of Oriental Research* 236:61–79.
1981   Excavations at Kadesh-barnea, 1976–1978. *Biblical Archaeologist* 44:93–115.
Cresson, B. C.
1972   The Condemnation of Edom in Post-exilic Judaism. In *The Use of the Old Testament in the New and Other Essays,* Festschrift for W. F. Stinespring, ed. J. M. Efrid, 125–48. Durham, N.C.: Duke University Press.
Crowfoot, J. W.
1934   An Expedition to Baluᶜah. *Palestine Exploration Quarterly* 1934: 76–84.
Glueck, N.
1935   *Explorations in Eastern Palestine II.* Annual of the American Schools of Oriental Research 15. New Haven, Conn.: American Schools of Oriental Research.
1967   Some Edomite Pottery from Tell el-Kheleifeh, Parts I and II. *Bulletin of the American Schools of Oriental Research* 188:8–38.

228 NANCY LAPP

1969 Some Ezion-Geber: Elath Iron II Pottery. *Eretz-Israel* 9:51–59.
1971 Iron II Kenite and Edomite Pottery. *Perspective* 12:45–56.

Hart, S.
1986 Sela^c: The Rock of Edom. *Palestine Exploration Quarterly* 1986: 91–95.
1987 Five Soundings in Southern Jordan. *Levant* 19:33–47.
1988 Excavations at Ghrareh, 1986: Preliminary Report. *Levant* 20:89–99.

Hart, S., and R. K. Falkner
1985 Preliminary Report on a Survey in Edom, 1984. *Annual of the Department of Antiquities of Jordan* 29:255–71.

Jobling, W. J.
1985 Preliminary Report of the Sixth Season of the Aqaba-Ma^can Epigraphic and Archaeological Survey. *Annual of the Department of Antiquities of Jordan* 29:211–20.

Kohavi, M.
1967 Tel Malhata. *Israel Exploration Journal* 17:272–73.
1977 Malhata, Tel. In *Encyclopedia of Archaeological Excavations in the Holy Land*, ed. M. Avi-Yonah and E. Stern, 3:771–75. Englewood Cliffs, N.J.: Prentice-Hall.

Lapp, N.
1976 Casemate Walls in Palestine and the Late Iron II Casemate at Tell el-Fûl (Gibeah). *Bulletin of the American Schools of Oriental Research* 223:25–42.

Lindner, M., and S. Farajat
1987 An Edomite Mountain Stronghold North of Petra (Ba^cja III). *Annual of the Department of Antiquities of Jordan*, 31:175–85.

Lindner, M.; S. Farajat; and J. P. Zeitler
1988 Es-Sadeh: An Important Edomite-Nabataean Site in Southern Jordan, Preliminary Report. *Annual of the Department of Antiquities of Jordan* 32:75–90.

Lugenbeal, E. N., and J. A. Sauer
1972 Seventh–Sixth Century B.C. Pottery from Area B at Heshbon. *Andrews University Seminary Studies* 10:21–69.

MacDonald, B.
1982a The Wadi el-Hasa Survey, 1979, and Previous Archaeological Work in Southern Jordan. *Bulletin of the American Schools of Oriental Research* 245:35–52.
1982b The Wadi el-Hasa Survey, 1981. *Annual of the Department of Antiquities of Jordan* 26:117–32.
1992 *Southern Ghors and Northeast Arabah Archaeological Survey 1985–1986, Southern Jordan*. Sheffield Archaeological Monographs, 5. Sheffield: J. R. Collis.

MacDonald, B.; G. A. Clark; M. Neely; R. Adams; and M. Gregory
1987 Southern Ghors and Northeast Arabah Archaeological Survey, 1986, Jordan: A Preliminary Report. *Annual of the Department of Antiquities of Jordan* 31:391–418.

Mazar, E.
1985   Edomite Pottery at the End of the Iron Age. *Israel Exploration Journal* 35:253–69.
Meshel, Z.
1977   Horvat Ritma—An Iron Age Fortress in the Negev Highlands. *Israel Exploration Journal* 4:110–35.
Oakeshott, M. F.
1978   A Study of the Iron Age II Pottery of East Jordan with Special Reference to Unpublished Material from Edom. Ph.D. dissertation, University of London.
1983   The Edomite Pottery. In *Midian, Moab, and Edom: The History of Late Bronze Age Jordan and North-West Arabia*, ed. J. F. A. Sawyer and D. J. A. Clines, 53–63. Journal for the Study of the Old Testament Supplement Series, 24. Sheffield: JSOT Press.
Pratico, G. D.
1985   Nelson Glueck's 1938–1940 Excavations at Tell el-Kheleifeh: A Reappraisal. *Bulletin of the American Schools of Oriental Research* 259:1–32.
Rast, W. E., and R. T. Schaub
1974   Survey of the Southeastern Plain of the Dead Sea, 1973. *Annual of the Department of Antiquities of Jordan* 19:5–53, 175–85.
Saller, S. J.
1966   Iron Age Tombs at Nebo, Jordan. *Liber Annuus* 16:165–298.
Schaub, R. T., and W. E. Rast
1989   *Bâb edh-Dhraᶜ: Excavations in the Cemetery Directed by Paul W. Lapp (1965–1967)*. Reports of the Expedition to the Dead Sea Plain, Jordan, vol. 1. Winona Lake, Ind.: American Schools of Oriental Research.
Tushingham, A. D.
1972   *The Excavations at Dibon (Dhiban) in Moab*. Annual of the American Schools of Oriental Research, 40. Cambridge, Mass.: American Schools of Oriental Research.
Weippert, M.
1982   Remarks on the History of Settlement in Southern Jordan during the Early Iron Age. In *Studies in the History and Archaeology of Jordan, 1*, ed. A. Hadidi, 153–62. Amman: Department of Antiquities.
Winnett, F. V., and W. L. Reed
1964   *The Excavations at Dibon (Dhiban) in Moab*. Annual of the American Schools of Oriental Research, 36–37. New Haven, Conn.: American Schools of Oriental Research.
Woolley, C. L., and T. E. Lawrence
1914–15   *The Wilderness of Zin*. Palestine Exploration Fund Annual, 3. London: Palestine Exploration Fund.

14 | Early Edom: The Relation between the Literary and Archaeological Evidence

BURTON MacDONALD

Over the centuries, information from outside the Bible has caused questioning of biblical statements that many had taken and continue to take literally. The findings of Copernicus (1473–1543) and Galileo (1564–1642), for example, regarding the sun as the center of the universe, caused scholars during the sixteenth and following centuries to question the biblical assertions and firmly held beliefs of the time that the earth was the center of the universe (Genesis 1—2). Again, Darwin's (1809–1882) theory of evolution caused scholars to reassess the biblical assertions on human creation. More pertinent to the subject under discussion, failure on the part of archaeologists to find evidence for a Late Bronze–Early Iron Age destruction level at Jericho caused biblical scholars to take a closer look at the story of the Israelite capture of Jericho and ask what type of literature we have in Joshua 6. Thus, down through the centuries, scientific discoveries have caused biblical scholars and others to examine more closely the literature that constitutes the Bible. This chapter will examine what is generally acknowledged to be the earliest literary evidence from Egypt and Israel on Edom/Edomites and see how it relates to recent archaeological findings in what is alleged to be the territory of Edom. The emphasis will be on those texts and archaeological findings that have to do with eastern Edom, that is, the part of Edom that is generally acknowledged to be located east of Wadi Arabah in what is now southern Jordan, and which deal with Edom/Edomites up to the time of Solomon. A straightforward presentation of the textual information will be followed by a summary of recent archaeological evidence from Edom, emphasizing again the region east of the Arabah. Finally, a comparison of these two types of information will be presented.

THE LITERARY SOURCES

The literary sources for our discussion come from Egypt and the Bible. The former are generally acknowledged to be older.

The Egyptian Sources

Although Egyptian scholars disagree as to the earliest literary reference to the word "Seir" for the territory of Edom (Kitchen 1992:26 and 31, n. 19), there is general agreement that it is used during the reigns of Ramesses II and Ramesses III. Ramesses II (1304–1237 BCE) describes himself as one who "has plundered the Shasu-land, captured the mountain of Seir" (Ward 1992:1165; see Kitchen 1992:26–27). In this context, Shasu and Seir are used in parallel phrases (Kitchen 1992:27). Ramesses III (1198–1166 BCE) claims: "I destroyed the Seirites, the clans of the Shasu" (Wilson 1969:262). These early Egyptian references indicate that both Ramesses II and Ramesses III thought that Seir and the Shasu people who lived there were worth either raiding or claiming as subdued (Kitchen 1992:27).

The word *Seir* means "hairy," that is, wooded, not necessarily well covered with trees but rather with scrub or bush. As early as the end of the second millennium BCE, "Seir" and "Mount Seir" are fixed expressions in Egyptian texts, reminiscent of the biblical phrase Mount Seir (Gen. 32:3; 36:8–9). The Egyptian sources do not give its location, but it would appear to be close to their territory. The Bible locates Seir both east and west of Wadi Arabah. The western part, in the eastern Negeb, is in proximity to the territory of the Israelite tribe of Simeon (1 Chr. 4:42–43). The territory conquered by Joshua in the south extended toward Seir (Josh. 11:17; 12:7). Moreover, the hill country of Seir is identified with Edom (Gen. 36:8–9, 21), and the land of Edom is repeatedly referred to as the land of Seir (Gen. 32:3; Num. 24:18; Josh. 24:4, etc.).

The Shasu were a people who lived, at least in part, in southern Palestine and southern Transjordan (Bartlett 1989:77–79; Ward 1992:1165). Indeed, Ward cites, on the basis of the Egyptian texts, an origin for the Shasu in Transjordan (1992:1166). The Shasu "represent a social class, partially nomadic and partially sedentary, members of which regularly left the Transjordanian homeland to hire out as mercenaries or engage in free-booting" (Ward 1992:1166).

The term *Edom* appears for the first time in Egyptian records during the reign of Merenptah (1236–1223 BCE). It occurs among a group of letters that served as models for schoolboys. One communication pre-

sents the form in which an official on the eastern frontier of Egypt might
report the passage of Asiatic tribes into the better pasture lands of the
eastern Nile Delta:

> We have finished with allowing the Shasu clansfolk of Edom to pass the
> Fortress of Merenptah that is in Succoth ['Tjeku'], to the pools (*brkt*) of
> Pi-Atum of Merenptah that (is/are) in Succoth, to keep them alive and
> to keep alive their livestock, by the will of Pharaoh, LPH, the good Sun
> of Egypt, along with the names from the other days on which the fort
> of Merenptah that is in Succoth was passed [by such people]. (Kitchen
> 1992:27; see Wilson 1969:259)

The fortress of Merenptah, in this particular case, would have been on
the eastern frontier of Egypt. Kitchen identifies Tjeku with Succoth, a
specific site in Wadi Tumilat in the east Nile Delta, while other scholars
would merely identify it with the region at the eastern end of Wadi
Tumilat near modern-day Ismailia. Pi-Atum is often identified with Tell
el-Retabeh, about 37 km east of Ismailia. The picture is one of pastoralists from Edom with their livestock. These Shasu people were, according
to Ward, a prominent part of the Edomite population (1992:1165).

The above agrees well with the inscription from the reign of Ramesses
III. Between accounts of his conflicts with the Sea Peoples and with the
Libyans, the following passage appears:

> I destroyed the Seirites, the clans of the Shasu, I pillaged their tents,
> with their people, their property, and their livestock likewise, without
> limit. (Kitchen 1992:27; see Ward 1992:1165 and Wilson 1969:262)

Kenneth Kitchen sees this as entirely consistent with the pastoralists of
Merenptah's time, and the raid on Seir by Ramesses III (an action repeat-
ing, as noted above, the claim of Ramesses II). He thinks that such actions
are possibly linked with Egyptian mining interests in Timna, on the western side of the Arabah, in both reigns, and the security of those interests
(1992:27). In his estimation, Seir/Edom was not just a deserted wilderness
in the Late Bronze–Iron Age transitional period (thirteenth–twelfth centuries BCE). There were enough people there to concern Egyptian official
interests, and the lifestyle was, at least in part, pastoral and with tents
(Kitchen 1992:27; Ward 1992:1166).

In a document from about 1000 BCE, or a little earlier, a persecuted
and oppressed Egyptian official asks for help. Near the end of the document he expresses the wish that his oppressor could be sent off to "the
back of beyond" to bring back an obscure person who would actually help

him. The writer adds that his oppressor had been with this person to the Seirites, literally, "those of Seir." What the document implies is that people lived in Seir/Edom about then ("those of Seir"), and also that Egyptians, from time to time, might have occasion to visit Seir, for whatever reason (Kitchen 1992:27). Thus, we have at least some evidence for an inhabited Edom/Seir, and at least intermittent relations with Egypt from the thirteenth into the tenth century BCE.

The Biblical Sources

The biblical evidence on Edom is not without its difficulties, since there is no consensus as to the period(s) from which it dates.

According to Genesis 25:24, Rebekah, the wife of Isaac, bears twins. The first twin born is called Esau, the second Jacob (Gen. 25:25–26). These two become the eponymous ancestors of the Edomites and the Israelites respectively. This text indicates that, at least in the mind of the biblical writer(s), these two peoples were closely related.

Some scholars, such as David Noel Freedman, see Exodus 15 and Judges 5, the so-called Song of the Sea and the Song of Deborah respectively, as two of the oldest passages in the Bible (Freedman 1975, especially 24, n. 2; 1976; 1979; 1987). In the Song of the Sea, "the chiefs of Edom," in parallel with the "leaders of Moab," are said to be "dismayed" when they see what Yahweh has done for Israel (Exod. 15:15). Freedman dates this song to the first half of the twelfth century, or about 1175 (1975:3; see also 1976; 1979:87–88; and 1987). If so, then there would be "chiefs of Edom" as early as this date. In the Song of Deborah, Yahweh is said to have gone "out from Seir . . . marched from the region of Edom" (Judg. 5:4). Freedman dates this song to the third quarter of the twelfth century, or not later than about 1125 (1975:3; see also 1976; 1979:88; and 1987). According to this dating, "Seir" and "Edom," as geographical indications, were known to the biblical writer(s) almost as early as to the scribes of Egyptian Dynasties 19 and 20.

Genesis 36:31–39 presents a list of "the kings who reigned in the land of Edom, before any king reigned over the Israelites" (v 31). Taken at face value, this text indicates that Edom had a series of kings who ruled before the Israelite and Judean kings. In the words of G. von Rad, "the Edomites reached statehood considerably earlier than did Israel" (1972:346).

The general background for understanding the next biblical presentation on Edom is the story of the Exodus, Israel's deliverance under the leadership of Moses from a condition of slavery in the land of Egypt, and

Israel's forty-year period of "wandering" in the area between Egypt and the land of Canaan. During this later phase, "Israel then sent messengers to the king of Edom, saying, 'Let us pass through your land'; but the king of Edom would not listen" (Judg. 11:17). Edom was so adamant in its refusal to let Israel pass through its land that it threatened to come out with sword against the Israelites (Num. 20:18) and "Edom came out against them with a large force, heavily armed" (Num. 20:20). God tells Israel not to engage Edom in battle "since I have given Mount Seir to Esau as a possession" (Deut. 2:5). Then, the Bible continues, Israel "journeyed through the wilderness, went around the land of Edom and the land of Moab, . . . and camped on the other side of the Arnon" (Judg. 11:18), that is, north of Wadi Mujib. What these texts imply is that at the time of Israel's journey from Kadesh to the plains of Moab, traditionally dated to the fifteenth or thirteenth centuries BCE, Edom had a king with a large fighting force. Moreover, this king was able to enforce the denial of permission to pass through Edomite territory. Thus, the generally accepted opinion that the Israelites were forced to detour around Edom.

Saul is said to have fought against all his enemies, one of whom was Edom (1 Sam. 14:47). When David became king, he subdued Edom, among other nations. More specifically, "he killed eighteen thousand Edomites in the Valley of Salt. He put garrisons in Edom; throughout all Edom he put garrisons, and all the Edomites became David's servants" (2 Sam. 8:13–14). According to 1 Kings 11:15–16, "when David was in Edom, and Joab the commander of the army went up to bury the dead, he killed every male in Edom (for Joab and all Israel remained there six months, until he had eliminated every male in Edom)." (John Bartlett gives a possible date of ca. 990 BCE for David's wars against Edom [1989:104].) However, Hadad, a young boy at the time and a member of the royal house of Edom (1 Kgs. 11:14), fled to Egypt with some Edomites (1 Kgs. 11:17) and married into the Egyptian royal house (1 Kgs. 11.19). He later became an adversary of Solomon (1 Kgs. 11:14), who "built a fleet of ships at Ezion-geber, which is near Eloth on the shore of the Red Sea, in the land of Edom" (1 Kgs. 9:26).

In summary, what some have thought to be the earliest biblical information on Edom relates how Edom is the descendant of Esau, the twin brother of Jacob/Israel. In the twelfth century BCE there were "chiefs in Edom," while the geographical references "Seir" and "Edom" are known to the biblical writer(s) at this time. Edom had kings before kings ruled over Israel. At the time of the biblical "wanderings" after Israel's departure from Egypt, Edom was so strong militarily that it prevented Israel from passing through its territory. Edom was of such a concern to both Saul and David that these two Israelite leaders had to subdue Edom to such an extent that every Edomite male was killed. Only Hadad, of the royal house of Edom, escaped and became an adversary to Solomon.

Difficulties with
a Literal Reading
of the Biblical Texts

Such literal interpretation of these biblical texts is made difficult by literary-critical analyses. Few biblical scholars today accept that both Edom and Israel are direct descendants of the figures Esau and Jacob. Furthermore, Bartlett, for example, dates the Song of the Sea to the tenth century BCE or later, and thus, in his opinion, it does not reflect contemporary knowledge of twelfth-century Edom (1992:13-14). Again, for Bartlett, the Song of Deborah is not to be dated to the premonarchic period but to a time during the divided monarchy when it was sung before the northern court of Israel (1989:93, 102; 1992:14). In any case, the names "Seir" and "Edom" are treated as mere geographical references in the Song of Deborah.

Bartlett sees the list in Genesis 36:31–39 as deriving "at the earliest from the monarchic period of Israel and Judah" (1992:14), while E. A. Knauf dates it to the early Persian period (1985). Critical analysis of this passage shows that the picture here is not a portrayal of a thirteenth-through tenth-century BCE situation but of a later period. The material in the list is not homogeneous, each king is connected with a different place, and no king is succeeded by his son. Thus, this is not a dynastic system of rule. It is possible that we should think of these "kings" as local rulers, controlling separate and independent regions, to be compared with the various local rulers mentioned in the books of Joshua and Judges. Bartlett thinks that the best we can do with the list is to point to the possibility of pre-Davidic rule in Edom being exercised on a regional basis (1989:102; 1992:15). He continues: "It is not impossible that the editor of the list was drawing on names which in reality belonged to the ninth–eighth centuries BC and the early days of the new monarchy of Edom, which began, according to the Deuteronomistic Historian (2 Kgs. 8:20), in the days of Jehoram of Judah, in the mid 840s BC" (1992:15).

There is a lack of consistency in the biblical presentation of Israel's journey from Kadesh to the "plains of Moab" (Num. 33:48–50). While

Numbers 20:14–21 indicates that the Israelites did not cross through Edomite territory, Deuteronomy 2:1–8 seems to imply that they did indeed travel through the territory (see especially Deut. 2:4, 8) (Bartlett 1989:91; 1992:15; Miller 1989:583). Bartlett concludes: "It is not easy to derive much evidence for the early history of the Edomites from these narratives. They tell us far more about late monarchic or even early exilic perceptions of Edom from the standpoint of Judah" (1992:16).

Bartlett does not think that Saul invaded or occupied Edom but that 1 Samuel 14:47 indicates "some growing contact between Edom and her neighbors" (1989:104). David is said to have annihilated the Edomites, but Solomon, nevertheless, had an adversary in Hadad the Edomite. The latter did not prevent Solomon, however, from having a sea port on the Red Sea.

THE ARCHAEOLOGICAL EVIDENCE

In the 1930s Glueck conducted archaeological surveys in Jordan that became the basis for interpreting its archaeological history, especially during the Bronze and Iron Ages. He was not the first, by any means, to carry out explorations of archaeological ruins in Jordan, but the new feature that characterized his work was the examination of surface pottery, which he collected from many of the sites he visited. He used this pottery to date the sites. He carried out this work to a large extent in what he called Ammon, Moab, and Edom, and he published his results in the *Annual of the American Schools of Oriental Research*, volumes 14, 15, 18–19, and 25–28 between 1934 and 1951. Our interest here is in Glueck's conclusions from his surveys pertaining to the Iron Age in southern Jordan; these conclusions have had a major influence for over half a century.

As background, it is important to note that Glueck held that during the Late Bronze Age (1550–1200 BCE) most of Jordan, especially south of Wadi Zarqa/Jabbok, was abandoned. At this time, he said, the population of Jordan was nomadic or seminomadic. During the thirteenth century BCE, however, Jordan began to be resettled. According to Glueck, these settlements reflected Ammonite, Moabite, Edomite, and Israelite cultures. Glueck used the Iron I (1200–918 BCE) archaeological evidence to reconstruct the growth of major kingdoms in the thirteenth century BCE. He viewed these kingdoms as continuing into Iron II (918–539 BCE). He emphasized, however, that most of the Iron II archaeological remains should be dated prior to 800 BCE in Moab and Edom and prior to the sixth century BCE in Ammon. He argued for a gap in settlement in Ammon, Moab, and Edom from the end of the Iron II period to the beginning of the Hellenistic and Nabataean periods, that is, until about 300 BCE. During the Iron Age (1200–539 BCE), according to Glueck, the kingdoms of Moab and Edom were well protected by a series of fortresses along their borders. On Edom specifically he wrote: "There was a highly developed Edomite civilization, which flourished especially between the thirteenth and the eighth centuries B.C. From the eighth century on there was a rapid disintegration of the power of Edom. . . . Their boundaries were well protected with a system of border fortresses in sight of each other" (1935:138–39).

Besides his surveys, Glueck excavated Tell el-Kheleifeh in the spring months of 1938–1940. He identified it with biblical Ezion-geber (Num. 33:35–36; Deut. 2:8; 1 Kgs. 9:26; 2 Chr. 8:17; 20:36) and assigned it to the period between the tenth and the fifth centuries BCE, beginning with the time of Solomon (Glueck 1970:109–10).

From the above it is easy to see how well the earliest biblical information on Edom, taken literally, and Glueck's findings agree, especially if one dates the Exodus and the "wanderings" to the thirteenth century BCE. (They do not suit so well a fifteenth-century BCE date for Israel's "wanderings.")

In the late 1960s and early 1970s Glueck revised somewhat his position on the archaeological histories of Ammon, Moab, and Edom in the light of new archaeological data (1970). These data, plus more recent information from archaeological excavations and surveys, outlined below, have led to further revisions in the archaeological history of Edom (Sauer 1985, 1986). Furthermore, Pratico's reassessment of Glueck's excavated material and reports from Tell el-Kheleifeh has led him to date the site from the eighth to the sixth centuries BCE, with some material dated to the fifth and early fourth centuries BCE (1985).

Over the past thirty years, several excavations and archaeological survey projects have been carried out in southern Jordan or in the region generally associated with the eastern segment of the territory of Edom. It is to this material that we now turn.

None of the excavated Iron Age sites—Tell el-Kheleifeh, Umm el-Biyara, Tawilan, Buseirah, Ghrareh, or Feifa (located east of Wadi Arabah and south of Wadi el-Hasa)—has yet been reported in final form. Furthermore, none appears to have a continuous Iron Age sequence (Bienkowski 1992b).

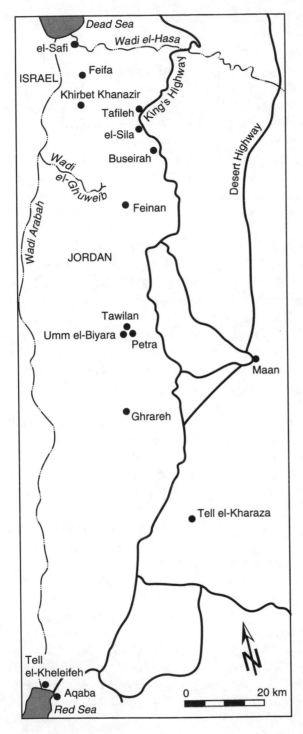

FIG. 14-1.
Sites east of the Wadi Arabah mentioned in the text.

Between 1960 and 1982, C. M. Bennett excavated three of them: Umm el-Biyara (in 1960, 1963, and 1965), Tawilan (in 1968–1970 and 1982), and Buseirah (in 1971–1974 and 1980). She dated none of these sites earlier than the Iron II period (1971, 1982; Bienkowski 1992b).

Umm el-Biyara is essentially a one-period site dating to the seventh century BCE. There is evidence for destruction and a reuse in the Hellenistic period. With the exception of possible Hellenistic sherds (Bennett 1966:382–83), the pottery throughout appears to be homogeneous Iron II (Bienkowski 1990:36; 1992b:99).

Tawilan was an unfortified town, essentially agricultural, with the major occupation in the seventh century BCE. In fact, all occupation at the site can be dated within Iron II, probably seventh–sixth centuries BCE. There is evidence of fire or destruction at the site (Bienkowski 1990:37–38; 1992b:99, 101). (The site is not biblical Teman [Jer. 49:7; Ezek. 25:13; Amos 1:12], which refers either to Edom, or to a particular region in Edom, rather than to a specific village/town.)

Buseirah's major buildings appear to date mainly to the seventh century BCE. Some of the later buildings may date to the Persian period (Bienkowski 1990:36; 1992b:101, 104). All phases at the site show evidence of destruction by fire (Bienkowski 1990:36). James Sauer points to some possible Iron I sherds in published reports from Buseirah (1986:10, 14). The site is generally identified with Bozrah (Isa. 34:6; 63:1; Jer. 48:24; 49:13, 22; Amos 1:12), the capital city of the Edomites.

S. Hart sounded Ghrareh in 1985 and excavated it in 1986. It is primarily a late Iron Age (seventh–sixth centuries BCE) site, most probably military in character. It is situated on an easily defended hilltop at the head of an important access route to Wadi Arabah. Strong defensive walls surround the site (Hart 1988).

Feifa, or at least its western segment, consists of an Iron II structure. There is not as yet a preliminary report on this site excavated by Rast and Schaub in 1989–1990 (but see Lapp, this volume). It appears, however, that the major architectural remains at the site are of a fortress from the Iron II period. This is particularly important for Iron Age presence in the area.

One further site, Khirbet Khanazir, deserves mention. Rast and Schaub also recently excavated (1989–1990) this site, which is a predominantly EB IV cemetery. The discovery in a later burial intrusive in an EB IV tomb of a scarab with hieroglyphic signs and a button seal with a carving of Anubis (the jackal-headed Egyptian god of embalming) on the flat side appears, on the basis of preliminary analyses, to indicate contacts with Egypt during the periods of Sethos I and Ramesses II (thirteenth–twelfth centuries BCE).

From the above summary of excavated Iron Age period sites south of Wadi el-Hasa, there is little evidence for sedentary occupation in eastern Edom prior to the Iron II period. Moreover, Pratico's reassessment of Glueck's work at Tell el-Kheleifeh does not support settlement at the site during the time of Solomon.

Several archaeological surveys have been carried out since the time of Glueck in the territory of eastern Edom: Manfred Weippert's 1974 survey, the Wadi el-Hasa Survey, the Edom Survey Project, the Southern Ghors and Northeast Arabah Survey, the Aqaba-Maan Archaeological and Epigraphic Survey, the Archaeometallurgical Explorations and Mining-Archaeological Studies in the Wadi Feinan region, and the Southern Jordan Survey. Several of these surveys produced evidence for occupation in the area prior to the Iron II period.

Weippert's 1974 survey reported no Late Bronze pottery, but he does list seven sites that yielded Iron I pottery in what is traditionally labeled as the Edomite "heartland." The majority of these sites are located in the north, that is, between Wadi el-Hasa and Tafileh (Weippert 1979:30; 1982:156–57). According to Weippert, there was an increase in settlement density throughout the Iron II period (1982:156).

The Wadi el-Hasa Archaeological Survey (WHS), along the south bank of the wadi, was in the field between 1979 and 1983 (MacDonald 1988, 1992a). The Late Bronze period is very poorly represented in the survey territory. However, there does appear to be the beginning of an increase in population at the very end of the period. This population increase continues during Iron I and reaches its greatest density during Iron II. There do appear to be permanent, albeit small, settlements along the south bank of Wadi el-Hasa by the twelfth century BCE, but only in the western portion. Even during Iron II, Wadi el-Ali seems to be the eastern frontier for sedentary occupation.

Hart carried out a survey in 1984 on the Edomite plateau (Hart and Falkner 1985) and in 1985 conducted soundings at five sites: Khirbet Qurein North, Ghrareh, Khirbet el-Megheitah, Khirbet Ishra, and Khirbet Ain Jenin (Hart 1987). He excavated Ghrareh, mentioned above, in 1986 (1988). One objective of the soundings and excavations was to show the continuity (or its lack) between the civilization of the Edomites and that of the Nabataeans. Hart concluded that in the historic periods the plateau was settled in any concentration in only two periods, the seventh–sixth centuries BCE (by the Edomites) and the first century CE (by the Nabataeans). He suggests that in the seventh century BCE organization was imposed by the Assyrians as part of a greater defensive plan against the desert tribes. The decline in settlement at the end of the sixth century BCE may be due, he thinks, to the same factor, namely, the desert tribes who had succeeded in becoming more effective.

The Southern Ghors and Northeast Arabah Archaeological Survey (SGNAS), in the southeast plain of the Dead Sea and in the northeast Arabah, was in the field in 1985 and 1986 (MacDonald 1992a, 1992b). It identified no Middle or Late Bronze period sites. The only exception to this is the possibility of MB I sherds at one site. Thus, the area seems to have been largely depopulated during these periods. The situation changes at the beginning of the Iron Age. The SGNAS found Iron I period sherds in the area as far north as Wadi el-Hasa and as far south as Wadi el-Ghuweib; it is in the latter wadi that the SGNAS surveyed the highest concentration of Iron I sites. Iron I period presence appears to be associated in this wadi with mining and smelting activities. Possibly there were several fortresses and/or watchtowers in the Southern Ghors during the Iron II period (see above on Feifa, for example). Moreover, there are indications of increased activity at the mining and smelting sites in the survey territory during this period. Natural resources, such as copper-manganese ores, were probably extensively exploited during the entire Iron Age period.

W. J. Jobling's extensive archaeological and epigraphic survey between Aqaba and Maan over the past ten years reported occupational evidence from several periods. Of interest here is the report of Iron Age sherds from his 1982 trial trench at Tell el-Kharaza, a rock shelter. This period was attested by surface sherds in the area around the rock shelter (Jobling 1983:189).

Andreas Hauptmann and his colleagues have examined, over the past decade, the mining and smelting sites of the eastern side of the Wadi Arabah, especially in the Wadi Feinan region, and attempted to date them more closely, paying particular attention to the ancient technology. They report pottery from the Late Bronze, Iron I, and Iron IIC, as well as from later periods, from the sites they investigated in the Wadi Feinan area (1985). Recent charcoal samples from houses at Khirbet el-Nahas, a smelting site in Wadi el-Ghuweib, have been radiocarbon-dated to 1200–950 BCE calibrated (Bienkowski 1992b:110, n. 1).

For more than two decades, Manfred Lindner has carried out explorations in southern Jordan, especially in the region of Petra. His work included a reexamination of el-Sila, an Edomite stronghold to the northwest of Buseirah; explorations in the area of Petra; Ba°ja III, an Edomite mountain stronghold north of Petra dating to the eighth–seventh centuries BCE, and el-Sadeh, an Edomite-Nabataean site southeast of Petra. With the possible exception of el-Sila, Lindner reports no Iron I pottery (1992).

P. Bienkowski rightly points out that evidence from these surveys for Iron I period presence in Edom is sparse. The material is ambiguous and not diagnostic, and could range from Late Bronze Age to Iron II, although there does appear to be some earlier Iron Age material (Bienkowski 1992a:6). Because of the nature of the work, none of the material claimed as Iron I was found in a stratified sequence. Thus, although there is no difficulty in positing Iron II presence in Edom, Iron I period presence is more elusive.

CONCLUSIONS

The Egyptian literary evidence indicates human presence in Edom in the thirteenth–twelfth centuries BCE. This presence consisted of at least a pastoral lifestyle. There is, moreover, evidence of intermittent relations between Egypt and Edom from the thirteenth through the tenth centuries BCE. One of the difficulties with this Egyptian literary evidence is that there is no indication as to whether it refers to west or east of Wadi Arabah, or both.

Both excavations and archaeological surveys south of Wadi el-Hasa support the position of a sedentary population in the area east of Wadi Arabah during the Iron II period. However, no firmly dated, excavated material from the Iron I period has been found. Iron I presence in the area is attested by archaeological survey work but only in the northern segment of the traditional, eastern Edomite territory. There is even less evidence for Late Bronze occupation of the area. As Israel Finkelstein and A. Perevolotsky (1990:67–69) point out, however, pastoralists leave little in the way of recoverable, archaeological remains.

The archaeological evidence on eastern Edom causes us to question the biblical texts on Edom/Edomites. It provides little support for a major Edomite presence in the area at the end of the Late Bronze and the beginning of the Iron Age. There is even less support for human presence in the area at the beginning of the Late Bronze period. There could have been local or regional "chiefs" but hardly "kings" in the area at the time under discussion. It is hard to envisage, on the basis of the present archaeological evidence, a strong fighting force in Edom that would have deterred a large group from passing—and forced the group to detour around—their territory. A large population in the territory would have been necessary to account for the numbers killed by David and/or Joab. Such evidence is not yet available. Moreover, archaeological evidence has not as yet brought to light firm support for a Solomonic sea port on the Red Sea.

In summary, archaeology can help place the Bible in the real world, that is, in its historical and cultural milieu. In addition, archaeology can help the scholar formulate questions to ask of the literary evidence, in our case of the Egyptian and biblical evidence that purport to refer to the thirteenth–tenth centuries BCE.

WORKS CITED

Bartlett, J. R.
1989   *Edom and the Edomites*. Sheffield: JSOT Press.
1992   Biblical Sources for the Early Iron Age in Edom. In *Early Edom and Moab: The Beginning of the Iron Age in Southern Jordan*, ed. P. Bienkowski, 13–19. Sheffield Archaeological Monographs, 7. Sheffield: J. R. Collis in association with National Museums and Galleries on Merseyside.

Bennett, C. M.
1966   Fouilles d'Umm El-Biyara: Rapport Préliminaire. *Revue biblique* 73:372–403.
1971   An Archaeological Survey of Biblical Edom. *Perspective* 12, no. 1/2:35–44.
1982   Neo-Assyrian Influence in Transjordan. In *Studies in the History and Archaeology of Jordan*, *I*, ed. A. Hadidi, 181–87. Amman: Department of Antiquities.

Bienkowski, P.
1990   The Chronology of Tawilan and the "Dark Age" of Edom. *ARAM* 2, no.1/2:35–44.
1992a   The Beginning of the Iron Age in Southern Jordan: A Framework. In *Early Edom and Moab: The Beginning of the Iron Age in Southern Jordan*, ed. P. Bienkowski, 1–12. Sheffield Archaeological Monographs, 7. Sheffield: J. R. Collis in association with National Museums and Galleries on Merseyside.
1992b   The Date of Sedentary Occupation in Edom: Evidence from Umm el-Biyara, Tawilan, and Buseirah. In *Early Edom and Moab:*

The Beginning of the Iron Age in Southern Jordan, ed. P. Bienkowski, 99–112. Sheffield Archaeological Monographs, 7. Sheffield: J. R. Collis in association with National Museums and Galleries on Merseyside.

Finkelstein, I., and A. Perevolotsky

1990   Process of Sedentarization and Nomadization in the History of the Sinai and the Negev. *Bulletin of the American Schools of Oriental Research* 279:67–88.

Freedman, D. N.

1975   Early Israelite History in the Light of Early Israelite Poetry. In *Unity and Diversity: Essays in the History, Literature, and Religion of the Ancient Near East*, ed. H. Goedicke and J. J. M. Roberts, 3–35. Baltimore: Johns Hopkins University Press.

1976   Divine Names and Titles in Early Hebrew Poetry. In *Magnalia Dei: The Mighty Acts of God*, ed. F. M. Cross, W. E. Lemke, and P. D. Miller, 77–80. Garden City, N.Y.: Doubleday.

1979   Early Israelite Poetry and Historical Reconstructions. In *Symposia Celebrating the Seventy-fifth Anniversary of the Founding of the American Schools of Oriental Research (1900–1975)*, ed. F. M. Cross, 85–96. Cambridge, Mass.: American Schools of Oriental Research.

1987   "Who Is Like Thee among the Gods?" The Religion of Early Israel. In *Ancient Israelite Religion: Essays in Honor of Frank Moore Cross*, ed. P. D. Miller, Jr., P. D. Hanson, and S. D. McBride, 315–35. Philadelphia: Fortress.

Glueck, N.

1935   *Explorations in Eastern Palestine, II*. Annual of the American Schools of Oriental Research 15. New Haven, Conn.: American Schools of Oriental Research.

1970   *The Other Side of the Jordan*. Rev. ed. Cambridge, Mass.: American Schools of Oriental Research.

Hart, S.

1987   Five Soundings in Southern Jordan. *Levant* 19:33–47.

Hart, S., and R. K. Falkner

1985   Preliminary Report on a Survey in Edom, 1984. *Annual of the Department of Antiquities of Jordan* 29:255–77.

1988   Excavations at Ghrareh, 1986: Preliminary Report. *Levant* 20:89–99.

1992   Iron Age Settlement in the Land of Edom. In *Early Edom and Moab: The Beginning of the Iron Age in Southern Jordan*, ed. P. Bienkowski, 93–98. Sheffield Archaeological Monographs, 7. Sheffield: J. R. Collis in association with National Museums and Galleries on Merseyside.

Hauptmann, A.; G. Weisgerber; and A. Knauf

1985   Archaeometallurgische und bergbauarchäologische Untersuchungen im Gebiet von Fenan, Wadi Arabah (Jordanien). *Der Anschnitt* 37:163–95.

Jobling, W. J.
1983   The 1982 Archaeological and Epigraphic Survey of the ᶜAqaba-
               Maᶜan Area of Southern Jordan. *Annual of the Department of
               Antiquities of Jordan* 27:185–96.
Kitchen, K. A.
1992   The Egyptian Evidence on Ancient Jordan. In *Early Edom and
               Moab: The Beginning of the Iron Age in Southern Jordan*, ed. P.
               Bienkowski, 21–34. Sheffield Archaeological Monographs, 7. Shef-
               field: J. R. Collis in association with National Museums and Gal-
               leries on Merseyside.
Knauf, E. A.
1985   Alter und Herkunft der edomitischen Königsliste Gen. 36:31–39.
               Zeitschrift für die alttestamentliche Wissenschaft 97:245–53.
Lindner, M.
1992   Edom outside the Famous Excavations: Evidence from Surveys in
               the Greater Petra Area. In *Early Edom and Moab: The Beginning of
               the Iron Age in Southern Jordan*, ed. P. Bienkowski, 143–66. Shef-
               field Archaeological Monographs, 7. Sheffield: J. R. Collis in asso-
               ciation with National Museums and Galleries on Merseyside.
MacDonald, B.
1988   *The Wadi el Ḥasā Archaeological Survey, 1979–1983, West-Central
               Jordan*. Waterloo, Ont.: Wilfrid Laurier University Press.
1992a   Evidence from the Wadi al-Hasa and Southern Ghors and North-
               east Arabah Archaeological Surveys. In *Early Edom and Moab: The
               Beginning of the Iron Age in Southern Jordan*, ed. P. Bienkowski,
               113–42. Sheffield Archaeological Monographs, 7. Sheffield: J. R.
               Collis in association with National Museums and Galleries on
               Merseyside.
1992b   *The Southern Ghors and Northeast ᶜArabah Archaeological Survey*.
               Sheffield Archaeological Monographs, 5. Sheffield: J. R. Collis.
Miller, J. M.
1989   The Israelite Journey through (around) Moab and Moabite
               Toponymy. *Journal of Biblical Literature* 108:577–95.
Pratico, G. D.
1985   Nelson Glueck's 1938–1940 Excavations at Tell el-Kheleifeh: A
               Reappraisal. *Bulletin of the American Schools of Oriental Research*
               259:1–32.
Rad, G. von
1972   *Genesis: A Commentary*. Rev. ed. Philadelphia: Westminster.
Sauer, J. A.
1985   Ammon, Moab, and Edom. In *Biblical Archaeology Today: Proceed-
               ings of the International Congress on Biblical Archaeology, Jerusalem,
               April 1984*, 206–14. Jerusalem: Israel Exploration Society.
1986   Transjordan in the Bronze and Iron Ages: A Critique of Glueck's
               Synthesis. *Bulletin of the American Schools of Oriental Research*
               263:1–26.

Ward, W. A.
1992   Shasu. In *The Anchor Bible Dictionary*, ed. D. N. Freedman, 5:1165–67. New York: Doubleday.

Weippert, M.
1979   The Israelite "Conquest" and the Evidence from Transjordan. In *Symposia Celebrating the Seventy-fifth Anniversary of the Founding of the American Schools of Oriental Research (1900–1975)*, ed. F. M. Cross, 15–34. Cambridge, Mass.: American Schools of Oriental Research.
1982   Remarks on the History of Settlement in Southern Jordan during the Early Iron Age. In *Studies in the History and Archaeology of Jordan*, I, ed. A. Hadidi, 153–62. Amman: Department of Antiquities.

Wilson. J. A.
1969   Egyptian Historical Texts. In *Ancient Near Eastern Texts Relating to the Old Testament*, ed. J. B. Pritchard, 229–64. 3d ed. with Supplement. Princeton, N.J.: Princeton University Press.

15 | The Northern Shephelah in the Iron Age: Some Issues in Biblical History and Archaeology

AMIHAI MAZAR

The Sorek Valley in the northern Shephelah of Israel and its environs have been the subject of intensive archaeological research in recent years (fig. 15-1). Twelve seasons of excavations at Tel Batash (biblical Timnah) between 1977 and 1989,[1] continuous work at Tel Miqne (biblical Ekron) since 1981, the excavations at Gezer and Beth-shemesh, and surveys of the valley have made this region one of the most intensively explored in the country (figs. 15-2, 15-3).[2] In this chapter, I shall discuss several issues in the biblical history and historical geography of this region in the light of archaeological research, with emphasis on the sites of Timnah and Ekron. Some of these issues have already been addressed in the preliminary reports on the excavations at Timnah and Ekron (Kelm and Mazar 1982, 1985, 1989, 1990; T. Dothan 1989; Gitin 1989), though from a different perspective.

THE IDENTIFICATION OF EKRON AND TIMNAH

The most important source for the identification of Tel Miqne (Khirbet el-Muqanna) with Ekron and Tel Batash with Timnah is the description of the northern border of Judah (Josh. 15:10–11). After it leaves the Judean Hills, the border in the Shephelah is described as follows: "[The boundary] goes down to Beth-shemesh, and passes along by Timnah; the boundary goes out to the shoulder of the hill north of Ekron" (RSV). Accordingly, Timnah should be located between Beth-shemesh and Ekron. In earlier studies, Ekron was identified with Qatra or even with Tel Batash (for references and discussion, see Kelm and Mazar 1982:2). In

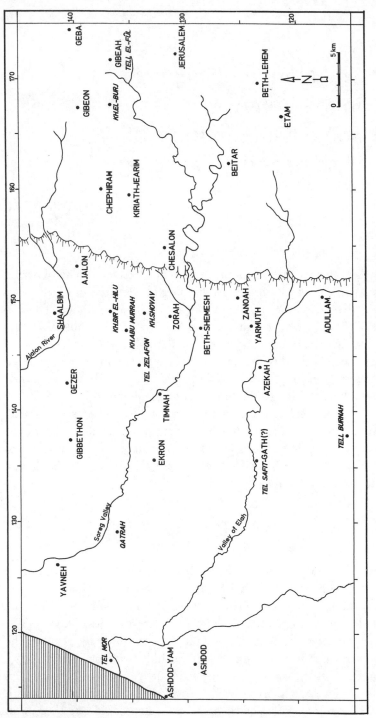

FIG. 15-1. Map of the northern Shephelah.

FIG. 15-2. Aerial view of the Sorek Valley, with Tel Batash at the center.

1957 Joseph Naveh described the lower city of Tel Miqne and suggested identifying this large site with Ekron (Naveh 1958). This resulted in the almost certain identification of Timnah with Tel Batash, since the latter is the only significant mound between Beth-shemesh and Ekron. These new identifications have been generally accepted (Aharoni 1958; 1979:256; B. Mazar 1960:66; Kallai 1958:145–46; Gitin 1989:24, 52, n. 4). As will be shown below, the identifications are supported by additional biblical sources and accord well with the archaeological discoveries at both Tel Miqne and Tel Batash.

THE IRON AGE I PERIOD

Extensive Iron Age I occupation levels have been found at all the major sites of the region (Ekron, Timnah, Beth-shemesh, and Gezer). All were urban centers, with several occupation phases related to this period, though Ekron differs considerably from the other sites. At Ekron, the Philistine city (Strata VII–V) grew from a modest Late Bronze town of about 4 ha (10 acres) to a huge city of about 20 ha (50 acres) (T. Dothan 1989; Dothan and Dothan 1992:239–52). This happened during the first part of the twelfth century BCE (Stratum VII). The pottery of this phase consists of forms made in the local Canaanite tradition, accompanied by the local decorated monochrome pottery, which is similar to the Mycenaean IIIC style known from the Aegean and Cyprus. Other Aegean elements of material culture at Ekron are domestic pottery (lakine kraters and cooking pots) and Aegean-type loom weights (T. Dothan 1989:6). It is evident that the sudden increase in population and the appearance of almost pure Aegean components of material culture are related to the foundation of the Philistine city-state of Ekron by immigrants of Aegean origin. In a later phase, the Philistines developed their bichrome ceramic

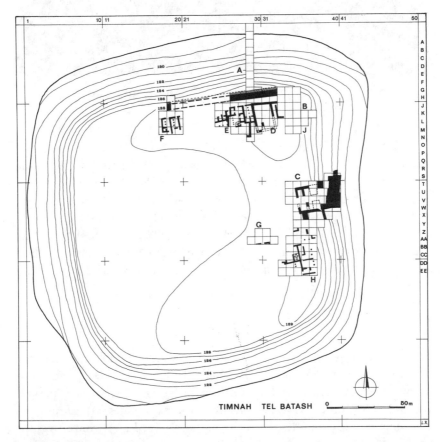

FIG. 15-3. Topographic map of Timnah (Tel Batash) with building remains of Stratum II (seventh century BCE). Letters designate excavation fields.

style, which appears at Ekron in Strata VI and V of the late twelfth and eleventh centuries BCE. During this period Ekron was a large city of about 20 ha (50 acres), surrounded by a city wall and containing elaborate buildings like that discovered in Field IV.

In contrast to Ekron, the other sites of the northern Shephelah lack the earliest phase of Philistine occupation (that marked by the appearance of locally produced "Mycenaean IIIC" pottery). The Iron Age I levels at these sites (Tel Batash Stratum V, Tel Beth-shemesh Stratum III, and Gezer Strata XIII–XI) contain a pottery assemblage similar to that of Ekron Strata VI–V: local Iron Age I pottery that developed from the Late Bronze Age Canaanite tradition, mixed with a certain amount of Philistine bichrome ware. All these occupation levels thus started during or after the last third of the twelfth century BCE, when Philistine bichrome ware was already in use, and the Philistines had started to expand their territory toward the east and north.

In spite of the identity of the material culture at these three sites, however, the ethnic character of their populations may have differed. Gezer is likely to have remained Canaanite for most of the period. The Philistine pottery there, about 5 percent of the assemblage, may point to trade and exchange with nearby Philistine territory (Dever 1986:87). The "Amorites" who forced the Danites into the hill country (Judg. 1:34) may have been the inhabitants of Gezer and its territory.

At Timnah, which is much closer to Ekron, the Philistine pottery in Stratum V constitutes a larger proportion of the assemblage than at Gezer (though exact figures are as yet unavailable). These data, combined with the Samson stories, which describe Timnah as a Philistine town, lead to the conclusion that in the Iron Age I Timnah was a "daughter" settlement of Ekron and was thus settled to a large extent by Philistines.[3] Though only a small area of the town has been excavated, the investigations yielded evidence of a city wall and well-built mud-brick houses, surrounded by courtyards that underwent several building phases.

The case of Beth-shemesh is more difficult to interpret. Though not mentioned in the Samson stories, Beth-shemesh is located very near to Zorah (Sarᶜah, on a ridge about 7 km east of Tel Batash), where Samson was born. The similarity between its material culture and that of Timnah inevitably leads to speculation about the identity of its inhabitants. If they were Danites, this would throw an interesting light on Yigael Yadin's suggestion that the tribe of Dan was related to the Dnn (Danuna) Sea Peoples, who eventually joined the Israelite confederacy (Yadin 1968; for a critical evaluation of this suggestion, see de Vaux 1978:780–83; on Dan, see also Spina 1977). If this suggestion is valid, then the Samson stories reflect conflict between two units of Sea Peoples, related to each other by origin and traditions. Indeed, the similarities between motifs in the Samson stories and those in early Greek legends, such as the Heracles stories, have often been cited (Licht 1982; Gordon 1971:58). Samson's marriage to a Philistine woman also hints at a close relationship between the Danites and the Philistines. It should further be recalled that in Judges 1:34 the Danites are described as being oppressed by the Amorites, and not by the Philistines, with whom they might have had peaceful relations. Such a background may explain why the material culture at Beth-shemesh Stratum III does not differ from that of Timnah, while both differ from the Israelite material culture known in the hill country. It must be remembered, however, that in the story of the return of the ark from Ekron through the Sorek Valley (1 Sam. 6) Beth-shemesh is described as an Israelite town. The Israelite historiographer thus considered the region of Beth-shemesh Israelite, and Dan was reckoned an Israelite tribe.

The main biblical source concerning this period is the Samson stories, "anecdotes with the character of sagas" (Eissfeldt 1975:558). As such, they have been treated as literary creations with no historical significance (see Licht 1982), yet it is likely that these stories retain kernels of historical reality. A chronological problem exists here, as Dan is mentioned in the Song of Deborah as one of the northern tribes (Judg. 5:17). This would date the immigration of Dan to the north to a time before the battle of Deborah, which is considered by many scholars to belong to an early phase of the period of the judges. If Samson lived before the migration of Dan to the north (Eissfeldt 1975:559), it would be before the Philistines were an important factor in the Shephelah, and probably before the foundation of Philistine Timnah in the late twelfth century BCE. This problem can be solved by claiming that the tribe of Dan mentioned in the Samson stories was only a remnant of the original tribe, left in the Beth-shemesh region after the immigration to the north of the tribe's main body (Licht 1982:196; Na'aman 1986a:116).

The absence of any mention of Ekron in the Samson stories needs explanation, especially as Ashdod, Ashkelon, and Gaza are mentioned. After all, Ekron was the main Philistine city in the Sorek Valley area and it probably controlled the western part of the valley, including Timnah. Indeed, in 1 Samuel 6 it is described as the main Philistine city in the region. It is difficult to explain this absence, unless one claims that the stories were written or edited at a time when Ekron was in decline, such as the period between the mid–tenth and the eighth centuries BCE, when the city's area and population shrank (Gitin 1989:24–26; see Kallai 1986:23 for a different, untenable solution).

THE PERIOD OF
THE UNITED MONARCHY

Stratum IV at Timnah represents a rebuilding of the town after the destruction (or abandonment?) of the Philistine city of Stratum V. The material culture of this new town differs from its predecessor in many aspects. It is characterized by red-slipped and hand-burnished pottery, belonging to a new ceramic tradition known throughout Israelite territory during the time of David and Solomon, particularly in the Shephelah and the coastal plain.[4] This pottery correlates Timnah Stratum IV with Tell Beit Mirsim Stratum B3, Beth-shemesh Stratum IIA, Gezer Stratum VIII, Lachish Stratum V, and Tell Qasile Strata IX–VIII. All these appear to be Israelite towns of the united monarchy, when the Israelite kings ruled the entire Shephelah and the coast north of Jaffa.

At Timnah Stratum IV, modest dwellings with large open spaces between them were found in all the excavation areas. The town was probably defended by the outer walls of houses constructed along the perimeter of the mound, and there was no real city wall. The entrance to the town was, however, probably through a gate with an L-shaped facade and two solid towers. Similar traits indicating the slow growth of urban life can be observed at many tenth-century BCE Israelite sites such as those mentioned above, as well as Tel Beer-sheba Strata VII–VI (V?) and northern sites like Megiddo VB and IVB-VA and Hazor Stratum X.

In contrast to the above-mentioned sites, the excavations at Ekron show that sometime in the early or mid–tenth century the large lower city was abandoned and the city shrank from an area of about 20 ha (50 acres) to a mere 3 to 4 ha (7 to 10 acres) (Gitin 1989:25). Stratum IV, which marks the last phase of the lower city before the gap in its occupation, contained pottery with dull red slip, mostly unburnished, while Philistine bichrome ware appears to have gone out of use in this phase. A date of about 1000 BCE, perhaps also covering the time of David (?), is acceptable for this stratum (T. Dothan 1989:9–11). Only in the seventh century BCE did Ekron return to its original size. This phenomenon, though difficult to explain, may have been the result of two factors: the rise of the Israelite kingdom of David and Solomon, which may have caused tensions in the border zone and adversely affected Ekron's economy (Gitin 1989:41), and, less plausibly in my opinion, the presumed Egyptian campaign in Siamun's reign, which resulted in the conquest of Gezer and its presentation to Solomon as a dowry gift (1 Kgs. 9:16). Kenneth Kitchen (1973:280–81) dates Siamun's assumed raid on Philistia and the conquest of Gezer to the beginning of Solomon's reign, about 970-960 BCE.

In contrast to Ekron, Ashdod grew from 8 to 20 ha (20 to 50 acres) during the tenth century BCE (M. Dothan 1975:90, 112). Moshe Dothan dated the beginning of the growth of the city to the mid–eleventh century BCE. This is based on the Philistine bichrome ware found in pits in Area M (local Stratum 11, general Stratum XB), though the finds from this period are very scarce. The actual growth of the city occurred when the fortifications of Stratum XA were constructed. This stratum was dated by Dothan to the first half of the tenth century BCE and its destruction was attributed to Siamun (Dothan and Porath 1982:52–56). The pottery from this stratum (pp. 115–19) can be dated to the entire tenth century BCE, however; it can thus be argued that Ashdod grew at the expense of Ekron, and that Israelite oppression caused many of Ekron's inhabitants to move to Ashdod, a process that resulted in the decline of Ekron and the growth of Ashdod.

Three geographical sources in the Bible concern this period: the list of Solomon's districts (1 Kings 4), the city list of Dan (Josh. 19:40–46), and the description of the northern border of Judah mentioned above. These sources and the relationships between them have been widely discussed in the past (see most recently Aharoni 1979:298–301, 309–20; Kallai 1986:40–71, 118–24, 361–71; Na'aman 1986a:75–117), so only a few comments on details related to the results of archaeological work in this region will be presented below.

A short inscription found at Tel Batash Stratum IV was incised on a bowl rim before firing. It reads: . . . *n ḥnn* and can be reconstructed: "(be)n Hanan = (belonging to)[the so]n of Hanan." A vertical divider separates the first *nun* from the name *ḥnn*. The letters can be assigned to the tenth century BCE, and are similar to those on the Gezer Calendar (Kelm and Mazar 1990:56). This inscription is one of a very small group of securely dated tenth-century BCE alphabetic inscriptions from Israel. Interestingly, the name Hanan appears as a component in the place name Elon-beth-hanan in Solomon's second district, which also includes the cities Makaz, Shaalbim, and Beth-shemesh (1 Kgs. 4:9). Makaz could be a

town in the region and is perhaps to be identified with one of the prominent sites in the vicinity of the valley of Aijalon, such as Khirbet Abu
Murrah (Hurvat Avimor), a prominent mound with tenth-century BCE
pottery, on a ridge between the valleys of Aijalon and Sorek.[5] Nadov
Na'aman (1986a:114–15) has suggested that the composite name Elon-
beth-hanan should be divided into two different names: Elon and Beth-
hanan. This suggestion leaves us with only four names that mark the four
most distant points of the district: Aijalon (east), Beth-shemesh (south),
Shaalbim (north), and Beth-hanan (west). "Elon," however, is mentioned
separately from Aijalon in the city list of Dan (Josh. 19:43), so there is no
reason to identify the two (as suggested by Na'aman), and they should be
considered two different towns. Elon, which appears before Timnah and
Ekron in Joshua 19:43, can thus be identified with Elon-beth-hanan in
1 Kings 10. The name "Hanan" in our inscription might thus be related
to a family of that name who dwelt in the region of Elon and Timnah
during the tenth century BCE; the name also occurs in the Beth-shemesh
ostracon of around 1200 BCE (Cross 1967:17*–18*). Elon-beth-hanan
might be one of the Iron Age sites discovered in the survey of the Sorek
Valley between Beth-shemesh and Timnah, such as the site at Khirbet
Hasan (map reference 1463/1344) or Tel Selafon (map reference 1443/
1342).

Israel controlled the entire territory covered by the city list of Dan
(Josh. 19:40–46) only during the united monarchy and perhaps the time
of Josiah. Most scholars date the list to the united monarchy and presume
that it reflects David's conquests in this region, which was previously
ruled by the Philistines and the "Amorites" (B. Mazar 1960:65–77; revised
in B. Mazar 1986:104–12; Kallai 1958:144–48; 1960:27–28; Aharoni
1976:7; 1979:298–99; de Vaux 1978:777; Na'aman 1986a:75–79, 107–17).
Only a few scholars would date the list to the reign of Josiah (Whitelam
1992:11).

The relationship between this list and Solomon's second district mentioned in 1 Kings 4:9 has been pointed out by several scholars. While
Benjamin Mazar suggested that Solomon's second district corresponded
only to the eastern part of the allotment of Dan, namely the eastern
Sorek Valley and the valley of Aijalon (B. Mazar 1960), Aharoni, Kallai,
and Na'aman suggested that the district covered the entire allotment of
Dan (Wright 1967:64*–65*; Aharoni 1976:6–10; Kallai 1986:49; Na'aman
1986a:114–16). In the city list of Dan, Timnah is mentioned in the form
Timnatah (Josh. 19:43) and appears between Elon and Ekron, after the

more easterly cities of Zorah, Eshtaol, Beth-shemesh, Shaalbim, and Yitlah. The appearance of Ekron in this list is problematic, since it was never conquered by Israel. I am inclined to accept Aharoni's suggestion that the original text read: "Timnath Ekron," in order to distinguish it from other towns named Timnah (Aharoni 1979:299); the affiliation originated, in his opinion, at the time of David, shortly after Timnah ceased to be a Philistine town of the kingdom of Ekron. This would agree with current archaeological research at Ekron, which shows that it lost much of its power during the tenth century BCE.

Shishak's invasion early in the reign of Rehoboam probably caused considerable destruction in this region as he passed on his way from the coastal plain to the hill country through Rubute, Aijalon, Beth-horon, K-r-t-m (Kirjath-jearim?), and Gibeon. No city in the region of the Sorek Valley is mentioned, however, in Shishak's list of conquered cities at Karnak, and even the mention of Gezer is disputed (Kitchen 1973:432–47 against Aharoni 1979:325–26; B. Mazar 1986). But we may assume that the destruction of Timnah Stratum IV and perhaps Beth-shemesh Stratum IIa occurred during this invasion.

THE EIGHTH CENTURY BCE

The border between Judah and Philistia during the period of the divided monarchy underwent several fluctuations. Rehoboam's westernmost fortified towns were Azekah, Adullam, Zorah, and Aijalon, located in the eastern Shephelah (2 Chr. 11:3–11). This list, however, probably does not mark the external border of the kingdom, which might have been slightly further west (see for example the map in Kallai 1971:253, which places Timnah within the border of Rehoboam's kingdom).

Timnah Stratum III inaugurates a new era in the history of the city: a massive fortification system was constructed, including a monumental gate (fig. 15-4), public buildings, and a large piazza next to the gate. This building campaign followed an occupational gap that lasted from the destruction of Stratum IV (by Shishak?) until the eighth century BCE.

Two verses in 2 Chronicles (26:6 and 28:18) are relevant to the fate of this region in the eighth century BCE. Since the reliability of the books of Chronicles for historical reconstruction is disputed, each event has to be checked against archaeological or other relevant sources (Na'aman 1991:24, n. 23 for appropriate literature). Second Chronicles 26:6 relates that Uzziah broke down the city walls of Gath, Jabneh, and Ashdod and

FIG. 15-4. Timnah, general view of the city gate of the Iron Age II period. On right, the outer gate; left, the inner gate.

that he "built cities in the territory of Ashdod and elsewhere among the Philistines." This description appears to be exaggerated, yet even so it may provide evidence of some territorial expansion of Judah during Uzziah's reign. Such an expansion probably enabled Judah to annex the region of the lower Sorek Valley, and permitted the building of Timnah as a fortified city on the western border of Judah. This may have been possible thanks to the weakness of Ekron between the mid-tenth and the early seventh centuries BCE (Gitin 1989:41, following Aharoni 1979:345, even suggests that Uzziah controlled Ekron; this is less plausible). The building techniques and plans of structures at Timnah Stratum III also support its identification as a Judahite town and stronghold.

Second Chronicles 28:18 records that during the reign of Ahaz the Philistines took the towns Beth-shemesh, Aijalon, Gederoth, Sochoh, Timnah, and Gimzo from Judah, and settled them. It is not clear which group of Philistines carried out this extensive conquest: Ekron was still a relatively small city, as shown by the archaeological investigations. This military campaign may have been carried out by a united force of Philistines who came from Ashdod and perhaps Ashkelon. The only archaeological indication for the historical validity of this source comes from Timnah. Here the pottery found in the destruction layer of Stratum III, which was destroyed by Sennacherib, is to a large extent coastal in type. This ceramic repertoire differs considerably from that of Judah and is probably similar to that of Ekron (though the eighth-century pottery of Ekron is as yet unknown in detail). Three molds for producing nude female figurines found in this stratum (Kelm and Mazar 1990:62–63) are also foreign to Judah and are related to coastal or Phoenician traditions. It thus appears that, in the time between the reign of Ahaz and 701 BCE, Timnah was inhabited by Philistines, as the book of Chronicles records.

Accepting 2 Chronicles 28:18 as a reliable source, Kallai used it as a major argument in favor of dating the town list of Judah (Josh. 15:21–62) to the reign of Hezekiah; according to his argument, Timnah and Beth-shemesh were not mentioned in the list of Judahite cities because they were under Philistine control at the time (Kallai 1986:374). But the date of the city list of Judah is disputed; a date in Josiah's reign appears to be more plausible (for a recent treatment, earlier literature, and support for the latter date, see Na'aman 1991:13–33).

The invasion of Judah by Sennacherib during Hezekiah's reign was a major event in the history of the region. It started with the occupation of the territories of Ashkelon in the Yarkon region and a clash with Egyptian troops at Eltekeh. Sennacherib then moved against Ekron, which was under Hezekiah's control. The conquest of Timnah preceded the capture of Ekron. The annals report: "I besieged Eltekeh [and] Timnah [*Ta-am-na-a*], conquered [them] and carried their spoils away. I assaulted Ekron . . ." (Oppenheim 1969:288). The mention of the conquest of Timnah in the context of the war against Ekron emphasizes the relationship between the two.

At Timnah, direct evidence of this confrontation has been found (Kelm and Mazar 1985:104–5). In the northeastern corner of the town, close to the city wall, we discovered a spacious building that may have served as a storehouse or barracks. One storage area in this building contained about thirty jars of the *lmlk* type. Several jar handles were stamped with the royal seal impression (though most of the handles were not sealed). As at Lachish Stratum III, both four-winged and two-winged symbols were found in the same context (see Ussishkin 1977). One handle was marked with the seal of an official: Zaphan (son of) Abimaaz (*spn 'bym's*), whose seal impressions have also been found at Jerusalem and Azekah. The context at Timnah enables us to examine several aspects of the use of *lmlk* jars, such as the proportion between stamped and unstamped handles. Only a few of the handles in this assemblage were stamped; the others remained unstamped, and only one stamp of an official was found in the entire assemblage. Such groups of jars were probably produced, sealed, and used in the framework of Hezekiah's preparations for the war against Sennacherib (A. Mazar 1981:47; Na'aman 1979, 1986b). They probably contained food for the troops and are thus found mainly in the northern Shephelah and in the Jerusalem area, where the war against Sennacherib took place. Fragments of several dozen clay scoops found in this building probably indicate activities like filling and emptying baskets or sacks containing wheat or the like (Gitin 1993).

The storeroom at Timnah may thus have been part of a barrack used by Hezekiah's troops in 701 BCE. But while at other Judahite sites *lmlk* jars appear as part of a Judahite cultural assemblage, at Timnah Stratum III most of the pottery found in other parts of the town is typical of the coastal plain, and only a minority of the pottery is Judahite in type. The finds from Stratum III thus show an interesting combination of cultural traits. The town's initial construction and the design of the fortifications may have been Judahite; from the reign of Ahaz onward, the town was occupied by Philistines who brought with them their own pottery and other components of material culture. Shortly before the war against Sennacherib, Hezekiah, who forced Ekron to join him, sent troops to Timnah. These soldiers probably brought with them *lmlk*-type jars containing their rations. The Judahite garrison stayed at Timnah for only a short time before and during 701 BCE, while the population of the city did not change.

The conquest of Timnah by Sennacherib led to the destruction of many buildings, such as the inner gate, the public complex south of the gate, and the *lmlk* jars building. Yet most of the city wall and the monumental outer gate were probably not destroyed, and they continued to be used when the town was rebuilt during the seventh century BCE.

The impact of Sennacherib's invasion at Ekron is not yet known. From the Assyrian documents one learns that the city was captured without violent battle, so a destruction level should not be expected. Bethshemesh, however, like many other Judahite cities in the Shephelah, was probably destroyed by Sennacherib and remained unsettled during the seventh century, since no seventh-century layer was found there. The fate of Gezer during this period is not clear: as part of the Northern Kingdom of Israel, it was conquered by the Assyrians together with the rest of the kingdom. Yet a considerable number of *lmlk* seal impressions were found there, and complete jars (though with no seal impressions) were found in Stratum VI of the Hebrew Union College excavations (Gitin 1990: pls. 15:11, 16:2). This level should thus be dated to the end of the eighth century BCE and first half of the seventh century BCE rather than before the Assyrian conquest of 733 as suggested by Gitin (1990:38). The finds of *lmlk* seal impressions and jars here may indicate that Hezekiah took over the city and turned it into a border fortress shortly before 701 BCE.

THE SEVENTH CENTURY BCE

It appears that Judah's rehabilitation after the widespread destruction caused by Sennacherib's invasion was slow and uneven. In our region, Beth-shemesh and perhaps other towns of the Shephelah stood in ruins. In contrast, both Ekron and Timnah were rebuilt during the seventh century BCE and flourished until their destruction by fire during the Babylonian invasion, between 604 and 600 BCE. During the first part of this period, the time of the Pax Assyriaca (until ca. 630 BCE), Gezer was probably the major Assyrian administration center in the region, as indicated by two Assyrian documents and various Assyrian objects found there (Brandl and Reich 1985). During this period Ekron (Stratum IC) expanded to its original area of over 20 ha (50 acres); industrial areas were constructed even beyond the limit of the lower mound, expanding the city to about 28 ha (70 acres). More than one hundred olive presses found close to the topsoil provide evidence of a thriving industry of olive oil production, based on the olive groves that probably covered the region (Gitin 1989). Two Assyrian references mention Ekron as one of the major city-states of the region (Gitin 1989:43); Gitin suggests that Ekron was one of the most important production centers of olive oil in the entire Near East, functioning in the framework of the planned imperialistic, centralized Assyrian economy. This suggestion, though, needs further proof. After the end of the Assyrian presence, between 630 and 603 BCE, Ekron was rebuilt (Stratum IB). In this phase the oil industry declined to some extent, as shown by the fact that some of the oil presses went out of use.

The major question concerning Timnah in the seventh century BCE is whether it belonged to Judah or to the kingdom of Ekron. Timnah Stratum II looks like a miniature of Ekron: the architecture is very similar, and two of the five buildings excavated contained olive oil presses similar

FIG. 15-5. Timnah: seventh-century BCE dwellings and olive oil press in Areas E and D, looking east.

to those of Ekron (fig. 15-5). The oil industry at Timnah appears to have been related that of Ekron. The major part of the ceramic assemblage from Timnah Stratum II is identical to that of Stratum IB at Ekron (Kelm and Mazar 1985:108–18; Gitin 1989:36–48). There is some difference between the two, however, as shown by comparative analysis of an assemblage of 377 vessels from Ekron and 89 vessels from one house at Timnah (Gitin 1989:51; Kelm and Mazar 1985:116). At Ekron, only 7 percent of the forms were defined as Judahite and 9 percent were defined as "southern," namely, forms that are common to both Judah and the coast. At Timnah, 17 percent of the assemblage was defined as Judahite and 50 percent as "Ekronite" forms. Among the Judahite forms at Timnah were the two types of Judahite cooking pots typical of the period, as well as storage jars of the *lmlk* type and of the rosette type. Most important is the presence at Timnah of six jar handles stamped with the Judahite rosette seal, which was probably a Judahite royal seal. No such stamped handles were found at Ekron.[6] Seven Judahite dome-shaped marked stone weights were found at Timnah. Only a few weights of this type have been found in Philistia (at Ekron and Ashdod). All these attributes support Timnah's affiliation with Judah. Small quantities of Phoenician, Transjordanian, and Greek pottery found at Timnah show that the town may have had its own trade connections, though such special vessels could have also been traded through Ekron.

Timnah's identity as either a Judahite or Ekronite town is crucial for the question of the extent of Josiah's kingdom. Since Albrecht Alt's study (1925), most scholars have agreed that Josiah gained control over large parts of Cisjordan, including parts of the coastal plain. This assumption has received most of its support from the discovery of Hebrew ostraca at Meṣad Hashavyahu (see, among others, Bright 1972:317; Aharoni 1979:403; Reviv 1979:203–4). It is agreed, however, that Ekron remained independent. Josiah thus controlled only a corridor north of Ekron, including the entire Sorek Valley and the coast near Meṣad Hashavyahu— a boundary that fits the description of the northern border of Judah in Joshua 15:10–12 (though it would be the southern border of the kingdom, if such a "corridor" existed). In contrast to this view, Na'aman recently suggested that Josiah's kingdom was limited to the territory listed in the city lists of Judah and Benjamin in Joshua 15:20–62 and 18:21–28. In his view, the region of Timnah as well as the entire coastal plain were outside Josiah's kingdom, and Meṣad Hashavyahu has nothing to do with Judahite control over the coast, in spite of the Hebrew ostraca found there (Na'aman 1991:44–51).

A clear-cut decision as to Timnah's affiliation could be of great importance in this debate: if it could be proved that Timnah was a Judahite town during Josiah's reign, this would support an extension of Josiah's territory to the coast. Unfortunately, I cannot offer a definite answer to this question. In a previous discussion I have argued that during Josiah's reign Timnah was probably part of the kingdom of Judah, though many of its inhabitants may have been of Ekronite origin (A. Mazar 1985:321; compare Kelm and Mazar 1985:118). I now suggest that the rebuilding of the town during the seventh century and the establishment of the oil industry in Timnah occurred before Josiah's reign, while Timnah still belonged to Ekron's sphere of influence. This is supported by the general similarity of the material culture of Timnah to that of Ekron, and the fact that olive oil production at Timnah may have been related to the larger industry at Ekron. Josiah, however, may have annexed Timnah and the territory to its west after the end of the Assyrian presence in the region. The local inhabitants may have been left in the town, while the connections with Judah became stronger. This would explain the nature of the finds in the destruction level of Stratum II at Timnah, where an "Ekronite" pottery assemblage is mixed with many Judahite attributes.

Following the violent destruction of both Ekron and Timnah, there came a short period of revival at Ekron—though probably only a few, scattered houses existed in this phase (Stratum IA). At Timnah evidence for postdestruction activity was found in only one place, in the form of an agricultural installation constructed above the destruction level of Stratum II. This phase was short and may indicate that a few farmers squatted in the ruined town for a short while in the early sixth century BCE (compare 2 Kgs. 25:12; Jer. 52:16).

The combined data from the excavations in the northern Shephelah and Ekron enable us to link the archaeological finds in the region with the biblical, historical, and geographical sources to produce a comprehensive picture, though some crucial questions remain unanswered. It is hoped that the detailed publication of the excavations at Ekron, Timnah, Beth-shemesh, and Gezer will throw a clearer light on the history of the region during the Iron Age.

NOTES

1. The excavations at Tel Batash were sponsored by the New Orleans Baptist Theological Seminary (between 1977 and 1979) and by Southwestern Baptist Theological Seminary (between 1981 and 1989), in collaboration with the Institute of Archaeology of the Hebrew University of Jerusalem. The expedition director was G. L. Kelm and the archaeological director was Amihai Mazar

2. Excavations at Beth-shemesh were resumed in 1990 under the direction of Shlomo Bunimovitz and Zvi Lederman. A partial survey of the Sorek Valley was carried out by Z. Kallai and the author in the 1970s, and since 1993 it has been continued by N. Appelbaum of the Institute of Archaeology of the Hebrew University. A survey of the Beth-shemesh region was carried out by Y. Dagan.

3. When using the term *Philistines*, one has to take into account the possibility that the true Philistine immigrants and their descendants formed only the dominant upper class in Philistia during this period, while much of the lower-class population were indigenous Canaanites under Philistine rule. This does not preclude the use of the term *Philistine culture* for the entire material culture assemblage that emerged in the Philistine cities during the twelfth–eleventh centuries BCE and that was inspired to a large extent by both Aegean and local Canaanite traditions. The trendsetters for this assemblage were the elite class, who were probably Philistines. For a different approach, see Bunimovitz 1990.

4. Light red slip and some hand burnish appear at Tell Qasile as early as mid-eleventh-century BCE contexts, together with Philistine bichrome ware (A. Mazar

1985:83–84). This contradicts the conclusions of John Holladay (1990), who dates the red-slipped and burnished pottery to the Solomonic era alone.

5. Na'aman (1986a:114–15), following F. Pintore, suggested that Makaz (*bmqz*) is not a toponym but is a misreading of the word *mqs[h]*, i.e., "from the end of," which appears elsewhere in the border descriptions.

6. In a comprehensive study of the rosette seal impressions from Judah, Jane Cahill has shown that there are several types of such impressions. All the impressions from Timnah belong to one type. In Cahill and Avi Ofer's opinion, the rosette jars were used by the kingdom of Judah in the framework of the preparations against the Babylonian invasion, just as the *lmlk* jars were used during the time of Hezekiah in the framework of the preparations against Sennacherib's invasion. The type used at Timnah, according to their view, is one of the earliest, used before the conquest of Timnah by the Babylonians, which according to them, should be dated to 603 BCE (Cahill forthcoming; Cahill and Ofer forthcoming).

WORKS CITED

Aharoni, Y.
1958   The Northern Border of Judah. *Palestine Exploration Quarterly* 90:27–31.
1976   The Solomonic Districts. *Tel Aviv* 3:5–15.
1979   *The Land of the Bible: A Historical Geography*. 2d ed. Philadelphia: Westminster.
Alt, A.
1925   Judas Gaue unter Josia. *Palästinajahrbuch des deutschen evangelischen Instituts für Altertumswissenschaft des Heiligen Landes zu Jerusalem* 21:100–116. (= *Kleine Schriften zur Geschichte des Volkes Israel*, 2:376–88. Munich: C. H. Beck).
Brandl, B., and R. Reich
1985   Gezer under Assyrian Rule. *Palestine Exploration Quarterly* 117:41–54.
Bright, J.
1972   *A History of Israel*. 3d ed. Philadelphia: Westminster.
Bunimovitz, S.
1990   Problems in the "Ethnic" Identification of the Philistine Culture. *Tel Aviv* 17:210–22.
Cahill, J. M.
Forthcoming   Rosette Stamp Seal Impressions from Judah. In *Judah in the Late Iron Age*, ed. D. V. Edelman. Chicago.
Cahill, J. M., and A. Ofer
Forthcoming   Rosette Stamp Seal Impressions from Ancient Judah: Historical Significance, Date and Comparison with LMLK Impressions. In *Israel Exploration Journal*.

Cross, F. M.
1967   The Origin and Early Evolution of the Alphabet. *Eretz-Israel* 8:8*–24*.
Cross, F. M., and G. E. Wright
1956   The Boundary and Province Lists of the Kingdom of Judah. *Journal of Biblical Literature* 75:202–26.
Dever, W. G.
1986   *Gezer IV: The 1969–71 Seasons in Field VI, the "Acropolis."* Jerusalem: Nelson Glueck School of Biblical Archaeology.
Dothan, M.
1975   Ashdod. In *Encyclopedia of Archaeological Excavations in the Holy Land*, ed. M. Avi-Yonah, 1:103–19. Jerusalem: Israel Exploration Society and Massada Press.
Dothan, M., and T. Dothan
1992   *People of the Sea.* New York: Macmillan.
Dothan, M., and Y. Porath
1982   *Ashdod Vol 4 (ʿAtiqot 15).* Jerusalem: Department of Antiquities and Museums.
Dothan, T.
1989   The Arrival of the Sea Peoples: Cultural Diversity in Early Iron Age Canaan. In *Recent Excavations in Israel: Studies in Iron Age Archaeology*, ed. S. Gitin and W. G. Dever. Annual of the American Schools of Oriental Research 49:59–70.
Eissfeldt, O.
1975   The Hebrew Kingdom. In *Cambridge Ancient History*, 2:2, 537–605. Cambridge: Cambridge University Press.
Gitin, S.
1989   Tel Miqne-Ekron: A Type Site for the Inner Coastal Plain in the Iron Age II Period. In *Recent Excavations in Israel: Studies in Iron Age Archaeology*, ed. S. Gitin and W. G. Dever. Annual of the American Schools of Oriental Research 49:23–58.
1990   *Gezer III: A Ceramic Typology of the Late Iron II, Persian, and Hellenistic Periods.* Jerusalem: Nelson Glueck School of Biblical Archaeology.
1993   Scoops: Corpus, Function, and Typology. In *Studies in the Archaeology and History of Ancient Israel in Honor of Moshe Dothan*, ed. M. Helzer, A. Segal, and D. Kaufman, 99–126. Haifa: Haifa University Press.
Gordon, C.
1971   Cultural and Religious Life. In *The World History of the Jewish People, Volume III: Judges*, ed. B. Mazar, 52–68. New Brunswick, N.J.: Rutgers University Press.
Holladay, J. S.
1990   Red Slip, Burnish, and the Solomonic Gateway at Gezer. *Bulletin of the American Schools of Oriental Research* 277/278:23–70.

Kallai, Z.
1958   The Town Lists of Judah, Simeon, Benjamin, and Dan. *Vetus Testamentum* 8:134–60.
1960   *The Northern Boundary of Judah*. Jerusalem: Magnes Press (Hebrew).
1971   The Kingdom of Rehoboam. *Eretz-Israel* 10:245–54 (Hebrew).
1986   *Historical Geography of the Bible*. Jerusalem: Magnes Press and Hebrew University, and Leiden: E. J. Brill.

Kelm, G. L., and A. Mazar
1982   Three Seasons of Excavations at Tel Batash-Biblical Timnah. *Bulletin of the American Schools of Oriental Research* 248:1–36.
1985   Tel Batash (Timnah) Excavations, Second Preliminary Report (1981–1983). *Bulletin of the American Schools of Oriental Research Supplement* 23:93–120.
1989   Excavating in Samson Country—Philistines and Israelites at Tel Batash. *Biblical Archaeology Review* 15, no. 1:36–49.
1990   Excavations at Tel Batash (Timnah), 1984–1988 (Third Preliminary Report). *Bulletin of the American Schools of Oriental Research Supplement* 27:47–67.

Kitchen, K. A.
1973   *The Third Intermediate Period in Egypt*. Warminster: Aris and Phillips.

Licht, J. S.
1982   Samson. In *Encyclopedia Biblica*, ed. E. L. Sukenik, et al., 8: cols. 190–96. Jerusalem: Bialik Institute (Hebrew).

Mazar, A.
1981   Archaeological Research on the Period of the Monarchy (Iron Age II). In *Recent Archaeology in the Land of Israel*, ed. H. Shanks and B. Mazar, 43–58. Washington, D.C.: Biblical Archaeology Society, and Jerusalem: Israel Exploration Society.
1985   *Excavations at Tell Qasile, Part Two. Various Finds, The Pottery, Conclusions, Appendices. Qedem* 20. Jerusalem: Institute of Archaeology, Hebrew University.

Mazar, B.
1960   The Cities of the Territory of Dan. *Israel Exploration Journal* 10:65–77.
1986   *The Early Biblical Period, Historical Studies*, ed. S. Ahiuv and B. A. Levine. Jerusalem: Israel Exploration Society.

Na'aman, N.
1979   Sennacherib's Campaign to Judah and the Date of the *lmlk* Stamps. *Vetus Testamentum* 29:62–86.
1986a   *Borders and Districts in Biblical Historiography*. Jerusalem: Simor.
1986b   Hezekiah's Fortified Cities and the LMLK Stamps. *Bulletin of the American Schools of Oriental Research* 261:5–21.
1991   The Kingdom of Judah under Josiah. *Tel Aviv* 18:3–71.

Naveh, J.
1958 Khirbet el-Muqanna^c—Ekron. *Israel Exploration Journal* 8:87–100, 165–70.
Oppenheim, A. L.
1969 Babylonian and Assyrian Historical Texts. In *Ancient Near Eastern Texts Relating to the Old Testament*, ed. J. B. Pritchard, 265–317. 3d ed. with Supplement. Princeton, N.J.: Princeton University Press.
Reviv, H.
1979 The History of Judah from Hezekiah to Josiah. In *The World History of the Jewish People, 4:1. The Age of the Monarchies: Political History*, ed. A. Malamat, 193–204. Jerusalem: Massada Press.
Spina, F.
1977 The Dan Story Historically Reconsidered. *Journal for the Study of the Old Testament* 4:60–71.
Ussishkin, D.
1977 The Destruction of Lachish by Sennacherib and the Dating of the Royal Judean Storage Jars. *Tel Aviv* 4:28–60.
Vaux, R. de
1978 *The Early History of Israel.* Trans. by D. Smith, from French. 1971–73. London: Darton, Longman and Todd.
Whitelam, K. W.
1992 Dan. In *Anchor Bible Dictionary*, ed. D. N. Freedman, 2:10–12. New York: Doubleday.
Wright, G. E.
1967 The Provinces of Solomon. *Eretz-Israel* 8:58*–68*.
Yadin, Y.
1968 And Dan, Why Did He Remain with the Ships? *Australian Journal of Biblical Archaeology* 1:9–23.

16 | Demography and Diatribes: Yehud's Population and the Prophecy of Second Zechariah

CAROL L. MEYERS
ERIC M. MEYERS

The use of archaeological materials in the interpretation or examination of biblical texts has all too often been a theologically tendentious or otherwise controversial enterprise (see, e.g., Dever 1985:31–74 and references cited). But removed from a theological agenda, the material remains of the biblical world can be invaluable in illuminating the context of many biblical passages, thereby making both the literary power and the socio-historical grounding of those passages available to modern readers in a way that would not otherwise be possible. By allowing a reconstruction of the reality of the biblical world and by testifying to the authenticity of many of its people, places, and events, archaeology enables us to contextualize biblical texts and also to investigate the particular configurations of public and private lives that generated Israel's distinctive self-understanding as recorded in scripture (see C. Meyers 1992).

In recent years the interpretation of archaeological remains in conjunction with biblical texts has, at its best, become a sophisticated process. Mindful of the goals and procedures of the "new archaeology" and now of postprocessual "contextual archaeology" (see Hodder 1986 and Trigger 1989) and of social archaeology (see Meyers and Meyers 1989), biblical archaeologists—those dealing with whatever material data can be used to contribute to an understanding of biblical times and the literature surviving from those times—can attempt to trace the life experience of the Israelites as members of social communities and also to reconstruct the dynamics of individual lives. At the same time, the sophisticated techniques of data procurement and analysis, the ethnoarchaeological analogies used to fill the inevitable and sizeable gaps in evidence, and the theoretical models that allow for plausible reconstructions can augment

268

the ongoing traditional modes of biblical archaeology. Thus, details of biblical texts can sometimes now be elucidated or verified in surprising ways.

One such example is William Dever's study of an eighth-century earthquake in relation to several prophetic texts (1992; see Meyers and Meyers 1993:424–29), a study that reverts to the notion of history as a legitimate goal of archaeology. Another case in point is this chapter, which will elucidate the shape of the demographic disaster of the Babylonian conquest in relation to one postexilic prophetic voice. Methods of calculating population, while inevitably somewhat conjectural, have made enormous strides in recent years thanks to ethnoarchaeological considerations of population density in rural and urban settings. Such calculations can be juxtaposed with the apparently stylized demographic information contained in the diatribes of Zechariah 13, and to a certain extent in Zechariah 14, to assess the extent to which Second Zechariah's otherworldly apocalyptic vision may nonetheless be grounded in acute awareness of historical reality.

SECOND ZECHARIAH'S REFERENCES TO POPULATION

Invoking the results of archaeological research to enrich or elucidate biblical prophecy is particularly difficult in the case of Zechariah 9—14 (Second Zechariah). No prophetic work is so devoid of specific historical markers. Indeed, it is characteristic of recent studies of this prophetic work to claim that neither its historical setting nor its social context can be recovered (e.g., Childs 1979:474–76). Some would even say that relating this book to sociohistorical reality should not be attempted and that modes of inquiry other than traditional historical-critical ones must be employed (Mason 1982:343–44). The widely divergent conclusions about social and political setting in the various commentaries and studies dealing with Second Zechariah underscore the paucity of information in that work that can be readily linked to historical data available for the late biblical period (that is, the end of the period of the Hebrew Bible). This being the case, other reading strategies and analytical procedures have emerged.

The value in using new strategies, especially ones concerned with literary features, in studying Second Zechariah does not mean that historical studies should be abandoned. The perceived impasse in historical analysis

and contextualizing processes can also be broken by the use of sophisticated new ways of handling archaeological data from the territory of
Yehud, the postexilic Persian province that encompassed the heartland of
the preexilic kingdom of Judah. Similarly, the application of social scientific models, as developed for the early centuries of the biblical period, to
the concluding centuries of that period helps to contextualize the signa-
ture literary features of Second Zechariah. In our work on this prophet
for the Anchor Bible (Meyers and Meyers 1993), we recognize that the
prophetic interweaving of past themes with future expectations, and
the reworking of authoritative texts to engender hope in ways those very
texts seemed to preclude, were features of identifiable dynamics and conditions in the postexilic community. The introduction to our commentary
lays out some of our insights into Second Zechariah's world.[1] Here we
highlight instances of the prophet's demographic perspectives, some of
which can be correlated with the results of recent archaeological surveys
and population calculations.

ZECHARIAH 10:
THE ESCHATOLOGICAL
POPULATION EXPLOSION

The overriding concern of Zechariah 9, which undoubtedly draws on
archaic poetic materials but which nonetheless speaks to the postexilic
community, is the eschatological recovery of the Promised Land and the
restoration of the exiles to their homeland. Zechariah 10 follows directly
from these concerns and in a way parallels them. If intervention by the
Divine Warrior is the only way that a powerless people can envisage
military-political redemption, so too is God's direct involvement the only
way for the underpopulated and territorially reduced homeland to acquire
its promised potential. According to chapter 9, Yahweh's control of the
cosmos will reverse the political status quo, empowering and restoring
autonomy to the exiled or dominated survivors of the foreign invasions of
Israel's homeland and restoring the full boundaries of that land (C. Meyers
1993). A similar cosmic reversal is portrayed in chapter 10. The eschatological restoration of all of God's people—those dispersed in Egypt and
Assyria and everywhere "among the peoples" (10:9; cf. 10:10), not just in
Babylon—will be the result of God's actions. Just as the surviving community could have had no dream of restored autonomy or power without

Yahweh's mighty deeds on its behalf, so too the dream of a populous homeland is unthinkable without Yahweh's gathering up the dispersed remnant.

The eschatological setting of Yahweh's military intervention in chapter 9 is a function of the painful awareness on the part of the postexilic community that it is utterly unable in its dependent, provincial status to contemplate the return of political-military autonomy and the restoration of a Davidic monarchy in historical time. Similarly, the eschatological setting of a divinely effected in-gathering in chapter 10 emerges from the sense that the population of Yehud is extraordinarily limited in size, and also in diversity with respect to the canonical, twelve-tribe inclusiveness in depictions of all Israel. The sense that the prophet is speaking from the context of a weak and much reduced population is highlighted by the eschatological emphasis of population growth and of expansion to hitherto unknown boundaries, even beyond what was known at the height of Israel's imperial extent in the early years of monarchy.

The emphasis on extreme demographic growth is found in several ways in Zechariah 10. For one thing, the prophet mentions "children" several times, thereby pointing to the younger generation. The progeny of verse 7 represent future growth, especially since the appearance there of "children" is closely followed by the Hebrew expression in verse 8, *wĕrābû kĕmô rābû*. The English translation "they will multiply as before" hardly does justice to the elegance of the Hebrew and its allusion to other biblical texts. The verb *rbh* ("to multiply, increase") evokes the anticipation of return from exile, as it does for both Jeremiah (23:3) and Ezekiel (36:11), who anticipate a future when the remnant "will be fruitful and multiply." Those two exilic prophets echo the language of Genesis (1:22, 28; 9:1, 7; 35:11). Second Zechariah, too, in coining a new expression while remaining in the mainstream of biblical thought, draws on the language of creation and of the patriarchal promise, asserting anew the idea that Israel was meant to be a great and populous people. This idea is particularly compelling in the postexilic period when the demographic reality is so removed from the age-old promise. Just how far removed will become clear below in our discussion of Yehud's population.

The great population density of the future age is also depicted in Zechariah 10:10. In setting forth the return of God's people from Egypt and Assyria, the prophet depicts them as settling in the land of Gilead and in Lebanon. That these two geographic designations appear is striking and bears examination, since neither singly nor together do they represent a return to historical Israelite settlement patterns, the preexilic core of Israel and Judah being the Cisjordanian highlands.

As a geographical term, Gilead designates land east of the Jordan. In some texts the term refers to a limited part of Transjordan. Yet it can also represent all of Transjordan (Deut. 3:12, 13; Josh. 12:2–6; see also Aharoni 1979:38–39) and was considered Israelite territory: southern Gilead, south of the Jabbok, occupied by Gad and Reuben; northern Gilead, north of the Jabbok, inhabited by the half tribe of Manasseh. Rugged and mountainous, Gilead has only a relatively narrow band of tableland and was probably densely forested in the biblical period. Without the same potential for agricultural development as the territory west of the Jordan, its importance for Israel lay more in political security and economic strategy. It was a buffer zone against the people of the east, and the King's Highway, one of the two major north-south arteries of the Levant, passed through it. Both its topography and its history (it came partially under Syrian control in the monarchic period; see 2 Kgs. 10:32–33; cf. Amos 1:3) indicate a somewhat marginal status for Gilead. In short, it was relatively empty territory; filling it with returning Israelite exiles could only mean that the heartland of Israel was full and that the number of returnees was large.

Lebanon has a similar significance. In the Bible this term refers to the chain of mountains that begin in northern Palestine and continue northward for about 160 km. These mountainous areas, unlike the Phoenician coast, were not settled in any significant way until the Roman period, and the eastern edge of the Lebanon—the Beqa Valley—has never been extensively settled. Like Gilead, it was considered Israelite (Deut. 1:7; 3:25; 11:24; Josh. 1:4; 13:5–6; 1 Kgs. 9:19) but was never really occupied, and at least part of it was controlled by non-Israelites for most of the monarchic period. It too was largely unsuitable for agriculture.

The marginal nature of Gilead and Lebanon as a pair is not new to Second Zechariah. A passage in Jeremiah (22:6) compares wayward Judah to Gilead and Lebanon; Judah will surely become uninhabitable, that is, like those areas that are quintessentially underpopulated. This Jeremiah text is often misunderstood, with the metaphoric use of Gilead and Lebanon construed as positive. Yet the following poetic line is introduced by 'im-lô', which is an emphatic affirmative, making it certain that Jeremiah considers Gilead and Lebanon uninhabited:

Gilead, you are to me the summit of Lebanon.
I will surely make you a wilderness, cities not inhabited.

For Second Zechariah as for Jeremiah, these two territories represent
empty territory, to be filled only when traditional population centers are
overflowing.

The last clause of Zechariah 10:10, "till no room is found for them," is
idiomatic and elliptical in the Hebrew: *wĕlo' yimmāṣē' lāhem*. The verb *mṣ'*
in the Nipᶜal means "will be found," that is, "will be [found] sufficient"
and appears in reference to demographic concerns in Joshua 17:16, which
records a complaint of the Josephites that their allotted territory in the
hill country "is not sufficient for us" (*lo'-yimmāṣē' lānû*). The use of this
language in Zechariah 10 in reference to the eschatological setting of
returnees in Gilead and Lebanon takes the repopulation of Israelite territory one step further—all of Israel's land, even the most marginal portions of it, will be filled to overflowing and will become inadequate to the
extraordinarily burgeoning population of the future age.

This depiction of demographic expansion clearly draws on the commands and promises of Genesis and on the language of exilic prophecy.
Yet the extreme to which it is carried in the eschatological future may
well be drawn from the historic extreme of low population in the prophet's
own time. The eschaton, in military-political matters and also in demography, will be a dramatic reversal of the dismal situation of the first half of
the postexilic period.

ZECHARIAH 13:
THE MEASURE OF
DEVASTATION IN JUDAH

One of the hallmarks of Second Zechariah, a feature that has made these
six prophetic chapters so difficult for traditional biblical scholarship to
understand, is the interweaving of retrospective language with allusions
to conditions of the prophet's own day and with vivid depictions of eschatological events. The conceptualization of time is thus exceedingly complex and defies the linear presentation that characterizes most Western
literature. But it is precisely this complexity that enables the prophetic
voice or voices of Second Zechariah to adhere to authoritative language
even when the promises and proclamations of authoritative texts do not
fit the experience of the postexilic community. With its multiplicity of

genres and its wide range of geographical and chronological concerns, Second Zechariah represents a highly creative and transitional work in the ongoing process of biblical prophecy.

Zechariah 13 is typical of Second Zechariah in its changing chronological referents and in its shift from retrospective elements to future-oriented language. Acute awareness of past events and future promise arises out of evaluation of present experience. The third section of 13:7–9 diverges in style and focus from the first two subunits (v 1 and vv 2–6) of the chapter, yet there are points of lexical contact and of shared thematic interest that connect all three. Nevertheless, the third section is unique in the specificity of its subject matter, imagery, and detail.

Whereas Second Zechariah's other oracles tend to be inclusive—dealing with the greater land of Israel, with both Judah and Ephraim, and even with an Israel with nearly cosmic dimensions—verses 7 to 9 of chapter 13 are apparently directed toward the Yehudites who had survived the Babylonian conquest and remained in the land. Although depicting an eschatological catastrophe, the prophet draws from the devastation well known to him: the realities of events of the sixth century, in which the Babylonians conquered Jerusalem and Judah, thereby terminating a half millennium of Israelite political autonomy.

In drawing upon the language of destruction, this subunit presents a tripartite scheme. It suggests that the inhabitants of subjugated Judah were subjected to one of three different fates. One group met death, another suffered displacement (exile), and the third remained in place but bereft of leadership and economic resources. The fates of each group are enumerated in verse 7, which continues the shepherd imagery that dominates Second Zechariah. Three actions are depicted: slaughtering, scattering, and turning against. These three actions reflect the results of the conquest: death, dispersion, and great difficulty.

The first verb, "slay" (nkh), is probably an abbreviated form of the idiom "to smite (nkh) with the edge of the sword" (see Deut. 13:16 [NRSV 13:15], hakkēh takkeh . . . lĕpî hāreb). The presence of "sword" in the first line of this verse, along with the fact that late biblical parlance tends to abbreviate the full Deuteronomic idiom, contributes to the sense that the term in 13:7 is used elliptically. In any case, with "shepherd" as object, it denotes loss of leadership through military confrontation with the enemy. Although the apostrophe at the beginning of this verse gives a future cast to it, the language is drawn from the prophet's awareness of the destruction of the past.

With that destruction went dispersion, as the next verbal idea ("that the flock may be scattered") asserts. The scattering of a flock is a figurative portrayal of all the people as a flock, thrust away from their own pastures, which provide sustenance and security (see 1 Kgs. 22:17; Ezek. 34:5, 6, 12; Jer. 10:21; 23:1, 2). It is probably no accident that the metaphoric use of "scattered" is found mainly in Ezekiel and Jeremiah, the two prophets of the exile and the two prophetic works most influential on Second Zechariah. Finally the last clause of verse 7—"I will turn my hand against the least"—conveys the idea of God's turning against the people. In addition to slaughter and exile, a third fate is possible: the "least," probably equivalent to the "poorest in the land" (2 Kgs. 25:11; Jer. 52:16), are left in their homeland to suffer the hardship of deprivation in a land ravished by conquest and deportation.

This threefold fate of the people that is to be (and has been) conquered is echoed in the following verse (8). The opening phrase, "in all the land," is a highly unusual metonymic use of "land" for "people." That people are implied is clear from the rest of the verse, so the use of "land" may function to connect the devastation described in this verse with the causes of divine punishment, the idolatry and impurity in the "land" of verse 2. The chief message of verse 7 is that the people will meet three different fates. A double portion (*pî šěnayim*) will together suffer two fates, that of being cut off or of perishing. While "cut off" (*krt*) can indicate destruction (e.g., Gen. 9:11; Isa. 29:20), it more often seems to indicate the living equivalent of death—to be cut off from one's people and/or land, as in the priestly excommunication texts (e.g., Lev. 7:20, 21, 25, 27; Num. 9:13). Here it is paired with "perish" (*gwʿ*), indicating that two-thirds of the whole will no longer live in their homeland; they will be either dead or dispersed.

The last third of the whole is specified in the last clause of this verse: "The third will remain in it." The verb *ytr* ("to be left over, remain"), when followed by *b* ("in") signifies those who are left in a place, that is, all those not killed or exiled. This is the group that most concerns the prophet, for the rest of the chapter, a long verse with a shift in imagery (to metallurgy) and a climactic expression of the covenant idea, depicts what will happen to the remnant.

The tripartite division of the people represented by the "two parts . . . third" language does not necessarily mean that the three possible fates of a conquered people involved three groups equal in size. Nor does it adequately indicate the fact that not all leaders were slain—many, in fact, were exiled. Nor does it indicate that not all people other than the poorest or the leaders were sent away from their homes. But it does indeed represent what could happen to a conquered people in the mid–first millennium BCE. And it strikingly represents the experience of the surviving remnant, their sense that they represented just a small proportion of what the population of Yehud, or rather Judah, had been before the Babylonians carried out their imperial strategy in the Levant.

Whether or not the concept of a threefold fate for the inhabitants of Judah, with one third surviving in the land, bears any relationship to demographic reality will be considered below. Here it is important to note that such an idea may be rooted in literary tradition as well as in actual population patterns. A number of biblical passages portray tripartite divisions that may be relevant. Ezekiel 5:1–12 describes a symbolic action in which the prophet divides hair shaved from his face and head into three parts and then destroys all parts (by burning, slaying, and scattering—to symbolize Jerusalem's punishment by pestilence, sword, and exile). Ezekiel's imagery may in turn depend upon that of 1 Kings 19:17–18 (so Greenberg 1983:126), which depicts Jehu's purge: some people are killed by Jehu, some by Elisha, and some survive. The connection between Ezekiel and 1 Kings seems a bit loose, since the Kings passage involves the survival of those innocent of Baal worship, whereas Ezekiel seems to see no innocence and depicts total devastation. Even if there are survivors, it is not because of innocence and not at the escape of divine punitive justice (Ezek. 12:10 and Greenberg 1983:140–41).

Second Zechariah's use of the idea of devastation differentially affecting portions, that is, thirds, of the population may echo Ezekiel's imagery. Yet Second Zechariah, as in so many other instances (see "Introduction" to Meyers and Meyers 1993), is not a slavish borrowing of existing authoritative materials. Zechariah 13 involves slaying and scattering, which are two of the causes of destruction in Ezekiel. Yet it apportions the three Ezekiel groups differently: two-thirds are killed or removed, and the remaining third suffers but remains in the land and survives. This revision of Ezekiel's sense of complete destruction may well be the result of Second Zechariah's perspective, well into the postexilic period, when the survival of some—a woefully small number in comparison to the preexilic kingdom—is apparent.

ZECHARIAH 14:
THE MEASURE OF
DEVASTATION IN JERUSALEM

Quantitative language in relation to the future cataclysmic onslaught against Jerusalem appears at the beginning of the last chapter of Second Zechariah. The focus on Jerusalem, in this final and extensive eschatological vision, is adumbrated by the attention it receives in previous chapters. There, however, its fate is linked with that of Judah; here it stands virtually alone (though note the appearance of Judah in 14:14 and 21). The intensity of interest in Jerusalem no doubt is a function of the depiction of the final stage of the eschatological process in Zechariah 14. The very universality of the end of chapter 14 presupposes a global structure of Yahweh's rule, with Jerusalem as the epicenter of that worldwide acknowledgement of Yahweh's might and the legitimacy of God's designated representative, the Davidic monarch on a throne in the capital. Both heavenly and earthly kings are based in Jerusalem, in temple and palace, and thus that city is used quite inclusively to denote all for whom Zion is the true and historic center of God's earthly domain.

In describing the onslaught against Jerusalem, with "all the nations" gathered "to Jerusalem, for war" (14:2), the prophet selects three items from the catalogue of the horrors of war. First, the city is captured (*lkd*), which may involve the slaughter of Jerusalem's warriors as well as some civilians. Then the vandalizing of property is specified: "the houses will be plundered." Finally, the sexual abuse of conquered females by the victorious soldiers is portrayed: "the women will be ravished." The fact that this listing of the horrors of war draws from Isaiah (13:15–16), who is focusing on the destruction to life and property involved in warfare, leads to an understanding of these three terms in Zechariah functioning in a similar way.

The fate of those who survive death (and rape?) at the hands of the enemy is then set forth in the last two clauses of verse 2:

> half the city will go into exile,
> but the rest of the people will not be cut off from the city.

Here we have a fifty-fifty division of all those people who will not have died in the great battle of Jerusalem. The numerical information here, however stylized it may be, does not conflict with the data of Zechariah 13:8–9. This verse in fact gives much the same information. The capture of Jerusalem involves death for its armed defenders and the taking of spoil (both material and human). Thereafter the conquering powers must resolve how to maintain their subjugation of the vanquished city. The political solution after the military phase involves exile for half of those left, with the remaining half allowed to stay in their city. Zechariah 13 has combined the military actions with those of the ensuing political era and has divided the fate of the people in thirds. In Zechariah 14, those two aspects of conquest are separated. The end result is the same: some die, and all who survive are divided into two parts, those to be deported and those allowed to remain in the ruined city.

As in chapter 13, the last group specified is the remnant, the "remainder," a word derived from the root *ytr*, which is used in 13:8 in much the same sense: to refer to the survivors in Judah who were not exiled. Similarly, the verb *krt* ("cut off") is used in 14:2 as well as in 13:8 to refer to deportations. These two lexical connections in passages dealing with the measure of devastation—delineating three different fates—suggest that the quantitative figures are different ways of saying the same thing. The fate of one part of the population is to be left in the city/the land. Just how that conceptualization of conquest fits with the demography of pre-exilic and postexilic Judah/Yehud remains to be considered.

DEMOGRAPHIC DATA RELEVANT TO
SECOND ZECHARIAH

This discussion has shown that for Second Zechariah, Yehud was inhabited by a population greatly diminished in comparison to the ideal posed by the promise traditions of the Pentateuch and/or to the reality of Judah on the eve of the Babylonian onslaught. The eschatological vision in chapter 10 of an overflowing, enlarged territory emerges, we suggest, from the hopeless and helpless condition of a sparsely populated Yehud. Similarly, the retrospectively conditioned diatribes of chapters 13 and 14 introduce quantitative language to the message that attacks by foreigners bring about demographic devastation to the land.

Clearly the language of Zechariah 13 and 14 is stylized, with the tripartite division of what happens to the vanquished at the hands of the victors perhaps drawing upon Ezekiel's symbolic actions. But can there be any numerical validity underlying the threefold fate of the conquered people? Can there be any basis in demographic reality for the proportions represented by the prophetic claim that some were killed in battle, some were exiled, and some were left behind? Such questions can be approached by considering current data used to estimate the population of Yehud, in its first phase, and the population of the equivalent territory of Judah at the end of the Iron Age, in the late seventh and early sixth centuries.

Before turning to the problem of population estimation, the extent of the territory involved in looking at Yehud and Judah must be addressed. As Charles Carter has pointed out (1991:53–64 and 1992), the lists in Ezra and Nehemiah, which have traditionally been used in scholarly attempts to delineate the extent of the postexilic province of Yehud, are not reliable indications of boundaries. Unlike the territorial descriptions and city lists of Joshua and Judges, the Ezra and Nehemiah materials contain names of sites to which exiles returned after Cyrus's decree and also names of places to which returnees had ancestral connections. In neither case do those lists provide a delineation of Yehud's extent.

Archaeological data are similarly inconclusive in providing an idea of Yehud's boundaries. Ephraim Stern claims that sites at which seals or coins bearing some variation of the *yhd* inscription were found should be considered part of Yehud. But some of the seals or coins he includes are probably Hellenistic (Carter 1992; see Lapp 1963). Furthermore, Stern's interpretation of a series of fortresses dating to the Persian period as boundary fortifications is problematic (Hoglund 1992:202–3). Those fortresses probably are more related to imperial Persian trade routes and communication arteries than they are to the borders of the province of Yehud.

With neither biblical nor archaeological data providing reliable information about the provincial boundaries of Yehud, geopolitical considerations become of paramount importance. Through a detailed and careful study of the terrain and resources of Yehud, in relationship to central place theory, a reasonable reconstruction of postexilic Yehud is possible (Carter 1992; 1991:53–92 and figs. 1–8, 20). This Yehud differs from most other reconstructions (such as that of Stern 1982:247 and Avi-Yonah 1966:13–23, map 1) in lacking the Shephelah. The western boundary is at the edge of the central hill country; the eastern extent probably reached to the Jordan River; the northern border must have followed tribal boundaries, that is, Benjamin's northern boundary; and the southern edge of Yehud likely stretched from En-gedi in the east toward Hebron and to the Shephelah.

This assessment of the size of postexilic Yehud reveals a rather tiny province in the central hill country of Palestine: an area of about 1700 km², which is less than one-half the area of Rhode Island (Carter 1992). It is roughly analogous to the hill country of Judah, including Jerusalem, which is separated out for population estimation by the most recent demographic study of the population of Palestine in the Iron Age (Broshi and Finkelstein 1992). In other words, postexilic Yehud was a province far smaller than preexilic Judah; perhaps its size was limited by the Persians because of its sensitive border situation.

The estimation of population for various epochs of the biblical period has come a long way from the naive reliance on literary sources that characterized an earlier generation of scholarship. Demographic studies such as those by Magen Broshi (1978), Broshi and Ram Gophna (1984, 1986), Israel Finkelstein (1988, 1990), and Yigal Shiloh (1980) have taken into account sophisticated modes of estimating premodern populations, including spatial analysis, carrying capacity, food remains analysis, water supply, and burial patterns. Perhaps the best strategy for estimations, however, is areal analysis, which seeks to establish the total number of dunams inhabited in a given period and then to use a carefully selected population coefficient (number of persons per dunam) to arrive at an approximation of population. Carrying out areal analysis effectively means utilizing survey data and excavation data in conjunction with ethnoar-chaeological assessments of population density with respect to site size and function as well in consideration of the rural, urban, and sedentary components of a population (London 1992).

The most recent studies use a population coefficient of twenty-five persons per dunam (250 per hectare), which is considerably lower than the figure used by Shiloh in his estimation (1980) of the Iron II popula-tion of Palestine. Although the twenty-five coefficient seems to be consis-tent with ethnographic studies, some believe that even that figure is too high (e.g., Carter 1991:158; see Finkelstein 1988). Gloria London, in a perceptive study calling for sensitivity to site function and location in relationship to size and domestic density, argues that a figure under 200 per hectare is preferable and that, in any case, the figure should vary with the nature of the site (1992:75).

While agreeing that twenty-five persons per dunam may be too high a coefficient, we nonetheless will use that figure because the two detailed studies that we will consult both employ it. Since our goal is to estimate the relative loss of population involved in the imperial conquest of Judah, the accuracy of absolute numbers is not critical. In any case, virtually all population estimates claim that the relative value of their figures is more significant than are the actual figures, given the lack of certitude about absolute numbers.

The population of Yehud in the Persian I period (539/38 BCE to ca. 450 BCE), which has fewer sites and thus a lower settled area than the Persian II period (ca. 450 BCE to 332 BCE), has been calculated by Carter, who has been careful to identify sites in relationship to this periodization of the postexilic period. His estimation is based on a total excavated area of 51 dunams, a surveyed area of 348 dunams, and a correction factor of 35 to account for undiscovered sites and other variables. The number of inhabited dunams is thus 434. Using a population coefficient of twenty-five, the resulting population estimation for Yehud in the Persian I period is 10,850 (Carter 1992; 1991:162), a population scattered unevenly among the eight individual environmental niches of Yehud.

Population estimates for the equivalent territory of preexilic Judah are difficult to locate in the demographic literature. Most studies of Iron II Palestine focus on eighth-century materials. And most do not break down their statistical data into groups that approximate environmental niches that can be correlated with those of Yehud. As we have suggested above, however, the recent study by Broshi and Finkelstein (1992) comes closest in providing figures that are meaningful for our purposes. They give separate figures for ten different geographical regions of Iron II western Palestine, excluding the Negeb south of Beer-sheba. One of those regions (region 7) is Judea, which they subdivide into four subregions plus Jerusalem. Their data for the Judean hill country, based on the surveys by Moshe Kochavi (1972) and Avi Ofer (1990), are particularly relevant. Although the calculations in Broshi and Finkelstein's assessment are for the Iron II without subphases, the eighth century is viewed as the critical part of the Iron II period and the apex of population for Palestine as a whole. That may be true, but subregional differences are probably significant, especially for Judah after the eighth century. Thus the fact that the Judean survey does include sites established in the hill country in the seventh century is important for estimating the population at the end of the monarchic era.

Using Kochavi's data, Broshi and Finkelstein (1992:287) estimate a population of 30,000 for the Judean hill country, but in light of Ofer's estimates, they suggest that 26,000 may be a more reasonable number. This figure is exclusive of Jerusalem, which they estimate to be 7500. However, if one takes the late preexilic size of Jerusalem as 500 dunams (Shiloh 1980:31; see Broshi 1974:21–26), allots only 50 percent of the urban area to settled space (London 1992:73, 75), and uses the same coefficient of twenty-five persons per dunam, then Jerusalem in the late preexilic period may have had a density of 6250, somewhat less than Broshi and Finkelstein's estimate.

These estimations of the population of the Judean hill country (26,000) and Jerusalem (6250) together thus provide a figure of 32,250 for the late seventh century.[2] That figure is almost precisely three times that of Persian I Yehud. Conversely if one were to take Second Zechariah literally and calculate one third of the preexilic population of 32,250, the resulting figure—10,750—would be strikingly close to the estimated population, 10,850, of Persian I Yehud.

This congruence of demographic estimations and prophetic language may be accidental. Indeed, the striking agreement of these two sources would dissipate somewhat if the area just north of Jerusalem were included. But even if the agreement is coincidental, or even if there is a greater discrepancy between Yehud and its preexilic equivalent than other calculations would have allowed for, the unmistakable impression is that the population of Yehud in the Persian period is dramatically smaller than that which occupied analogous territory at the end of the preexilic period. For Jerusalem, the change in population is even more marked. Our low estimate of 6250 for Josiah's day is ten times larger than the 625 to 750 estimated to have been the population in the provincial capital before Nehemiah's mission (Carter 1992).

With depopulation of such magnitude, it is no wonder that the prophetic gaze of the fifth century would deem it just as improbable for a populous restored Israel as for a restored monarchy and independent nation-state to become realities. Using the historical specificity of a Yehud one-third the size of its predecessor, Second Zechariah portrays an eschatological resolution of unprecedented expansion. But all along, he is aware that the key to that expansion is the remnant, the third who survive war and deportation. The remnant is subjected to testing and purification through the hardships they must endure in their reduced size and status. Thus they will be present when Yahweh fights the last cosmic battle and changes the very climate and landscape of Judah and Jerusalem so that Yahweh's people will at last prosper in their land and all other nations will acknowledge the sovereignty of Israel's god. With his demographic sensibility, as with many other aspects of Zechariah 9—14, the prophet is keenly aware of past circumstances; and he weaves them into his projections of a future that is radically different while still rooted in Israel's historic heritage of authoritative tradition and promised land.

NOTES

1. Many of the assumptions in this chapter, such as the postexilic date for Second Zechariah, and also the specific readings of the texts examined below, are based on materials that are developed in detail in Meyers and Meyers 1993. The reader is referred to that work for further information about our interpretive strategies, our readings of the relevant Zechariah passages, our assessment of the nature and significance of the prophecies of Zechariah 9—14, and our suggestions about the work's authorship.

2. This estimation excludes one subregion of Broshi and Finkelstein's region 7, namely that of the territory between Jerusalem and Ramalleh, which perhaps ought to have been included. It is not clear, however, how much overlap there may be in the subdivisions or whether the demarcation of the Shephelah is the same as in Carter's work. Adding this subdivision would only contribute to the sense of a population for Yehud less than that of equivalent preexilic Judah.

WORKS CITED

Aharoni, Y.
1979   *The Land of the Bible.* 2d ed. Philadelphia: Westminster.
Avi-Yonah, M.
1966   *The Holy Land.* Grand Rapids: Baker House.
Broshi, M.
1974   The Expansion of Jerusalem in the Reigns of Hezekiah and Manasseh. *Israel Exploration Journal* 24:21–26.
1978   Estimating the Population of Ancient Jerusalem. *Biblical Archaeology Review* 4:10–15.
Broshi, M., and I. Finkelstein
1992   The Population of Palestine in Iron Age II. *Bulletin of the American Schools of Oriental Research* 287:47–60.
Broshi, M., and R. Gophna
1984   The Settlement and Population of Palestine during the Early Bronze II–III. *Bulletin of the American Schools of Oriental Research* 253:41–53.
1986   Middle Bronze Age II Palestine: Its Settlement and Population. *Bulletin of the American Schools of Oriental Research* 261:73–90.
Carter, C. E.
1991   A Social and Demographic Study of Post-Exilic Judah. Ph.D. dissertation, Duke University.
1992   The Province of Yehud in the Post-Exilic Period: Soundings in Site Distribution and Demography. Paper presented at the annual meeting of the American Academy of Religion/Society of Biblical Literature/American Schools of Oriental Research, San Francisco.
Childs, B. S.
1979   *Introduction to the Old Testament as Scripture.* Philadelphia: Fortress.

Dever, W. G.
1985   Syro-Palestinian and Biblical Archaeology. In *The Hebrew Bible and Its Modern Interpreters*, ed. J. A. Knight and G. M. Tucker, 31–74. Philadelphia: Fortress Press; and Chico, Calif.: Scholars Press.
1992   A Case-Study in Biblical Archaeology: The Earthquake of Ca 760 BCE. *Eretz-Israel* 23:27*–35*.

Finkelstein, I.
1988   The Value of Demographic Data from Recent Generations for Environmental Archaeology and Historical Research. Paper presented at the Society for Biblical Literature International Meeting, Sheffield, England.
1990   Environmental Archaeology and Social History: Demographic and Economic Aspects of the Monarchic Period. Paper presented at the Second International Congress on Biblical Archaeology, Jerusalem.

Greenberg, M.
1983   *Ezekiel 1–20*. Anchor Bible 22. Garden City, N.Y.: Doubleday.

Hodder, I.
1986   *Reading the Past: Current Approaches to Interpretation in Archaeology*. Cambridge: Cambridge University Press.

Hoglund, K.
1992   *Achaemenid Imperial Administration in Syria-Palestine and the Missions of Ezra-Nehemiah*. Society of Biblical Literature Dissertation Series, 125. Atlanta: Scholars Press.

Kochavi, M.
1972   The Land of Judah. In *Judaea, Samaria, and the Galilee: Archaeological Survey, 1967–1968*, ed. M. Kochavi, 19–89. Jerusalem: Carta (Hebrew).

Lapp, P.
1963   Ptolemaic Stamped Handles from Judah. *Bulletin of the American Schools of Oriental Research* 177:22–35.

London, G.
1992   Tells: City Center or Home? *Eretz-Israel* 23:71*–79*.

Mason, R.
1982   Some Examples of Inner Biblical Exegesis in Zechariah 9–14. *Studia Evangelica* 7:343–54.

Meyers, C.
1992   The Contributions of Archaeology. In *The Oxford Study Bible*, ed. M. J. Suggs, K. D. Sakenfeld, and J. R. Mueller, 48–56. New York: Oxford University Press.
1993   Foreign Places, Future World: Toponyms in the Eschatology of Zechariah 9. *Eretz-Israel* 24:164*–72*.

Meyers, C., and E. Meyers
1989   Expanding the Frontiers of Biblical Archaeology. *Eretz-Israel* 20:140–47.
1993   *Zechariah 9–14*. Anchor Bible 25C. New York: Doubleday.

Ofer, A.
1990   The Judean Hill Country—From Nomadism to a National Mon-
               archy. In *From Nomadism to Monarchy: Archaeological and Historical
               Aspects of Early Israel*, ed. N. Na'aman and I. Finkelstein, 155–214.
               Jerusalem: Yad Ben Zvi (Hebrew).

Shiloh, Y.
1980   The Population of Iron Age Palestine in Light of a Sample Analy-
               sis of Urban Plans, Areas, and Population Density. *Bulletin of the
               American Schools of Oriental Research* 239:25–35.

Stern, E.
1982   *Material Culture of the Land of the Bible in the Persian Period, 538–
               332 B.C.* Warminster: Aris and Phillips.

1984   The Persian Empire and the Political and Social History of Pales-
               tine in the Persian Period. In *The Cambridge History of Judaism*,
               Vol. 1, Introduction; The Persian Period, ed. W. D. Davies and L.
               Finkelstein, 70–87. Cambridge: Cambridge University Press.

Trigger, B. G.
1989   *A History of Archaeological Thought*. Cambridge: Cambridge Uni-
               versity Press.

17 | King Solomon's Shields

ALAN MILLARD

The biblical descriptions of King Solomon give a picture of conspicuous wealth that arouses the incredulity of commentators. J. B. Pritchard wrote of "the extravagant detail which is so characteristic of the writings about the Solomonic Age . . . the imagination which the writers about the Age of Solomon had allowed full rein" (1974:32). Others draw attention to a tendency "to exaggerate the richness of the original furnishings," specifically of the Temple (Miller and Hayes 1986:94). Scholars are at liberty to suppose that the accounts may be exaggerated or even fictitious, yet before they relegate them to the realms of folklore, it is just to investigate the possibility that these accounts reflect a real situation. This chapter concentrates on one element, the shields in Solomon's palace.

> King Solomon made two hundred large shields of beaten gold; six hundred shekels of gold went into each shield. And he made three hundred shields of beaten gold; three minas of gold went into each shield; and the king put them in the House of the Forest of Lebanon. (1 Kgs. 10:16–17)

Together these shields accounted for almost two tons of gold. Whether they were of wood, overlaid with gold, or of base metal so embellished, is unstated, and matters little here.

Golden shields sound unlikely, and were certainly worthless in war. Their replacements in bronze, after Shishak removed Solomon's treasure to Egypt, were used for ceremonial parades, as 1 Kings 14:26–28 makes clear. Earlier, Hadadezer of Damascus had been attended by courtiers who carried golden shields, which David captured (2 Sam. 8:7). Beside these biblical references can be set discoveries of gold work that is just as useless in battle. Golden swords and golden axes seem ridiculous, yet there are examples from the Royal Cemetery at Ur in the mid–third millennium BCE, from the Royal Tombs at Byblos in the Middle Bronze Age, and from Achaemenid Hamadan (Ecbatana) (Woolley 1934: pls. 151–52, 153*b*, 156*a*, 157*b*; Dunand 1950: pls. 133, 135; Porada 1965: pl. 47). Ur also yielded the famous gold helmet of Meskalamdug, clearly a piece of parade armor for show, not combat, yet reproducing in precious metal what was made presumably in base for real protection. (The king wears a somewhat similar helmet in two war scenes on the Stele of Vultures from Girsu [Tello] of slightly later date [Amiet 1980: nos. 45, 328].) Golden shields, however, have not been found in ancient Near Eastern sites.

Reports of golden shields have long been available in Greek sources. In the second century CE the traveler Pausanias saw hanging in the temple of Zeus at Olympia "a golden shield, with Medusa the Gorgon in relief." The inscription on the shield declares who dedicated it and the reason why they did so:

> The temple has a golden shield; from Tanagra
> The Lacedaemonians and their allies dedicated it.
> A gift taken from the Argives, Athenians and Ionians,
> The tithe offered for victory in war.
> (translation from Jones and Ormerod 1926)

Pausanius also observed: "On the outside of the frieze that runs round the temple at Olympia, above the columns, are gilt shields one and twenty in number, an offering made by the Roman general Mummius when he had conquered the Achaeans in war, captured Corinth, and driven out its Dorian inhabitants" (*Description of Greece* V, Elis, 1.10.4–5). Remote in time from King Solomon and different in purpose as these shields were, being votive gifts to the temple, nevertheless they are evidence that the concept of golden shields was not alien to antiquity. Pausanias also visited Delphi, where he noted there was an iron stand for a bowl presented by the Lydian king Alyattes (*Description of Greece* 10.16.i). That was the only relic of the treasures sent to Delphi by the Lydian kings eight centuries before. Herodotus had recorded those in detail, including a silver bowl and dish of welded iron from Alyattes. Croesus's donations were the most lavish. Golden shields did not figure among his offerings at Delphi, but Herodotus tells of a golden spear and a golden shield that Croesus sent to another shrine, which he himself saw in an Apollo temple in Thebes (*The*

Histories 1.50–52). Contemplation of these Greek accounts might lead some to conclude the Hebrew writers were reflecting practices of Greek times, the sixth century BCE and later. (Such reasoning led Eduard Meyer to suppose the boundaries of David's kingdom reflected the extent of the Persian province of Abr-Nahrain.) While this conclusion is theoretically possible, evidence from the ancient Near East makes it unlikely.

An echo of the shield Pausanias described at Olympia can be seen in the fragment of a bronze example unearthed at Olympia (Kunze 1956:46–50; see Snodgrass 1964:37–68) and in another excavated at Carchemish on the Euphrates in 1911. That lay in the ruins of a house in the outer town which had been burnt, there is little room to doubt, when Nebuchadrezzar's forces took the city in 605 BCE. Cleaned and reconstructed, it has a gorgon's face embossed in the center of concentric rings of animals running toward some hoops, possibly caves, in an east Greek (Ionian) style. The whole design is almost identical to the Olympia fragment. The shield, 80 cm (27½ in) in diameter, was made of very thin bronze fixed to a wooden or leather base (Woolley 1921:125, 128, pl. 24). It is hard to believe it had any truly defensive function (see fig. 17-1).

Other shields dating from the seventh century BCE came to light during Henry Layard's excavations at Nimrud. One room in the North-West Palace was full of metal objects, among them bronze shields.

> The shields stood upright, one against the other, supported by a square piece of brick work, and were so much decayed that with great difficulty two were moved and sent to England. They are of bronze, and circular, the rim bending inwards, and forming a deep groove round the edge. The handles are of iron, and fastened by six bosses or nails, the heads of which form an ornament on the outer face of the shield. The diameter of the largest and most perfect is 2 feet 6 inches [76.2 cm]. (Layard 1853:194)

These were plain, military shields.

The thirst for antiquities created by the sensational discoveries P. E. Botta and Layard made in Assyria led to digging in many other places. In 1880 a hoard of bronze work was taken from Toprak Kale, east of Lake Van. This included one plain and two decorated bronze shields, and pieces of others. Later another decorated shield was recovered. The shields range from 0.48 to 1 m (19 to 39 in) in diameter. Their ornamentation comprises a central rosette surrounded by two or three concentric rings of animals walking in procession, embossed and chased (fig. 17-2a, b). Cuneiform inscriptions on some of these shields declare their dedication

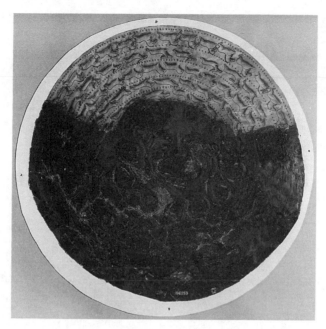

FIG. 17-1. Fragmentary bronze shield decorated in Ionian style with a gorgon's head at the center and concentric rows of animals. Late seventh century BCE, found at Carchemish. Diameter 80 cm. British Museum WAA 116253. Photograph courtesy of the Trustees of the British Museum.

by Rusas, an Urartian king ruling late in the seventh century BCE (Barnett 1960: pls. 9, 10, 22.4). A bronze shield 1 m (39 in) in diameter rewarded Russian excavators at another Urartian citadel, Karmir Blur, dedicated by an earlier king, Argishti, in the eighth century BCE. It has a conical boss in the center. Elsewhere on the site there were bronze bosses with remnants of wicker shields, the bosses inscribed by the same king (Barnett and Watson 1952:135–36). Other shields have been found in Urartian sites (Van Loon 1966:116–18; Azarpay 1960:21–24).

These Urartian shields especially, but the Carchemish and Olympia ones, too, enable us to envisage the concept conveyed by Rehoboam's bronze replacements for Solomon's golden shields.

From Urartu, again, comes illumination of those golden shields. In 714 BCE, King Sargon of Assyria marched from his palace to quell rebel tribes in the mountains to the east. As happens frequently, he was drawn farther into foreign territory than he intended to go, until he found himself attacking one of the chief cities of Urartu, Musasir, southwest of

FIG. 17-2a. Bronze shield decorated with concentric rows of lions and other animals and inscribed with the name of Rusas, king of Urartu, ca. 629 to 615 BCE, found at Toprak Kale near Lake Van. Diameter 85.2 cm. British Museum WAA 22481. Photograph courtesy of the Trustees of the British Museum.

FIG. 17-2b. Bronze shield similar to the above. Diameter 77 cm. British Museum WAA 22482. Photograph courtesy of the Trustees of the British Museum.

Lake Urmia. His soldiers took the city and looted it. Following the usual custom in ancient wars, a large share of the booty went to King Sargon. When he arrived home victorious, he gave a lengthy report of his campaign to the national god Assur, and a copy of this letter, written on a large clay tablet, was found by the German expedition at the city of Ashur in 1912. It was itself looted from the site during the First World War and sold through the antiquities market to the Musée du Louvre in Paris. In it Sargon lists the spoils of Musasir's palace and of the temple of Haldi, chief god of Urartu, giving a fascinating glimpse through ancient doorways. Of most interest here are lines 370–71, recounting the rich embellishments the Assyrians removed, including: "6 shields of gold which hung to the right and left of his shrine, gleaming brightly, with heads of fierce dogs protruding from the centres, by weight 5 talents and 12 minas of red gold" (Thureau-Dangin 1912; Mayer 1983; 1979:586). The weight is equivalent to about 25 kg (55 lbs) for each; for comparison, King Solomon's larger gold shields weighed about 6.8 kg (15 lbs) each, the smaller 2 kg (4.5 lbs) each. The list continues with many other treasures, some initially surprising, like a bolt and two keys of gold and a large golden sword weighing 26 minas and 3 shekels (about 25 kg [55 lbs] each).

As well as describing his success in words, King Sargon had a pictorial record of it carved on stone slabs lining the walls of his palace at Dur-Sharruken, now Khorsabad, north of Nineveh. The panel bearing the relief of Musasir's temple being pillaged was dug up in 1843, but only a fragment of it survives. A drawing made at the time preserves the scene (Botta and Flandin 1849: pl. 141; Albenda 1986:149, pl. 134, 163 AO198892, fig. 90; C. B. F. Walker in Albenda 1986:110–11). Assyrian soldiers are ransacking a building that appears to have a domed roof, and running off with its treasures (fig. 17-3). Some of them carry shields; other shields hang on the walls of the temple. Some shields are shown from the front, with a central boss and an outer flange; others are shown in profile, the central boss clearly being a snarling animal's head. Thus the sculpture complements the written record, and both together supply a complete analogy for Solomon's golden shields. They were made, in every case, for display, either in a royal procession or in devotion to deity.

The surviving bronze shields from Assyria and Urartu and the reliable contemporary witness for golden ones in eighth-century Urartu are still two centuries later than Solomon's reign and many hundreds of miles distant from his palace. At present earlier examples, closer to Jerusalem, have not come to light. Is the analogy satisfactory? Certainly it proves the

FIG. 17-3. Drawing of a relief carving from the palace of Sargon II of Assyria, at Khorsabad, showing Assyrian soldiers looting shields that decorated the temple of Haldi in the Urartian town of Musasir. Reproduced from Botta and Flandin 1849: pl. 141.

use of shields to decorate a royal building, and that golden shields were made for that purpose in the Near East two hundred years before the manufacture of the shield for Croesus that Herodotus saw. The situation is one Near Eastern archaeology frequently meets. A written record asserts the existence of something at a certain time and place, but there is no physical evidence for it there and then. When some specimens do emerge from the appropriate context, the texts gain in reality, whether or not their statements have been believed on their own merit. A relevant case is the references to gold and silver drinking vessels in cuneiform tablets from Mari, Alalakh, and other Old Babylonian or Middle Bronze Age sites, which describe these goblets as animal shaped. Texts from the Late Bronze Age give similar information. Until twenty years ago the only hint at what these texts were describing came from pottery vessels formed as animal heads, found at Kanesh (Kültepe) and a few other sites, dating from the Middle Bronze Age, and from others of the Late Bronze Age. Not unexpectedly, precious metal was constantly recycled, so most ancient plate has disappeared. However, a private collector acquired two remarkable silver vessels, one worked as a stag's head, the other as a bull's, dated about 1400 to 1200 BCE, and originating in a Hittite workshop (Muscarella 1974: nos. 123–24; 1992:6, 7, 54). From the pottery pieces and from these silver ones, some idea of the objects the texts described can be gained (Dalley 1984:59–62). In the same way, while Assyrian records list golden vessels in large quantities, and the reliefs depict some examples, not a single Assyrian gold goblet or dish was discovered until an Iraqi workman struck the tomb of a royal lady at Nimrud in 1989, revealing a hoard of golden treasure, and other tombs nearby then yielded much more. There are several pieces of gold plate, including at least one golden drinking bowl inscribed with the name of a high official active early in the eighth century BCE (Fadhil 1990:182, pl. 39).

No one had seriously doubted the accuracy of those records because they were contemporary, and many of them are the mundane products of clerks and accountants; an element of suspicion always attaches to the royal inscriptions, for ancient kings inevitably wanted to present themselves in the richest colors to their own age and to posterity. Partly because the present form of 1 Kings comes from the sixth century BCE, or later, and partly because of the lavish terms of the description of Solomon's reign, the Hebrew text about King Solomon's shields has lacked contextual examination. To prove it is factually accurate is all but impossible; to demonstrate that it could be a reliable record of an ancient decoration in Jerusalem has been the purpose of this chapter. Anyone is at liberty to reject 1 Kings 10:16–17 as patriotic invention, an attempt by theological authors long after Solomon's time to produce propaganda for their own ends, or a fairy tale, if they can provide solid grounds for doing so; to dismiss this or any other part of the Solomonic story simply because some elements occur in reports about other ancient kings is an illogical process which, if followed freely, would deny the validity of many ancient records upon which our knowledge of ancient history depends (Miller and Hayes argue in this way, 1986:195). That Solomon did the same things as other ancient kings does not necessarily prove his story is a pastiche; it may well imply that he was a prominent ruler who behaved in the way expected of such a ruler, for had he not done so, his contemporaries would not have recognized his status. Only if adequate, careful examination of all ancient sources indicates that an ancient text, biblical or other, is quite at variance with the period it claims to describe, or produces contrary witnesses whose evidence is indisputable, can modern scholars jettison the testimony of that text with impunity. Any other action is, to a greater or lesser extent, a distortion of the evidence handed down to us from antiquity.

WORKS CITED

Amiet, P.
1980   *Art of the Ancient Near East*. New York: Harry N. Abrams.
Albenda, P.
1986   *The Palace of Sargon King of Assyria*. Paris: Editions Recherches sur les Civilisations.
Azarpay, G.
1960   *Urartian Art and Artifacts*. Berkeley and Los Angeles: University of California Press.
Barnett, R. D.
1960   The Excavations of the British Museum at Toprak Kale near Van. *Iraq* 12:1–43.
Barnett, R. D., and W. Watson
1952   Russian Excavations in Armenia. *Iraq* 14:132–47.
Botta, P. E., and E. Flandin
1849   *Monuments de Ninive* II. Paris: Imprimerie Nationale.
Dalley, S.
1984   *Mari and Karana*. London: Longman.
Dunand, M.
1950   *Fouilles de Byblos*, II. Paris: Maisonneuve.
Fadhil, A.
1990   Die Grabinschrift der Mullissu-mukanniŝat-Ninua aus Nimrud/ Kalhu und andere in ihrem Grab gefundene Schriftträger. *Baghdader Mitteilungen* 21:471–82.
Jones, W. H. S., and H. A. Ormerod, eds.
1926   Pausanius. *Description of Greece*. Loeb Classical Library. London: Heineman.

Kunze, E.
1956   *V Bericht über die Ausgrabungen in Olympia*. Berlin: de Gruyter.
Layard, A. H.
1853   *Nineveh and Babylon*. London: Murray.
Mayer, W.
1979   Die Finanzierung einer Kampagne. *Ugarit-Forschungen* 11:571–95.
1983   Sargons Feldzug gegen Urartu-714 v. Chr.: Text und Überset-
            zung. *Mitteilungen der deutschen Orient-Gesellschaft* 115:65–132.
Miller, J. M., and J. H. Hayes
1986   *A History of Ancient Israel and Judah*. Philadelphia: Westminster.
Muscarella, O. W.
1992   Ancient Art: Gifts from the Norbert Schimmel Collection. *Bulle-
            tin of the Metropolitan Museum of Art* 49.4.
Muscarella, O. W., ed.
1974   *Ancient Art: The Norbert Schimmel Collection*. Mainz: Philip von
            Zabern.
Porada, E.
1965   *Ancient Iran*. New York: Crown.
Pritchard, J. B.
1974   *Solomon and Sheba*. London: Phaidon.
Snodgrass, A.
1964   *Early Greek Armour and Weapons*. Edinburgh: University Press.
Thureau-Dangin, F.
1912   *Une relation de la huitième campagne de Sargon*. Textes cunéiformes
            du Louvre 3. Paris: Paul Geuthner.
van Loon, M. N.
1966   *Urartian Art*. Istanbul: Nederlands Historisch-Archaeologisch
            Instituut.
Woolley, C. L.
1921   *Carchemish II*. London: British Museum.
1934   *Ur Excavations, II: The Royal Cemetery*. London: British Museum.

18 | The Cenacle and Community: The Background of Acts 2:44–45

JEROME MURPHY-O'CONNOR, O.P.

It is not surprising that there has been no serious discussion of the authenticity of the Cenacle, a rather dilapidated building outside the south wall of the Old City of Jerusalem where the Upper Room of Pentecost and the Last Supper rises above the Tomb of David.

According to the Bible, David was buried in the City of David (1 Kgs. 2:10), which is identified with the city of the Jebusites on the Ophel Ridge (2 Sam. 5:6–9). The two great shafts running horizontally into the bedrock, discovered by Raymond Weill (1920) in 1913–14, were immediately identified as the royal tombs, an identification that has been accepted by some (Vincent 1921; Mazar 1975:183–85) but refused by others (Kenyon 1967:188; Ussishkin 1993:299). Throughout the Byzantine period, however, the tomb of David was located in Bethlehem (Wilkinson 1977:151). Fourth- and fifth-century lectionaries reveal that in those centuries a memorial service for David and James, the brother of the Lord, founders of the old and new Jerusalem respectively, was celebrated in the Church of Mount Zion on December 25 (subsequently 26). The liturgical memorial eventually gave rise to physical memorials (Limor 1988), namely tombs, that of James in the Armenian cathedral and David beneath the Cenacle.

If the foundations of this building are so insecure, what chance can the Upper Room have? Its features are so specifically Lusignan gothic that it can only have been constructed by craftsmen from Cyprus recruited by the Franciscans, when they returned as Guardians of the Holy Land in 1335. A papal bull of Clement VI dated 21 November 1342 notes the construction there of a monastery for twelve monks (Vincent and Abel 1922:423, 465).

Nothing visible, therefore, has the slightest claim to authenticity. Does this mean that the site is totally devoid of interest? On the contrary, it throws new light on the circumstances of the first Christian community in Jerusalem. After discussing the archaeological and textual evidence for the existence of a second-century Christian building on Mount Zion, I shall argue that the determination of the strong Christian community in Aelia Capitolina to maintain contact with the site, despite severe obstacles, betrays an attachment to the building that is explicable only in terms of the importance the site had in the first century, when the quarter was the home of the most affluent residents of the city.

A SECOND-CENTURY CHURCH
ON MOUNT ZION

The Muslims took possession of the Cenacle in 1524 and transformed it into a mosque (Vincent and Abel 1922:471). In 1948 heavy fighting around the Zion Gate forced closure of the mosque. It was not reopened after the cease-fire because the site was immediately on the frontier with Jordan. It was some time before the situation stabilized and Orthodox Jews moved in. The interval was put to good advantage by J. Pinkerfeld, who in 1951 conducted the only excavation on the site. Fortunately he produced a preliminary report before he was killed in the terrorist attack on the Archaeological Convention of 1956 at Ramat Rahel, but no final report ever appeared. J. Hirschberg (1975) offers no more than a bland summary of Pinkerfeld's work. Moreover, he approached his investigation with the mistaken conviction that the building was a synagogue oriented to the Temple by a niche in the north wall.[1]

About 12 cm beneath the present floor of the burial chamber Pinkerfeld found the floor corresponding to the Crusader sarcophagus. The next floor appeared 48 cm deeper. It was "a colored mosaic decorated with geometric designs characteristic of the late Roman or early Byzantine period" (1960:42). Ten cm below that was another floor, "quite possibly the remains of a stone pavement," but it too might have been mosaic (1960:43). While the information is sketchy, nonetheless one important conclusion can be drawn: there was a building on this site in the late Roman period, that is, in the second or third century.

The three groups of Greek graffiti of the earliest period passed through the hands of Moise Schwabe and Baruch Lifshitz before being given to the Franciscans where they were interpreted by Emmanuel Testa. He read the most specific as "Oh, Jesus, that I may live, O Lord of the autocrat" (Bagatti 1971:121). This bizarre reading is rejected by Emile Puech (1989), who nonetheless finds a mention of Jesus and insists that the context is Christian. The proposed reading "Jesus" for *I* written above *OY* commands awe but not conviction.

Writing in 394, Epiphanius of Salamis noted that when the emperor Hadrian visited Jerusalem in 130 he found the city in ruins

> except for a few houses, and the little church of God (*kai tēs tou theou ekklēsias mikras*) on the spot where the disciples went to the upper room on their return from the Mount of Olives after the Ascension of the Redeemer. It was built there, namely on Sion, which escaped the destruction, and the houses around Sion and seven synagogues (*synagōgai*) which remained isolated in Sion like huts, one of which survived into the time of bishop Maximos and of the emperor Constantine, like a shanty in a vineyard, as the Scripture says [Isa. 1:8]. (*De mensuris et ponderibus* 14; *PG* 43:261)

Despite his name, acquired only in 367 when he was consecrated Metropolitan of Salamis, Epiphanius was a Palestinian born of Christian parents in 315 in Eleutheropolis (Bet Guvrin), where he directed a monastery for over thirty years (*LTK* 3.944–45). His contacts with Jerusalem must have been frequent, making him an eyewitness of the situation in Jerusalem at the beginning of the Byzantine period. That his information in fact stems from this period rather than his later visit in 393 is suggested by his slightly older contemporary, the Bordeaux Pilgrim, who arrived in Jerusalem in 333; regarding Mount Zion the latter wrote, "Inside Sion, within the wall, you can see where David had his palace. Seven synagogues were there, but only one is left—the rest have been 'ploughed and sown' as was said by the prophet Isaiah [1:8]" (Wilkinson 1981:157–58).

The identical reference to Isaiah 1:8 makes it certain that Epiphanius and the Pilgrim drew on precisely the same local tradition, which mentioned the survival of a single synagogue into the third decade of the fourth century. When taken at face value, this is highly improbable. After the Second Jewish Revolt (132–35), Hadrian decreed the city and territory of Jerusalem to be off-limits for all Jews: "From that time on, the entire race has been forbidden to set foot anywhere in the neighbourhood of Jerusalem, under the terms and ordinances of a law of Hadrian which ensured that not even from a distance might Jews have a view of their ancestral soil" (Eusebius, *HE* 4.6.3; Williamson 1989:108). The decree has been reconstructed by Michael Avi-Yonah: "It is forbidden for all circumcised persons to enter or stay within the territory of Aelia Capitolina; any person contravening this prohibition shall be put to death" (1976:50–51). There is no evidence that this edict was subsequently rescinded. On the contrary, the exception mentioned by both Origen[2] and the Bordeaux Pilgrim[3] attests that it was in force in the third and fourth centuries.[4] Even if individual Jews occasionally took the risk of living in Jerusalem (Avi-Yonah 1976:76), it is impossible that there should have been a functioning synagogue.

A European visitor, such as the Bordeaux Pilgrim, who recognized the religious character of the building but found it alien to his religious experience, might be forgiven for thinking it a synagogue rather than a church of indigenous Christians (so rightly Walker 1990:286, 290). A native like Epiphanius, however, could not have made this sort of mistake. Another explanation must be sought.

A strange feature of Epiphanius's report is its repetitiousness. Although the passage is very short, the second part duplicates the first. It opens by recalling the survival of a few houses and the little church of God, and concludes by evoking the survival of a few houses and a single synagogue. There are two mentions of Zion in close proximity. It would appear that the author has combined two slightly different descriptions of the same locality, one reflecting Palestinian, the other Diaspora language. Alternatively, Epiphanius might have given his own interpretation—"little church of God" implies that he knew greater churches—to a report from another source. In either case the church and the synagogue would be one and the same building, but looked at from two different perspectives, which reflect the change introduced by the legalization of Christianity. The edifice had not been built as a church; it was a Jewish Christian place of assembly that in fact served as a church.[5] Now the point of mentioning that the synagogue survived into the time of Maximus becomes evident. It was during his period of episcopal office (335–49) that the first church on Mount Zion was consecrated, sometime before 348, when Cyril of Jerusalem speaks of the Upper Church of the Apostles (*Catechetical Lectures* 16:4; Vincent and Abel 1922:472). Evidently it was well known in the fourth century that an earlier building had been transformed, because Egeria (43:1; Wilkinson 1981:141) casually notes that "it has now been altered into a church." The absence of any synagogue in 370 was noted by Optatus of Mileve (*De schismate Donatistarum* 3:2; Vincent and Abel 1922:473).

THE CHRISTIAN COMMUNITY OF
AELIA CAPITOLINA

When correctly understood, therefore, both Epiphanius and the Bordeaux Pilgrim assert the existence of a Christian church on Mount Zion
from the second to the fourth century. Is this credible? Two conditions
must be fulfilled for an affirmative answer to be plausible: (1) the continuous presence in Aelia Capitolina of Christians (2) whose public activity
was in no way circumscribed. That both these conditions were in fact met
can be demonstrated from Eusebius.

Continuity is guaranteed by the unbroken succession of bishops from
the time of Hadrian to the early fourth century.[6] The substantial accuracy
of this list cannot be impugned.[7] The character of the Christian presence
is illustrated by the figure of Alexander. While a bishop in Cappadocia,
he had already been imprisoned for the faith (Eusebius, *HE* 6.11.5). He
made a pilgrimage to Jerusalem in 212, where, against his will, he was
forced to become the auxiliary of the aged bishop of Narcissus, whom he
succeeded. He died in prison in Caesarea in 251 (*HE* 6.39.2–3; Vincent
and Abel 1922:896). During his long pontificate of thirty-nine years he
constructed the library of Aelia, which was used by Eusebius: "Prominent
at that period were a number of learned churchmen, who penned to each
other letters still surviving and easy of access, as they have been preserved
to our own time in the library established at Aelia by the man who then
presided over the church there, Alexander—the library from which I
myself have been able to bring together the materials for the work now in
hand" (*HE* 6.20.1; Williamson 1989:198).

This library should be understood as an institution of the city rather
than as a purely ecclesiastical library, although a concern for theological
resources may have been its primary motivation. It was a time when cities
felt that they owed themselves libraries, and the initiative of citizens was
welcomed (Wendel 1954; Granger 1933). Apart from certain basic books,
such as the Bible, the selection was haphazard. It is most probable that
the letters mentioned by Eusebius reached Jerusalem as part of the private collections of individuals given or willed to the library. It would be
most extraordinary if it did not contain much more than letters.

A hint of its scope is provided by Julius Africanus in a work written
about 230 (Viellefond 1970:278). He notes apropos of a bizarre incanta-
tion in which the name of Yahweh is combined with the gods of the
Greek and Egyptian pantheons: "This passage appears intact in the

archives [*archeiois*] of our ancient homeland, the colony of Aelia Capitolina in Palestine, as well as in that of Nysa in Caria, and as far as verse 13 at Rome in the beautiful library [*bibliothēkē*] of the Pantheon near the Baths of Alexander for which I drew up the plans for the emperor" (*Papyrus Oxyrhynchus* 3.412; Veillefond 1970:288–91). While one cannot be absolutely certain that this is a reference to the library of Alexander, that is the simplest hypothesis. Despite the use of *archeion*, the contrast with *bibliothēkē* is only apparent because the nature of the text shows that it could never have belonged to the "public records" of Aelia. Moreover, the allusion to Nysa suggests a public library, whereas the contents and the circumstances of the Hadrianic decree of expulsion militate against a Jewish collection. Even though Julius evokes the Jewish heritage that he shares with his readers, "our ancient homeland" (Viellefond 1970:17), it cannot be forgotten that he was a Christian when he wrote.

The situation of Christianity in the second and third centuries, therefore, was as follows. There were sporadic persecutions, but they failed to block the growth of the church or to intimidate its members. The ability of the diocese of Aelia to fund a library, and its interest in so doing, betray the strength of the church in the colony. Local efforts, of course, were assisted by pilgrims from abroad (Vincent and Abel 1922:896–902).

THE CAMP OF
THE TENTH LEGION

The next step in the argument is to highlight the significance of the location on Mount Zion of the little church of God. It was cut off from the city by the camp of the Tenth Legion.

One of the most significant discoveries made by Nahman Avigad in the Jewish Quarter was the southern portion of the Cardo Maximus of Aelia. Though at first debated, his dating of the foundation of this section of the main street to the sixth century is now accepted (1980:225–26). The Hadrianic Cardo Maximus of Aelia terminated somewhere in the area of the present David Street. If it did not go farther south, that can only be because the line of its extension was blocked by the camp of the Tenth Legion *Fretensis*.

It is known from Josephus that Titus established the legion in the area of the palace of Herod the Great: "Caesar gave orders that they should now demolish the entire city and temple, but should leave as many of the towers standing as were of the greatest eminence, that is, Phasaelus, and

Hippicus, and Mariamne, and so much of the wall as enclosed the city on the west side. This wall was spared in order to afford a camp for such as were to be the garrison" (*History of the Jewish War* 7.1–2). This report suggests that three towers of the palace constituted the northwest corner of the legion camp. At this time the west wall of Herodian Jerusalem followed the curve of the Hinnom Valley to the east, but it is improbable that all its length was utilized by the legion.[8] The sixth-century Mosaic map from Madaba in Jordan shows an interior east-west wall on approximately the line of the present south wall of the Old City. The simplest explanation of its origins is that on the west it represents the south wall of the legion camp, which was subsequently prolonged to the east to join the Temple Mount when the legion was definitively withdrawn by Diocletian (284–305).[9] Only at that time did Aelia need or acquire a wall.

The line of the eastern wall of the legion camp is much more difficult to determine. The average size of a permanent Roman legion camp housing six thousand men was 20 ha (50 acres) (Saglio 1899; von Domaszewski 1899). In order to come anywhere near this dimension, the camp of the Tenth Legion would have had to go as far east as the escarpment of the Tyropoeon Valley, which moreover would have offered the same defensive advantage as the Hinnom Valley on the west.[10]

Since the residential area of Aelia Capitolina was north of the legion camp, the Christians of Aelia Capitolina would have had to go around the legion camp either on the east or on the west in order to reach the little church on Mount Zion.

The former route would have been extremely difficult, if not impossible. In order to defend the Temple the Zealots demolished the bridge crossing the Tyropoeon. Benjamin Mazar (1975:221) cites the early homiletic Midrash *Ekha Rabbati* 4:7: "Said Rabbi Abba bar-Cahana: The aqueduct which came from Etam was destroyed one day by the Sicarii." The huge mass of debris that this dumped on the road below was increased to a height of almost fifteen meters when the Romans pushed out the external walls projecting above the platform of the temple (Mazar 1975:217). The slope to the west up to the escarpment was a scree of loose stones from the ruined buildings. To scramble through this mess would have been both laborious and dangerous. Conditions might have improved to the southeast but not by much. The area immediately south of the Temple Mount was resettled only in the fourth century.

The alternative route around the western side of Aelia offered other difficulties. It would have been much easier physically, the only difficulty being the rather steep eastern slope of the Hinnom Valley. The danger came from Roman sentries. The Mount Zion segment of the south wall of the legion camp was one of its weakest points, being unprotected by a valley. In consequence it was guarded more securely. Between the two great revolts there were moments of high tension, possibly in 86, certainly in 115 (Schürer 1973:514–18), when Christians assembling on Mount Zion would have been seen as a threat and severely questioned. After 135 there was no further danger.

Such difficulties make it impossible that Jerusalem Christians should have invented a holy place on Mount Zion in the second century. If, despite all obstacles, they maintained contact with a site there, it must have been of extreme importance to them. This means that veneration of the site must be pushed back into the first century and prior to the fall of Jerusalem.[11]

THE MYTH OF THE FLIGHT
TO PELLA

The implication of this conclusion is that there must have been constant Christian presence in the Holy City in the period between the two great Jewish revolts. In this respect the tradition of the flight of the Christian community to Pella creates a problem, because the suggestion is that the believers never returned to Jerusalem.

H. J. Lawlor (1912:30) has shown that the three allusions to the event in Epiphanius (*Panarion* 29.7.7; 30:2.7; *De mensuris* 15) all depend on Eusebius (similarly Luedemann 1989:203–4), who thus becomes the one explicit witness: "The people of the church in Jerusalem were commanded by an oracle given by revelation before the war to those in the city who were worthy of it to depart and dwell in one of the cities of Perea which they called Pella" (*HE* 3.5.3). As G. Leudemann (1989:205) has shown, the only likely source for this information is Aristo of Pella (*HE* 4.6.3), and one is forced to ask whether he is reporting a historical fact, as E. Schürer maintains (1979:147–48), or making a propaganda claim on behalf of his hometown to have inherited the mantle of the Jerusalem church. The latter is certainly the more probable.

The possibility of special pleading diminishes the credibility of Aristo's late and lone voice. His reliability is further undermined by the unsuitability of Pella as a place of refuge (Luedemann 1989:211). A Gentile city that had been laid waste by Alexander Jannaeus (Josephus, *History of the*

Jewish War 1.104; *Antiquities of the Jews* 13.397), and again by Jews at the beginning of the First Revolt (*History of the Jewish War* 2.458), would have been most unlikely to offer a welcome to Jewish Christians, however desperate their plight.

On the positive side, Eusebius elsewhere provides evidence that there was no break in the Christian presence in Jerusalem from the time of the episcopate of James the brother of the Lord: "I have received documentary proof of this, that up to Hadrian's siege of the Jews there had been a series of fifteen bishops there" (*HE* 4.5.1). This is complemented by a further assertion: "Until the time of the siege by Hadrian there was an extremely significant church of Christ at Jerusalem which consisted of Jews" (*Demonstratio Evangelica* 3.5.108). Epiphanius's note that the stay of the Jerusalem Christians in Pella was only temporary (*De mensuris* 15) is manifestly an attempt to reconcile the internal contradictions of Eusebius.

THE QUALITY OF LIFE
IN FIRST-CENTURY MOUNT ZION

Having established that there was a constant Christian presence in Jerusalem to carry the tradition from the first to the second century, the next question is, what event in the life of Jesus or the early church was associated with Mount Zion?

Epiphanius, as we have seen, simply identifies the site of the little church of God as the residence of the disciples in Jerusalem (Acts 1:13). A certain plausibility accrues to this assertion because of its very modesty. More significant spiritual associations appear much later. First Pentecost (Acts 2:1–4) is localized there in the fourth century,[12] and early in the next century it becomes the place of the Last Supper.[13] A debate about the name of the owner of the building began very early. In the fifth and sixth centuries at least three candidates had their partisans, John/Mark, Mary, and James (for details, see Wilkinson 1977:171–72). Such speculation, however, is pointless, since no definitive answer will ever be possible. It is more fruitful to ask if the location of the building says anything about the social status of the owner.

Although his street layout has only the slenderest evidence to recommend it, J. Wilkinson (1989:81) is certainly correct in supposing that the western hill was extensively remodeled when Herod the Great, about 24 BC, built his palace there (*History of the Jewish War* 1.402, 5:156–83). Whereas previously the houses of the wealthy clustered around the Hasmonaean palace,[14] now those who could afford it erected their mansions in the vicinity of the new royal seat. The palace of Agrippa and Berenice burnt by the rebels in 66 (*History of the Jewish War* 2:426) is to be identified with the Hasmonaean palace (*Antiquities of the Jews* 20:189–90). The palace of Ananias, the high priest (47–59), burnt on the same occasion, has not been located. He was not from the four great high priestly families. Thus he did not have a traditional residence, so if he built it is likely to have been further up the hill in the vicinity of the new palace.

Certainly that is the area where the earliest Byzantine tradition locates the palace of the high priest Caiaphas (18–36).[15] From the Bordeaux Pilgrim we learn only that it was a ruin on Mount Zion (Wilkinson 1981:157). Writing sometime before 518, Theodosius is much more precise in his *The Topography of Jerusalem*: "From Holy Sion to the House of Caiaphas which is now the Church of St Peter it is about 50 paces [*passus*]" (Wilkinson 1977:66; see also p. 60 and Maps 18 and 21). F.-M. Abel reckons a *passus* at its Roman value equivalent to about 1.5 meters; hence the distance was about 75 meters (ca. 245 ft.) (Vincent and Abel 1922:485), almost exactly the distance between today's Cenacle and the Armenian Monastery of Saint Saviour, which enshrines a house of Caiaphas.

Mosaic floors, one with the geometric patterns typical of the fifth century (Broshi 1976:86), and a well-constructed apse oriented to the east (Vincent and Abel 1922:489, 499), came to light in the courtyard of the Armenian Monastery of Saint Saviour, between the Cenacle and the present south wall of the Old City. Whether these represent traces of Saint Peter's Church is no more certain than that the Herodian material brought to light by Broshi on the same site belongs to the palace of Caiaphas. This, however, is less important than the character of the structures. Following the earthquake of 31 BC (*Antiquities of the Jews* 15.121–22), the area was rebuilt of two- and possibly three-story buildings with barrel-vaulted cisterns. Some rooms were decorated with *fresco secco* murals depicting birds, trees, stylized tendrils, garlands, and architectural elements, which, according to Broshi, "leave no doubt that this quarter was occupied by the more affluent residents of Jerusalem" (1976:83–84).

If the building that subsequently became known as "the little church of God" was located in a wealthy quarter of the city, its owner must have had significant financial resources. The highly idealistic common life (Acts 2:44–45) revealed by the most primitive source of the Acts of the Apostles (Boismard and Lamouille 1990:2.31–32) necessarily presupposes a spacious house and a generous host. It was the lifestyle of Jesus' immediate companions (Matt. 19:27), whose internal financial organization (John 12:6; 13:29) was primed by gifts from female supporters (Luke 8:1–3). This may point to the Mary mentioned in Acts 12:12 as the owner of the house. What number might have been involved no one can say, but such fervor is unlikely to have been shared by a great number.

How long this lifestyle lasted is easier to determine, because at a later stage, represented by Acts 4:32, 34–35 (Boismard and Lamouille 1990:2.159–63), we find that idealism has been tempered by practicality. A lived ideal has been transformed into Platonic theory (Cerfaux 1939:26–28). The church has grown. There is no longer any question of living together, nor of complete community of goods. The apostles act as the channel between the haves and the have-nots. That the same edifice which once housed a community should now have become an administrative center would not have diminished its value in the eyes of believers. Through good times and bad the little church of God was cherished as the first place of assembly for the church in Jerusalem.

NOTES

1. His assertion (p. 41) that "the niche pointed north with an eastern deviation of several degrees, i.e., exactly towards the Temple Mount" is incorrect. B. Pixner (1991:293, 298) is more correct in claiming that the niche is directed toward the Holy Sepulcher, but Pixner produces no parallels to prove intention. Moreover, the architectural parallel to the niche that Pinkerfeld offers is that of the synagogue at Eshtemoa, which is dated to the fourth century AD. A synagogue on Mount Zion at that period is inconceivable, and orienting niches are not attested in first-century synagogues (e.g., Gamla, Masada). On the whole issue, see Wilkinson 1984.

2. "O Jew, when you come to Jerusalem . . . do not weep as you do now 'after the fashion of infants.' Do not lament. . . . When you see the altar abandoned I do not wish that you should suffer. When you do not find priests, I do not wish that you should despair" (Homélies sur Josué: Jesu Nave 17.1; Sources chrétiennes 71, 373). This text is dated to 249–50.

3. "There is a pierced stone which the Jews come and anoint each year. They mourn and rend their garments and depart" (Wilkinson 1981:157).

4. No historical value can be given to the legend that the decree of expulsion was rescinded by Marcus Aurelius (161–180) in gratitude for a miracle worked by a Jew (Bacher 1897).

5. I find implausible B. Bagatti's suggestion (1971:118) that "there were two separate rooms: one for the celebration of the Eucharist on the upper floor, and one on the lower floor for ritual prayers. The first represented the church, the second the synagogue."

6. *HE* 5.12 (from Hadrian to the early third century); 6.10–11; 6.39.3; 7.14; 7.32.29 (to the early fourth century).

7. The only problematic point is *HE* 5.12, which claims to list fifteen bishops but in fact mentions only thirteen. As R. Bauckham (1990:71, n. 79) points out, however, "the names of Maximus and Antoninus can be supplied, after Capito, from Eusebius, *Chronicon*." Moreover the duplication of some names might suggest that the list was expanded to match the list of fifteen Judeo-Christian bishops. Be this as it may, history is not immune to coincidence.

8. *Pace* Geva 1984:247, 249. His study, which is essentially an argument from silence, is internally contradictory in that he assigns far too great a space to far too few soldiers. In addition he ignores Epiphanius and the Bordeaux Pilgrim.

9. Excavations on this line near Zion Gate have not brought to light any traces of the Roman wall (Broshi and Tsafrir 1977:34–36).

10. In this respect (but not in others) Vincent and Abel's plan (1922: pl. I) is more accurate than those proposed by D. Bahat (1983:35) and K. Prag (1989:31). An intermediate position is taken by Wilkinson (1989:91).

11. Although Joan Taylor (1993:212) admits this possibility, she is more impressed by the fact that Eusebius never mentions a Christian site on the southwest hill. Peter Walker interprets Eusebius's silence differently, as a manifestation of historical skepticism and scholarly ambivalence (1990:290). One loses confidence in Taylor's judgment when she makes Eusebius (*Demonstratio Evangelica* 6.13.15–17; 8.3.1–15) and Cyril of Jerusalem (*Catechetical Lectures* 16.18) say that the area with which we are concerned was given over to agriculture (1993:210–11); both in fact were referring to the Temple Mount.

12. Cyril of Jerusalem, *Catechetical Lectures* 16.4; *Egeria* 43.3.

13. The earliest hint is provided by the content of the readings (1 Cor. 11:23–32; Mark 14:1–26) assigned by the Old Armenian Lectionary; see Wilkinson 1981:267.

14. The hints given by Josephus (*History of the Jewish War* 2.344; 6:325; *Antiquities of the Jews* 20.189–96) place this palace in the vicinity of the residences excavated by Avigad (1980:83–139). See the reconstruction by Leen Ritmeyer in Pritchard 1987:166–67.

15. A priori the top of the ridge is much more probable than the site halfway down the eastern slope, now occupied by Saint Peter in Gallicantu, which is defended by E. Power (1934).

WORKS CITED

Avi-Yonah, M.
1976   *The Jews of Palestine: A Political History from the Bar Kokhba War to the Arab Conquest.* Oxford: Clarendon.
Avigad, N.
1980   *Discovering Jerusalem.* Nashville: Thomas Nelson.
Bacher, W.
1897   La légende de l'exorcisme d'un démon par Simon b. Yohaï. *Revue des études juives* 35:285–87.

Bagatti, B.
1971   *The Church from the Circumcision: History and Archaeology of the Judaeo-Christians*. Jerusalem: Franciscan Press.
Bahat, D.
1983   *Carta's Historical Atlas of Jerusalem: An Illustrated Survey*. Jerusalem: Carta.
Bauckham, R.
1990   *Jude and the Relatives of Jesus in the Early Church*. Edinburgh: T. and T. Clark.
Boismard, M.-E., and A. Lamouille
1990   *Les Actes des Deux Apôtres: II Le Sens des Récits*. Paris: Gabalda.
Broshi, M.
1976   Excavations on Mount Zion, 1971–72. Preliminary Report. *Israel Exploration Journal* 26:81–88.
Broshi, M., and Y. Tsafrir
1977   Excavations at the Zion Gate, Jerusalem. *Israel Exploration Journal* 27:28–37.
Cerfaux, L.
1939   La première communauté chrétienne à Jérusalem (Act., II, 41—V, 42). *Ephemerides theologicae lovanienses* 16:5–31.
Domaszewski, A. von
1899   Castra. In *Pauly Real-Encyclopädie der classischen Altertumswissenschaft*, ed. G. Wissowa, vol. 3, cols. 1762–66. Stuttgart: Metzler.
Geva, H.
1984   The Camp of the Tenth Legion in Jerusalem: An Archaeological Reconsideration. *Israel Exploration Journal* 34:239–54.
Granger, F.
1933   Julius Africanus and the Library of the Pantheon. *Journal of Theological Studies* 34:157–61.
Hirschberg, J.
1975   The Remains of an Ancient Synagogue on Mount Zion. In *Jerusalem Revealed: Archaeology in the Holy City, 1968–1974*, ed. Y. Yadin, 116–17. Jerusalem: Israel Exploration Society.
Kenyon, K. M.
1967   *Jerusalem: Excavating 3000 Years of History*. New York: McGraw-Hill.
Lawlor, H. J.
1912   *Eusebiana*. Oxford: Clarendon.
Limor, O.
1988   The Origins of a Tradition: King David's Tomb on Mount Sion. *Traditio* 44:453–62.
Luedemann, G.
1989   *Opposition to Paul in Jewish Christianity*. Minneapolis: Fortress.
Mazar, B.
1975   *The Mountain of the Lord*. Garden City, N.Y.: Doubleday.

Pinkerfeld, J.
1960   "David's Tomb": Notes on the History of the Building. Prelimi-
            nary Report. In *Louis M. Rabinowitz Fund for the Exploration of
            Ancient Synagogues, Bulletin III*, 41–43. Jerusalem: Hebrew Univer-
            sity/Department of Antiquities.
Pixner, B.
1991   Die apostolische Synagogue auf dem Zion. In *Wege des Messias und
            Stätten der Urkirche: Jesus und das Judenchristentum im Licht neuer
            archäologischer Erkenntnisse*, ed. R. Riesner, 287–326. Giessen/Basel:
            Brunnen.
Power, E.
1934   Eglise Saint Pierre et Maison de Caïphe. In *Dictionnaire de la
            Bible, Supplément*, vol. 2, cols. 691–756. Paris: Letouzey.
Prag, K.
1989   *Jerusalem*. Blue Guide. London: Black.
Pritchard, J. B., ed.
1987   *The Times Atlas of the Bible*. London: Times Books.
Puech, E.
1989   La synagogue judéo-chrétienne du Mont Sion. *Monde de la Bible*
            57:19.
Saglio, E.
1899   Castra. In *Dictionnaire des antiquités grecques et romaines*, ed. C.
            Daremberg and E. Saglio, vol. 1, part 2, 940–59. Paris: Hachette.
Schürer, E.
1973   *The History of the Jewish People in the Age of Jesus Christ (175 BC–AD
            135)*, ed. G. Vermes, F. Millar, and M. Black, vol. 1. Edinburgh:
            T. and T. Clark.
1979   *The History of the Jewish People in the Age of Jesus Christ (175 BC–AD
            135)*, ed. G. Vermes, F. Millar, and M. Black, vol. 2. Edinburgh:
            T. and T. Clark.
Taylor, J.
1993   *Christians and the Holy Places. The Myth of Jewish–Christian Origins*.
            Oxford: Clarendon Press.
Ussishkin, D.
1993   *The Village of Silwan. The Necropolis from the Period of the Judean
            Kingdom*. Jerusalem: Israel Exploration Society.
Viellefond, J.-R.
1970   *Les "Cestes" de Julius Africanus: Etude sur l'ensemble des fragments
            avec édition, traduction, et commentaires*. Firenze: Sansoni, and Paris:
            Didier.
Vincent, L.-H.
1921   La Cité de David d'après les fouilles de 1913–1914. *Revue biblique*
            30:410–33, 541–69.
Vincent, L.-H, and F.-M. Abel
1922   *Jérusalem nouvelle*. Paris: Gabalda.

Walker, P.
1990   *Holy City, Holy Places? Christian Attitudes to Jerusalem and the Holy
                Land in the Fourth Century.* Oxford: Clarendon Press.
Weill, R.
1920   *La Cité de David: Compte rendu des fouilles exécutées à Jérusalem, sur
                le site de la ville primitive: Campagne de 1913–1914.* Paris: Paul
                Geuthner.
Wendel, C.
1954   Bibliothek. In *Reallexikon für Antike und Christentum,* ed. T. Klaus-
                ner, vol. 2, cols. 231–74. Stuttgart: Hiersemann.
Wilkinson, J.
1977   *Jerusalem Pilgrims before the Crusades.* Jerusalem: Ariel.
1981   *Egeria's Travels to the Holy Land,* rev. ed. Jerusalem: Ariel.
1984   Orientation, Jewish and Christian. *Palestine Exploration Quarterly*
                116:16–30.
1989   Jerusalem under Rome and Byzantium 63 BC–637 AD. In *Jerusalem
                in History,* ed. K. J. Asali, 75–104. London: Scorpion.
Williamson, G. A., trans.
1989   Eusebius. *The History of the Church from Christ to Constantine,* with
                notes by A. Louth. London: Penguin.

19 | Medical Discoveries of Biblical Times

ROBERT NORTH, S.J.

My research for a recent symposium on medicine in the Bible (North 1992) uncovered numismatic evidence published independently a half-century ago in Boston and Vienna but virtually unmentioned in medico-archaeological literature. Equally intriguing are the "votive X rays" or statuettes of a torso with enough of the skin peeled back to disclose the internal organs. A third area is surgical instruments, for many of which information is already well published but often in specialized periodicals not widely known; this corpus is being continually augmented by more recent excavations. Fourth, and most directly relevant to biblical study, are the medical materials or instruments discovered in or near Palestine itself. These four topics are the subject of this chapter.

MATERIA MEDICA ON COINS

The author of a general work on disease in antiquity (Hart 1983) earlier published "The Diagnosis of Disease from Ancient Coins" (Hart 1973). A coin from the British Museum of Phraates IV shows the Parthian king with what is called a "forehead nodule." It resembles a wart, but is doubtless important to the medically initiated. More obviously diagnostic is the "goiter" claimed to be identified on a coin published by P. C. Kraay (1956:31–96B) and perhaps also on a coin of Cleopatra (Hart 1973:127). This numismatic evidence pertains more directly to medical diagnosis than to treatment.

In 1931, Horatio R. Storen, a gynecologist, published *Medicina in Nummis*, a survey of the coins, medals, and slugs known to him relating to surgery and other medical specialties. A half-century earlier, Joseph Bret-

311

tauer, an ophthalmologist in Trieste, had gathered a collection of coins that he found variously relevant to medicine. In 1907 he donated this collection to the University of Vienna, which mounted an exposition of the coins in 1928, along with a catalog prepared by Eduard Holzmair in 1937, coincidentally with the same title, *Medicina in Nummis* (Holzmair 1989).

Most of Holzmair's publication is devoted to coins with portraits of physicians and natural scientists (nos. 1–1347, pp. 1–99). Holzmair's second section (nos. 1348–2280, pp. 100–175) deals with plagues and epidemics but includes also "votive memorials" (treated in more detail below). No. 1892 is described as the swarm of a locust plague, as in Joel 1:4. It is not illustrated, but the cognate coin, number 1891 (pl. 18), shows a single grasshopper.

The third section is closer to the biblical domain. This section, "Patrons of Medicine and Amulets," has three subdivisions: healing gods of antiquity (nos. 2280–2335, pp. 175–78), Christian patrons of medicine and places of miraculous cures (nos. 2336–62, pp. 178–80), and kabbalistic and astrological or alchemical medallions (nos. 2366–68, p. 180).

Holzmair's remaining sections deal with more modern developments: meetings, hospitals, the Red Cross, lifesaving, biology and physics (often allegorical or satirical, p. 307), circumcision (nos. 4544–49). The oculist section describes, though with insufficient clarity, the "blinding of Tobias" (Tob. 2:10, no. 4663, p. 319). Among the remaining coins, some are veterinary (nos. 5218–82, pp. 353–58).

Apart from the very few and peripheral items specified, none of this collection, nor indeed the other works cited, offers much that is properly medical and related to the Bible. The chief usefulness of these publications may lie in directing the attention of archaeologists to this material hitherto overlooked.

EX-VOTOS SHOWING INTERNAL ORGANS

A second surprise was the prominence of the votive statuettes that I have called "X rays," and their relevance for discussion of the brain in biblical physiology. Those statuettes could be called "dissections," because they show a torso with enough of the skin folded back to give a glimpse of the organs lying beneath, but they are definitely not "autopsies" or medical dissections made after death. The presence of garments and other factors show that it was the donors' intention to indicate the organs for whose healing they were desirous or grateful.

The simplest and perhaps the most satisfying of these examples is a statuette discussed by A. Krug (1993:35; here fig. 19-1). The exposed portion, rather below the level of the lungs and heart, shows a jumbled mass. To experts who have examined and discussed it, however, it is possible to distinguish various organs and identify them by their proper modern medical terms. Still, the statuette is a product of imagination rather than of actual dissection or X ray. This interesting statuette (fig. 19-1) is photographed from the Museo Arqueológico of Madrid, where it is attributed to the Etruscans of the second century BCE. One may question what relevance the Etruscans could have to medical practice related to the Bible. I will explain below how the dominance of ancient medicine was transferred from Egypt to Greece around the time of the definitive composition of the Bible, and thence passed to Rome after 200 BCE. The Etruscans were at the time well attested from Rome northward to Florence (Bonfante 1991). There must have been interaction between them and the Romans, especially in matters of such importance as medical care.

P. Decouflé (1964) described a series of terra-cotta statuettes similar to the one from Madrid. The most interesting of these (his fig. 19, here fig. 19-2) shows a youth, clothed, with his arm beneath his tunic, but with an oval of skin folded back between the breastbone and navel, revealing his internal organs. These are shown enlarged in Decouflé's figure 20. In Decouflé's figure 21 each of the organs is numbered 1 to 28, and the presumed modern medical name for each is given (p. 31) (see fig. 19-3).

The largest organ visible in the center (no. 16) is labeled "Liver, left lobe." Above it to the right is the "right lobe" (no. 11). The heart is number 6 (*oreillettes*) and number 7 (*ventricules*). The lungs are number 3. Number 2 is the clavicle and number 1 "perhaps" the thyroid; numbers 4, 5, and 27 are merely the incision. Number 12 is the diaphragm or midriff. Farther down at left, number 18 is expressly labeled the right kidney ("*rein droit, surrenal*"). The intestine is number 24 and doubtfully also 25 and/or 22. The large organ number 21 near the bottom is called "gallbladder" ("*vésicule*") or "rectum." Number 20 is the sacrum, and number 22 below is "penis or prostate." Number 25 farther up at right is the peritoneum.

Decouflé's analysis remains the most informative. Unfortunately the editors of *Latomus* could furnish no details of the statuette's provenance

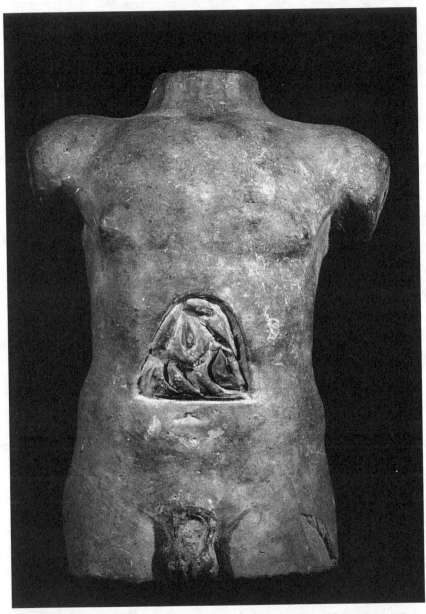

FIG. 19-1. The "internal organs of cognition" (Hebrew *lēb*), Etruscan circa 150 BCE; scale not indicated. Museo Arqueológico Nacional of Madrid. Reproduced by permission.

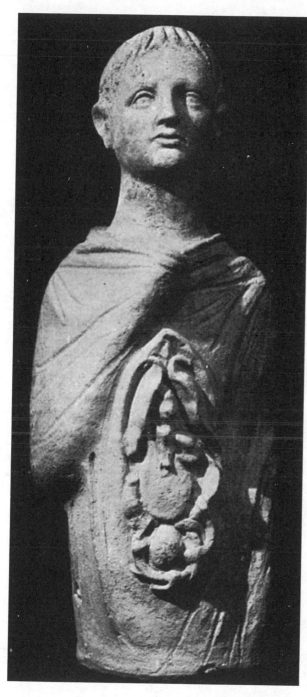

FIG. 19-2. Decouflé's Etruscan ex-voto. (Decouflé 1964: fig. 19, scale not indicated.) Reproduced by permission.

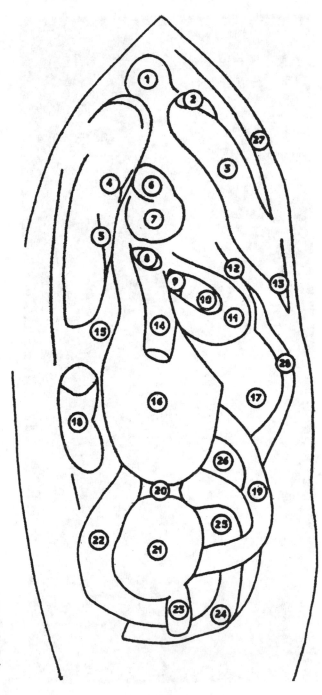

FIG. 19-3. Decou-flé's anatomical analysis of his ex-voto. (Decouflé 1964: fig. 21.) Reproduced by permission.

or present whereabouts except that it is "Decouflé's private property." But more or less similar items from several other collections have been published. Some, including Decouflé's polyvisceral Etruscan and Roman ex-votos, have been studied comparatively by M. Tabanelli (1962). Those from Palestrina, now in Ghent, have been compared with other examples from Veio by S. de Laet and M. Desittere (1969). There are a few torsos without "windows" in the Lavinio collection published by N. Fenelli (1975a). In the Esquiline deposit known as Minerva Medica, found in Rome in 1887, are some plaques vaguely resembling Decouflé's togaed youth, but without "windows" (Gatti Lo Guzzo 1978: pl. 51, no. R-15; p. 54, V-1; p. 16, E-14). There are older studies of cognate materials by T. Meyer-Steineg (1912).

Ex-voto Organs
as "Heart" or "Brain"

The Madrid statuette with its "window" on the internal organs is perhaps of chief importance to biblical research as an illustration of what is really meant by the Hebrew word *lēb* or *lēbāb*, usually translated "heart." It must be noted first of all that of the 850 occurrences of this word in the Bible, not a single one indicates specifically the organ for pumping blood. It is doubtful that biblical peoples were even aware of the circulation of the blood. Passages like 2 Kings 9:24 and Psalms 45:6 and 37:15 attributing death to a weapon piercing the *lēb* are actually applicable to other vital internal organs. Equally indefinite are Job 41:24, Jeremiah 4:29, and Hosea 13:8.

What *lēb* really means was already sufficiently clear from dictionaries of biblical Hebrew, but the word has been recently researched by Á. Gil Modrego (1992), relying partly on E. Dhorme (1963). In most instances the meaning is the internal organs (chiefly the area that we call loosely the "stomach"), which are clearly identified as the organs of cognition and control. Biblical Hebrew had no word for "brain," and the functions of knowledge and will were not located inside the head (North 1993). Rather, knowledge and will were linked with what we call "emotions," the heightening of which is observable in the increase not only of the heart-beat but also of breathing ("lungs" is likewise a word absent in biblical Hebrew) and in less obvious effects on such organs as the kidneys, liver, and spleen.

Thus in the Bible the functioning of the *lēb* or "internal organs" corresponds largely to the functioning of the "nervous system," located loosely inside the torso, but not excluding what we today consider to be the principal part of the nervous system, the brain inside the skull. "Nerve" itself, insofar as it existed even in postbiblical Hebrew, is not easily distinguished from "tendon" or even "vein." The *gîd* in Jacob's thigh is described as a tendon in Genesis 32:26 and 33, though there is merit in the recent exegetical trend to identify *gîd* with the sciatic nerve, as already in the Septuagint.

Admitting that it is inappropriate to translate *lēb* simply as "brain," or even as "nervous system," I am nevertheless suggesting that when we look at the opened Madrid torso we see what in biblical Hebrew was termed *lēb*, the internal organs of cognition and control, which are known today as the nervous system including the brain. The outlook of the ancient Egyptians was not dissimilar, as the title of H. Schipperges's recent work, *The World of the Heart: Symbol, Organ, Center of the Human Being* (1989, in German), indicates. As for the Israelites, as Aubrey Johnson wrote a half-century ago: "Even if they knew nothing of the nervous system as such, they were well aware of its presence and operation . . . and as a result we find [the *lēb*, "heart"] taking the place of the brain in their thinking" (1949:77).

Other X-ray–Type Artifacts

Apart from torsos showing the internal organs, there are several other interesting examples in G. Penso's brilliantly illustrated book on Roman medicine. His color plate 20 (opposite p. 257) shows what he calls "trachea, lungs, heart, liver, stomach, intestinal coils, abdominal organs," the latter looking rather like an X ray. He illustrates (p. 215, fig. 109) an X-ray–type ex-voto from the Rome National Museum, with what he describes as "organs partly displaced in the lower abdomen" (see also p. 208, fig. 107).

A somewhat similar statuette in Penso's plate 37 (opposite p. 448) has the ribs clearly showing. The legend states that because the person was so emaciated, the skin is shown sticking to the bones, but there is a remote resemblance to an X ray of the chest.

Penso also offers a different type of representation of the body's hidden interior (p. 186, fig. 93): a fifth-century BCE Etruscan skeleton in bronze, from the National Museum of Florence. The skeleton on a vase painting (p. 190, fig. 96) looks caricatured by comparison. Even in mosaics, there is a stylized skeleton from Pompeii now in the Naples National Museum (p. 189, fig. 94). From Rome's National Museum (fig.

95) is an X-ray–like drawing of a skeleton inside a body. From the photo it is not clear whether the skeleton itself is tesselated or is painted in black on the surface of a white mosaic. In a mosaic from Pompeii (pl. 19, p. 256) only a skull is shown.

Finally perhaps relevant here is the "Anatomy Lesson," a fresco from Rome's Via Latina Catacomb, Room 1 (arcoscolium to the right): a bare-chested person and thirteen other students watch the master with pointer touching a nude body on the floor before them (Penso 1984:242, pl. 18).

SURGICAL INSTRUMENTS

For ancient Israel, several excellent recent surveys (Seybold and Müller 1981; Wiseman 1986; Kudlien 1988; Brown 1990) have hardly a word about surgical instruments. Concrete illustrative material is scant from Mesopotamia as well, partly because there, as in Israel, illness was regarded as work of good or evil spirits (Avalos 1991).

Such instruments might be expected from Egypt, which also had a highly developed medical literature, such as the surgical papyri edited by J. H. Breasted (1930), B. Ebbell (1937, 1939), H. Grapow (1956), Grapow and others (1958), and W. R. Dawson (1967) and succinctly illustrated by J. V. Kinnier Wilson (1982) and J. T. Rowling (1989). A statue of the alleged "father of medicine," the pharaoh Joser's vizier Imhotep (ca. 2700 BCE), is almost the only object illustrating doctors in pharaonic Egypt (Jonckheere 1958: frontispiece; Estes 1989).

The link between Egypt and Greece and Rome is by way of Alexandria. At the time the Hebrew Bible was being edited (Pentateuch, Ezra, Chronicles, all ca. 400 BCE), there was an amazing development of medical science in the Greek world linked with Hippocrates of Cos who practiced on Cnidus on the southeast coast of Asia Minor (Deichgräber 1983; Gourévitch 1984; Hillert 1990). After the founding of Alexandria in 331, the medical establishment was transferred there and linked with Herophilus. Thus the stage was set for the transition from ancient Egyptian to Greek medicine (Saunders 1963), and thus it is justifiable to speak of the surgical instruments of Greco-Roman Egypt (Marganne-Mélard 1987).

Pliny the Elder (*Natural History* 29.12) cites from Cassius Hemina the name of Agatharchus of Peloponnesus, who in 219 BCE was the first doctor to transfer his medical practice to Rome (André 1987:16). For long after that, all doctors in Rome were of Greek origin. Hence the focus here on surgical instruments of the Roman Empire is relevant not only to the encomium to physicians in Sirach 38 and to the New Testament generally, but also to the gradual development of Egyptian thought as a tacit background for the Hebrew Bible.

The major authority on collections of Roman surgical instruments is Ernst Künzl. In *Operating Rooms inside Roman Thermal Baths: A Surgical Tool Kit from the Colonia Ulpia Traiana* (1986, in German), he begins with the observation that while a large public open space would not seem suited to delicate surgical operations, that is where instruments have been found.

Another major study by Künzl, *Medical Instruments Found in Burials of the Roman Empire* (Künzl, Hassel, and Künzl 1983, in German) gives a brief classification and description of the various types of medical instruments in museum collections and a word on their manufacture. Examples include a "speculum," an instrument to divide and hold open an incision (Künzl, Hassel, and Künzl 1983: fig. 7; so Borobio 1992); long thin instruments from Ephesus (fig. 19-5, nos. 17–21) and elsewhere in Asia Minor (fig. 19-5, no. 15) in the Mainz Roman-German Museum; and objects from the Bingen Museum (here figs. 19-4, 19-5).

Other important studies with illustrations are by P. H. Goerke (1984), G. Penso (1984), and H. Matthäus (1989). R. Jackson (1988:127) and Penso (1984: pl. 1) both reproduce the remarkable fresco from Pompeii of Japyx removing an arrowhead from the leg of Aeneas. Familiarity with the complete photo is essential for appreciating the excellent enlarged color closeup of the wound and the instrument in the surgeon's hand given by L. Capasso (1989:94).

Mario Tabanelli describes eleven tools found in 1940 in an Etruscan tomb near Volterra (1958). He also devotes special attention to the instruments that gave name to the "Surgeon's House" near the Herculaneum gate at Pompeii (1958:36, 34; see also Eschebach 1984).

Another set of Roman medical instruments from Italy (purchased, not excavated) includes several rare types, including three catheters (Jackson 1986:119). L. J. Bliquez traces the Roman surgical instruments now in the V. Merlo Collection of the University of Mississippi. Merlo was known as Misucuro in Naples till 1930, where his connections with "replica-makers" are discreetly noted (Bliquez 1988:11, n. 29).

Drawing nearer to Syria-Palestine, there is the Roman surgeon's tomb from Cyprus (Michaelides 1984: pl. 74). I present it here (fig. 19-6) not only because of its proximity to Palestine but also because it gives a representative sampling of the surgical tools found in the Roman collections described above. Of further interest is the claim that this tomb also contained ancient medicines, powders, and salts that were the by-products of copper mining in Cyprus (Foster 1988). Such medical products intended for internal consumption are less likely to have survived. The meager evidence has recently been surveyed by J. Scarborough (1991).

Special attention is merited by surgical tools found in shipwrecks. Among those recently noted is the wreck near Syracuse in Sicily (Gibbins 1988, 1989; cf. Buckler and Caton 1914).

Finally there are the magnificently humane scenes on Trajan's Column in Rome, showing Roman soldiers caring for their wounded, notably a *capsarius* bandaging the thigh of a comrade (Penso 1984:149, fig. 73; Davies 1989:208).

MEDICAL MATERIALS DISCOVERED
IN PALESTINE

Despite the intense interest shown in the practice of medical healing by both doctors and exegetes, archaeologists have been able to provide only a few random examples of medical *realia* from Palestine.

Best known among these are the trephined skulls of Lachish from the eighth century BCE (Harrison 1962) to which must now be added the claimed discovery of similar practices at Jericho (Zias 1982), and another example from Early Bronze Arad (Smith 1990). Similar cases are found in Kom Ombo, Egypt (Stettler 1982), though there is no mention of trephination in Egyptian medical literature (Pahl 1985) nor in the Bible.

This raises the question whether excavators have too hastily applied the medical term "trephination" to their discoveries. There can of course be no doubt whatever that these openings were made in these skulls by surgical instruments. Possibly some were made after death, perhaps as part of a burial ritual similar to the Neolithic practice of beading around the skull. Assuming that the skull perforations were made during the subject's lifetime and with the intention of remedying pain, the explanation in closest accord with Mesopotamian and biblical references is that the opening was made to release the evil spirits supposed to be causing the individual's physical or mental illness.

The claim that these skulls exhibit trephining as a form of surgical operation intended to reduce pressure on the brain must take into account the arguments above that the brain itself is completely unmentioned in

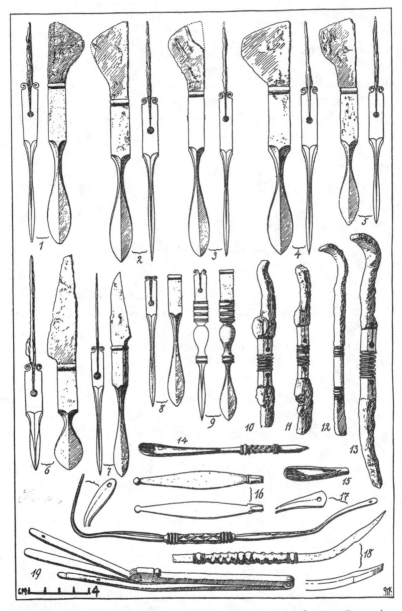

FIG. 19-4. Bingen Museum tools. (Como 1925:156–58, fig. 56.) Deutsches Archäologisches Institut, Romische Germanische Kommission. Reproduced by permission.

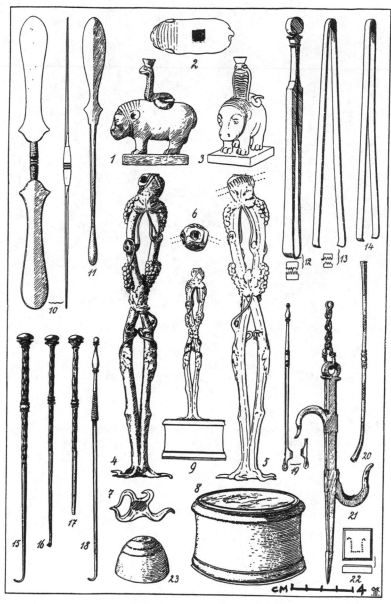

FIG. 19-5. Bingen Museum medical instruments. (Como 1925: fig. 57.) Reproduced by permission. (See also Künzl, Hassel, and Künzl 1983: 82–83, fig. 56–57.)

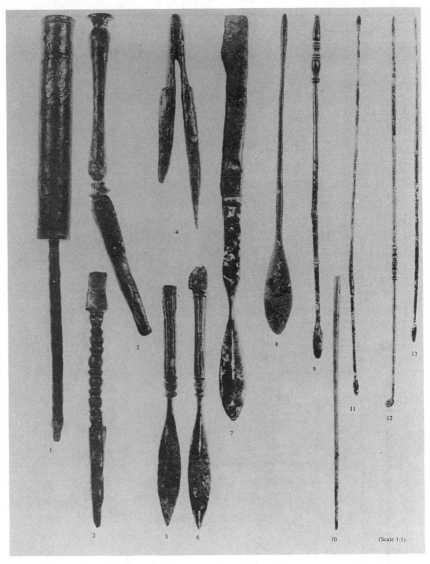

FIG. 19-6. Tools from a Roman surgeon's tomb of Nea Paphos, Cyprus. (Michaelides 1984: pl. 74.) Reproduced by permission.

biblical or Mesopotamian literature and that cognitive and nervous processes were ascribed rather to the *lēb*. The *lēb*, as explained above, was not only or chiefly the heart but rather all the internal organs generally surrounding the stomach, and *not* specifically including the contents of the skull. Despite these factors, however, it is likeliest that the skulls were perforated as a form of healing.

A second type of excavated materials are those claimed to be actual medical instruments. Spatulas of bone found near Gaza are plausibly interpreted to have been used for the treatment of eye disorders (Van Beek and Van Beek 1990). A Roman-era cupping vessel (*cucurbitula*) from Masada is perhaps in the category of the "headcuppers" of the German collections (Hershkovitz 1989).

At Gadara of the Decapolis, T. Weber (1991) describes medical instruments including forceps, tweezers, and spatulas from a Byzantine crypt tomb. Further study of these finds by Künzl and Weber (1991) revealed that these were largely dental tools dating from around 350 CE. These instruments demonstrate the extreme conservatism of ancient dentistry, as identical tools are attested at least three centuries earlier. For comparison there is the recent study of dental instruments and practice in ancient Egypt (Bardinet 1990).

The third and last type of medical discovery within Palestine is a pottery flask from Qumran shown by analysis to have contained "probably" balsam oil, which very likely had medicinal purposes (Patrich and Arubas 1989). Even though such oil may also have been used as perfume or another cosmetic, it is fair to admit that "pharmacy" and "perfumery" were not sharply distinguished in antiquity but combined into a single industry (Crocker 1989). Noted above was the claim of similar medicaments from Cyprus and small likelihood of such materials surviving for excavation.

Also from Qumran is the spurious claim that one of the scrolls is to be called "Therapeia," a compendium of medical data. This claim was short-lived; support given by J. H. Charlesworth (1985) was promptly and prudently withdrawn (1987) in the face of emphatic objections by Joseph Naveh (1986) and others.

By focusing attention on this hitherto largely neglected area of biblical research, this modest investigation may lay the groundwork for archaeologists and exegetes to explore further more significant medical discoveries of biblical times.

WORKS CITED

André, J.
1987   *Être médecin à Rome.* Realia 9. Paris: Belles Lettres.

Avalos, H. I.
1991   Illness and Health Care in Ancient Israel: A Comparative Study of the Role of the Temple. Ph.D. dissertation, Harvard University.

Bardinet, T.
1990   *Dents et mâchoires dans las représentations religieuses et la pratique médicale de l'Egypte ancienne.* Studia Pohl 15. Rome: Pontifical Biblical Institute.

Bliquez, L. J.
1988   *Roman Surgical Instruments and Minor Objects in the University of Mississippi.* Studies in Mediterranean Archaeology, Pocketbook Series 58. Göteborg: Paul Åströms Förlag.

Bonfante, L.
1991   Recent Books from Italy on the Etruscans. *American Journal of Archaeology* 95:157–64.

Borobio Melendo, E. L.
1992   Instrumentos médicos hispanoromanos: El espéculo y los ginecólogos romanos. *Revista de Arqueología* 13/140:6–7.

Breasted, J. H.
1930   *The Edwin Smith Surgical Papyrus.* Oriental Institute Publications 3. Chicago: University of Chicago Press.

Brown, M. L.
1990   Rapa'. In *Theologisches' Wörterbuch zum Alten Testament,* ed. H.-J. Fabry and H. Ringgren, vol. 7, cols. 617–25. Stuttgart: Kohlhammer.

Bucaille, M.
1990   *Mummies of the Pharaohs: Modern Medical Investigations.* New York: St. Martin's.

Buckler, W. H., and R. Caton
1914   Account of a Group of Medical and Surgical Instruments Found at Kolophon. *Proceedings of the Royal Society of Medicine* 7/6:235–42.

Capasso, L.
1989   I Romani in farmacia. *Archeo* 57:55–99.

Castrén, P., ed.
1989   *Ancient and Popular Healing: Symposium on Ancient Medicine, Athens, 9–10 October 1986.* Helsinki: Finnish Institute at Athens.

Charlesworth, J. H.
1985   *The Discovery of a Dead Sea Scroll (4Q Therapeia): Its Importance in the History of Medicine and Jesus Research.* International Center for Arid and Semi-Arid Land Studies, Publication No. 85-1. Lubbock, Tex.: Texas Tech University Press.

1987   A Misunderstood Recently Published Dead Sea Scroll (4QM 130). *Explorations* 1.2:2.

Cockburn, A., and E. Cockburn
1980   *Mummies, Disease, and Ancient Cultures.* Cambridge: Cambridge
            University Press.
Como, J.
1925   Das Grab eines römischen Arztes in Bingen. *Germania* 9:152–62.
Crocker, P. T.
1989   Apothecaries, Confectionaries, and a New Discovery at Qumran.
            Buried History 25:36–46.
David, A. R.
1984   *Evidence Embalmed: Modern Medicine and the Mummies of Egypt.*
            Manchester: Manchester University Press.
Davies, R. W.
1989   *Service in the Roman Army.* Edinburgh: Edinburgh University
            Press.
Dawson, W. R.
1967   The Egyptian Medical Papyri I. In *Diseases in Antiquity*, ed. D.
            Brothwell and A. Sandison, 98–111. Springfield, Ill.: Charles C
            Thomas.
Decouflé, P.
1964   *La notion d'ex-voto anatomique chez les Étrusco-Romains: Analyse et
            synthèse.* Collection Latomus 72. Brussels: Latomus.
Deichgräber, K.
1983   *Der hippokratische Eid.* 4th ed. Stuttgart: Hippokrates-Verlag.
Dhorme, E.
1963   *L'emploi métaphorique des noms de parties du corps en hébreu et en
            akkadien.* Paris: Paul Geuthner.
Ebbell, B.
1937   *The Papyrus Ebers, the Greatest Egyptian Medical Document.* Copen-
            hagen: Munksgaard.
1939   *Die alt-ägyptische Chirurgie: Die chirurgischen Abschnitte Smith und
            Ebers.* Norsk Videnskaps-Akademi 2. Oslo: Dybwad.
Eschebach, H.
1984   *Die Arzthäuser in Pompeii.* Sondernummer 15, Antike Welt. Mainz:
            Philipp von Zabern.
Estes, J. W.
1989   *The Medical Skills of Ancient Egypt.* Canton, Mass.: Watson.
Fenelli, N.
1975a   Contributo per lo studio del votivo anatomico: I votivi anatomici
            di Lavinio. *Archeologia Classica* 27:206–52.
1975b   Votivi anatomici in Le Tredici Are. *Lavinium* 2:253–55.
Fischer, P. M.
1986   *Prehistoric Cypriot Skulls: A Medico-anthropological, Archaeological,
            and Micro-analytical Investigation.* Studies in Mediterranean Archae-
            ology 75. Göteborg: Paul Åströms Förlag.
Foster, G. V.; K. Kanada; and D. Michaelides
1988   A Roman Surgeon's Tomb from Nea Paphos, Part 2: Ancient

Medicines: By-Products of Copper Mining in Cyprus. *Report of the Department of Antiquities of Cyprus* 1988 (Part 2):229–34.

Gatti Lo Guzzo, L.
1978   *Il deposito votivo dell'Esquilino detto di Minerva Medica.* Studi e Materiali di Etruscologia e Antichità Italiche 17. Florence: Sansoni.

Gibbins, D.
1988   Surgical Instruments from a Roman Shipwreck off Sicily. *Antiquity* 62:294–97.
1989   The Roman Wreck of c. AD 200 at Plemmirio, Near Siracusa: Medical Equipment and Pottery Lamps. *International Journal of Nautical Archaeology* 18:1–25.

Gil Modrego, Á.
1992   Estudio de lēb/āb en el Antiguo Testamento: Analisis sintagmático y paradigmático. Dissertation, Universidad Complutense, Madrid.

Goerke, P. H.
1984   *Arzt und Heilkunde: Vom Asklepiospriester zum Klinikarzt, 3000 Jahre Medizin.* Munich: Callwey.

Gourévitch D.
1984   *Le triangle hippocratique dans le monde gréco-romain: Le malade, sa maladie, et son médecin.* Rome: École Française.

Grapow, H.
1956   *Grundriss der Medizin der alten Ägypter, 3: Kranker, Krankheiten, und Arzt.* Berlin: Akademie.
1958   *Grundriss der Medizin der alten Ägypter, 4: Übersetzung der medizinischen Texte.* Berlin: Akademie.

Grmek, M. D.
1989   *Diseases in the Ancient Greek World.* Translated by M. and L. Muellner, from French, 1983. Baltimore: Johns Hopkins University Press.

Halpern, D. J.
1982   The Book of Remedies, the Canonization of the Solomonic Writings, and the Riddle of Pseudo-Eusebius. *Jewish Quarterly Review* 72:269–92.

Harrison, R. K.
1962   Disease. In *Interpreter's Dictionary of the Bible*, ed. G. A. Buttrick, 1:847–54. Nashville: Abingdon Press.

Hart, G.
1973   The Diagnosis of Disease from Ancient Coins. *Archaeology* 26, no. 2:123–27.
1983   *Disease in Ancient Man.* London: Clarke Irwin.

Hershkovitz, M.
1989   A Roman Cupping Vessel from Masada. *Eretz-Israel* 20:275–77 (Hebrew with English summary, p. 204*).

Hibbs, V. A.
1991   Roman Surgical and Medical Instruments from La Cañada Honda (Gandul). *Archivo Español de Arqueología* 64:111–34.

Hillert, A.
1990   *Antike Ärztedarstellungen.* Marburger Schriften zur Medizin-
            geschichte 25. Frankfurt: Lang.
Hogan, L. P.
1992   *Healing in the Second Temple Period.* Novum Testamentum et Orbis
            Antiquus 21. Fribourg: Universität; and Göttingen: Vandenhoeck
            and Ruprecht.
Holzmair, E.
1989   *Medicina in Nummis, Sammlung Dr. Josef Brettauer.* Numismatische
            Kommission 22. Vienna: Österreichische Akademie.
Jackson, R.
1986   A Set of Roman Medical Instruments from Italy. *Britannia* 17:119–
            67.
1988   *Doctors and Diseases in the Roman Empire.* London: British Museum.
Johnson, A.
1949   *The Vitality of the Individual in the Thought of Ancient Israel.* Cardiff:
            University of Wales.
Jonckheere, F.
1958   *Les médecins de l'Égypte pharaonique.* La médecine égyptienne 3.
            Brussels: Fonds Égyptologique Reine Élisabeth.
Kee, R. C.
1992   Medicine and Healing. In *The Anchor Bible Dictionary*, ed. D. N.
            Freedman, 4:659–64. New York: Doubleday.
Kinnier Wilson, J. V.
1982   Medicine in the Land and Times of the Old Testament. In *Studies
            in the Period of David and Solomon and Other Essays*, ed. T. Ishida,
            337–65. Tokyo: Yamikawa.
Kottek, S., ed.
1988   Proceedings of the Third International Symposium on Medicine
            in Bible and Talmud, Jerusalem, December 7–9, 1987. *Koroth* 9
            (Special Issue).
Kraay, P. C.
1956   *Greek Coins.* London: Thames and Hudson.
Krug, A.
1993   *Heilkunst und Heilkult: Medizin in der Antike.* 2d: ed. Munich:
            C. H. Beck.
Kudlien, F.
1979   *Der griechische Arzt im Zeitalter des Hellenismus.* Mainz: Akademie.
1986   *Die Stellung des Arztes in der römischen Gesellschaft.* Forschungen
            zur antiken Sklaverei 18. Stuttgart: Steiner.
1988   Heilkunde. In *Reallexikon für Antike und Christentum*, ed. E. Dass-
            mann, 14:223–49. Stuttgart: Hiersemann.
Künzl, E.
1986   Operationsräume in römischen Thermen. Zu einem chirurgischen
            Instrumentarium aus der Colonia Ulpia Traiana, mit einem
            Auswahlkatalog römischer medizinischer Instrumente im rö-
            mischen Landesmuseum, Bonn. *Bonner Jahrbücher* 186:491–509.

Künzl, E., and D. Ankner
1986   Eine Serie von Fälschungen römischer Instrumentarien. *Archäolo-*
             gisches Korrespondenzblatt 16:333–39.
Künzl, E.; F. Hassel; and S. Künzl
1983   *Medizinische Instrumente aus Sepulkralfunden der römischen Kaiser-*
             zeit. Bonner Jahrbücher 182. Cologne: Rheinland.
Künzl, E., and T. Weber
1991   Das spätantike Grab eines Zahnarztes zu Gadara in der Dekapo-
             lis. *Damaszener Mitteilungen* 5:81–118.
de Laet, S., and M. Desittere
1969   Ex voto anatomici di Palestrina nel Museo Archeologico
             dell'Università di Gand. *L'Antiquité Classique* 38:16–27.
Leca, A.-P.
1983   *La médecine égyptienne au temps des Pharaons.* 3d. ed. Paris: Dacosta.
Majno, G.
1975   *The Healing Hand: Man and Wound in the Ancient World.* Cam-
             bridge, Mass.: Harvard University Press.
Marganne-Mélard, M.-H.
1987   Les instruments chirurgicaux de l'Égypte gréco-romaine. In
             Archéologie et médecine, VIIᵉ rencontres internationales d'archéologie et
             d'histoire d'Antibes, 23–25 October 1986, pp. 403–12. St. Juan-les-
             Pins: Association pour la promotion et diffusion des connaissances
             archéologiques.
Matthäus, H.
1989   *Der Arzt in römischer Zeit, Medizinischel Instrumente und Arzneien:*
             Archäologische Hinterlassenschaft in Siedlungen und Gräbern. Limes-
             museum Aalen 43. Stuttgart: Landesmuseum.
Meyer-Steineg, T.
1912   Darstellungen normaler und krankhaft veränderter Körperteile an
             antiken Weihgaben. *Jenaer Medizinhistorische Beiträge* 2:22–24.
Michaelides, D.
1984   A Roman Surgeon's Tomb from Nea Paphos. *Report of the Depart-*
             ment of Antiquities of Cyprus 1984:315–32.
Naveh, J.
1986   A Medical Document or a Writing Exercise? The So-Called 4Q
             Therapeia. *Israel Exploration Journal* 36:52–55.
North, R.
1992   Medicina y terapías en el Antiguo Testamento. Forthcoming in
             Universidad Complutense cursos de verano, ed. A. Piñero. Almeria:
             Universidad Complutense.
1993   "Brain" and "Nerve" in the Biblical Outlook. *Biblica* 74: 577–97.
Pahl, W. M.
1985   Trepanation. In *Lexikon der Ägyptologie,* ed. W. Helck and E. Otto,
             6:756–57. Wiesbaden: Harrassowitz.
Patrich, J., and B. Arubas
1989   A Juglet Containing Balsam-Oil(?) from a Cave near Qumran.
             Israel Exploration Journal 39:43–55.

Penso, G.
1984   *La médecine romaine*. Paris: Dacosta.
Preuss, J.
1983   *Biblical and Talmudic Medicine*. Translated by F. Rosner, from German, 1911. New York: Hebrew Publishing.
Rowling, J. T.
1989   The Rise and Decline of Surgery in Dynastic Egypt. *Antiquity* 63:312–19.
Saunders, J. B. de C. M.
1963   *The Transitions from Ancient Egyptian to Greek Medicine*. Clendening Lecture 10. Lawrence, Kans.: University of Kansas.
Scarborough, J.
1969   *Roman Medicine*. London: Thames and Hudson.
1991   The Pharmacology of Sacred Plants, Herbs, and Roots. In *Magika Hiera*, ed. C. A. Faraone and D. Obbink, 138–74. New York: Oxford University Press.
Schipperges, H.
1989   *Die Welt des Herzens: Sinnbild, Organ, Mitte des Menschen*. Frankfurt: Knecht.
Seybold, K. P., and U. B. Müller
1981   *Sickness and Healing*. Translated by D. W. Stott, from German, 1978. Biblical Encounters. Nashville: Abingdon.
Smith, P.
1990   The Trephined Skull from the Early Bronze Age Period at Arad. *Eretz-Israel* 21:89*–93*.
Snyder, G.
1972   *Instrumentum Medici: Der Arzt und sein Gerät im Spiegelbild der Zeiten*. Ingelheim am Rhein: Boehringer.
Stettler, A.
1982   Der Instrumentenschrank von Kom Ombo. *Antike Welt* 13.3:48–54.
Storen, H. R.
1931   *Medicina in Nummis, a Descriptive List of Coins, Medals, Jetons relating to Medicine, Surgery, and the Allied Sciences*. Boston.
Tabanelli, M.
1958   Lo strumento chirurgico e la sua storia dalle epoche greca e romana al secolo decimosesto. *Romagna Medica* 9. Forlì: Valbonesi.
1962   *Gli ex-voto poliviscerali etruschi e romani*. Florence: Olschki.
Temkin, 0.
1971   Griechische Medizin als Wissenschaft und Handwerk. In *Antike Medizin*, ed. H. Flasher, 1–28. Wege der Forschung 221 = Greek Medicine as Science and Craft. Translated by D. Flashar. *Isis* 44(1953):213–25.
Van Beek, G., and O. Van Beek
1990   The Function of the Bone Spatula. *Biblical Archaeologist* 53:205–9.
Weber, T.
1991   Gadara of the Decapolis. Preliminary Report on the 1990 Season

at Umm Qeis. *Annual of the Department of Antiquities of Jordan* 35:223–31.

Wiseman, D. J.
1986   Medicine in the Old Testament World. In *Medicine and the Bible*, ed. B. Palmer, 13–42. Exeter: Paternoster.

Zias, J.
1982   Three Trephinated Skulls from Jericho. *Bulletin of the American Schools of Oriental Research* 246:55–58.

20 | Hezekiah's Reform and the Altars at Beer-sheba and Arad

ANSON F. RAINEY

The views for and against the historicity of Hezekiah's cultic reform as described in 2 Kings 18:4 and 2 Chronicles 31:1 are well known, but there is no reason to doubt that a dismantling of altars throughout the kingdom of Judah took place during Hezekiah's reign (Oded 1977:442–46; Miller and Hayes 1986:357). This action can be seen as part of Hezekiah's plan to unify the kingdom of Judah, to centralize the cultic apparatus (with its fiscal infrastructure) in the Jerusalem Temple, and to attract northerners to Jerusalem's cause.

In 2 Kings 18:4 it is said that Hezekiah *hēsîr 'et habbāmôt*, "removed the high places"; in 2 Chronicles 31:1, we are told *wayĕnattĕṣû 'et-habbāmôt wĕ'et-hammizbĕḥôt*, "and they pulled down the high places and the altars." Despite all that has been written on the subject and all the examples of ritual installations that have been found in excavations (Vaughn 1974), no one can say with certainty of a specific architectural feature, "This is a biblical *bāmâ*." Altars are considerably easier to define since the construction of both licit and forbidden types is described (Exod. 20:24–25).

The reform of Hezekiah is to be dated between 715 and 701 BCE. The fact that Sennacherib came in the fourteenth year of Hezekiah (2 Kgs. 18:13; Isa. 36:1) means that Hezekiah began his rule in 715 BCE. E. R. Thiele's explanation of the discrepancies in the "synchronisms" of 2 Kings 17:1; 18:1; 18:9, 10 (1983:134–38) is still the only satisfactory one (despite attempts by Laato 1986, 1987; Becking 1992; and others): failure to realize the nature of Pekah's reign, with twelve years in Gilead prior to his seizing power in Samaria, has caused a twelve-year discrepancy in the synchronisms of these four passages.

THE SIGNIFICANCE OF
TEL BEER-SHEBA STRATUM II

The principal result of Yohanan Aharoni's excavations at Tel Beer-sheba was the exposure of a large percentage of the site's latest urban stratum. According to Aharoni's practice of naming the stratigraphic horizons according to their cultural periods and then numbering them within each category (1973:4–8), the Roman fort (Stratum R_1, Fritz 1973) and the Herodian/Hellenistic/Persian phases of occupation (Strata H_1, H_2, and H_3) were preceded by a squatter settlement, Israelite I, during which some people apparently tried to live on the ruins of the destroyed city. That city, in its latest phase, he called Israelite Stratum II. Everywhere it was uncovered, there were signs that the town had been destroyed by fire and left exposed for a considerable time (except perhaps for the squatter settlement of Israelite I in the gate area).

Dating

We went to Tel Beer-sheba with high expectations of finding a late seventh-/early sixth-century BCE city. Not only is Beer-sheba mentioned in the Bible with relation to the reign of Josiah (2 Kgs. 23:8), it also appears in one of the ostraca from the Elyashib archive that was found in the last Judahite fortress at Arad (Y. Aharoni 1981:17, Inscription 3:3–4). Therefore, it was assumed that a stratum of occupation comparable to Arad VII–VI and Lachish II would be found. Subsequently, it became apparent that only at the ancient site upon which modern Beer Sheva stands are there seventh–sixth-century remains (Gophna and Yisraeli 1973). But during the first and second seasons at Tel Beer-sheba, Aharoni and the rest of us had to struggle with the fact that our topmost destruction level was producing, not seventh–sixth-century pottery, but only ceramics comparable to those of Lachish III and Arad VIII.

On his sabbatical leave in 1965–66, Aharoni had spent considerable time going over Lachish III pottery with Olga Tufnell. In a letter to me he mentioned that he was more than ever convinced that Arad VIII and Lachish III were contemporary and that their destruction, especially that of Lachish, was at the hands of Sennacherib in 701 BCE, contrary to the prevailing view that Lachish III was destroyed in 597 BCE. The bitter controversy on that issue is now history since the later excavations at Lachish have demonstrated conclusively that Lachish III must have been destroyed by Sennacherib (Ussishkin 1977).

Even after Yohanan and Miriam Aharoni presented a convincing demonstration that the pottery repertoire of Tel Beer-sheba Israelite Stratum II was comparable to Lachish III and Arad VIII (Aharoni and Aharoni 1976), and after the final proof that Lachish III is the stratum destroyed by Sennacherib, there is still dispute about Tel Beer-sheba. Kenyon (1976) argued that the pottery of Tel Beer-sheba might be earlier than Lachish III (which she still dated to 597). Comparing the published wares from the storehouses at Tel Beer-sheba with a few vessels in burial caves at Lachish and Jerusalem, she argued not that the shapes of the vessels were different, but rather that the relative percentages of certain types of vessels were different at the two sites. The methodological weakness of making statistical comparisons from such radically different selections of pottery was invalid in itself; but beyond that, she presumed to have demonstrated archaeologically that Tel Beer-sheba must have been destroyed in the seventh century, during the reign of Manasseh, even though such an event is not compatible with the written sources. Surprisingly, Nadav Na'aman (1979a, 1979b) agreed, even though he also knew by then that Lachish III was destroyed by Sennacherib. Seeking an explanation for a destruction of Tel Beer-sheba Stratum II earlier than Sennacherib's campaign, to Kenyon's arguments he added the almost total lack of *lmlk* seal impressions from the Negeb in general and Tel Beer-sheba in particular.

As a matter of fact, I found the one *lmlk* seal impression to come from Tel Beer-sheba (Y. Aharoni 1973:76–77) when uncovering a plastered floor of Stratum II during the first season in 1969. The next year's work in that same area by Ze'ev Herzog proved that the plastered floor had belonged to one of the gate chambers, the walls of which had been severely robbed out. The vessel that had borne the impression was a pithos, not one of the usual jars so abundant at Lachish. The clay of this pithos evidently came from the Jerusalem area (Mommsen, Perlman, and Yellin 1984:107–9). In a subsequent study of the *lmlk* impressions I pointed out that the paucity of *lmlk* handles in the Negeb was obviously due to the different logistic arrangements there (Rainey 1982). The strong points in the Shephelah and in the hill country were supplied with wine from the royal vineyards located at the four hill country sites of Hebron, Ziph, Socoh, and *Mmšt*. Cities like Arad and Beer-sheba were receiving wine shipments from other places nearby, as witnessed, for example, by a small inscribed sherd found in the storehouse at Tel Beer-sheba that recorded shipments of wine from Tolad and Beth-amam (Y. Aharoni

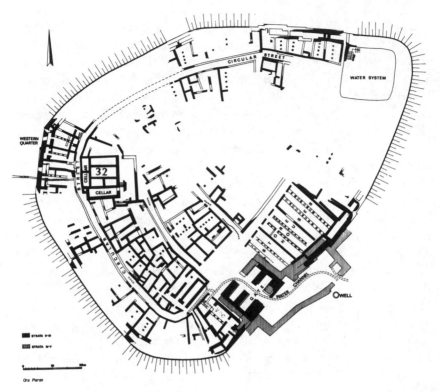

FIG. 20-1. Tel Beer-sheba Stratum II, overall plan of the town. Note the location of Building 32.

1973:71–73). The four place names on the *lmlk* seal impressions have nothing to do with administrative divisions of the kingdom (Aharoni and Avi-Yonah 1993:116–17).

Layout

The overall ground plan of Stratum II has been revealed in almost all its main elements (fig. 20-1): its integral design with the casemate walls, the dwelling units built against it, and the circular street on which all these dwellings front. Within the inner blocks one notes the presence of some larger structures, such as the building nicknamed the "governor's palace," just inside the gate. A lateral street running from the gate area led directly to Building 32 (see below). It should be obvious that the location of

Building 32 is significant with regard to the central axis of the city, as may also be its direct east-west orientation.

Identification

Aharoni always believed that he had found the administrative center of biblical Beer-sheba. None of us ever doubted that there was a civilian settlement under the industrial area of modern Beer Sheva; at my suggestion the summary of excavations in the modern town was added to the first excavation report (Gophna and Yisraeli 1973). It has been asserted that Tell es-Seba^c, our Tel Beer-sheba, is not the site of biblical Beer-sheba at all but rather the Shema/Sheba of Joshua 15:26 and 19:2 (Na'aman 1980:149–51). But the tell is the only prominent site in the area of modern Beer Sheva where a fortified center could have stood in the Iron Age. The small town at Beer-sheba during the seventh century (i.e., after the destruction of Stratum II at the tell) needed supplies from Arad (which is much smaller than the town of Stratum II at Tel Beer-sheba), as attested in the ostracon mentioning Beer-sheba (Y. Aharoni 1981: no. 3). The well-organized city at Tel Beer-sheba was, in our view, the major fortified administrative center in the biblical Negeb, standing between the Beer-sheba valley and the Besor basin. There is no reason why it could not have borne the name Beer-sheba as well as the civilian settlement by that name five kilometers away. Other doublets are known from this region, such as Anim and Arad.

Recently, Volkmar Fritz has proposed to identify Tel Beer-sheba with biblical Ziklag (Fritz 1993). His main argument is archaeological. He claims that the finds at Tel Sera^c (Tell esh-Sharî^cah) are not suitable for Ziklag. On the contrary, I find that they are strikingly appropriate (see Oren 1992). The deciding factors in identifying Tel Sera^c with Ziklag (Rainey 1988:1196) are its location in the Negeb (according to Joshua 15:31); its place in that list (which runs from east to southeast to west to northwest, Alt 1935:114 = 1959:426; Noth 1953:93), indicating that it should be in the western Negeb, close to Philistia; its association with the Negeb of the Cherethites (1 Sam. 30:1–3), suggesting that it was within the Philistine-controlled sphere of the western biblical Negeb; and the improbability that it was located within those areas where David claimed to be making attacks on behalf of Achish, king of Gath (1 Sam. 27:10). These considerations rule out Tel Halif (Tell el-Khulweilfeh), Tel Masos (Khirbet el-Meshâsh), and Tel Beer-sheba (Tell es-Seba^c).

FIG. 20-2. Reconstructed altar from Tel Beer-sheba; the width and breadth could be greater than three cubits if more stones should be found.

THE ALTAR AT TEL BEER-SHEBA

Probably the most famous discovery during the excavations at Tel Beer-sheba was that of the ashlar stones from a dismantled horned altar (Y. Aharoni 1974b). The reconstructed altar today (fig. 20-2) includes additional stones found by Herzog during the 1976 season (Herzog, Rainey, and Moshkovitz 1977:57, fig. 4). The black stain marks on these stones show that the altar originally must have had a metal grill on top; there the fires for the periodic sacrifices would have been kindled. Such a grill must have been used with the Arad altar as well. Our suggestion is that the biblical term *'ărî'ēl* (Ezek. 43:15–16; also *'r'l* in line 12 of the Mesha Stone) refers to such a metal installation. There is no reason to doubt that both altars, at Arad and at Tel Beer-sheba, were for animal sacrifices and not merely for incense (contra Yadin 1976:11; Fowler 1982:8–9; 1984). The dimensions of the Arad altar conform to the instructions in Exodus 27:1.

The height of the altar at Tel Beer-sheba was about three royal cubits (Y. Aharoni 1974b:3). As reconstructed, the length and width were also three royal cubits. The Arad altar, on the other hand, was five by five cubits square and three cubits high; it thus conformed to the biblical dimensions for the wooden altar to be used with the tabernacle (Exod. 27:1). It was also made of unhewn stones in accordance with another biblical injunction (Exod. 20:24–25); the latter passage does not specify the dimensions of the stone altars to be built wherever the Lord would put his name. The Tel Beer-sheba altar contrasts both in size and in materials with the two altar traditions mentioned above; it is of hewn stone and apparently only three by three cubits square.

On the other hand, only the most radical skeptic (e.g., Fowler 1982) can doubt that the discovery of the altar stones indicates that a ritual center had existed at the site of Tel Beer-sheba. It is also significant that the altar had been dismantled and at least some of its stones disposed of carefully: built into a repaired storehouse wall or buried under the rampart outside the gate. Other stones may still be hidden around the site under the latest phase of the earthen rampart. In any case, there was once an installation for sacrifice there and it was later dismantled.

This is reminiscent of how carefully the incense altars at the entrance to the holy of holies at Arad had been laid on their sides when the shrine went out of use. The Arad sacrificial altar had been put out of commission by being covered by a fill during Stratum VIII (Herzog et al. 1984:19), the same stratum that was contemporary with Lachish Stratum III and Tel Beer-sheba Stratum II. It has long been my view that in fact the entire shrine went out of use at that time. The substantial fortification wall (assigned by Aharoni to Stratum VI) that cut through the holy place (hêkal) probably so disrupted the meager stratified debris on each side of it that it was impossible to discern that the holy place had been covered along with the altar and the courtyard. There had been a Hellenistic pit just above the holy of holies and under that pit the flint stelae and other installations were found. Therefore, it would have been difficult to determine just when the holy of holies ceased to be used. This, in turn, suggests that the Levitical names and the "sons of Korah" on ostraca from rooms adjacent to the temple, which came from Stratum VIII, might represent new personnel posted there by Hezekiah. These details will be clarified in the final report.

House 430

The major question at Tel Beer-sheba is the original location of the ashlar altar. Considerable controversy has arisen over this issue, mainly because of a proposal by Yigael Yadin. Shortly after Aharoni's untimely death,

FIG. 20-3. House 430 with Yadin's proposed altar (in black) and the actual size of the altar discovered at Tel Beer-sheba (in white).

Yadin published an attempt to prove that the altar had stood in the court-yard of House 430, a dwelling located beside the city gate (Yadin 1976; Shanks 1977). My colleagues and I replied with alacrity (Herzog, Rainey, and Moshkovitz 1977; Rainey 1977), but our arguments have not been sufficiently appreciated. Therefore, another picture has been prepared using Yadin's old photograph, on which his altar has been outlined (in black) but on which the true size of the real altar has been superimposed (fig. 20-3). It is obvious that Yadin's proposed altar is about one-quarter the size of the actual excavated altar. If the excavated altar had been placed in the courtyard of House 430, there would have been little space to pass from the entryway to the door of the next inner room. I personally excavated the floor of that courtyard and uncovered the oven in the corner (fig. 20-4). Furthermore, there was a stone-lined pit (Pit 441) of Hellenistic date that cut the staircase, breaking its connection with the central walls of the house (fig. 20-5). Obviously the staircase was built to give access to the second floor or the roof of House 430. It could serve no function, but would only impede the acts of sacrifice.

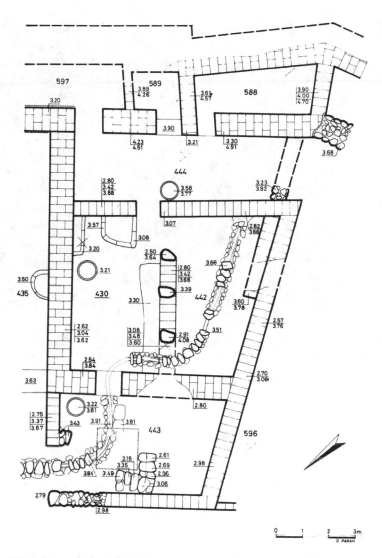

FIG. 20-4. Ground plan of House 430 with true dimensions of the altar sketched in (dotted lines).

The plan of the building (fig. 20-4), prepared by S. Moshkovitz, reveals not only the true size of the altar and that it would have virtually filled the courtyard, but also the water drain under the paved floor of the inner court of the house. This water drain was the continuation of a roof drain in the wall of the courtyard (fig. 20-6). These details prove that the paved

FIG. 20-5. Hellenistic stone-lined pit, which must have cut the line of the ascending staircase.

area was really a courtyard open to the sky. In Yadin's reconstruction it was a roofed stall in which sacrificial animals were kept (Yadin 1976:1, Fig. 9), and his theory that House 430 was a "high place" with the sacrificial altar in its courtyard and sacrificial animals in an inner stall is erroneous.

Building 32

In our rebuttal of Yadin's theory, we pointed to Building 32 as the possible site of the original structure marking the place of the altar (Herzog, Rainey, and Moshkovitz 1977:56–57). The story of how this building was discovered and some details of its stratigraphic position will shed some light on our proposal. During the first season of excavations at Tel Beersheba, Aharoni selected the main excavation area, where the domestic buildings of the "Western Quarter" (Beit-Arieh 1973) were uncovered, because it was at the westernmost side of the tell, just about where a temple might be expected if the arrangement at Arad could be used as

FIG. 20-6. The drain that was under the floors of House 430; note that it begins at the bottom of a roof drain in the far wall. It was originally covered by a stone pavement in a courtyard that must have been open to the sky.

a precedent. In 1969, it appeared that Aharoni's intuition had misled him. The casemate wall, and the dwellings built against it, were purely domestic in nature. But there was one anomaly: across the circular street from the dwellings was what appeared to be a room of the same stratum (now Locus 1262), but it had no floor. We kept going down in burnt brick debris, below the contemporary street level. Deep foundations of what later proved to be part of a Herodian-period fortified "castle" bounded it on one side, and the pool from the same Herodian complex was on the other. So the locus was abandoned at the end of the season.

Only in 1972 did we begin to get some indications of what might be in that immediate area. I was excavating under the second-century Roman fort excavated by Fritz (1973); John Lawrentz, under my tutelage, was excavating the adjacent area on the west. In my area the eastern corner of the massive Herodian fortress, mainly outlined by robber trenches, and the courtyard of the Hellenistic temple complex, with its altar platform (Y. Aharoni 1975:163–65), were coming to light. Lawrentz was finding its extension to the west. The stairs and fragments of a room that we take as

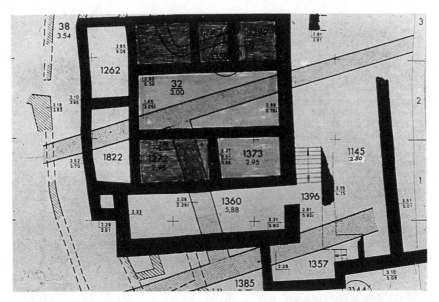

FIG. 20-7. Plan of Building 32; the structure faces due east. Rooms with dark shading had dirt floors; those with light shading had crushed chalk floors, including the central inner court (Locus 32). The court on the eastern (1145) side had a floor surface of gray material (cf. fig. 20-9, no. 10 in the section) laid over a previous crushed chalk floor. The Iron Age building is outlined over the wall outlines and the pool of the later Herodian building and also over the Persian period grain silo (1358). Compare figure 20-10, where these later elements appear in the photograph.

the "holy place" had been uncovered by Itzhaq Beit-Arieh (along with a pit containing the collection of Egyptian votive objects and a Mesopotamian votive cylinder seal) during the 1971 season. In spite of the massive robber trenches of the Herodian building, it was possible for Lawrentz to uncover a substantial segment of a courtyard area from the Iron Age. A wall (D 203) running north-south came to light, which subsequently was identified as the eastern wall of the courtyard of Building 32. In the courtyard were large areas of a crushed chalk surface. The surface did not abut the line of the wall, because the foundation trenches for the walls had cut the crushed chalk surface; thus the surface was older than the walls (fig. 20-7).

In 1973, I opened the area between the courtyard on the east and the residential quarter on the west. As for the courtyard, it became clear that the chalk had later been covered with a layer of about 30 cm of the gray material (fig. 20-9 for the section) so ubiquitous at Tel Beer-sheba (Rainey 1974). The gray material was the surface of the courtyard during the life of Building 32. As soon as its walls began to be exposed, it was clear that the building was not a temple, but rather a "four-room house" of impressive dimensions with an additional fifth room added on the south side (fig. 20-8). The building was oriented exactly east-west. Considering the circular nature of the overall ground plan of Israelite Stratum II, it was apparent that the location of Building 32 was not accidental. It was placed just at the east-west axis of the radial walls of the outer line of dwellings that went with the casemate wall (see fig. 20-1).

What was more surprising, however, was that the fifth room had no floor. We kept digging in heavily burnt brick debris containing numerous vessels of various types, such as jugs, juglets, and cooking pots. After a day or so of digging, it became clear that we were dealing with a basement into which had collapsed the debris of an upper story. Steps led down from the courtyard level to the entryway to the basement. From there one evidently descended by a wooden ladder. At the bottom there was a stone, probably the brace for such a ladder. When the room was completely excavated, we found that in its northwest corner there was a doorway that led in the direction of the locus that we had begun back in 1969. We reopened that locus and soon realized that it too was a basement. It was divided into two units by a brick wall in which was a window. On the far side of that wall, the jug with the inscription ḥṣy lmlk, "a half measure for the king," was found (Y. Aharoni 1975:158–63, pl. 33). Now we understood why we had not found a floor there at street level in 1969. Building 32 had deep basements on two sides, the south and the west. The building itself is reminiscent of Albright's "northwest tower" at Tell Beit Mirsim (Albright 1975:176, lower figure).

After finding that on two sides the building had basements going down to virgin rock, we decided to excavate under the floors of the other rooms in the house to look for earlier stratigraphy. In every case, we found that the fills beneath the floors went down to bedrock. The resulting picture was surprising. When the builders came to construct Building 32, they excavated a huge rectangle, about 17 by 12 m, down to bedrock. Then they began to build their walls up to the level of the street in Israelite Stratum II. On two sides, they left the spaces empty to serve as basements. But in the other rooms and also in the inner courtyard (where we found a large grinding stone and a smaller basalt grindstone), we found that the fill added by the builders began at bedrock and went all the way

FIG. 20-8. Crushed chalk surfaces badly disturbed by Hellenistic pits, Herodian foundation and robber trenches, and especially by the foundation trench of Wall D 203, the eastern courtyard wall of Building 32. The left end of the meter stick is pointing to the balk face drawn as the section in figure 20-9.

FIG. 20-9. Section showing the crushed chalk surface (Israelite Stratum III) and the layer of gray material laid over it to form the courtyard surface of Building 32 (Israelite Stratum II): (1) bedouin graves; (2) loess accumulation; (3) robber trenches of Herodian building; (4) ashy material, top of eroded Hellenistic occupation layers; (5) ashy material; (6) brown bricky debris; (7) ashy material; (8) yellowish bricky debris of Building 32, Israelite Stratum II; (9) burnt material with pottery, destruction of Building 32; (10) gray ashy material, courtyard makeup of Building 32; (11) crushed chalk surface, evidently from courtyard surface of Israelite Stratum III.

up to floor level (fig. 20-10)! Incidentally, there was another basement on the south inner side of the western courtyard, reached by a staircase (Locus 1357). On the western side, we found that the foundation trench for Building 32 had cut the street levels of Strata III, IV, and V (figs. 20-11, 20-12).

During the last excavation season in 1976, after Yohanan Aharoni's untimely death, we excavated under the sections of chalk floor in the courtyard. There we found fragments of walls that conformed to the pattern of houses in Stratum V. Strata V, IV, III, and II had all been exposed in the area immediately adjacent to Building 32 on the south side. Thus, we had some Stratum V houses with which to compare the scanty walls found under the courtyard of Building 32.

It was now certain that, although the builders of Building 32 had excavated to bedrock where they wanted to found the house itself, they

FIG. 20-10. Rooms of Building 32 excavated to bedrock. Note steps leading to the entrance of the deep basement (the "fifth unit," Locus 1360). The person is standing on the partially dismantled foundation of the Herodian fortified palace, the foundations of which bisect Building 32 at several places. Behind him is a brick-lined grain silo (Locus 1358) from the Persian period and in the square beyond it is the pool of the Herodian Fort.

had left large parts of the crushed chalk floor of the western courtyard untouched. The foundation trenches for their courtyard walls cut through the chalk surface (fig. 20-8).

The Location of the Altar

When seeking a suitable location for the ashlar altar of sacrifice, it is unlikely that such a finely built artifact would be hidden in the relatively modest courtyard of a structure like Building 430. The altar should have occupied a prominent place, approachable by visitors but possibly within a temenos area. The precedent of Arad, if it may be allowed, would suggest that the altar should stand in a courtyard on the east side of a building whose main axis was east-west. Not only Arad but the Jerusalem temple, the Pentateuchal tabernacle, and two Hellenistic temples (the wrongly called Solar Shrine at Lachish and the temple found at Tel Beersheba) all follow the same pattern.

FIG. 20-11. Dame Kathleen Kenyon visits Tel Beer-sheba. The author is showing her and Professor Aharoni a probe cut through the street levels behind Building 32. The foundation trench of Wall A-16 was seen to cut through the street levels of the previous strata. Compare figure 20-12.

CONCLUSION

Therefore, we still stand behind our original suggestion that the temple to which the altar belonged had formerly stood in the place where we found Building 32. Herzog has shown how such a temple could fit in the area now occupied by the foundations of Building 32 (fig. 20-13). When the building was destroyed and replaced by Building 32, the altar was also dismantled and its stones hidden in various places around the tell. This, we maintain, took place in the reign of Hezekiah, when Stratum II was constructed.

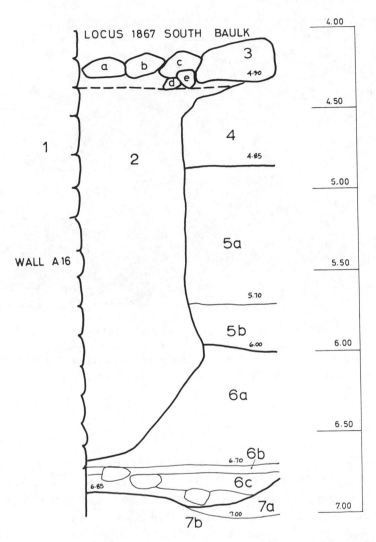

FIG. 20-12. Section drawing showing how the foundation trench (Locus 1867) of Wall A-16 (the western wall of Building 32) cut through the street levels of previous strata: (1) Wall A-16 of Building 32; (2) foundation trench of Wall A-16, bricky fill; (3) stub of drain from Stratum III cut by foundation trench of Building 32 (some of its stones, a, b, c, d, e were tossed on top of the trench fill); (4) gray material, street makeup of Israelite Stratum IV; (5a) very solid bricky material, debris of Stratum V; (5b) gray material, street makeup of Stratum V; (6a) very solid bricky material, debris of Stratum VI; (6b) crushed chalk surface of Stratum VI; (6c) gray material, fill of Stratum VI; (7a) bricky material, debris of Stratum VII; (7b) hard white surface.

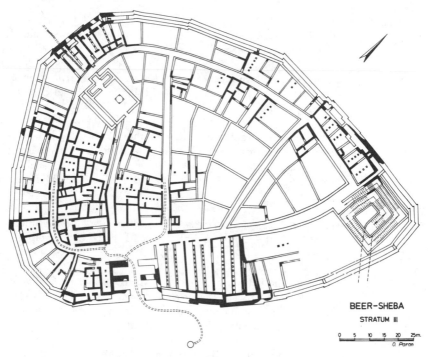

FIG. 20-13. Tel Beer-sheba Stratum III as reconstructed by Herzog (1978:40); note that a temple building like that at Arad could have stood in place of Building 32 from Stratum II.

WORKS CITED

Aharoni, M., and Y. Aharoni
1976   The Stratification of Judean Sites in the Eighth and Seventh Centuries B.C.E. *Bulletin of the American Schools of Oriental Research* 224:73–90.

Aharoni, Y.
1974a   Excavations at Tel Beer-sheba, Preliminary Report of the Fourth Season, 1972. *Tel Aviv* 1:34–42.
1974b   The Horned Altar of Beer-sheba. *Biblical Archaeologist* 37:2–6.
1975   Excavations at Tel Beer-sheba. Preliminary Report of the Fifth and Sixth Seasons, 1973–1974. *Tel Aviv* 2:146–68.
1981   *Arad Inscriptions*. Jerusalem: Israel Exploration Society.

Aharoni, Y., ed.
1973   *Beer-sheba I: Excavations at Tel Beer-sheba, 1969–1971 Seasons*. Publications of the Institute of Archaeology, 2. Tel Aviv: Institute of Archaeology, Tel Aviv University.

Aharoni, Y., and M. Avi-Yonah
1993   *The Macmillan Bible Atlas.* 3d ed., rev., ed. A. F. Rainey and Z.
                Safrai. New York: Macmillan.
Albright, W. F.
1975   Beit Mirsim, Tell. In *Encyclopedia of Archaeological Excavations in the
                Holy Land*, ed. M. Avi-Yonah, 1:171–78. Jerusalem: Israel Explora-
                tion Society and Massada Press.
Alt, A.
1935   Historische Geographie und Topographie des Negeb, III: Saru-
                hen, Ziklag, Horma, Gerar. *Journal of the Palestine Oriental Society*
                15:294–324.
1959   *Kleine Schriften zur Geschichte des Volkes Israel.* Band III. München:
                C. H. Beck.
Becking, B.
1992   *The Fall of Samaria: An Historical and Archaeological Study.* Studies
                of the Ancient Near East, Vol. 2, ed. M. and H. E. Weippert.
                Leiden: Brill.
Beit-Arieh, I.
1973   The Western Quarter. In *Beer-sheba I, Excavations at Tel Beer-sheba,
                1969–1971 Seasons: The Early Iron Age Settlements*, ed. Y. Aharoni,
                31–37. Publications of the Institute of Archaeology, 2. Tel Aviv:
                Institute of Archaeology, Tel Aviv University.
Fowler, M. D.
1982   The Excavation of Tell Beer-sheba and the Biblical Record. *Pales-
                tine Exploration Quarterly* 114:7–11.
1984   Excavated Incense Burners. *Biblical Archaeologist* 47:183–86.
Fritz, V.
1973   The Roman Fortress. In *Beer-sheba I, Excavations at Tel Beer-
                sheba, 1969–1971 Seasons*, ed. Y. Aharoni, 83–89. Publications of
                the Institute of Archaeology, 2. Tel Aviv: Institute of Archaeology,
                Tel Aviv University.
1993   Where Is David's Ziklag? *Biblical Archaeology Review* 19,
                no. 3:58–61, 76.
Gophna, R., and Y. Yisraeli
1973   Soundings at Beer Sheva (Bir es-Seba^c). In *Beer-sheba I, Excava-
                tions at Tel Beer-sheba, 1969–1971 Seasons*, ed. Y. Aharoni, 115–18.
                Publications of the Institute of Archaeology, 2. Tel Aviv: Institute
                of Archaeology, Tel Aviv University.
Herzog, Z.
1978   Israelite City Planning in the Light of the Beer-sheba and Arad
                Excavations. *Expedition* 20:38–43.
Herzog, Z.; M. Aharoni; A. F. Rainey; and S. Moshkovitz
1984   The Israelite Fortress at Arad. *Bulletin of the American Schools of
                Oriental Research* 254:1–34.
Herzog, Z.; A. F. Rainey; and S. Moshkovitz
1977   The Stratigraphy at Beer-sheba and the Location of the Sanctu-
                ary. *Bulletin of the American Schools of Oriental Research* 225:49–58.

Kenyon, K. M.
1976   The Date of the Destruction of Iron Age Beer-sheba. *Palestine Exploration Quarterly* 108:63–64.

Laato, A.
1986   New Viewpoints on the Chronology of the Kings of Judah and Israel. *Zeitschrift für die alttestamentliche Wissenschaft* 98:210–21.

Miller, J. M., and J. H. Hayes
1986   *A History of Ancient Israel and Judah.* Philadelphia: Westminster.

Mommsen, H.; I. Perlman; and J. Yellin
1984   The Provenience of the *lmlk* Jars. *Israel Exploration Journal* 34:89–113.

Na'aman, N.
1979a   The Brook of Egypt and Assyrian Policy on the Border of Egypt. *Tel Aviv* 6:68–90.
1979b   Sennacherib's Campaign to Judah and the Date of the LMLK Stamps. *Vetus Testamentum* 29:61–86.
1980   The Inheritance of the Sons of Simeon. *Zeitschrift des deutschen Palästina-Vereins* 96:136–52.

Noth, M.
1953   *Das Buch Josua.* Handbuch zum Alten Testament, Erste Reihe 7, ed. O. Eissfeldt. Tübingen: J. C. B. Mohr (Paul Siebeck).

Oded, B.
1977   Judah and the Exile. In *Israelite and Judaean History*, ed. J. H. Hayes and J. M. Miller, 435–88. Philadelphia: Westminster.

Oren, E.
1992   Sera[c], Tel. In *The New Encyclopedia of Archaeological Excavations in the Land of Israel*, ed. E. Stern, 4:1563–70. Jerusalem: Israel Exploration Society, Ministry of Defence, and Carta Publishers; and New York: Simon and Schuster.

Rainey, A. F.
1974   Dust and Ashes. *Tel Aviv* 2:77–83.
1975a   The Fate of Lachish during the Campaigns of Sennacherib and Nebuchadnezzar. In *Investigations at Lachish: The Sanctuary and the Residency (Lachish V)*, ed. Y. Aharoni, 47–60. Publications of the Institute of Archaeology, 4. Tel Aviv: Institute of Archaeology, Tel Aviv University.
1975b   Sacrifice and Offerings. In *The Zondervan Pictorial Encyclopedia of the Bible*, 194–211. Grand Rapids: Zondervan.
1977   No Bama at Beer-Sheva. *Biblical Archaeology Review* 3, no.3:18–21, 56.
1982   Wine from the Royal Vineyards. *Bulletin of the American Schools of Oriental Research* 245:57–62.
1984   Early Historical Geography of the Negeb. In *Beer-Sheva II: The Early Iron Age Settlements*, ed. Z. Herzog, 88–104. Publications of the Institute of Archaeology, 7. Tel Aviv: Tel Aviv University, Institute of Archaeology and Ramot Publishing Co.

1988   Ziklag. In *The International Standard Bible Encyclopedia*, ed. G. W.
               Bromiley, 4:1196b. Grand Rapids: Eerdmans.

Shanks, H.
1977   Yigael Yadin Finds a Bama at Beer-Sheva. *Biblical Archaeology
               Review* 3, no. 1:3–12.

Thiele, E. R.
1983   *The Mysterious Numbers of the Hebrew Kings*. Grand Rapids:
               Zondervan.

Ussishkin, D.
1977   The Destruction of Lachish by Sennacherib and the Dating of the
               Royal Judean Storage Jars. *Tel Aviv* 4:28–60.

Vaughn, P. H.
1974   *The Meaning of 'Bāmâ' in the Old Testament: A Study of Etymological,
               Textual, and Archaeological Evidence*. London: Cambridge University Press.

Yadin, Y.
1976   Beer-sheba: The High Place Destroyed by King Josiah. *Bulletin of
               the American Schools of Oriental Research* 222:5–17.

21 | Priestly Families and the Cultic Structure at Taanach

WALTER E. RAST

In his archaeological commentary on Amos, Hosea, and Micah, Philip King writes: "Worship and cult are basically the same, just as the worship of God and the service of God are synonymous terms. In earlier times it was thought that the deity had needs, and the deity's servants ministered to these needs" (King 1988:88). Human action in cult (what the Bible terms *ʿăbōdâ*) is a subject of interest to the archaeologist, since it suggests that ancient sites may yield evidence of how people ministered to the deity's needs as well as their own through worship.

Two problems have bedeviled this aspect of archaeological research, however. One has been the difficulty of isolating such cultic material during fieldwork, while a second has been the lack of necessary conceptualization to guide the search for such data. Because of these difficulties and the tenuous grounds on which objects have sometimes been held to be cultic, a common way of introducing this subject has been to caution against assigning data too quickly to this sphere (May 1935:1; Shiloh 1979:147), and scholars have questioned several proposals of supposed cultic materials (Yeivin 1973; Fowler 1984; Coogan 1987).

The Cultic Structure at Taanach is one example whose identification as a building containing ceremonial objects has been questioned (Yeivin 1973; Fowler 1984), although others have accepted the cultic interpretation advanced by Paul Lapp (1964:26–32, 35–39; Shiloh 1979:151–52; Dever 1990:134–37). It should be said at the outset that S. Yeivin's conclusion (1973:28*, 172–73 [Hebrew]), to which M. D. Fowler (1984:34) assents, that the ceramic types found in the Taanach Cultic Structure are simply examples of ordinary household pottery, is dubious. One should consider the unusual character of the material from this structure, its archaeological context, and comparisons that can be made with parallels at other sites, especially Megiddo. I shall return below to some of the supposedly ordinary household pottery.

The most striking objects from the Cultic Structure area were a number of highly decorated ceramic stands, two of which have elaborate motifs with parallels in art and literature of the ancient Near East (May 1935:13–17). There is, first of all, the stand discovered by E. Sellin, which he termed an "incense altar," but which was more likely used for some other purpose, possibly libation (Sellin 1904:76–78; Herbert G. May [1935:13–15] referred to similar examples from Megiddo as pottery "shrines," or "houses," with windows and doors). Sellin (1904:76) recorded that he found various pieces of this incense altar 8 m southeast of the large stone and rectangular basin (Basin 75 in fig. 21-1)[1] that have also been considered a possible cultic installation (for a drawing of Sellin's stand, see Graham and May 1936:248, fig. 47, and Glock 1993:1431; for a photograph, see Glock 1978:1144). According to Sellin's description, this would have put the location near Silo 16, or perhaps slightly south of the latter (fig. 21-1). Since Sellin's report provided no stratigraphic information, no evidence is available to establish the relation of this object to the other finds in and around the Cultic Structure, but the decorative features on the stand and the fact that it was found in the vicinity of the building itself make it likely that it was connected with this complex.

The second stand (TT 1500) was discovered in the lower part of Cistern 69 by the expedition to Taanach directed by Paul Lapp (Lapp 1969:42–44). Based on the dating of associated pottery, this stand was also apparently in use during the tenth-century use phase of the Cultic Structure. Since detail about this stand will be published by Nancy Lapp, its mythic and artistic features will not be discussed here (for a discussion of the motifs on this stand see Dever 1990:135–36).

This stand, like that found by Sellin, was almost certainly associated with the Cultic Structure complex, as was also a third stand, damaged and less elaborate, which also came from Cistern 69 (Rast 1978:36, fig. 54). The size, the shape, and the motifs depicted on these ornate objects point to one of the determinative characteristics Michael Coogan has proposed for designating archaeological finds as cultic, namely their exotic features (Coogan 1987:2–3). This, together with the striking parallels between materials from the Cultic Structure and those from Locus 2081 and Building 10 at Megiddo (Rast 1978:34, table 1; Loud 1948:44, fig. 102), allows us to proceed with the assumption that we have here information about

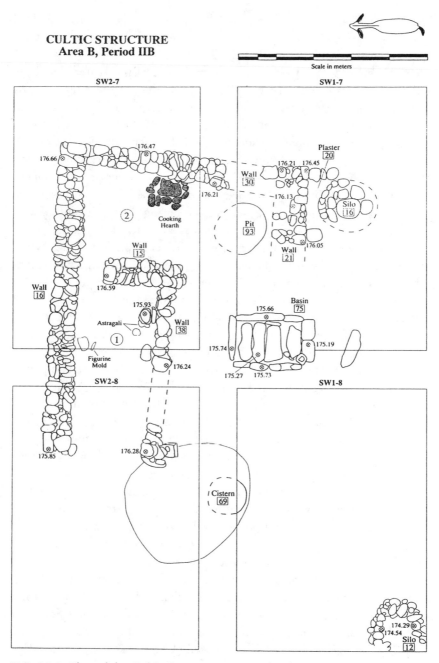

FIG. 21-1. Plan of the Cultic Structure at Taanach, showing various features of the area (credit: Mark Meehl).

the cult at Taanach during the days of Solomon, that is, in the third quarter of the tenth century BCE. The arguments for this date have been spelled out previously (Rast 1978:24–27).

In this study I wish to pursue the significance of this material and the building itself from a different angle, accepting the fact that these materials and the building represent some sort of connection with the organized cult of tenth-century BCE Taanach. Thus it is important to ask what these data might indicate about the socioreligious character of Taanach during the time of Solomon, and how they might relate to biblical information about this period. To answer such questions it is necessary to consider both the Taanach material and parallel data, especially from Megiddo, with regard to the social changes occurring during the tenth century BCE.

The progression of early Israel from a tribal society to a chiefdom and then to a state that reached its fruition in the tenth century under David and Solomon has been the focus of a great deal of discussion in recent biblical scholarship devoted to the social study of the monarchy. This kind of study is based on the dynamics of the formation of chiefdoms and states. C. Renfrew, for example, building on the work of Elman Service and Marshall Sahlins, has identified twenty basic traits that characterize a chiefdom (Renfrew 1984:228–29), all of which would pertain as well to a state society, although in the latter case they would be more complex.

Each of Renfrew's twenty traits can be applied to what the biblical texts reveal about Israelite society during the monarchy under Solomon, and to some degree David. These include, to name a few: ranking; the redistribution of produce organized by the chief; greater population density and size; specialization; organization and deployment of public labor; potential for territorial expansion; and pervasive inequality. For the problem of cult, these features are particularly important: centers that coordinate social and religious as well as economic activity; frequent ceremonies and rituals serving wide social purposes; and the rise of a priesthood.

Despite the difficulties for historical reconstruction introduced by later redaction, the Bible has probably preserved, at least in outline, the developments that accompanied the establishment of the monarchy in Israel, including information about ceremonial activities in various parts of the country at the time. The reorganization of the kingdom under Solomon not only brought about political and economic change but also produced transformations in the cultic *realia* as well (1 Kgs. 4:1–19). The descriptions of Solomon's installation of new personnel in the higher and subordinate positions of the priesthood, some of these being newly created positions, and his own presiding over the building and dedication of the Jerusalem Temple (1 Kgs. 8:22–64), bring to mind those very features that Renfrew associates with the founding of chiefdoms (and states), principally increased involvement of the rulership in matters of cult, and the assignment of a priesthood tied to the governing power. All of these developments, beginning with Jerusalem, also had an effect upon the local cult places of the countryside, including the central and northern parts of the country (see Ahlström 1982:44–51).

Under the new monarchy the priesthood became increasingly the prerogative of select families, with members of the Abiathar group competing with those of Zadok for such positions (Abba 1962:881; Schiffman 1985:821–22; Cody 1969:88–93). It is in this regard that information found in Numbers 4 may be significant regarding the cultic material at Taanach, Megiddo, and other sites. Although the final composition of this passage dates to a later time, its descriptions of the specific activities of priestly families may apply to some degree throughout most of the monarchy in Israel, and even to the period of reconstruction following the destruction of Jerusalem in 587/86 BCE.

Numbers 4 contains the account of a census of the Levites with regard to their duties in the cult. The setting is the wilderness at a time prior to the conquest of Canaan, when the Tabernacle is the sole shrine. But the prismlike character of such a text no doubt reflects some part of the activity of the Levitical groups in the Jerusalem Temple and in outlying sanctuaries. Of the assignment of cultic duties to the three families of Levi, the Kohathites, the Gershonites, and the Merarites, we are particularly concerned with the first of these, the Kohathites (Num. 4:1–20).

The family of Kohath was given the responsibility of overseeing the transport of the sacred vessels found within the Tabernacle (Milgrom 1990:24–29), while the families of Gershon and Merari had perhaps a less important and certainly less threatening task of overseeing the Tabernacle curtain and the structure itself—its posts, poles, and pegs. Thus it is in the list of vessels presided over by the Kohathites that we are given a glimpse of the kinds of cultic vessels used, not only for the earlier period of Israelite history supposedly represented in the Tabernacle, but most likely also during the age of the monarchy (see 2 Chron. 24:14).

The vessels that needed to be wrapped before they could be lifted by the Kohathite priests were those on the table of the presence (Num. 4:7–8), those associated with the lampstand (Num. 4:9–10), and those found on the golden altar (Num. 4:11–14). Because they were fully recognized priests (see Num. 3:9–10), "Aaron and his sons" had the authority to approach and cover the vessels, after which they could be carried by the Kohathites.

The group of vessels found on the table of the presence that are especially relevant here consists of bowls (qĕʿārōt), ladles (kappōt), jars (mĕnaqqiyyōt), and libation jugs (qĕśôt hannesek) (following the translation of Milgrom 1990:26). Ironically, if Yeivin's conclusions noted above were followed, an archaeologist unearthing these vessels at an Israelite site could just as well conclude that they were domestic rather than ceremonial, since the biblical list records vessel types quite similar to those found in the excavated examples from Taanach and Megiddo. Yeivin had trouble seeing how jars and jugs could represent anything other than mundane functions (see Yeivin 1973:172, col. 2, where he writes that the rooms from which they came were "ordinary storage rooms," one probably being a "kitchen"). My contention is that even though Rooms 1 and 2 of the Taanach Cultic Structure might have been for storage, with one of them perhaps a kitchen, neither interpretation would negate that we are dealing with cultic material. After all, storage facilities and kitchens were needed in a number of social settings.

In studying the vessels from Taanach, therefore, we need to look more closely at the building in which they were found. Lapp's decision to call the building a "Cultic Structure" left open the question of how to understand its function. This is a nuance apparently missed by Yeivin, who lumped the Taanach remains together with buildings designated as temples in his article "Temples That Were Not." Lapp's conclusion was not based on the architecture of the building, of which only fragments remained due in large part to Sellin's trenching. Nor did Lapp ever claim that this building was a temple or sanctuary.

A key point is that the pottery group found in the Taanach Cultic Structure is one of several assemblages of this type from north central Palestine, dating to the tenth century. The close similarities between the materials from Locus 2081 at Megiddo and the Taanach Cultic Structure assemblage are now apparent. The ceramic stands, for example, were constructed and decorated in very similar ways, and the mythical motifs found on them are very much alike (see Lapp 1969: fig. 29, p. 43, and May 1935: figs. 13 and 15). The stand with down-turned tabs found in Cistern 69 at Taanach could have been fashioned by the same artisan who made a similar stand at Megiddo (see Rast 1978:54 with May 1935: fig. 20). Indeed, the assemblages from Locus 2081 at Megiddo and the Cultic

Structure at Taanach as a whole, including the fine pottery, have so many features in common that they could have come from the same workshop (see Loud 1948:44, fig. 102).

What is important, however, is that these similar assemblages were found not in large public buildings like sanctuaries or temples, but rather in what Yigal Shiloh (1979:149–51) termed "cult corners located in residential sections and buildings." This fact raises the question of the meaning of such a context for understanding the religious practices at Taanach or Megiddo in the tenth century.

Shiloh understood this to mean a type of worship in which religious activities were practiced in small, private buildings, such as dwellings, rather than in temples (Shiloh 1979:156). The data from the cultic corners of residential units might then be envisioned as evidence of widespread domestic religious activities rather than as proof of a more public cult (cf. Åhlström 1982:44).

My proposal takes a different approach. The very fact of almost identical assemblages in the "cult corners" at Megiddo and Taanach suggests the management of cult and religion by the emerging state society of the tenth century, whose integrating power also brought this aspect of social life under strong national influence, if not direct control.

Thus an alternative explanation of the similar kinds of cultic material found in these smaller buildings would be that we have material evidence of specific priestly families at Megiddo and Taanach being entrusted with materials belonging to the public cult, something akin to the situation described in Numbers 4. Indeed, if it is true that "a *kohen* was essentially the attendant of a sanctuary with the objects contained therein" (Cody 1969:101), then cultic material might be expected to turn up not only in larger sanctuary buildings but also in residential quarters occupied by priestly families. What we may have, then, in the case of the local rooms or parts of buildings at Taanach, Megiddo, and other sites that Shiloh (1979:149) has called "cult corners" or "little chapels," were houses belonging to priestly groups. Thus the Cultic Structure at Taanach, Locus 2081 at Megiddo, and Building 10 also at Megiddo, near which were found the "horned altars," were probably not structures in which these items were used, but were places where traditional cultic material was stored, repaired, or perhaps even manufactured, either by the priests themselves or by artisans under their jurisdiction.

The problem of where the sanctuaries of the tenth-century BCE sites were located, and what they were like, is something about which we thus far have little information. We cannot conclude from the sparse data, however, that no such sanctuaries were built, or that there existed only loosely organized institutions of worship at the domestic rather than the public level. Much of the lack of information about public cult buildings during Iron I may be due to the vagaries of excavation. Apart from the much debated date of the "sanctuary" at Iron Age Arad, excavation has thus far not produced clear information on public structures related to worship. But it would indeed be strange to find that the widespread reorganization of the kingdom in the tenth century, with greater involvement of government in the daily life of the people, did not affect public religion (Åhlström 1982:44).

I now return to the pottery from the Cultic Structure, an assemblage that Yeivin characterized as being nothing more than domestic pottery. First, I reiterate that the presence in the Cultic Structure of common types such as storage jars and cooking pots (Rast 1978:30–35, 49) does not negate the cultic use of these vessels in a different context, especially if the notion of priestly quarters is kept in mind. Other vessels in the Cultic Structure assemblage deserve closer attention. The fact that fine, red-slipped burnished bowls are the most predominant group in the Cultic Structure suggests some specialized activity regarding these vessels (Rast 1978:42–49). Of the jugs and juglets, one example may have been used for pouring wine (Rast 1978:28–29, fig. 37:2), perhaps ceremonially, while two other jugs were made of extremely fine, thin ware, lustrously burnished, and decorated (Rast 1978:39:2, 4). Two amphoras indicate possible special usage (Rast 1978: fig. 36:3–4). The large krater that contained a heap of clay loom weights (Rast 1978: fig. 41:1), which could have been used in an ordinary textile industry, might indicate the weaving of textiles for cultic purposes. The lamps, the perforated vessel (possibly a censer), and the stand with window (Rast 1978: fig. 51:1–4) also suggest specialized vessels for cultic use.

Also significant, though overlooked by Yeivin and Fowler in their discussions, are the vessels found in Cistern 69, a feature that I have shown above to be part of the Cultic Structure complex. Not only the two elaborate stands, but also three chalices, or parts thereof, came from this cistern (Rast 1978: fig. 52:4–6). It also seems possible that the unusual carinated bowl from Cistern 69 (Rast 1978: fig. 52:9) may have fit into the stand from the Cultic Structure (Rast 1978: fig. 51:4). This could explain the function of this atypical bowl form in the tenth century. The cumulative evidence of the ceramic groups from this entire area thus speaks against their interpretation as domestic pottery.

My conclusions, then, are the following: (1) The similar assemblages from the Cultic Structure at Taanach, together with those at nearby Megiddo as well as those at several other tenth-century sites such as Beth-shan and Lachish, show a new type of uniformity in the management of cultic *realia*, which is expressive of a more controlled society emerging under the developing monarchy. (2) This uniformity was fostered with the blessing of the state authorities by a process in which the management of cult came into the hands of select families serving as priests or their associates. (3) Such priestly families oversaw the paraphernalia used in public worship, such as altars and consecrated storage vessels. (4) Either these priestly functionaries themselves, or specialized artisans commissioned by them, were active in the production of new types of ceremonial objects to be used in public worship. Thus the figurine mold at Taanach was intended for making copies to be used in public as well as private worship. (5) Finally, the curious presence of sheep *astragali* in both the Taanach Cultic Structure and Locus 2081 at Megiddo (see Lapp 1964:35 [where they are identified as pig *astragali*] and parallels from Megiddo listed there; for their identification as sheep/goat *astragali*, see Stager and Wolff 1981:100, n. 7) may point not so much to the fact that these items were used directly in cult, but that they had special significance as remains from acts of animal sacrifice well known from the Bible and contemporary texts (cf. Lev. 8:18–21).

I have not dealt with the question of how the apparently Canaanite motifs found on several of the elaborately decorated stands could square with whatever emerging Yahwism had developed by the tenth century. But the Bible's own rather detailed picture of conditions in the following century (1 Kgs. 18) makes clear that priests in the northern part of Israel took over a variety of practices derived from native Canaanite worship for their ministrations to the God of Israel.

NOTE

1. I am grateful to Mark Meehl, who generously supplied a copy of the plan of the Cultic Structure from his Johns Hopkins University doctoral dissertation, in preparation. Meehl's study treats the overall Iron Age stratigraphy of Taanach and is a valuable complement to my study of the Iron Age pottery (Rast 1978).

WORKS CITED

Abba, R.
1962   Priests and Levites. In *The Interpreter's Dictionary of the Bible*, ed.
                G. A. Buttrick, 3:876–89. New York: Abingdon.
Ahlström, G. W.
1982   *Royal Administration and National Religion in Ancient Palestine.*
                Leiden: E. J. Brill.
Cody, A.
1969   *A History of Old Testament Priesthood.* Analecta Biblica 35. Rome:
                Pontifical Biblical Institute.
Coogan, M. D.
1987   Of Cults and Cultures: Reflections on the Interpretation of
                Archaeological Evidence. *Palestine Exploration Quarterly* 119:1–8.
Dever, W. G.
1990   *Recent Archaeological Discoveries and Biblical Research.* Seattle: Uni-
                versity of Washington Press.
Fowler, M. D.
1984   Concerning the "Cultic" Structure at Taanach. *Zeitschrift des
                Deutschen Palästina-Vereins* 100:30–34.
Glock, A. E.
1978   Taanach. In *Encyclopedia of Archaeological Excavations in the Holy
                Land*, ed. M. Avi-Yonah and E. Stern, 4:1138–47. Jerusalem: Mas-
                sada Press.
1993   Taanach. In *The New Encyclopedia of Archaeological Excavations in
                the Land of Israel*, ed. E. Stern, 4:1428–33. Jerusalem: Israel Explo-
                ration Society, Ministry of Defence, and Carta Publishers; and
                New York: Simon and Schuster.
Graham, W. G., and H. G. May
1936   *Culture and Conscience: An Archaeological Study of the New Religious
                Past in Ancient Palestine.* Chicago: University of Chicago Press.
King, P. J.
1988   *Amos, Hosea, Micah: An Archaeological Commentary.* Philadelphia:
                Westminster.
Lapp, P. W.
1964   The 1963 Excavation at Taᶜannek. *Bulletin of the American Schools
                of Oriental Research* 173:4–44.
1969   The 1968 Excavations at Tell Taᶜannek. *Bulletin of the American
                Schools of Oriental Research* 195:2–49.
Loud, G.
1948   *Megiddo II: Seasons of 1935–39.* Oriental Institute Publications, 62.
                Chicago: University of Chicago Press.
May, H. G.
1935   *Material Remains of the Megiddo Cult.* Oriental Institute Publica-
                tions, 26. Chicago: University of Chicago Press.

Meehl, M.
In   A Stratigraphic Analysis of the Unpublished Iron I Material from
preparation Tell Taᶜannek in Light of Recent Jezreel Valley Excavations. Ph.D.
             dissertation, Johns Hopkins University.
Milgrom, J.
1990   *The JPS Torah Commentary: Numbers.* Philadelphia and New York:
             Jewish Publication Society.
Rast, W. E.
1978   *Taanach I: Studies in the Iron Age Pottery.* Cambridge, Mass.: Amer-
             ican Schools of Oriental Research.
Renfrew, C.
1984   *Approaches to Social Archaeology.* Cambridge, Mass.: Harvard Uni-
             versity.
Schiffman, L. H.
1985   Priests. In *Harper's Bible Dictionary*, ed. P. J. Achtemeier, 821–23.
             San Francisco: Harper and Row.
Sellin, E.
1904   *Tell Taᶜannek.* Denkschriften der Kaiserlichen Akademie der
             Wissenschaften in Wien, Philosophisch-historische Klasse, 50.
             Vienna: Carl Gerolds Sohn.
Shiloh, Y.
1979   Iron Age Sanctuaries and Cult Elements in Palestine. In *Symposia
             Celebrating the Seventy-fifth Anniversary of the Founding of the Amer-
             ican Schools of Oriental Research*, ed. F. M. Cross, 147–57. Cam-
             bridge, Mass.: American Schools of Oriental Research.
Stager, L. E., and S. R. Wolff
1981   Production and Commerce in Temple Courtyards: An Olive Press
             in the Sacred Precinct at Tel Dan. *Bulletin of the American Schools
             of Oriental Research* 243:95–102.
Yeivin, S.
1973   Temples That Were Not. *Eretz-Israel* 11:163–75 (Hebrew with
             English summary, 28*).

22 | A New Climatic and Archaeological View of the Early Biblical Traditions

JAMES A. SAUER

Between 1982 and 1986, I published several articles related to archaeology and biblical studies (Sauer 1982b, 1985, 1986) in which I noted that firm connections between the Hebrew Bible and archaeological evidence did not predate Merneptah's mention of Israel in about 1230 BCE. I did agree, however, with Albright's original ideas about the Israelite conquest and the Philistine invasion and with his correlations with the biblical periods of the judges, the united monarchy, and the divided monarchies (see, e.g., Albright 1940, 1960, 1963, 1968).

I also went on to observe that Albright and many of his students (e.g., Glueck 1940, 1946, 1959; Wright 1961, 1962; Bright 1981) had been too optimistic about making connections between archaeology and the biblical sources before the thirteenth century BCE, especially going back as far as Early Bronze III–IV times. This was the time of the original tablet discoveries at Ebla, when claims were being made (e.g., Freedman 1978; Pettinato 1979, 1981; Shanks 1980) that such biblical names as Sodom and Gomorrah were attested at Ebla. I felt that the existing evidence was simply not compelling enough to warrant those earlier connections, but I also indicated that future discoveries might change my viewpoint. Although I still do not believe that the names themselves are attested at Ebla (see below), my current work on climate change has now led me to conclude that Albright and his students were clearly correct to look for such connections in the early biblical traditions.

From 1973 to 1981, I had been involved with surveys in Jordan, both my own joint project in the East Jordan Valley in 1975–76 (Ibrahim, Sauer, and Yassine 1976; Yassine, Ibrahim, and Sauer 1988) and the reading of the pottery for many other projects, including the 1973–76 survey of the Hesban region (Ibach 1987), the 1978–82 survey of Central Moab (Miller 1991), and the 1979–83 survey of the Wadi el-Hasa in Edom (MacDonald 1988). In the East Jordan Valley, like Albright (1960:68–69), I immediately noticed that the major Chalcolithic site of Teleilat el-Ghassul was located near wadis that today were quite dry (average annual rainfall at the site itself less than 100 mm—desert), while in Jordan's hills (average annual rainfall of 200 to 600 mm—Mediterranean) there were only much smaller sites. I soon concluded that the climate must have been wetter in the Chalcolithic period. In the East Jordan Valley, I was also struck by the appearance of numerous Islamic sugar mills, which required a great deal of water both to grow the sugar cane and to turn the mills, but which today were sometimes located near only modest wadis. Again I concluded that Jordan's climate may have been wetter in those centuries (up to ca. 1400 CE).

During those same years, I also made numerous trips into the northeastern desert regions of Jordan (average annual rainfall of 0 to 200 mm—steppe-desert), where I observed numerous hunting kites attesting primarily Early Neolithic (Pre-Pottery Neolithic B—PPNB) flint arrowheads. This also implied a wetter environment in Jordan at that time.

In addition to this work in Jordan, from 1977 to 1979 I also conducted survey work in Syria, especially near the site of Qarqur in the Ghab along the Orontes River (for an article based on these surveys, see Sauer 1982a). In the Ghab (average annual rainfall in excess of 800 mm—Mediterranean), I had been impressed by the distinctively dark soil on the surface of the former marshy lake bed in that region. I also had noted the numerous ceramic Dark-Faced Burnished Ware (DFBW) sites that continued to prosper after the end of the Early Neolithic (PPNB) period in this region, which was much better watered than most of Jordan.

Between 1982 and 1987, I was the Chief Archaeologist of the American Foundation for the Study of Man (AFSM) Wadi al-Jubah Archaeological Project in Yemen. The Wadi al-Jubah (average annual rainfall of 0 to 200 mm—steppe-desert) is a small eastward-flowing wadi along the caravan route between Timna (capital of ancient Qataban) and Marib (capital of ancient Sheba). In the very first season (1982), while doing initial reconnaissance work with M. R. Toplyn, I immediately noticed a thick dark organic soil layer visible on the surface in some eroded locations. It was obvious in the eroded sections of the wadi floor beneath the later culturally modified light-colored irrigation soils. It reminded me immediately of the dark marshy lake bed of the Ghab in northern Syria. For this reason and because I was also aware of the evidence for lakes in the Empty Quarter of Saudi Arabia (see below), I suggested that during the pluvial periods, it is possible that the Wadi al-Jubah was a lake or a swamp so the valley floor would have been unusable (Blakely, Sauer, and Toplyn 1985:149). In 1985, geologists W. C. Overstreet and M. J. Grolier studied the Wadi al-Jubah (Overstreet, Grolier, and Toplyn 1988). At that time, I indicated to them that there was a dark soil layer in the wadi that might provide evidence for a wetter phase sometime in the wadi's history. They concluded that this paleosol did reflect wetter conditions, but probably those of a savannah grassland rather than a marsh (Overstreet, Grolier, and Toplyn 1988:190–226, 446–52). The uncalibrated radiocarbon dates from the paleosol were 9520 +/- 280 BP (bottom) to 5270 +/- 90 BP (ca. 0.65 m below top), but there was also one later date that came from a different upper paleosol (see below). I immediately noted that the end date for the main paleosol was parallel to the date for the end of the Chalcolithic period in the Levant, which would explain the wetter Chalcolithic evidence at Teleilat el-Ghassul in Jordan and the Beer-sheba sites in Israel (Sauer and Blakely 1988:97–99).

Throughout, I had accepted the prevailing assumption that the climate in the Near East had changed little if at all since about 10,000 BP (old uncalibrated date = the end of the last glacial; new calibrated date = ca. 11,000/11,500 BP?) (see especially Braidwood and Howe 1960; Glueck 1940, 1946, 1959; Wright 1961, 1962; Harding 1959; Kenyon 1960). This position of climate stability is still held by the vast majority of scholars working in the Near East, especially in Israel (see, e.g., Aharoni 1982; A. Mazar 1990), despite the fact that some of the best contradictory data have come from research conducted there (e.g., Horowitz 1971, 1974, 1978, 1979; Goldberg and Bar-Yosef 1982). Recent work by Thomas Levy (1986) and P. Goldberg and A. M. Rosen (1987) have, however, allowed for climate change as a factor in cultural change (in the Chalcolithic particularly), but none has given it the full weight that it deserves in that and other periods. Of these researchers, only Rosen (1986, 1989) has given the evidence for climate change adequate attention, and her work has not gained wide acceptance.

In the spring of 1993, while preparing a report on the Hesban pottery (Sauer 1994), I began to explore the possibility that climatic change might have been a (if not the) dominant force shaping the history of Jordan (and the rest of the Near East) in Holocene times. At the same time, I had read a paper on Holocene climate change and the domestication of beasts of burden at the Fifth International Conference on the History and Archaeology of Jordan in the spring of 1992 in Irbid, Jordan.

The relative importance of Holocene climate change had been argued earlier in works by E. Huntington (1911) and C. E. P. Brooks (1922, rev. ed. 1970). Later K. W. Butzer wrote extensively on this topic from about 1958 on (e.g., 1958, 1971), and I am in general agreement with him. He did conclude, however, that broad generalizations about Holocene climate change could not be made, and I disagree with that. He also published (1958: diagram 2) one of the first attempts to reconstruct Late Glacial and Postglacial precipitation in the Near East. His reconstruction is quite good for many periods but he concluded that the second millennium BCE (the Middle and Late Bronze Ages) was generally more arid. For Egypt and beyond, B. Bell (1971) was essentially correct concentrating on the First Intermediate evidence for aridity in Egypt (but see below). Concerning the Near East, A. D. Crown (1972) correctly argued for a wetter Chalcolithic period and for a drier First Intermediate period (see below). H. H. Lamb (1972–77) has written excellent volumes on the subject, and we share some conclusions as well, even including hints about connections with the early biblical traditions (see below). In Israel, the best work has been that of A. Horowitz (e.g., 1971, 1974, 1978, 1979), and I usually find myself in agreement with him. His data are the best, and they document the entire Holocene climatic history for Israel, Jordan, the Near East, and beyond. However, his diagrams have been criticized and revisions proposed, especially the calibration of his radiocarbon dates (see, e.g., Rosen 1989). This has resulted in some significant uncertainties that will be discussed below. W. C. Brice (1978) covered the evidence for Holocene environmental history in the various regions of the Middle East. In Israel, P. Goldberg and O. Bar-Yosef (1982) have discussed climate change and settlement patterns, and I am in essential agreement with them as well. N. Shehadeh (1985) was also correct in discussing climate change for Jordan; but he followed Butzer's ideas about the more arid Middle Bronze and Late Bronze periods, which he correlated with some archaeological "gap evidence" in parts of Jordan. Using a variety of evidence in Israel, Rosen (1986, 1989) argued for a drier Early Bronze IV period (but see below) and a wetter Chalcolithic period. F. L. Koucky (1987) was the first to combine American dendrochronology, data on international sea levels and glacials, and the astronomical theories

of Milutin Milankovitch to present a model for 1134-year climatic cycles.
He also properly concluded that the climate of the Kerak region in Jordan today is very different from that in ancient times. Sometimes, however, he used historical data uncritically, in continuing to trust a much
later (and probably exaggerated) report of a 33-year famine in Cyprus, in
using inaccurately Josephus's references to the famines at the times of
Ahab and Herod the Great, and in referring to Heshbon as being especially dry in Iron II times. In Syria Harvey Weiss is currently doing
innovative climatic work at Tell Leilan that will provide important information to support the suggestion of an increase in aridity in at least part
of the Early Bronze IV period (Weiss et al. 1993).

The Holocene climate changes can be detected in the changing global
sea levels (fig. 22-1), about which there are many different theories (e.g.,
Gifford 1976; Hillaire-Marcel and Vincent 1980; Masters and Flemming
1983; Koucky 1987).

These climatic changes are also reflected in the recent ice cores taken
from around the world (fig. 22-2), including sites in Greenland (e.g.,
Dansgaard, Johnsen, and Møller 1969; Dansgaard et al. 1993; Greenland
Ice-Core Project Members 1993) and Antarctica (e.g., Lorius et al. 1985;
Barnola et al. 1987; Jouzel et al. 1993). Most of these researchers consider
the current Holocene interglacial, in contrast to earlier interglacials, to be
relatively stable (see, e.g., White 1993), but I disagree. There is considerable variation in the Holocene data, especially when looked at in detail.
Although the Holocene fluctuations may have been more modest than
those of earlier epochs, they were still significant enough to affect human
activities in important ways throughout the world.

Orbital phenomena in the solar system probably explain some of these
cyclical phenomena, as suggested originally by Milankovitch (see e.g.,
NATO 1982), but there are other possible causes (see, e.g., Lamb 1972–
77; Oliver and Fairbridge 1987). Some specialists who acknowledge climatic variation, but who do not agree with cycles, evoke concepts such as
chaos theory to explain climate change (e.g., Burroughs 1992).

Two key features of climate change, namely a wet phase in the Chalcolithic period (with a terminal dry oscillation before a wetter Early
Bronze I, and a somewhat drier but still moist phase during Early Bronze
II–III) and a more arid phase in at least part of the Early Bronze IV
period, fit well the early biblical traditions in Genesis. The first was the
wetter environment of the Mesopotamian flood in Genesis 6—9, and
the second was the drier environment of the extended famine at the time

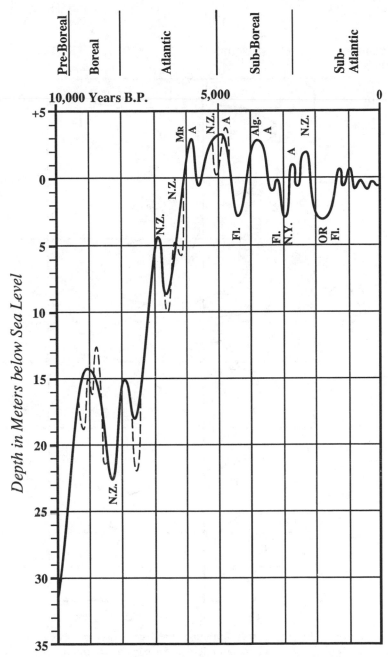

FIG. 22-1. Sea level changes. Uncalibrated. After R. W. Fairbridge, in International Symposium 1966: fig. 2. Computer-generated image by C. Andrews. Courtesy of Royal Meteorological Society.

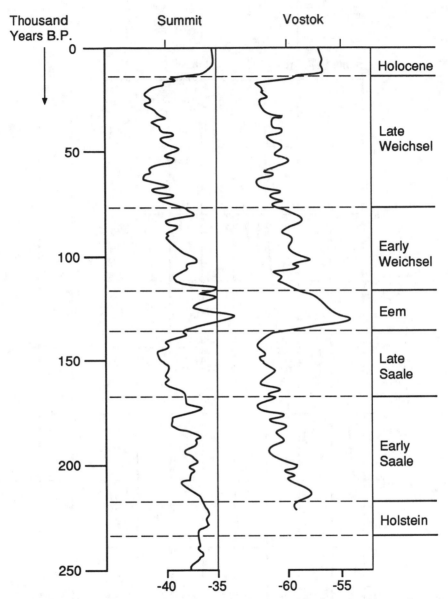

FIG. 22-2. Two climate records spanning the last glacial cycles, from about 250,000 BP. A. Summit, Greenland ice-core Oxygen 18 record. B. Vostok, Antarctica ice-core Oxygen 18 record. Uncalibrated. After Dansgaard et al. 1993: fig. 2. Computer-generated image by C. Andrews. The lines represent only the averages of the extremes recorded. For the most accurate drawings, see the original publication. Reprinted with permission from *Nature*.

of Joseph (Genesis 41—47). Some of these ideas had already been partially hinted at by other researchers, such as Butzer (1958) and Lamb (1972–77). If these correlations are correct, then some of the views of David Noel Freedman (1978) about the patriarchs in the third millennium BCE, although wrongly connected to the names at Ebla, would fit this period as well. The Early Bronze sites located near the southeastern plain of the Dead Sea (Bab edh-Dhra^c, Numeira, and so forth) would also agree with this reconstruction (see below). The river bed Farouk El-Baz has found running from Hijaz in western Arabia to Kuwait could fit the enigmatic reference to the Pishon River located near Eden in Genesis 2:11–12. If correct, this would have very important implications not only for biblical history but for the history of the whole Near East.

Most of the Albright school had been opposed to using climate change in this way, but in fact it is more supportive of the early biblical traditions than any other existing data. Therefore I am now willing to consider the pre-1200 BCE materials in the Bible as preserving fairly accurate historical memories back even as far as the fourth to third millennium BCE. My perspective is very different from those of Nelson Glueck, G. E. Wright, and John Bright, although Albright seems to have allowed for the possibility of some climate change (e.g., 1960:68–69). I thus disagree with Martin Noth (1960), T. L. Thompson (1974), John Van Seters (1975, 1992), Benjamin Mazar (1986), J. Maxwell Miller and John H. Hayes (1986), and William Dever (e.g., 1990) in their treatment of these periods, and feel that more archaeological, climatic, geographical, literary, and artistic evidence from as early as the fourth–third millennia BCE will be forthcoming in the future. Thus, "biblical archaeology" can and should be extended back to that date and to regions as far apart as Mesopotamia and Egypt, as Albright originally suggested.

I begin with a partial topographic map of Israel and Jordan (Horowitz 1979: fig. 2.2), which shows the topographic features of Israel and part of Jordan (though not all of the highest elevations in Jordan; see fig. 22-3). In figure 22-4, a rainfall map (Zohary 1973: map 5), the current climatic situation in the modern Middle East is shown. With these figures it is possible to compare the locations of archaeological sites of various periods with the current rainfall and vegetation at those sites today.

I include here (fig. 22-5) also pollen diagrams published by Horowitz (1971, 1974, 1978, 1979) from cores in Lake Hula and the Mediterranean, since they reflect, in my opinion, the entire climatic Holocene history of the region. To my knowledge, this is the first time that these

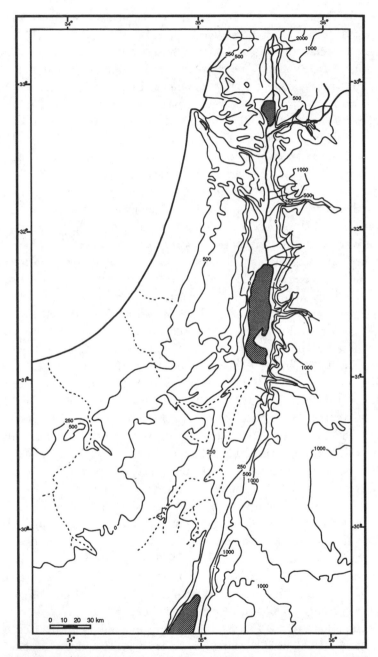

FIG. 22-3. Partial topographic map of Israel and Jordan. After Horowitz 1979: fig. 2.2. Computer-generated image by C. Andrews. Courtesy of Academic Press.

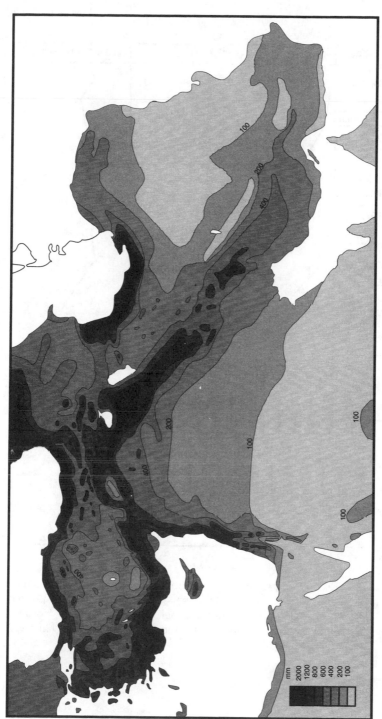

FIG. 22-4. Rain map of the Middle East. After Zohary 1973: map 5. Computer-generated image by C. Andrews. Courtesy of Gustav Fischer Verlag.

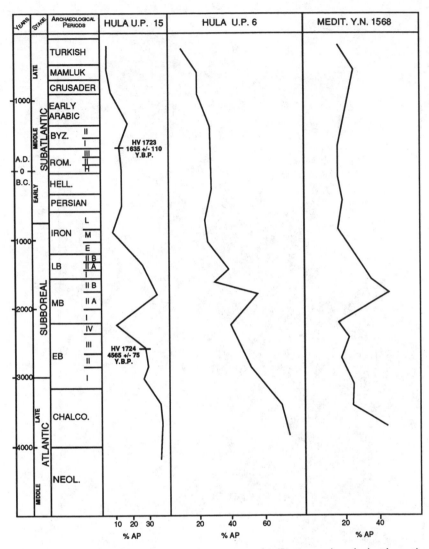

FIG. 22-5. Arboreal pollen percentages in samples from two boreholes from the Hula Valley and one from the Mediterranean offshore, correlated by radiocarbon with the archaeological sequence in Israel. Uncalibrated. After Horowitz 1978: fig. 1. Computer-generated image by C. Andrews. Courtesy of A. Horowitz.

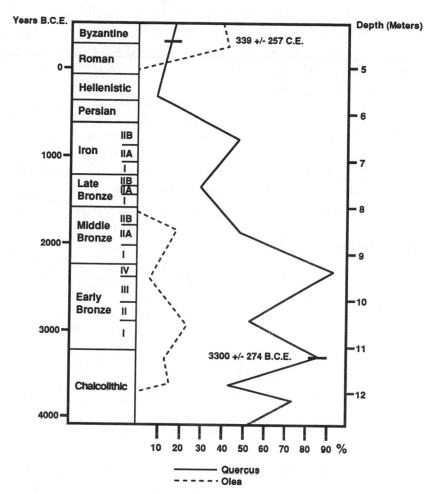

FIG. 22-6. Pollen diagram from Borehole U.P. 15 at Lake Hula, revised by L. Stager from Horowitz 1971. After Rosen 1989: fig. 2. Calibrated but with Chalcolithic period listed as ending in 3200 BCE. Computer-generated image by C. Andrews. Courtesy of A. M. Rosen.

crucial diagrams have been taken seriously by an archaeologist working in the Holocene periods of the Near East. Rosen (1986, 1989) is the sole exception.

The radiocarbon dates on these diagrams have not been calibrated. Such calibration would alter these diagrams significantly (see L. E. Stager in Rosen 1989: fig. 2; see here fig. 22-6). For example, the Chalcolithic period ends in about 3200 BCE (fig. 22-6). Calibration would raise that date to about 3500 BCE (see Stager 1992). Similarly, the dates for the Early Bronze IV period (shown on fig. 22-6 as both Early Bronze IV and Middle Bronze I) have recently been recalibrated from about 2250–1950 BCE (old uncalibrated) to about 2350–2000 BCE (see, e.g., Richard and Boraas 1988). In my opinion, it is not unlikely that the calibrated Bronze Age dates will be raised proportionally even higher prior to about 3500 BCE (the calibrated date for the end of the Chalcolithic period). This would also affect these diagrams in many significant ways, improving them considerably.

Although the two versions of Horowitz's diagrams (uncalibrated, fig. 22-5; and calibrated, fig. 22-6) are not in full agreement, it is still possible to offer a general overview of climate change based on them. Thus, the Chalcolithic period was wetter, and it seems to have ended in a more arid oscillation. During the Early Bronze I period, a wetter interval is again attested, which may have continued through the Early Bronze II–III periods (fig. 22-5), or may have been marked by an arid decline prior to Early Bronze II (fig. 22-6). Early Bronze II–III continued to be fairly wet, but in figure 22-5, the climate is presented as becoming drier toward Early Bronze IV, while in figure 22-6 the climate is shown as becoming wetter until Early Bronze IV. In figure 22-5, aridity is shown peaking in Early Bronze IV, while in figure 22-6 the beginning of Early Bronze IV is shown as being very wet with a sharp increase in aridity following in Early Bronze IV (termed by some "Middle Bronze I"). Following figure 22-5, the Middle Bronze Age I–II would have witnessed a return to much wetter conditions, which would have tapered off gradually through Late Bronze and Iron Age. In figure 22-6, the Middle and Late Bronze Ages are shown as continuing to become more arid, until the Late Bronze II. In figure 22-5, a slight arid dip is shown in the Iron II period, but then the Persian to Roman periods are presented as fairly constant. In figure 22-6, a rise in precipitation is shown starting again in Late Bronze II and peaking in Iron II, reaching its nadir in the Hellenistic period. In figure 22-5, a slight increase in moisture is shown in the Byzantine and Islamic periods, continuing until about 1400 CE, and then declining until modern times. The decline after 1400 CE has sometimes been attributed to Ottoman tax policies or unregulated wood cutting, but in fact the process began even earlier with a period of greater aridity in Late Mamluk times (see Ghawanmeh 1985). The modern climate is substantially drier than most previous Holocene periods, indicating that current conditions in the Near East are not reflective of earlier periods in its history. I turn now to two periods of particular interest with respect to the early biblical traditions, the Chalcolithic and the Early Bronze Ages.

CHALCOLITHIC

The first line of evidence to be noted comes from the Holocene pollen diagrams from two cores at Lake Hula and one from the Mediterranean coast of Israel (Horowitz 1978: fig. 1). The cores were originally dated by uncalibrated radiocarbon methods. In the diagrams (fig. 22-5 [uncalibrated], fig. 22-6 [calibrated, but with the Chalcolithic period starting in 3200 BCE rather than 3500 BCE]), the arboreal pollens are shown as markedly higher in the Chalcolithic period than in the present, indicating that there was then heavier forest cover and greater rainfall. More arboreal pollens have been found in soils collected at Chalcolithic sites in southern Israel than are present there today (Horowitz 1974: table 1). These and other lines of evidence (see, e.g., Rosen 1986; Goldberg and Rosen 1987) agree with the observation that the major Chalcolithic sites in Jordan (Teleilat el-Ghassul in the southeastern Jordan Valley) and in southern Israel (e.g., the Beer-sheba sites and Shiqmim) are located in topographically low areas (see fig. 22-3) with little modern rainfall (generally between 0 and 200 mm annually—steppe-desert) (see fig. 22-4). They must have had more rainfall when these sites were occupied. By contrast, very few and much smaller Chalcolithic sites have been found in the higher (ca. 1000+ m) plateau regions of Jordan. These were not located near water (e.g., Hanbury-Tenison 1986). In general, the same seems to be true in Israel, at least as far as site size and frequency are concerned. Toward the end of the Chalcolithic period, there was a marked drop in arboreal pollens (see figs. 22-5, 22-6) indicating a decline in wooded vegetation and thus in rainfall.

In the Wadi al-Jubah in Yemen, the dark paleosol is the most striking evidence for climate change that I have encountered in my years of fieldwork in the Middle East. This dark paleosol was exposed in the sides of the wadi beneath the later lighter-colored soils produced by irrigation. Owing to erosion, the full thickness of the paleosol could not be established, but it was at least 3 m thick in some locations. It was also visible on the surface of the wadi floor, where some small stone-built circular structures were found on and in the paleosol. One such installation consisting of an ashy hearth lying about 0.65 m below the top of the paleosol produced an uncalibrated radiocarbon date of 5270 +/- 90 BP. Four addi-

tional uncalibrated dates came from the paleosol: 9520 +/- 280 BP; 7410
+/- 160 BP; 6560 +/- 120 BP; and 5770 +/- 110 BP (but see below). The
first was from a low exposure and the second from an intermediate exposure at the same sampling location. The last two came from upper levels
of the paleosol. Uncalibrated dates put the earliest deposit of paleosol as
early as about 10,000 BP. The climate at that time resembled a savannah
rather than a lake or a swamp, and A. Ghaleb later recovered human
artifacts (especially obsidian flakes) within the layers of the paleosol. Our
team also observed small rocky mounds constructed on it, and they are
probably to be found within the paleosol as well. The paleosol clearly
reflects a wetter phase down to an uncalibrated date of about 5000 BP
(calibrated: ca. 3500 BCE). After that, a drier period (but one still wetter
than today) probably followed (Overstreet, Grolier, and Toplyn 1988:190–
226, 446–52).

In Saudi Arabia, it has long been known that Pleistocene and Holocene
lakes existed in the Empty Quarter (see, e.g., McClure 1976). These lakes
had two main phases, with some possible intermediate activities between
the two phases. The latest of the two phases was radiocarbon dated from
about 10,000 BP to about 5000 BP (uncalibrated). Following calibrated
dates, these Holocene lakes would have ended about 3500 BCE. This is
almost identical to the dates of the paleosol in Wadi al-Jubah, confirming
that the Chalcolithic period was wetter. H. A. McClure (1976) argued
that a period of full aridity followed after about 5000 BP, while I will
argue that the evidence from Yemen and elsewhere suggests that the
period after about 5000 BP was still somewhat wet, at least in some areas.

A core taken from the Arabian Sea (Van Campo, Duplessy, and
Rossignol-Strick 1982) contains pollen indicating that there was a humid
phase which began around 10,000 BP (uncalibrated), which peaked by
about 8000 BP, and which concluded by about 4000 BP (see fig. 22-7). In
addition, there is now some recently published evidence from a core from
the Arabian Sea not far from Yemen (Sirocko et al. 1993). This core gave
evidence of a wetter environment in about 9000 to 7000 BP (uncalibrated
radiocarbon dates). It also seems to reflect a drier climate after about
5000 BP, but that evidence was less clear than the earlier wet phase.
F. Sirocko and his colleagues concluded that Arabia was virtually abandoned after about 5000 BP (calibrated: ca. 3500 BCE), and that the former
inhabitants fled into river valleys of the Fertile Crescent, but that does
not seem likely.

In Africa (Butzer et al. 1972), there are major lakes lacking outlets

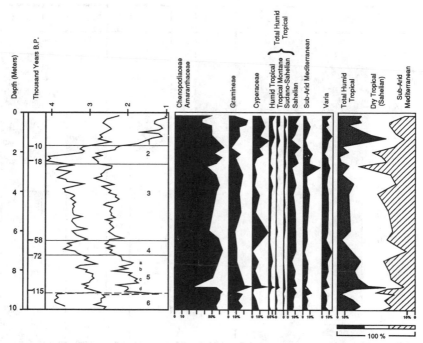

FIG. 22-7. Oxygen isotope and pollen record of core MD76135 in the Arabian Sea. Uncalibrated. After Van Campo; Duplessy; and Rossignol-Strick 1982: fig. 2. Computer-generated image by C. Andrews. Reprinted with permission from *Nature*.

(Lake Rudolf/Turkana, Lake Nakuru, and Lake Chad) whose levels exhibited an expected wet phase starting around 10,000 BP (uncalibrated), and another wetter climatic oscillation between about 6000 and 4000 BP (see fig. 22-8). These wet phases correspond to the occurrence of the dark paleosol in Wadi al-Jubah.

In the Sahara, certain "Neolithic" occupations have been associated with various pluvial periods (Butzer 1971:581–94), and some of them correspond chronologically with the evidence from the Near East.

Like the evidence from the African lakes, there is uncalibrated evidence from a Mediterranean core (Oeschger et al., in Jado and Zötl 1984: pl. 6), which appears to show a wetter environment for the periods representing both the Chalcolithic and the Early Bronze periods, after which follows a drier phase.

In Arabia (El-Baz 1993, 1994), there is important new evidence for a

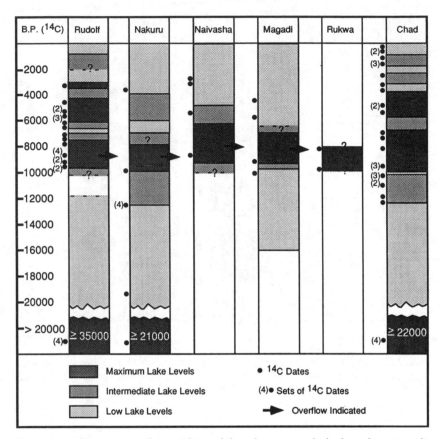

FIG. 22-8. Fluctuations of East African lakes that presently lack outlets. Uncalibrated. After Butzer et al. 1972: fig. 4. Computer-generated image by C. Andrews. Courtesy of K. W. Butzer.

Holocene river (fig. 22-9). Using remote sensing, El-Baz has traced a major river channel from the mountains of Hijaz to Kuwait. This river, which he named the "Kuwait River," was dated by associated geology to the Holocene, about 11,000 BP to about 5000 BP (uncalibrated). This river clearly is a relic of a wetter phase in Arabia during this period, which gradually dried up after about 3500 BCE (calibrated).

Pollen and uncalibrated radiocarbon dates from one particular core in a large marshy lake bed in the Ghab of Syria (noted above) also indicate an increase in arboreal pollen from about 10,000 BP (Niklewski and van Zeist 1970). These data indicate the beginning of a wet phase around

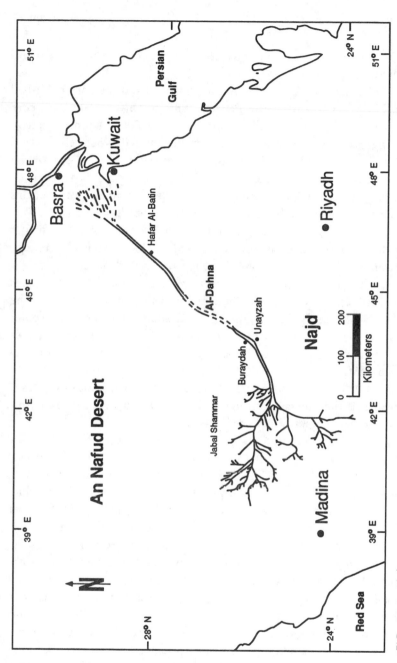

FIG. 22-9. Holocene river detected by remote-sensing in Arabia. After El-Baz 1994. Computer-generated image by C. Andrews. Courtesy of Gordon and Breach Science Publishers.

10,000 BP, but the later periods are not so clear because they are incomplete.

In Mesopotamia, there is important evidence from the core published by W. Nützel (1976) from the Persian Gulf (see fig. 22-10). This core exhibits a wetter phase from about 5500 to about 3000 BCE (uncalibrated). This range includes the Chalcolithic, and if calibrated, would end around 3500 BCE. H. J. Nissen accepted this evidence in his synthesis of the Neolithic period (1988). Nützel (1976, 1979) and Nissen (1988) postulated that part of southern Mesopotamia would have been under water at this time owing to higher Gulf sea level during the wet phase.

In addition, earlier excavations in southern Mesopotamia at such sites as Ur, Kish, and Shuruppak revealed stratified flood deposits (see, e.g., Mallowan 1964: pl. 20). At Ur, Woolley discovered an almost three-meter-thick sterile layer above the fourth millennium BCE Ubaid remains (Moorey 1982). Woolley originally considered this layer evidence of the Flood of Noah (see fig. 22-11), though he later abandoned that viewpoint because the level in question dated too early to fit the flood chronologies of Mesopotamia. There were flood deposits at higher levels at some of these sites (Mallowan 1964: pl. 20). One of these, dated (uncalibrated) to about 2900 BCE (Early Dynastic I–II), agreed better with both the Meso-potamian and the biblical versions of the Flood. This conclusion domi-nates the archaeological literature today.

All of the evidence cited above supports the view that a global wet phase began around 10,000 BP (uncalibrated). This wet phase was proba-bly interrupted by some drier periods but was predominantly wet prior to at least 3500 BCE (calibrated), equivalent to the end of the Chalcolithic. Major lakes were full, at least one river flowed in Arabia, part of Arabia was grassland, and the southern part of Mesopotamia was under water. Rivers such as the Nile, Tigris, and Euphrates had more flow than today.

In Mesopotamia, this mid-fourth-millennium BCE evidence probably corresponds to the biblical (Genesis 6—9) and other ancient Near East-ern traditions of floods. These floods were localized phenomena, not global catastrophes. At present, it is uncertain if the biblical Flood should be dated to the mid–fourth millennium or to the late fourth or third millennia BCE (calibrated), but the former possibility should not be auto-matically discounted. It does mesh both with the evidence for the wetter climate of the Chalcolithic and of the Early Bronze Age. Thus it could fit in either period.

In this respect, the "Kuwait River" is also important. Running from

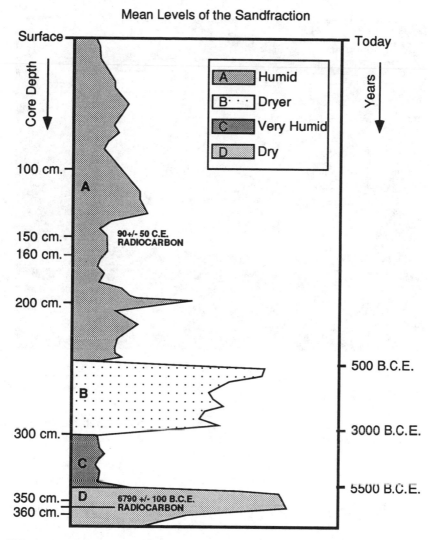

FIG. 22-10. Core 1056 in the Persian (Arabian) Gulf. Uncalibrated. After Nützel 1976: fig. 3. Computer-generated image by C. Andrews. Courtesy of State Organization of Antiquities and Heritage.

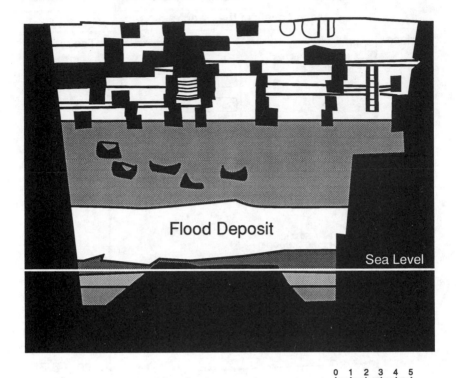

FIG. 22-11. Section through the Flood Pit F at Ur. After Mallowan 1964: pl. 17. Computer-generated image by C. Andrews. Courtesy of British School of Archaeology in Iraq.

near Medina in the Hijaz to Kuwait at the head of the Persian Gulf, it certainly was active down to about 3500 BCE. This raises the possibility of human movement between Mesopotamia and western Arabia along the river. If El-Baz is correct and the river does not much postdate 3500 BCE (calibrated), and if after that date Arabia became so arid that no one could cross it, then there could have been no communication along it in the Early Bronze Age periods that followed. But if the Kuwait River continued to flow during the Early Bronze I–IV and if Arabia was only somewhat more arid than previously, then the river could have continued in use as a route of communication. At present, it is not possible to know which of these options is correct, but I favor the second. El-Baz urged that archaeological surveys be conducted along the route of the river (wherever it is not covered by Holocene sands) to determine the types of archaeological sites associated with the route of the river and their periods of occupation.

The Kuwait River brings to mind Genesis 2:10–14 very well, where four rivers are mentioned flowing out of Eden. Verses 11 and 12 read:

> The name of the first is Pishon; it is the one that flows around the whole land of Havilah, where there is gold; and the gold of that land is good; bdellium and onyx stone are there. (NRSV)

Although the details of the translation are uncertain, the description in general fits a river flowing into the head of the Persian Gulf from the low mountains of western Arabia. First, and most important, the text mentions "good gold." There is only one place in Arabia which has such a deposit, the famous site of Mahd edh-Dhahab ("Cradle of Gold"). This ancient and modern gold mining site is located about 170 km south of Medina (see, e.g., Twitchell 1958; Nawwab, Speers, and Hoye 1981:143), near where El-Baz has traced the headwater areas of the "Kuwait River." There are aromatic resins (bdellium) in Yemen to the southwest, and, although they are not known to be produced in the vicinity of Medina, they could have been brought there from the south, along what is later known to be the main north-south caravan route. Semiprecious stones such as alabaster also come from these areas, but it is uncertain if other precious stones, such as onyx, do.

No other river at the moment would seem to fit the biblical description, although in such an early setting it would not be impossible for other less geographically literal interpretations to be considered. The Wadi Hadhramawt in Yemen is a candidate; however, there is no gold there and it does not connect to the Gulf. Evidence of other inland rivers may yet be found in southwestern Arabia where higher elevations produce (even today) more rainfall than in the northerly Hijaz. If such other rivers are indeed found, they probably would drain into other parts of the Persian Gulf south of Kuwait.

At present, therefore, I am inclined to think that the "Kuwait River" could well be the Pishon of the Bible. If so, it implies extraordinary memory on the part of the biblical authors for a river that went out of existence as early as the end of Chalcolithic or as late as Early Bronze I–IV.

Such a river may have provided a route for limited trade between Mesopotamia and western Arabia before the widespread introduction of donkeys or camels as beasts of burden. Precious items of small weight and bulk could have been carried by humans walking. By the Chalcolithic/ Ubaid period, the donkey is attested as a beast of burden (see Stager 1992:27); by the Early Bronze Age it is very common.

Finally, it should be emphasized that it is likely a wetter climate continued through the Early Bronze I–IV periods. Supporting the postulation of a still somewhat wetter climate in Arabia is evidence from the African lakes (Butzer et al. 1972), which seemed to remain wet down to about 4000 BP; the Mediterranean core, which indicates a wet phase until that date (Oeschger et al. 1980 in Jado and Zötl 1984: pl. 6); one late, uncalibrated (but possibly important) radiocarbon date from Wadi al-Jubah, 4120 +/- 175 BP (not from the dark paleosol but from a different, upper paleosol [Overstreet and Grolier in Overstreet, Grolier, and Toplyn 1988:221, 451]); the continuation of so-called "Neolithic" occupations in the Sahara down to about 2200 BCE (uncalibrated, Butzer 1971:581–94); and, most important, continued occupation at large village sites in Yemen radiocarbon-dated to Early Bronze Age (e.g., Ghaleb oral communication; de Maigret 1984). All of Arabia clearly was not abandoned about 5000 BP (uncalibrated) as asserted by F. Sirocko and colleagues (1993) and as implied by McClure (1976).

Continued occupation in some parts of Arabia into the Early Bronze I–IV periods probably also correlates with the Kuwait River. By the Early Bronze I–IV, donkeys had been domesticated and were in widespread use as beasts of burden. Donkey bones have been found at the Bronze Age sites in Yemen excavated by de Maigret (1984). Since this was the period of the rise of major urban centers, the first use of full writing, and the emergence of complex civilizations in Mesopotamia and Egypt, trade with western and southwestern Arabia would be expected by this time.

EARLY BRONZE IV

At the end of Early Bronze III (or Early Bronze IVA), most major urban sites in Israel and Jordan were abandoned until Middle Bronze II. The Lake Hula, Mediterranean, and Persian Gulf cores; the soil data from Leilan in Syria; the settlement patterns in Israel and Jordan; and the literary evidence from Egypt and the Bible combine to provide some climatic insights into this phenomenon. Those data accord with the contentions of Rosen (1989), who has argued persuasively for a period of major aridity at the end of the third millennium BCE. But they also agree with evidence from Jordan and Israel that at least part of this period may have been wet.

First, according to uncalibrated dates (see fig. 22-5), there was a very steep decline in the arboreal pollen (reflecting drier conditions) in the Lake Hula and the coastal Mediterranean cores in the Early Bronze IV, followed by a sharp rebound to wetter conditions in the Middle Bronze Age. Goldberg and Bar-Yosef (1982) argued that an increase in aridity caused the abandonment of Early Bronze II–III urban sites in Israel, such as Arad. Clearly this is a possibility, although some Early Bronze III sites seem to have been destroyed by human action. After this period of aridity, Goldberg and Bar-Yosef suggested that the Middle Bronze I period was wetter, because of the many MB I sites discovered in the Negeb. That reconstruction would agree with uncalibrated dates shown in figure 22-5, but the reverse would be the case following the calibrated dates shown in figure 22-6.

In the Persian Gulf, Nützel (1976) noted an increase in aridity about this time (fig. 22-10).

In northern Syria, Weiss has recently shown that the climate was drier in about 2200 to 1900 BCE. He has postulated that the collapse at the end of the Old Akkadian period may have been caused primarily by prolonged drought, citing in support other affected areas in the Near East and the Aegean (Weiss et al. 1993).

In Jordan, Early Bronze IVA remains are attested in the terminal phase at Bab edh-Dhra^c and at occupation sites on the plateau such as Ader, ^cAra^cir, Lehun, and Khirbet Iskander. Most of these are small sites not located near adequate modern water, but Iskander was a major urban site near a strong modern wadi. Occupation at these sites may indicate a continuation of slightly wetter conditions at the beginning of Early Bronze IV, or perhaps a migration of population eastward from Israel (where few occupation sites are attested) with the onset of arid conditions in the Early Bronze IV. The Transjordanian plateau is on average at a somewhat higher elevation than the hill country of Israel, enough to attract settlement there during a drier phase in the Cisjordanian highlands. Such a circumstance may be reflected in Ruth 1:1, where, during an Iron I famine, a man from Bethlehem is said to have gone to Moab. Early Bronze IVB–C remains on the high plateau of Jordan, though present, are not as well attested there, but they are well represented in the East Jordan Valley near rivers and secondary wadis. These latter occupations perhaps reflect either a drier or a wetter phase in this part of the period.

In Egypt, there are historical records of serious famines in the First Intermediate period, and Bell (1971) attributed the near collapse of the Egyptian state to the reduced flow of the Nile during this time. In this drier period, equivalent to the Early Bronze IV/Middle Bronze I in Israel and Jordan, the movement of Asiatics into Egypt is also well documented.

There can be little doubt then that the Early Bronze IV was an arid period. It may have been so for most of its duration or for only part of it, and additional data and further analyses of existing evidence will be needed to work out the exact details. This aridity explains some of the shifts in settlement in Israel and Jordan as well as in Syria, Mesopotamia, and Egypt. Climatic change was probably the main cause of these shifts (so Rosen 1989).

Although the famines in Egypt had been noted by Butzer (1958) and Lamb (1972–77), they did not connect them directly to the biblical traditions of Joseph. In my opinion, however, this period of aridity is reflected in the descriptions of the severe famines at the time of Joseph (Genesis 41—47). It is not impossible that they could belong to the Middle or Late Bronze Ages, since it is still uncertain if those periods were wetter or drier (in my opinion, the Middle Bronze Age was wet, with drying commencing in the Late Bronze Age). It is likely that the famine reported at the time of Joseph is probably another accurate fragment of climatic memory reflected in the early biblical traditions.

Proceeding from these considerations is the likely conclusion that the Early Bronze sites of Bab edh-Dhraᶜ, Numeira, and so forth probably were some of the "Cities of the Plain" (see Rast and Schaub 1974, 1980; Rast and Schaub 1981; Coogan 1984; Schaub and Rast 1984, 1989). I agree with David Noel Freedman (1978) about the third-millennium BCE date for the patriarchs, although the names were wrongly identified at Ebla. Giovanni Pettinato (1979, 1981; see Shanks 1980) was incorrect about the names (see Archi 1981), and Ebla was a much smaller site than usually described (see Diakonoff 1990). Though impressive for the period (see Matthiae 1980), it was by no means the only large site in Syria. The Ebla tablets themselves name sites located mostly near Ebla in northern Syria. To obtain better epigraphic data about the southern Levant, what is needed is written evidence from a site in or near that region. Such a discovery has not yet been made, but in the meantime, evidence from sites throughout the Near East should continue to be studied for the light they can shed on the early histories of Israel and Jordan.

CONCLUSIONS

This is a very preliminary assessment and, although based on the best evidence now available, it will certainly be revised in the future. The greatest difficulty is the issue of radiocarbon calibration; thus two different versions of Horowitz's pollen diagrams are presented here (figs. 22-5 and 22-6). A new (third) version of Horowitz's diagrams should be prepared, which would permit the possible further raising of Iron Age I and Bronze Age calibrated dates prior to 3500 BCE, that is, the calibrated date for the end of the Chalcolithic period. The current chronological framework for these periods has been established through a combination of historical data and uncalibrated radiocarbon dates, but as argued here, the dates for some early periods should be raised (e.g., 3500 BCE instead of 3200 BCE for the end of the Chalcolithic period), in accordance with the higher calibrated radiocarbon dates. These higher dates may also affect the other periods from 3500 BCE to 1200 BCE, resulting in a slightly higher date for the start of the Iron Age I, and concomitant raising of dates throughout the Bronze Age. This will require a careful assessment of the existing historical data from all of the regions of the ancient Near East.

These conclusions are not only in agreement with Albright's views, but they push his ideas about the historical backgrounds of the biblical traditions back even further. To be sure, these traditions are still very much cast in the worldview of the Iron Age, but that has led too many scholars to ignore the possibility that the biblical texts accurately preserve many earlier traditions. Since the memories of climatic change and of early geography seem so accurate, it could even be suggested that some of these traditions may not have been written down for the first time in the tenth century BCE but were in fact written down much earlier.

Climatic change has been taken for granted in the preceding Paleolithic periods (see, e.g., Cauvin and Sanlaville 1981; Bintliff and van Zeist 1982; Garrard and Gebel 1988; Henry 1989), but it is time that it be recognized as a continuing factor in human existence down to the present day.

WORKS CITED

Aharoni, Y.
1982   *The Archaeology of the Land of Israel.* Philadelphia: Westminster.

Albright, W. F.
1940   *From the Stone Age to Christianity*. Baltimore: Johns Hopkins University Press.
1960   *The Archaeology of Palestine*. Baltimore: Penguin.
1963   *The Biblical Period from Abraham to Ezra*. New York: Harper and Row.
1968   *Yahweh and the Gods of Canaan*. Garden City, N.Y.: Doubleday.

Archi, A.
1981   Notes on Eblaite Geography 2. *Studi Eblaiti* 4:1–17.

Barnola, J. M.; D. Raynaud; Y. S. Korotkevich; and C. Lorius
1987   Vostok Ice Core Provides 160,000-Year Record of Atmospheric C02. *Nature* 329:408–14.

Bell, B.
1971   The Dark Ages in Ancient History 1: The First Dark Age in Egypt. *American Journal of Archaeology* 75:1–26.

Bintliff, J. L., and W. van Zeist, eds.
1982   *Palaeoclimates, Palaeoenvironments, and Human Communities in the Eastern Mediterranean Region in Later Prehistory*. British Archaeological Reports International Series, 133(i-ii). Oxford: British Archaeological Reports.

Blakely, J. A.; J. A. Sauer; and M. R. Toplyn
1985   *Site Reconnaissance in North Yemen, 1983: The Wadi al-Jubah Archaeological Project*, vol. 2. Washington, D.C.: American Foundation for the Study of Man.

Braidwood, R. J., and B. Howe
1960   *Prehistoric Investigations in Iraqi Kurdistan*. Chicago: University of Chicago Press.

Brice, W. C., ed.
1978   *The Environmental History of the Near and Middle East since the Last Ice Age*. London: Academic Press.

Bright, J.
1981   *A History of Israel*. 3d ed. Philadelphia: Westminster.

Brooks, C. E. P.
1922   *The Evolution of Climate*. London: Benn.
1970   *Climate through the Ages*. New York: Dover Publications.

Burroughs, W. J.
1992   *Weather Cycles: Real or Imaginary?* New York: Cambridge University Press.

Butzer, K. W.
1958   *Quaternary Stratigraphy and Climate in the Near East*. Bonn: Dummlers.
1971   *Environment and Archeology*. Hawthorne, N.Y.: Aldine.

Butzer, K. W.; G. L. Isaac; J. L. Richardson; and C. Washbourn-Kamau
1972   Radiocarbon Dating of East African Lake Levels. *Science* 175:1069–76.

Cauvin, J., and P. Sanlaville, eds.
1981   *Préhistoire du Levant*. Paris: Éditions du CNRS.
Coogan, M. D.
1984   Numeira 1981. *Bulletin of the American Schools of Oriental Research* 255:75–81.
Crown, A. D.
1972   Toward a Reconstruction of the Climate of Palestine, 8000 B.C.– 0 B.C. *Journal of Near Eastern Studies* 31:312–30.
Dansgaard, W.; S. J. Johnsen; and J. Møller
1969   One Thousand Centuries of Climatic Record from Camp Century on the Greenland Ice Sheet. *Science* 166:377–80.
Dansgaard, W.; S. J. Johnsen; H. B. Clausen; D. Dahl-Jensen; N. S. Gundestrup; C. U. Hammer; C. S. Hvidberg; J. P. Steffensen; A. E. Svein- björnsdottir; A. E. Jorzel; and G. Bond
1993   Evidence for General Instability of Past Climate from a 250-kyr Ice-Core Record. *Nature* 364:218–20.
Dever, W. G.
1990   *Recent Archaeological Discoveries and Biblical Research*. Seattle: Uni- versity of Washington.
Diakonoff, I. M.
1990   The Importance of Ebla for History and Linguistics. *Eblaitica* 2:3–29.
El-Baz, F.
1993   Boston University Scientist Discovers Ancient River System in Saudi Arabia. *Boston University News* March 25:1–2.
1994   Gulf War Disruption of the Desert Surface in Kuwait. In *Gulf War and the Environment*, by F. El-Baz. New York: Gordon and Breach.
Freedman, D. N.
1978   The Real Story of the Ebla Tablets, Ebla, and the Cities of the Plain. *Biblical Archeologist* 41:143–64.
Garrard, A. N., and H. G. Gebel, eds.
1988   *The Prehistory of Jordan: The State of Research in 1986*. British Archaeological Reports International Series, 396(i–ii). Oxford: British Archaeological Reports.
Ghawanmeh, Y.
1985   The Effect of Plague and Drought on the Environment of the Southern Levant during the Late Mamluk Period. In *Studies in the History and Archaeology of Jordan 2*, ed. A. Hadidi, 315–22. Amman: Department of Antiquities.
Gifford, J. A.
1976   Sea Levels and Ancient Seafaring. *American Institute of Nautical Archaeology Newsletter* 3.2:1–3.
Glueck, N.
1940   *The Other Side of the Jordan*. New Haven, Conn.: American Schools of Oriental Research.

1946   *The River Jordan.* Philadelphia: Westminster Press.
1959   *Rivers in the Desert.* New York: Farrar, Straus and Cudahy.
Goldberg, P., and O. Bar-Yosef
1982   Environmental and Archaeological Evidence for Climatic Change
                in the Southern Levant. In *Palaeoclimates, Palaeoenvironments, and
                Human Communities in the Eastern Mediterranean Region in Later
                Prehistory,* ed. J. L. Bintliff and W. van Zeist, 399–414. British
                Archaeological Reports International Series, 133(ii). Oxford: Brit-
                ish Archaeological Reports.
Goldberg, P., and A. M. Rosen
1987   Early Holocene Palaeoenvironments of Israel. In *Shiqmim 1:
                Studies Concerning Chalcolithic Societies in the Northern Negev Desert,
                Israel (1982–1984),* ed. T. E. Levy, 23–33. British Archaeological
                Reports International Series, 356(i–ii). Oxford: British Archaeo-
                logical Reports.
Greenland Ice-Core Project (GRIP) Members
1993   Climate Instability during the Last Interglacial Period in the GRIP
                Ice Core. *Nature* 364:203–7.
Hanbury-Tenison, J. W.
1986   *The Late Chalcolithic to Early Bronze I Transition in Palestine and
                Transjordan.* British Archaeological Reports International Series,
                311. Oxford: British Archaeological Reports.
Harding, G. L.
1959   *The Antiquities of Jordan.* New York: Thomas Y. Crowell.
Henry, D. O.
1989   *From Foraging to Agriculture: The Levant at the End of the Ice Age.*
                Philadelphia: University of Pennsylvania Press.
Hillaire-Marcel, C., and J.-S. Vincent
1980   *Holocene Stratigraphy and Sea Level Changes in Southeastern
                Hudson Bay, Canada.* Paleo-Quebec 11. Montreal: Laboratoire
                d'archéologie de l'UQAM.
Horowitz, A.
1971   Climatic and Vegetational Developments in Northeastern Israel
                during Upper Pleistocene-Holocene Times. *Pollen et Spores*
                13:255–78.
1974   Preliminary Palynological Indications as to the Climate of Israel
                during the Last 6000 Years. *Paleorient* 2:407–14.
1978   Human Settlement Patterns in Israel. *Expedition* 20.4:55–58.
1979   *The Quaternary of Israel.* New York: Academic Press.
Huntington, E.
1911   *Palestine and Its Transformation.* Boston: Houghton Mifflin Co.
Ibach, R. D., Jr.
1987   *Archaeological Survey of the Hesban Region: Catalogue of Sites and
                Characterization of Periods.* Hesban 5. Berrien Springs, Mich.:
                Institute of Archaeology and Andrews University.

Ibrahim, M. M.; J. A. Sauer; and K. Yassine
1976   The East Jordan Valley Survey, 1975. *Bulletin of the American Schools of Oriental Research* 222:41–66.
International Symposium on World Climate
1966   *World Climate from 8000 to 0 B.C.* London: Royal Meteorological Society.
Jado, A. R., and J. G. Zötl, eds.
1984   *Quaternary Period in Saudi Arabia*, vol. 2. Vienna: Springer.
Jouzel, J.; N. I. Barkov; J. M. Barnola; M. Bender; J. Chappellaz; C. Genthon; V. M. Kotlyakov; V. Lipenkov; C. Lorius; J. R. Petit; D. Raynaud; G. Raisbeck; C. Ritz; T. Sowers; M. Stievenard; F. Yion; and P. Yiou
1993   Extending the Vostok Ice-Core Record of Palaeoclimate to the Penultimate Glacial Period. *Nature* 364:407–12.
Kenyon, K. M.
1960   *Archaeology in the Holy Land.* London: Ernest Benn.
Koucky, F. L.
1987   The Regional Environment. In *The Roman Frontier in Central Jordan: Interim Report on the Limes Arabicus Project, 1980–1985*, ed. S. T. Parker, 11–40. British Archaeological Reports International Series, 340(i). Oxford: British Archaeological Reports.
Lamb, H. H.
1972-77   *Climate: Present, Past, and Future.* London: Methuen.
Levy, T. E.
1986   The Chalcolithic Period. *Biblical Archaeologist* 49:82–108.
Lorius, C.; J. Jouzel; C. Ritz; L. Merlivat; N. I. Barkov; Y. S. Korotkevich; and V. M. Kotlyakov
1985   A 150,000-Year Climatic Record from Antarctic Ice. *Nature* 316:591–96.
MacDonald, B.
1988   *The Wadi el Hasa Archaeological Survey, 1979–1983, West-Central Jordan.* Waterloo, Ont.: Wilfrid Laurier University.
de Maigret, A.
1984   *The Bronze Age Culture of Hawlan at-Tiyal and Al-Hada (Republic of Yemen).* ISMEO Reports and Memoirs, 24. Rome: ISMEO.
Mallowan, M. E. L.
1964   Noah's Flood Reconsidered. *Iraq* 26:62–82.
Masters, P. M., and N. C. Flemming, eds.
1983   *Quaternary Coastlines and Marine Archaeology.* London: Academic Press.
Matthiae, P.
1980   *Ebla: An Empire Rediscovered.* London: Hodder and Stoughton.
Mazar, A.
1990   *Archaeology of the Land of the Bible, 10,000–586 B.C.E.* New York: Doubleday.

Mazar, B.
1986   *The Early Biblical Period.* Jerusalem: Israel Exploration Society.
McClure, H. A.
1976   Radiocarbon Chronology of Late Quaternary Lakes in the Arabian
                Desert. *Nature* 263:755–56.
Miller, J. M., ed.
1991   *Archaeological Survey of the Kerak Plateau.* American Schools of
                Oriental Research Archaeological Reports, 1. Atlanta: Scholars
                Press.
Miller, J. M., and J. H. Hayes
1986   *A History of Ancient Israel and Judah.* Philadelphia: Westminster.
Moorey, P. R. S.
1982   *Ur "of the Chaldees": A Revised and Updated Edition of Sir Leonard
                Woolley's "Excavations at Ur."* Ithaca, N.Y.: Cornell University
                Press.
NATO Advanced Research Workshop on Milankovitch and Climate
1982   *Milankovitch and Climate: Understanding the Response to Astronomical
                Forcing,* ed. A. Berger. Boston: D. Reidel.
Nawwab, I. I.; P. C. Speers; and P. F. Hoye, eds.
1981   *Aramco and Its World.* Washington, D.C.: Arabian-American Oil
                Company.
Niklewski, J., and W. van Zeist
1970   A Late Quaternary Pollen Diagram from Northwestern Syria.
                Acta Botanica Neerlandica 19:737–54.
Nissen, H. J.
1988   *The Early History of the Ancient Near East: 9000–2000 B.C.* Chicago:
                University of Chicago Press.
Noth, M.
1960   *The History of Israel.* New York: Harper and Row.
Nützel, W.
1976   The Climate Changes of Mesopotamia and Bordering Areas:
                14000–2000 B.C. *Sumer* 32:11–24.
1979   On the Geographical Position of as yet Unexplored Early Mesopo-
                tamian Cultures. *Journal of the American Oriental Society* 99:288–96.
Oliver, J. E., and R. W. Fairbridge, eds.
1987   *The Encyclopedia of Climatology.* New York: Van Nostrand Reinhold.
Overstreet, W. C.; M. J. Grolier; and M. R. Toplyn
1988   *Geological and Archaeological Reconnaissance in the Yemen Arab
                Republic, 1985: The Wadi al-Jubah Archaeological Project,* vol. 4.
                Washington, D.C.: American Foundation for the Study of Man.
Pettinato, G.
1979   *Catalogo dei Testi Cuneiformi di Tell Mardikh–Ebla.* Materiali Epi-
                graphici di Ebla, 1. Naples: Istituto Universitario Orientale
                di Napoli.
1981   *The Archives of Ebla.* Garden City, N.Y.: Doubleday.

Rast, W. E., and R. T. Schaub
1974   Survey of the Southeastern Plain of the Dead Sea 1973. *Annual of the Department of Antiquities of Jordan* 19:5–53.
1980   Have Sodom and Gomorrah Been Found? *Biblical Archaeology Review* 6, no. 5:26–36.
Rast, W. E., and R. T. Schaub, eds.
1981   *The Southeastern Dead Sea Plain Expedition: An Interim Report of the 1977 Season*. Annual of the American Schools of Oriental Research, 46. Cambridge, Mass.: American Schools of Oriental Research.
Richard, S., and R. S. Boraas
1988   The Early Bronze IV Fortified Site of Khirbet Iskander, Jordan: Third Preliminary Report, 1984 Season. *Bulletin of the American Schools of Oriental Research Supplement* 25:107–30.
Rosen, A. M.
1986   *Cities of Clay: The Geoarchaeology of Tells*. Chicago: University of Chicago Press.
1989   Environmental Change at the End of the Early Bronze Age. In *L'urbanisation de la Palestine à l'age du Bronze ancien*, ed. P. de Miroschedji, 247–56. British Archaeological Reports International Series, 527. Oxford: British Archaeological Reports.
Sauer, J. A.
1982a   Prospects for Archeology in Jordan and Syria. *Biblical Archeologist* 45:73–84.
1982b   Syro-Palestinian Archeology, History, and Biblical Studies. *Biblical Archeologist* 45:201–9.
1985   Closing Session. In *Biblical Archaeology Today*, 490–91. Jerusalem: Israel Exploration Society.
1986   Transjordan in the Bronze and Iron Ages: A Critique of Glueck's Synthesis. *Bulletin of the American Schools of Oriental Research* 263: 1–26.
1994   The Pottery at Hesban and Its Relationships to the History of Jordan. In *Hesban after 25 Years*, ed. D. Merling and L. T. Geraty. Berrien Springs, Mich.: Andrews University Press.
Sauer, J. A., and J. A. Blakely
1988   Archaeology along the Spice Route of Yemen. In *Araby the Blest*, ed. D. T. Potts, 90–115. Copenhagen: Carsten Niebuhr Institute.
Schaub, R. T., and W. E. Rast
1984   Preliminary Report of the 1981 Expedition to the Dead Sea Plain, Jordan. *Bulletin of the American Schools of Oriental Research* 254:35–60.
1989   *Bab edh-Dhra': Excavations in the Cemetery Directed by Paul W. Lapp (1965–67)*. Reports of the Expedition to the Dead Sea Plain, Jordan 1. Winona Lake, Ind.: Eisenbrauns.
Shanks, H.
1980   BAR Interviews Giovanni Pettinato. *Biblical Archaeology Review* 6, no. 5:46–52.

Shehadeh, N.
1985   The Climate of Jordan in the Past and Present. In *Studies in the History and Archaeology of Jordan 2*, ed. A. Hadidi, 25–37. Amman: Department of Antiquities.

Sirocko, F.; M. Sarnthein; H. Erlenkeuser; H. Lange; M. Arnold; and J. C. Duplessy
1993   Century-Scale Events in Monsoonal Climate over the Past 24,000 Years. *Nature* 364:322–64.

Stager, L. E.
1992   The Periodization of Palestine from Neolithic through Early Bronze Times. In *Chronologies in Old World Archaeology*, ed. R. W. Ehrich, 22–41. Chicago: University of Chicago Press.

Thompson, T. L.
1974   *The Historicity of the Patriarchal Narratives*. Berlin: Walter de Gruyter.

Twitchell, K. S.
1958   *Saudi Arabia*. Princeton, N.J.: Princeton University Press.

Van Campo, E.; J. C. Duplessy; and M. Rossignol-Strick
1982   Climatic Conditions Deduced from a 150-kyr Oxygen Isotope–Pollen Record from the Arabian Sea. *Nature* 296:56–59.

Van Seters, J.
1975   *Abraham in History and Tradition*. New Haven, Conn.: Yale University Press.
1992   *Prologue to History*. Louisville, Ky.: Westminster/John Knox.

Weiss, H.; M.-A. Courty; W. Wetterstrom; F. Guichard; L. Senior; R. Meadow; and A. Curnow
1993   The Genesis and Collapse of Third Millennium North Mesopotamian Civilization. *Science* 261:995–1004.

White, J. W. C.
1993   Don't Touch That Dial. *Nature* 364:186.

Wright, G. E.
1961   The Archaeology of Palestine. In *The Bible and the Ancient Near East*, ed. G. E. Wright, 73–112. Winona Lake, Ind.: Eisenbrauns.
1962   *Biblical Archaeology*. Rev. ed. Philadelphia: Westminster.

Yassine, K.; M. M. Ibrahim; and J. A. Sauer
1988   The East Jordan Valley Survey, 1976 (Part Two). In *Archaeology of Jordan: Essays and Reports*, ed. K. Yassine, 189–207. Amman: Department of Archaeology, University of Jordan.

Zohary, M.
1973   *Geobotanical Foundations of the Middle East*. Stuttgart: Gustav Fischer.

23 | The Eastern Border of the Kingdom of Judah in Its Last Days

EPHRAIM STERN

Judah, under Josiah, began to enjoy its final period of prosperity around 630 BCE, after the Assyrians retreated from the country. The king, who had ascended the throne by 639 BCE, reorganized his kingdom, incorporating into it the territory of Benjamin and the southern part of the former Assyrian province, from Jericho in the east through Gibeon, Beth Horon, and Gezer to Meṣad Hashavyahu on the coast (Pritchard 1961, 1964; Naveh 1962; Stern 1975; Malamat 1968, 1974, 1975, 1979).

All of these sites, including Jericho (see below), have produced artifacts that clearly belong to the last period of the kingdom of Judah. Josiah also organized and fortified the southern border of his kingdom, as is evidenced in the many excavations recently carried out in the Beer-sheba valley (see, for example, Aharoni and Aharoni 1976; Y. Aharoni 1981; Biran and Cohen 1981; Biran 1985; Beit-Arieh 1985, 1991; Cohen 1988; but see Na'aman et al. 1987; Tatum 1991).

Even more impressive are Josiah's accomplishments along his eastern border, in the region extending from Jericho down to En-gedi, which recently have been clarified. We can state with confidence that during the entire Iron Age this whole area was not settled (except perhaps the town of Jericho itself) until the arrival of Josiah. It now seems certain that these sites, without exception, are to be dated from the time of Josiah down to the Babylonian conquest. In what follows we shall list them one by one.

Relying on the biblical sources, we can assume that Jericho and its region were part of the Northern Kingdom of Israel until its conquest by the Assyrians in 720 BCE; Hiel of Bethel, who rebuilt Jericho in the ninth century BCE, was a citizen of the kingdom under Ahab; and furthermore, the prophets Elijah and Elisha, both Israelites, were also active there (1 Kgs. 16:34; 2 Kgs. 2:4–5, 15–18). We can also assume that during the period of Assyrian rule, Jericho (if still in existence) was part of the Assyrian province that replaced the Israelite kingdom (Forrer 1921; Cogan 1974; Eph'al 1979).

As is now well known, in all the various stages of the Tell es-Sultan excavations, remains were revealed of a flourishing town from the end of the Iron Age (Sellin and Watzinger 1913; Garstang 1940; Tushingham 1965; Weippert and Weippert 1976; Kenyon and Holland 1981:11–13, 171–73, 219; 1982:455–533, 537–39, fig. 220:1; 1983:58–84, 179–81).

A recent survey of the area, however, uncovered a large (2.4 ha [6 acre]) site only a few kilometers south of the mound on the southern side of Wadi Qilt. Avraham Eitan, who reported the discovery, has even suggested that it was probably the "town of Jericho" at the end of the Iron Age (Eitan 1983). The site has not yet been excavated, but two other sites that protected Jericho on the roads leading to the city have been investigated during the past few years.

One is Ḥorvat Shilḥah (Universal Transverse Mercator map ref. 7146/5248), located north of Wadi Qilt on the road leading from Jericho to Mukhmas (ancient Michmash) along the modern road called "Tariq Abu Hindi." This is possibly the biblical "border road" (1 Sam. 13:18). The excavations at Ḥorvat Shilḥah uncovered

> a single large Iron Age building, almost square in plan. It contains a large central courtyard with rooms on three sides. An architectural unit resembling a "four-room house" was found to be incorporated into the southwestern part of the building, including pillar bases and built-up mangers [see fig. 23-1]. The building was poorly preserved and probably existed only for a short time, since no floor raising or other architectural renovations were observed. The pottery is homogeneous, and can be dated to the late 7th–early 6th centuries BCE. It is typical Judean pottery, quite similar to that known from Jerusalem. Among the other finds was a stamped *lamelekh* jar-handle with a two-winged impression (Ziph)—one of the few such stamped handles found in a clear late 7th century-BCE context. The building is interpreted either as a royal citadel/military center, or a caravanserai. (Mazar, Amit, and Ilan 1983)

The second late Judahite site was uncovered by Eitan in 1982 at Vered Jericho, about 5 km south of Tell es-Sultan and 3 km south of the late Iron Age town mentioned above. It is also a fortress or perhaps even a temple and today stands beside the modern main road leading from Jericho to Jerusalem at the point where Wadi es-Sweid opens into the Jordan

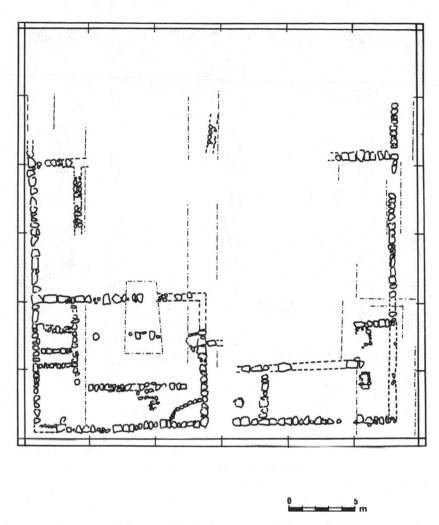

FIG. 23-1. Plan of the large Iron Age building at Ḥorvat Shilḥa.

Valley. The building was found in an excellent state of preservation. Its remains formed a small mound, 25 by 30 m, and 2.5 m high.

The building itself was a rectangular structure, 20 by 24 m (fig. 23-2). The outer wall, 0.9 m wide, is still standing today to a height of 2 m and in some places even more. The building was constructed on a stone foundation coated with mud and topped with a mud-brick superstructure. The building is distinguished by its symmetrical plan. The finds at the

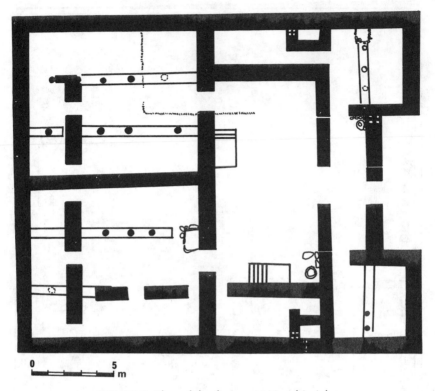

FIG. 23-2. Plan of the fortress at Vered Jericho.

site were dated by the excavator from the late seventh century BCE to the beginning of the sixth (Eitan 1983).

Further to the south, Frank Cross and J. T. Milik already in the 1950s were investigating three additional sites in the Buqêᶜah: Khirbet Abu Tabaq, Khirbet es-Samrah, and Khirbet el-Maqari (Cross and Milik 1956; fig. 23-3). At the time, they dated these three eastern Judean settlements to the Iron Age and assigned them to quite a considerable time range. Later, Lawrence Stager, who reexamined the material, came to the conclusion that:

> In the 7th century B.C. Judah incorporated the "desert province" (Josh 15:61–62) into its eastern frontier. This gave Jerusalem access to minerals in and around the Dead Sea (salt, sulfur, and bitumen being the most important) and control over date-palm plantations first developed

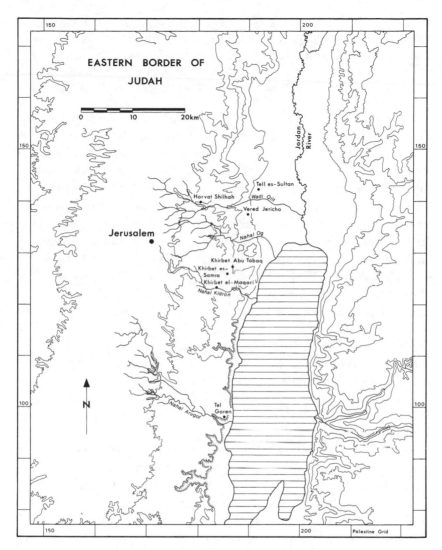

FIG. 23-3. Map of the eastern Judean sites.

along the western littoral in the 7th century BCE. These plantations extended from Khirbet Qumran in the north to ᶜÊn Gedi in the south.

To secure these economic advantages, Judah had to keep the Buqêᶜah route from becoming the "haunt of robbers." For these reasons, a string of three paramilitary outposts—Khirbet Abu Ṭabaq, Khirbet es-Samrah, and Khirbet el-Maqârī—with outliers and nearby desert farms was established in the Buqê‘ah wasteland in the 7th century B.C. These forts lasted no more than a few decades, abandoned when the kingdom of Judah fell to the Neo-Babylonians early in the 6th century BCE. They were not occupied again until the 1st century BCE. (Stager 1976:145; see also Stager 1975:171–269)

Outside of Jericho, the major Judahite settlement in this region that has been extensively excavated and probably presents the best and clearest picture is the Judahite settlement at En-gedi. Archaeological excavations were carried out at En-gedi on behalf of the Hebrew University and Israel Exploration Society, in the first two seasons (1961–62) directed by Benjamin Mazar, Immanuel Dunayevsky, and Trude Dothan, and in the following three (1963–65) by Mazar, Dunayevsky, and the writer. During the five seasons, the excavations were concentrated mainly on Tel Goren, the most prominent site in the oasis (Aharoni 1958; Mazar 1963; Mazar and Dunayevsky 1964; Mazar, Dothan, and Dunayevsky 1966; Mazar 1976).

Five occupation levels were distinguished at Tel Goren, of which the earliest (Stratum V) was dated to the end of the Iron Age (630–582 BCE). This earliest settlement at Tel Goren was built on the top of the hill and on the terraces on its slopes. On the southern slope, the remains cleared consisted mostly of courtyards with adjoining buildings. The numerous finds made here under the brick debris and a layer of ashes included large pottery vessels (pithoi) shaped like barrels or vats and with their bases sunk into the ground.

Benjamin Mazar observed that in one of the courtyards was uncovered a row of seven such pithoi set close together. Around them was an abundance of pottery vessels, such as jars, bowls, cooking pots, jugs, juglets, decanters, lamps, etc., as well as a basalt mortar, perforated clay balls, and lumps of bitumen. All the vessels belong to types characteristic of the second half of the seventh century BCE and the beginning of the sixth century BCE. To this period also belong the buildings on a wide terrace in the middle of the northern slope of the mound. These structures had a uniform plan. They consisted of a courtyard with two interconnected small rooms along one side. Stairs leading up from the street on the lower terrace gave access to these houses (fig. 23-4).

Along this street were discovered a group of installations, including ovens. Pithoi, similar to those found on the southern slope, pottery, as well as metal and bone objects were found in one of the courtyards (fig.

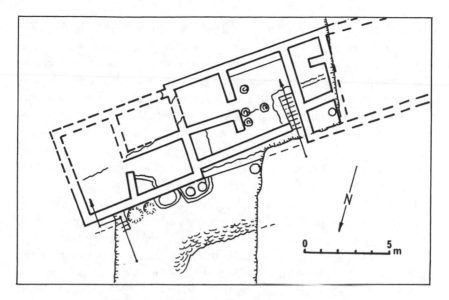

FIG. 23-4. Tel Goren: houses in Stratum V.

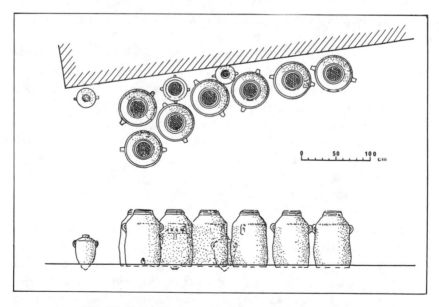

FIG. 23-5. Tel Goren: row of vats on southern slope.

23-5). The excavators assumed that these structures were used for some special industry, most probably for the production of perfume. En-gedi was known as a center for the cultivation of perfume-producing plants, especially the balsam (*opobalsamum*). It can be assumed that the workshops processing such costly products were concentrated at Tel Goren and that the local growers and perfume workers were employed in the royal service. A gloss of Rabbi Joseph on Jeremiah 52:16 ("But Nebuzaradan . . . left certain of the poor of the land to be vinedressers and husbandmen") states that these were the "balsam gatherers from En-gedi to Ramtha" (in the southern Jordan Valley; Babylonian Talmud, *Shabbat* 26a).

Individual finds included a small square seal with the Hebrew inscription that can perhaps be read *l'ryhw czryhw* ("belonging to Uriyahu [son] of Azaryahu"). A larger stamp made of limestone bears the name *tbšlm* ("Tobshalom"). Near the name is a design resembling the plan of the building in which the seal was found. Another find was a fragment of a store jar inscribed *lptyhw* ("belonging to Putiyahu"). Numerous jar handles with rosette stamps were also discovered. One jar handle was found with the seal impression of the double-winged symbol, above which are the words *lmlk* ("belonging to the king") and *zyp* (Zyph). Beside the seal are incised concentric circles, made with a compass. Also found was a jar handle stamped with the figure of a horse.

Other finds were stone weights, each marked with the sign representing the shekel with the numerals "one," "four," or "eight." In a building on the northern slope (where the stamp of Tobshalom was found) was a pot covered with a lamp. Inside it was a hoard of silver ingots of various shapes, which must have served as a form of currency. In various buildings, silver jewelry, such as rings, beads, and earrings, was discovered. These finds can be dated with certainty to the end of the kingdom of Judah.

This early settlement was completely destroyed by a conflagration, perhaps in the year 23 of the reign of Nebuchadrezzar (582/81 BCE; see also Jer. 52:30; Josephus, *Antiquities of the Jews* 10.181; B. Mazar 1976).

The overall picture emerging from the above survey of Jericho and the settlements along the eastern border of Judah indicates clearly that from the days of Josiah the entire eastern border of the kingdom from Jericho to En-gedi (and perhaps including Tell es-Sultan itself, which at that time was probably also incorporated into the kingdom) had been populated according to a careful plan with a dense line of settlements, agricultural estates, and fortresses, in an area that had been previously completely uninhabited. All these new sites were presumably based on the cultivation of perfume-producing plants, especially balsam. Date palm plantations were probably also developed and minerals extracted from the Dead Sea.

The reason for such an undertaking in this desert region may have been the renewal in Josiah's time of commercial ties with Greece and the Aegean, which was always an important client for these products. From this time onward, these newly established relations with the west were of great significance for the material culture of the entire country.

WORKS CITED

Aharoni, M., and Y. Aharoni
1976   The Stratification of Judahite Sites in the Eighth and Seventh Centuries BCE. *Bulletin of the American Schools of Oriental Research* 224:73–88.

Aharoni, Y.
1958   Archaeological Survey of En-Gedi. *Bulletin of the Israel Exploration Society* 22:27–45 (Hebrew).
1981   *Arad Inscriptions.* Jerusalem: Israel Exploration Society.

Beit-Arieh, I.
1985   Tel ʿIra; A Fortified City of Judah. *Qadmoniot* 18:17–25 (Hebrew).
1991   A Small Frontier Citadel at Horvat Radum in the Judean Negev. *Qadmoniot* 24:86–89 (Hebrew).

Biran, A.
1985   Tel ʿIra. *Qadmoniot* 18:25–28 (Hebrew).

Biran, A., and R. Cohen
1991   Aroer in the Negev. *Eretz-Israel* 17:250–73 (Hebrew).

Cogan, M.
1974   *Imperialism and Religion: Assyria, Judah, and Israel in the Eighth and Seventh Centuries BCE.* Missoula, Mont.: Scholars Press.

Cohen, R.
1988–89   Ein Haseva. *Excavations and Surveys in Israel* 7–8:52.

Cross, F. M., and J. T. Milik
1956   Explorations in the Judaean Buqêʿah. *Bulletin of the American Schools of Oriental Research* 142:2–17.

Eitan, A.
1983   Vered Jericho. *Excavations and Surveys in Israel* 82:106–7.

Eph'al, I.
1979   Assyrian Domination in Palestine. In *The World History of the Jewish People, 4:1. The Age of the Monarchies: Political History,* ed. A. Malamat, 276–89. Jerusalem: Massada Press.

Forrer, E.
1921   *Die Provinzeinteilung des Assyrischen Reiches.* Leipzig.

Garstang, J.
1940   *The Story of Jericho*. London: Marshall, Morgan and Scott.
Kenyon, K. M., and T. A. Holland
1981   *Excavations at Jericho, Volume 3: The Architecture and Stratigraphy of the Tell*. London: British School of Archaeology at Jerusalem.
1982   *Excavations at Jericho, Volume 4: The Pottery Type Series and Other Finds*. London: British School of Archaeology at Jerusalem.
1983   *Excavations at Jericho, Volume 5: The Pottery of Phases at the Tell and Other Finds*. London: British School of Archaeology at Jerusalem.
Malamat, A.
1968   The Last Kings of Judah and the Fall of Jerusalem. *Israel Exploration Journal* 18:137–56.
1974   Josiah's Bid for Armageddon. T. H. Gaster Festschrift. *Journal of the Ancient Near Eastern Society* 5:267–79.
1975   The Twilight of Judah in the Egyptian-Babylonian Maelstrom. *Vetus Testamentum Supplements* 28:123–45.
1979   The Last Years of the Kingdom of Judah. In *The World History of the Jewish People, 4:1. The Age of the Monarchies: Political History*, ed. A. Malamat, 205–21, 249–53. Jerusalem: Massada Press.
Mazar, A.; D. Amit; and Z. Ilan
1983   The "Border Road" between Michmash and Jericho and Excavations at Horvat Shilhah. *Eretz-Israel* 17:236–50. (Hebrew with English summary, pp. 10*-11*).
Mazar, B.
1963   Excavations at the Oasis of En Gedi. *Archaeology* 16:99–107.
1976   En-Gedi. In *Encyclopedia of Archaeological Excavations in the Holy Land*, ed. M. Avi-Yonah, 2:370–75. Jerusalem: Israel Exploration Society and Massada Press.
Mazar, B.; T. Dothan; and I. Dunayevsky
1966   En-Gedi: The First and Second Excavations, 1961–1962. *'Atiqot* 5:1–38, 53–59 (English Series).
Mazar, B., and I. Dunayevsky
1964   En-Gedi: The Third Season of Excavations, Preliminary Report. *Israel Exploration Journal* 14:121–28.
Naveh, J.
1962   The Excavations at Mesad Hashavyahu. *Israel Exploration Journal* 12:89–99.
Na'aman, N.; A. F. Rainey; A. Biran; and I. Beit-Arieh
1987   The Negev in the Last Days of the Judean Kingdom. *Cathedra* 42:4–38 (Hebrew).
Pritchard, J. B.
1961   *The Water System of Gibeon*. Philadelphia: University Museum.
1964   *Winery, Defenses, and Soundings at Gibeon*. Philadelphia: University Museum.
Sellin, E., and C. Watzinger
1913   *Jericho*. Leipzig: J. C. Hinrichs.

Stager, L. E.
1975   Ancient Agriculture in the Judean Desert: A Case Study of the Buqêᶜah Valley. Ph.D. dissertation, Harvard University.
1976   Farming in the Judean Desert during the Iron Age. *Bulletin of the American Schools of Oriental Research* 221:145–58.
Stern, E.
1975   Israel at the Close of the Period of the Monarchy: An Archaelogical Survey. *Biblical Archaeologist* 38:26–54.
Tatum, L.
1991   King Manasseh and the Royal Fortress at Horvat Usa. *Biblical Archaeologist* 54:136–45.
Tushingham, A. D.
1965   Tombs of the Early Iron Age. In *Excavations at Jericho, Volume 2: The Tombs Excavated in 1955–58*, ed. K. M. Kenyon, 479–515. London: British School of Archaeology at Jerusalem.
Weippert, H., and M. Weippert
1976   Jericho in der Eisenzeit. *Zeitschrift des deutschen Palästina-Vereins* 92:105–48.

24 | Gate 1567 at Megiddo and the Seal of Shema, Servant of Jeroboam

Gate 1567, the gatehouse leading to the compound of Palace 1723, is one of the finest monumental structures of the period of the kingdom of Israel uncovered at Megiddo. Here I will discuss the stratigraphy and character of Gate 1567, which leads to a fresh evaluation of the stratigraphic context and date of some Hebrew seals found here, notably the seal of Shema, servant of Jeroboam. The date of the seals has far-reaching archaeological and historical implications. And in an appendix to this chapter, I will touch upon the questions of the date and function of Storage Pit 1414, a huge public silo situated near Gate 1567, questions elucidated with reference to the stratigraphy of the gatehouse.

GATE 1567

In 1904 Gottlieb Schumacher excavated part of a monumental structure at the southern part of Megiddo, extending to the west of his main trench, which crossed the site from north to south. He labeled it "der Palast" (the Palace), this term being a technical term rather than a definition of the function of the building (fig. 24-1; Schumacher 1908:91–99, pls. 29–30). The Oriental Institute expedition completed the excavation of the structure, which was found to be the gatehouse of the entrance to Courtyard 1693, in which Palace 1723 was situated. The monumental gatehouse was termed Gate 1567 (fig. 24-2; Lamon and Shipton 1939:10–17).

Neither Schumacher nor R. S. Lamon or G. M. Shipton fully understood Gate 1567. Schumacher did not identify it as a gatehouse; he uncovered only part of the structure, and gatehouses of this type were not yet known at other sites at the time of his excavations. Lamon and Shipton identified Gate 1567 as a gatehouse, but they misinterpreted some structural elements and the stratigraphy of the gate. Furthermore, as I have discussed in detail elsewhere (Ussishkin 1989:149–54), the American excavators did not fully coordinate their finds with those of the German expedition, and this also affected the study of Gate 1567. Lamon and Shipton were familiar with Schumacher's excavation report (1908) but they did not make full use of the data included in it in their analysis of the gatehouse. Also, structural elements of "the Palace" uncovered by Schumacher and recorded by him, which were destroyed prior to the renewal of excavations at Megiddo by the American expedition, are not shown in the plan of Courtyard 1693 and Gate 1567 published by Lamon and Shipton.

Lamon and Shipton believed that two phases, or periods of use, can be discerned in Gate 1567. In the first phase the gatehouse was built as a monumental entrance to the palatial compound that included Courtyard 1693 and Palace 1723 (fig. 24-2: no. 1). They believed that the palace compound, including Gate 1567, had never been completed or in use, and that Palace 1723 was demolished before completion. Lamon and Shipton (1939:8–11, 59) considered the palace compound as a separate archaeological stratum, and labeled it Stratum IVB. According to the corrected stratigraphy of W. F. Albright, G. E. Wright, and Yigael Yadin (see Ussishkin 1980 with further bibliography), the compound of Palace 1723, that is, Stratum IVB, is contemporary with remains of Stratum VA, and so this archaeological level is now generally known as Stratum VA–IVB (or simply Stratum VA by some scholars). Stratum VA–IVB is assigned by most scholars to the reign of Solomon (965–928 BCE). (The dates of the kings of Israel in this study are after Tadmor 1962).

Lamon and Shipton (1939:14–15) assigned to Gate 1567 in its first phase two proto-Ionic capitals. One of the capitals was undecorated, and Lamon and Shipton interpreted it as an indication that the carving of the capital had not been completed, supporting their view that the construction of the palace compound was abandoned before completion. Both capitals, however, should probably be restored in the entrance to Palace 1723 rather than in the gatehouse (Ussishkin 1970).

Following the destruction of Stratum VA–IVB, a new city was built, labeled "the main phase of Stratum IV" by Lamon and Shipton, but now generally known as Stratum IVA (Stratum IV according to some scholars). Stratum IVA is characterized by City Wall 325 and the "stable compounds"; it is assigned by most scholars to the period of the divided

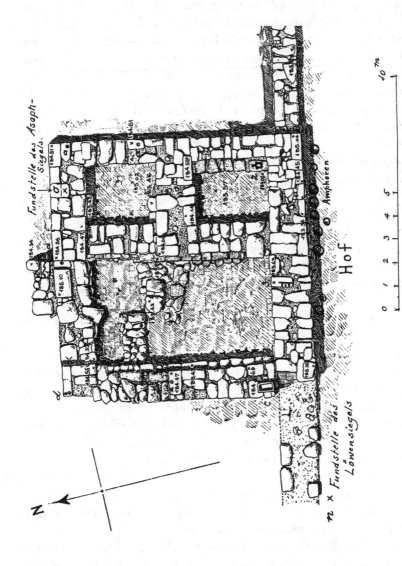

FIG. 24-1. "The Palace" dug by Schumacher (after Schumacher 1908: pl. 29, A).

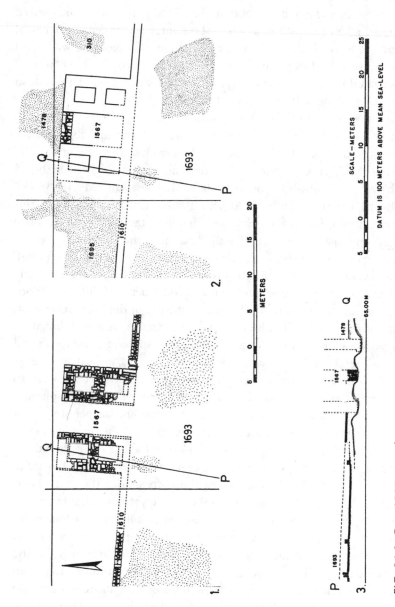

FIG. 24-2. Gate 1567 according to Lamon and Shipton: (1) Plan of first phase (Stratum IVB); (2) Plan of second phase (Stratum IV); (3) Section P-Q (after Lamon and Shipton 1939: figs. 12, 34–35).

monarchy, prior to the Assyrian conquest in 732 BCE. The second phase in the history of Gate 1567, according to Lamon and Shipton, is associated with Stratum IVA. They believed that Gate 1567 continued to be used in this period, albeit not as a gatehouse. The outer and inner entrances of the structure were blocked at that time by stone-built blocking walls, and the gatehouse served as a "single tower" (fig. 24-2: no. 2). This "tower" was associated with Courtyard 1693, which contained a building built in place of the now-demolished Palace 1723.

In my opinion, Gate 1567 is a gatehouse of the kind typical of Palestine in the Iron Age, which is constructed on "built-up" foundations. Before discussing Gate 1567, let me briefly introduce the structural characteristics of this type of gate (for detailed discussions of six-chambered gates based on "built-up" foundations at Lachish and Megiddo, see, respectively, Ussishkin 1978:58–61 and 1980:7–12). Gatehouses of this type contain two, four, or six chambers flanking the gate passage. They are based on massive foundation walls laid upon the surface of the site (i.e., the surface of the site at the time of construction of the gatehouse). The spaces between the foundation walls, and the area immediately around the structure, were filled with a constructional fill. The floor elevation of such a structure was level with the top of the foundation walls and the constructional fill. The walls of the superstructure were based on the foundations, and followed their lines, but are sometimes narrower and built in a different style. A number of foundation walls, known as "sleeper walls," did not support walls of the superstructure; they were intended to connect the foundation walls physically and to create a box-like foundation structure. Typical in gatehouses of this type are sleeper walls that connect both piers of the outer entrance, both piers of the inner entrance, and the edges of the piers along the left side and along the right side of the gate passage. These sleeper walls extend across the outer and inner entrances of the gatehouse, and across the entrances to the gate chambers; hence they served as solid thresholds to the various entrances in the structure. Significantly, in many cases the sleeper walls are not bonded to the proper foundation walls, as the latter walls, meant to support walls of the superstructure, are more solidly built with ashlar stones while the adjoining sleeper walls are constructed from inferior masonry. Finally, an important point must be emphasized: the floor of such a gatehouse would have been laid at an elevation much higher than that of the surface on which the foundations of the structure were laid. Once the floor and the constructional fill covering the foundation walls have been excavated, that is, removed, the exposed foundation structure, made of "built-up" walls, would misleadingly appear to be a perfectly normal, above-ground structure whose floor is the lower surface, which is earlier in date.

Gate 1567 is a four-chambered gatehouse based on massive "built-up" foundation walls (fig. 24-3). The foundations were constructed with carefully dressed ashlars. Two sleeper walls connect the edges of the piers to the right and left of the gate passage, forming the thresholds of the entrances to the four chambers of the gate. These sleeper walls were rightly assigned by Lamon and Shipton to the original structure. Two more sleeper walls extend across the outer and inner entrances of the gatehouse, forming thresholds to the entrances. These sleeper walls were wrongly considered by Lamon and Shipton to be a later structural addition, and form the basis for their mistaken conclusion that the gatehouse had been blocked at a later period and used as a "tower." The sleeper wall crossing the outer entrance of the gatehouse, which was still extant during the American excavation, is built in inferior style and hence is not bonded to the proper foundation walls (see Schumacher 1908: fig. 142; Lamon and Shipton 1939: fig. 14). The sleeper wall crossing the inner entrance had been uncovered by Schumacher and was destroyed later, prior to the American excavation. An examination of Schumacher's plans and photographs (figs. 24-1, 24-4, 24-5) indicates that this sleeper wall was built with ashlar stones and appears similar in character to the foundation structure, but only the stones of its lowest course were in fact bonded to the foundation walls.

The floor elevation of Gate 1567 is generally indicated by two pieces of data. First, Schumacher recorded the elevation (above sea level, according to his own calculations) of the flat top of a stone topping the sleeper wall which crosses the outer entrance (fig. 24-1). The elevation given here is 185.10 m; we assume that this stone belongs to a step or a threshold projecting above the floor level, hence the floor elevation must have been at about 184.90 m. This estimated elevation also fits that of an external stone threshold in front of the outer entrance, which is 184.84 m. Second, Section P-Q published by Lamon and Shipton (fig. 24-2: no. 3), includes the lime floor of Courtyard 1693 adjoining the inner edge of the gatehouse, and lime Floor Segment 1478, which adjoins the outer entrance. (Floor Segment 1478 was associated by Lamon and Shipton with the "later phase" of the gatehouse as it adjoined the "blocking wall" of the gate [1939:28]; however, assuming that the "blocking wall" forms the original threshold of the outer entrance, Floor Segment 1478 forms part

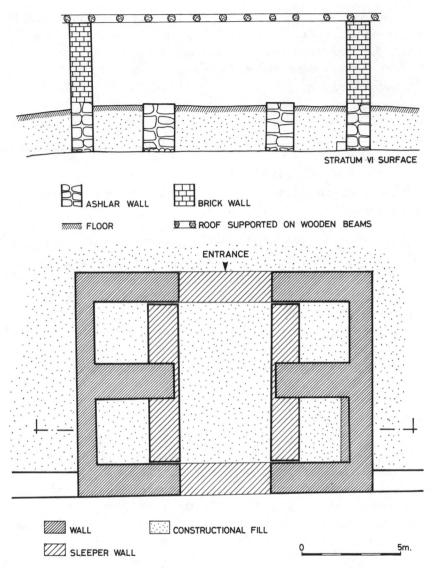

FIG. 24-3. A suggested schematic reconstruction of Gate 1567, plan and section (drawing: Ora Paran).

FIG. 24-4. The inner, left gate chamber and the "sleeper wall" across the inner entrance; from northwest (after Schumacher 1908: fig. 135).

of the original floor in front of the gatehouse.) Both floor segments extend about 3 m higher than the datum line of Section P-Q at elevation 165 m (above sea level, according to the calculations of the American expedition). The American elevation system can be adjusted to Schumacher's elevation system by adding 18 m, as we calculated on the basis of data published by Loud (1948: fig. 415). Thus, adding 18 m to 165 m, the floor shown by Lamon and Shipton is at an elevation of about 186 m, according to Schumacher's system of elevations.

The foundation walls of the gatehouse were laid on a layer or course of small stones, above the destruction debris of Stratum VI. Remains of Stratum VB were preserved in the spaces between the foundation walls and were incorporated in the constructional fills dumped there. The foundations were made of three or four courses of carefully dressed ashlars (as can be observed also in Lamon and Shipton's Section P-Q). The uppermost course of ashlars apparently projected slightly above floor level, as the elevation of the top of the ashlars in the southeast corner was 185.04 m, and that of the south wall to the west of the inner entrance

FIG. 24-5. The southern, inner facade of the gatehouse (after Schumacher 1908: pl. 29, B).

was 185.36 m (according to Schumacher's elevation system; see fig. 24-1). In the southeast corner the ashlar structure rose to a height of 2.36 m.

Detailed information on the superstructure of the gatehouse above the ashlar structure is given by Schumacher (but not by Lamon and Shipton): The walls were built of bricks and wood; brick walls were still standing to a height of 70 cm at the time of excavation (thus, according to the data given above, their tops were at elevation ca. 186 m); and the brick debris reached elevation 187 m. The roof was made of wooden beams, and their remains mixed with straw were found above the brick debris. The gatehouse suffered destruction by a violent fire, evidence for which was detected in the hardened bricks and burnt wood remains found here.

The stratigraphic evidence in the area of Gate 1567 can be summarized as follows. The gatehouse is based on a massive structure of "built-up" foundations. The foundation walls, built of ashlar stones, were laid above the destruction debris of Stratum VI, between remains of Stratum VB that were incorporated in the constructional fill of the foundations. The superstructure of the gatehouse was built of bricks and wooden beams. The gatehouse formed the main entrance to the compound of Palace 1723, part of Stratum VA–IVB, whose construction is generally assigned to the reign of Solomon. The gatehouse was destroyed by a violent fire, the debris covering the remains of the structure. This destruction probably occurred at the time when other structures of Stratum VA–IVB—notably Palace 6000, Shrine 2081, and Building 10—met their end.

THE SEALS OF SHEMA,
SERVANT OF JEROBOAM,
AND OF ASAPH

Two Hebrew seals, one belonging to Shema, servant of Jeroboam, and one belonging to Asaph, were found by Schumacher during the excavation of "the Palace." I shall now turn to these seals and analyze their stratigraphical context and date.

The seal of Shema is an unpierced scaraboid of jasper measuring 37 by 27 by 17 mm; it portrays a roaring lion and contains the inscription *lšmʿ ʿbd yrbʿm*, "(belonging) to Shema, servant of Jeroboam" (fig. 24-6a). This beautiful seal was sent by Schumacher to the Ottoman capital Constantinople (modern Istanbul), where it was kept in the collection of the sultan. It was later mislaid or lost, and its present whereabouts are unknown.

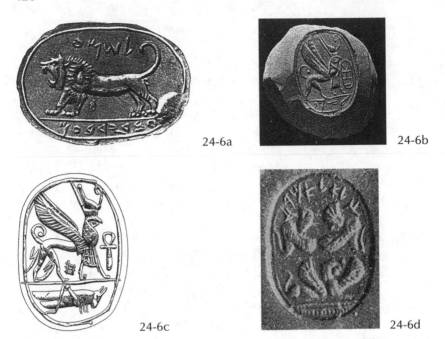

FIG. 24-6. Hebrew seals (or their impressions) from Megiddo: (a) the seal of Shema, Servant of Jeroboam; (b) the seal of Asaph; (c) the seal of Haman; (d) the seal of Elamar.

Information about the seal of Shema was published first by E. Kautzsch (1904a, 1904b), then by S. A. Cook (1904), Schumacher (1908:99–100), and C. Watzinger (1929:64–67). As it is one of the most famous and finest Hebrew seals, it has been discussed and reproduced in many publications since then (e.g., Galling 1941: no. 17; Pritchard 1954: no. 276). The seal must have belonged to an official of King Jeroboam of Israel, and since its discovery scholars have generally agreed that Jeroboam should be identified with Jeroboam II (784–748 BCE) rather than Jeroboam I (928–907 BCE).

S. Yeivin (1960) and G. W. Ahlström (1993), dissenting from the accepted scholarly view, advocated the identification of Jeroboam with Jeroboam I, thus dating the seal to the last quarter of the tenth century BCE. Their arguments are based on stylistic, paleographic, and stratigraphic criteria. Regarding the roaring lion carved on the seal, and other seals depicting similar lions, see the recent studies by André Lemaire (1990) and Nahman Avigad (1992), who date all of them relatively late, thus supporting the attribution of Shema's seal to the eighth century BCE.

The seal of Shema was uncovered in Courtyard 1693, near its northern wall, about 1 m from the southwest corner of Gate 1567. Its find spot is accurately marked in Schumacher's plan (fig. 24-1). It was uncovered at elevation 186.50 m, 1 m beneath the surface of the site, which was therefore at about elevation 187.50 m. According to Schumacher, the stone-built northern wall of the courtyard here rose to a height of approximately 60 cm beneath the surface of the site, that is, accordingly, elevation 186.90 m. Since the brick debris of the nearby gatehouse reached elevation 187.00 m, Schumacher concluded that the seal belongs "without doubt" to the period of this structure.

When considering the seal of Shema on the basis of the above data, and independently of the seal of Asaph to be discussed below, its stratigraphic position is ambiguous. On the one hand, Gate 1567 is the only substantial structure in the area, and, significantly, Schumacher states without reservation that the seal was found "without doubt" in the context of this building. On the other hand, the seal was uncovered at elevation 186.50 m, about 1.50 m above the floor level of the gatehouse as estimated on the basis of Schumacher's data, and about 50 cm above floor level as based on the data of Lamon and Shipton. Schumacher's statement that the stone-built wall of the courtyard rose at this point to a height of 186.90 m is difficult to accept, as the stone substructure of the gatehouse rose only to an elevation of 185.36 m or less. Moreover, this particular wall segment is marked on Schumacher's plan as largely missing. It seems that either Schumacher here uncovered a wall segment of Strata III–II, or that there is an error in the given elevation. Finally, Schumacher was not familiar with the technique of stratigraphic excavation, and we have to consider the possibility that the seal had been dumped at a later period into a pit dug in the debris of the gatehouse, a pit not discerned by Schumacher.

The seal of Asaph is an unpierced scaraboid of lapis lazuli, 18 mm long (fig. 24-6b). It portrays a winged griffin wearing the double crown of Lower and Upper Egypt and contains the inscription *l'sp*, "(belonging) to Asaph." It was first published by A. Erman and E. Kautzsch (1906) and later by Schumacher (1908:99–101), and Watzinger (1929:64–67). The seal was found on top of the northern ashlar wall of the gatehouse, at elevation 185.00 m, at a depth of 2.50 m beneath the surface. The exact find spot is marked in Schumacher's plan (fig. 24-1).

The seal of Asaph seems to be associated with the gatehouse. It was found at the elevation of the floor near the front, left chamber of the gate in an area covered by brick debris of the fallen gatehouse. The fact that it was found on top of the stone wall of the gatehouse can be easily explained. The uppermost course of ashlars of that wall was missing when Schumacher uncovered it, apparently robbed in a later period. Objects lying on the floor of the gate chamber nearby could have easily slipped into the robber trench left when the stones of the wall were extracted. On the other hand, it is also possible that the seal of Asaph was dumped into the robber trench from above, at the time when the ashlars were removed from the wall or even later.

In my opinion, however, the stratigraphic context of the two seals should be considered together. The two seals are very similar typologically. Both of them are unpierced, a relatively unusual feature in Hebrew seals, and must have been mounted on rings. The rings were not found, and it must be assumed that the seals were torn from their mounts in antiquity. The seal of Asaph seems to have belonged to an official comparable to Shema. Both seals were uncovered in association with a single public building used in a single period and not replaced by similar structures in later periods. A priori it would seem an extraordinary coincidence that two similar seals would have been left in the same place under different circumstances. Hence, if the seal of Asaph most likely belonged to the stratigraphic context of Gate 1567, so then did the seal of Shema, even if its stratigraphic position is ambiguous. It seems quite possible that the two seals were kept in the gatehouse, or even in Palace 1723, to be used there by government officials. At the time of the palace's destruction, someone took the seals; tore away the rings, which were probably of precious metal; and discarded the scaraboids before leaving the (already burning?) compound.

The alternate interpretation, less convincing although stratigraphically possible, is that, in a later period, the two seals were each dumped independently into a separate pit cut into the debris of fallen Gate 1567, possibly when ashlars were robbed to build the structures of Stratum IVA, or when domestic units of Strata III and II were erected in the area formerly occupied by the monumental compound. Also, when considering the alternatives, we must allow the possibility, though remote, that one or both of these scaraboid seals, being very small in size, could have been removed from their original context and brought to their respective findspots by burrowing animals.

In summary, on the basis of stratigraphic considerations alone, the seals of Shema and of Asaph most likely were in use in the compound of Palace 1723 at the time of its destruction, at the end of Stratum VA–IVB.

Other chronological considerations, such as paleography or stylistic criteria, are beyond the scope of this study, and are, at any rate, secondary to stratigraphy.

THE SEALS OF HAMAN AND ELAMAR

Two more Hebrew seals, the seals of Haman and Elamar, were found in this general area out of stratigraphical context, but they too may be related to the seals just discussed.

The seal of Haman (Staples 1931; Lamon and Shipton 1939: pl. 67, no. 10) is an unpierced scaraboid of serpentine measuring 15.75 by 11.00 by 5.25 mm (fig. 24-6c). The seal depicts a winged griffin wearing the crown of Lower and Upper Egypt and a locust, and contains the inscription *ḥmn*, "Haman." The seal was found by the Oriental Institute expedition "on the surface in square N 9, about 30 meters west of the main trench excavated by Schumacher in 1905, and had probably been washed down from his dump" (Staples 1931:49). Square N 9 is located about fifty meters northwest of Gate 1567, and the dump located there could have also originated in the gatehouse area rather than in Schumacher's large trench.

The seal of Elamar (May 1935–36; Lamon and Shipton 1939: pl. 67, no. 34) is of lapis lazuli, measuring ca. 22 by 15 mm, and is also unpierced (fig. 24-6d). It shows a winged sphinx and two winged uraei, and contains the inscription *l'l'mr*, "(belonging) to Elamar." The seal was found "above the 'palace' area, about a foot behind a retaining wall erected by Schumacher at the edge of his trench. If in situ, the scaraboid is to be placed in Stratum II. . . . The possibility of a disturbed area, however, must be considered" (May 1935–36:198). The findspot is defined as "Locus Q9, SE=1405, Stratum II?" (May 1935–36:197), situated a short distance west of the point where the seal of Shema was found (see Lamon and Shipton 1939: figs. 73, 122).

The seals of Haman and Elamar show typological similarity to the seals of Shema and Asaph. All four seals are unpierced scaraboids, and their rings were not found. All four seals are elaborately decorated. Similar winged griffins decorate the seals of Asaph and Haman. The seals of Haman and Elamar both seem to have originated from Schumacher's excavation, possibly from the area of "the Palace." In summary, the circumstantial evidence suggests the possibility that all four Hebrew seals belonged to government officials and stemmed from the same context.

Perhaps they all originated in the compound of Palace 1723 belonging to Stratum VA–IVB.

POSSIBLE ARCHAEOLOGICAL AND HISTORICAL IMPLICATIONS

If indeed the seal of Shema, servant of Jeroboam, as well as the other seals under discussion, should be assigned to Stratum VA–IVB, the following corollaries emerge.

First, the seal of Shema belonged to an official of Jeroboam I rather than Jeroboam II, as already suggested by Yeivin and Ahlström.

Second, Stratum VA–IVB at Megiddo, or at least the compound of Palace 1723, was not destroyed shortly after the death of Solomon and the division of the united monarchy, nor even during the campaign of Shoshenq I, circa 925 BCE, but at a later date. The compound of Palace 1723, and probably the rest of the contemporary city, still functioned during the reign of Jeroboam I, and it was destroyed either toward the end of the tenth century or during the earlier part of the ninth century BCE. This corollary supports the conclusion discussed elsewhere (Ussishkin 1990:71–74) that the erection of a stele of Shoshenq I at Megiddo is an indication of conquest and domination of an existing city rather than of an overall destruction of the place; hence the conclusion that Shoshenq I did not destroy Megiddo Stratum VA–IVB.

Third, two (perhaps as many as four) fine Hebrew seals can be dated to the last quarter of the tenth century or the first part of the ninth century BCE.

Fourth, the pottery assemblage of Stratum VA–IVB, in particular the red-slipped, irregularly burnished pottery, is to be dated to later than the reign of Solomon. This conclusion is significant as the pottery assemblage of Stratum VA–IVB serves as a cornerstone in the study of Iron Age pottery in northern Israel (see Rast 1978; Zimhoni 1992).

APPENDIX: STORAGE PIT 1414

A large public silo, labeled Storage Pit 1414, was built in front of and adjacent to the west wing of Gate 1567 (Lamon and Shipton 1939:66–68). It is a huge stone-lined pit, 11 m in diameter at its top, 7 m in diameter at its bottom, and at least 7 m deep; its capacity is about 450 m^3.

FIG. 24-7. Storage Pit 1414 (after Lamon and Shipton 1939: fig. 77).

Remains of chaff and grains were found inside, and the structure has rightly been interpreted as a public silo (fig. 24-7).

The stratigraphic position of the storage pit is as follows. Its location near the facade of Gate 1567, and the fact that its edge nearly obstructs the entrance to the monumental gatehouse, indicate that the storage pit must have been erected after Gate 1567 had fallen into disuse, that is, after the destruction of Stratum VA–IVB. On the other hand, two super-imposed domestic structures, assigned to Strata II and I, were built above the disused storage pit (Lamon and Shipton 1939:66, figs. 73, 78–79, 98). Hence the storage pit must have been erected after Stratum VA–IVB and before Stratum II, that is, in Stratum IVA or III.

Lamon and Shipton assigned the storage pit to Stratum III. We can guess that their attribution was based on the assumption, erroneous, as discussed above, that Gate 1567 had been still in use during Stratum IVA, albeit secondarily as a "tower."

Here I would like to raise the possibility that the storage pit in fact belongs to Stratum IVA. In Stratum III this area of the tell contained a residential quarter, with domestic structures and streets intersecting in a regular pattern; a huge public storage pit does not fit the character of these surroundings. Significantly, Building 1418 (assigned to Stratum II) is built along the same orientation as the residential quarter of Stratum III and resembles in size and character the other buildings in that quarter.

Storage Pit 1414 fits the character of Stratum IVA, which is marked by public buildings. It is located midway between the southern and the northern "stable compounds" (Lamon and Shipton 1939:32–47). The function of these compounds is controversial, and weighty arguments have been presented by James Pritchard (1970), Ze'ev Herzog (1973), Volkmar Fritz (1977), and Larry Herr (1988) in favor of their identification as barracks, storehouses, or market places. Following the American excavators as well as Yigael Yadin (1976) and John Holladay (1986), I believe that these compounds were royal stables. On that basis I suggest that Storage Pit 1414 was a central granary for feeding horses. The pit had a huge capacity (450 m³), and from the remains of chaff and grain found inside it, the excavators estimated that it still contained a certain amount of chaff when it fell into disuse. Assuming, as calculated by Holladay (1986:118), that each horse consumed about 9.6 l of fodder per day, the pit could have held provisions sufficient for feeding 300 to 330 horses for about 130 to 150 days.

WORKS CITED

Ahlström, G. W.
1993   The Seal of Shema. *Scandinavian Journal of the Old Testament* 7:208–15.

Avigad, N.
1992   A New Seal Depicting a Lion. *Michmanim* 6:33*–36*.

Cook, S. A.
1904   A Newly Discovered Hebrew Seal. *Palestine Exploration Fund Quarterly Statement*, pp. 287–91.

Erman, A., and E. Kautzsch
1906   Ein Siegelstein mit hebräischer Unterschrift vom Tell el-Mutesellim. *Mittheilungen und Nachrichten des Deutschen Palästina-Vereins* 12:33–35.

Fritz, V.
1977   Bestimmung und Herkunft des Pfeilerhauses in Israel. *Zeitschrift des deutschen Palästina-Vereins* 93:30–45.

Galling, K.
1941 Beschriftete Bildsiegel des ersten Jahrtausends v. Chr., vornehmlich aus Syrien und Palästina. *Zeitschrift des deutschen Palästina-Vereins* 64:121–202.

Herr, L. G.
1988 Tripartite Pillared Buildings and the Market Place in Iron Age Palestine. *Bulletin of the American Schools of Oriental Research* 272:47–67.

Herzog, Z.
1973 The Storehouses. In *Beer-Sheba I: Excavations at Tel Beer-Sheba, 1969–1971 Seasons*, ed. Y. Aharoni, 23–30. Tel Aviv: Tel Aviv University.

Holladay, J. S.
1986 The Stables of Ancient Israel. In *The Archaeology of Jordan and Other Studies Presented to Siegfried H. Horn*, ed. L. T. Geraty and L. G. Herr, 103–66. Berrien Springs, Mich.: Andrews University Press.

Kautzsch, E.
1904a Ein althebräisches Siegel vom Tell el-Mutesellim. *Mittheilungen und Nachrichten des deutschen Palästina-Vereins* 10:1–14.
1904b Zur Deutung des Löwensiegels. *Mittheilungen und Nachrichten des deutschen Palästina-Vereins* 10:81–83.

Lamon, R. S., and G. M. Shipton
1939 *Megiddo I: Seasons of 1925–34, Strata I–V*. Oriental Institute Publications 42. Chicago: University of Chicago Press.

Lemaire, A.
1990 Trois sceaux inscrits inédits avec lion rugissant. *Semitica* 39:13–22.

Loud, G.
1948 *Megiddo II: Seasons of 1935–39*. Oriental Institute Publications 62. Chicago: University of Chicago Press.

May, H. G.
1935–36 Seal of Elamar. *American Journal of Semitic Languages and Literatures* 52:197–99.

Pritchard, J. B.
1970 The Megiddo Stables: A Reassessment. In *Near Eastern Archaeology in the Twentieth Century: Essays in Honor of Nelson Glueck*, ed. J. A. Sanders, 268–76. Garden City, N.Y.: Doubleday.

Pritchard, J. B., ed.
1954 *The Ancient Near East in Pictures Relating to the Old Testament*. Princeton, N.J.: Princeton University Press.

Rast, W. E.
1978 *Taanach I: Studies in the Iron Age Pottery*. Cambridge, Mass.: American Schools of Oriental Research.

Schumacher, G.
1908 *Tell el-Mutesellim I: Fundbericht*. Leipzig: Rudolf Haupt.

Staples, W. E.
1931   An Inscribed Scaraboid from Megiddo. In *New Light from Arma-geddon*, by P. L. O. Guy, 49–68. Oriental Institute Communications 9. Chicago: University of Chicago Press.

Tadmor, H.
1962   Chronology. In *Encyclopaedia Biblica*, ed. E. L. Sukenik, U. M. D. Cassuto, B. Mazar, N. H. Tur-Sinai, C. H. Rabin, and S. Yeivin, vol. 4, cols. 245–310. Jerusalem: Bialik Institute (Hebrew).

Ussishkin, D.
1970   On the Original Position of Two Proto-Ionic Capitals at Megiddo. *Israel Exploration Journal* 20:213–15.

1978   Excavations at Tel Lachish—1973–1977, Preliminary Report. *Tel Aviv* 5:1–97.

1980   Was the "Solomonic" City Gate at Megiddo Built by King Solomon? *Bulletin of the American Schools of Oriental Research* 239:1–18.

1989   Schumacher's Shrine in Building 338 at Megiddo. *Israel Exploration Journal* 39:149–72.

1990   Notes on Megiddo, Gezer, Ashdod, and Tel Batash in the Tenth to Ninth Centuries B.C. *Bulletin of the American Schools of Oriental Research* 277/278:71–91.

Watzinger, C.
1929   *Tell el-Mutesellim II: Die Funde*. Leipzig: J. C. Hinrichs.

Yadin, Y.
1976   The Megiddo Stables. In *Magnalia Dei: The Mighty Acts of God: Essays on the Bible and Archaeology in Memory of G. Ernest Wright*, ed. F. M. Cross, W. F. Lemke, and P. D. Miller. Garden City, N.Y.: Doubleday.

Yeivin, S.
1960   The Date of the Seal "Belonging to Shema (the) Servant (of) Jeroboam." *Journal of Near Eastern Studies* 19:205–12.

Zimhoni, O.
1992   The Iron Age Pottery from Tel Jezreel: An Interim Report. *Tel Aviv* 19:57–70.

General Index

Aaron, 360
ʿăbōdâ (cult), 355
abecedaries, 162
Abiathar, 359
Abraham/Abram, 204
  adoption of Eliezer, 203
  visit to Dan, 1, 3
Abr-Nahrain (Persian province), 288
Abu Murrah, Khirbet (Hurvat Avimor)
    (Makaz), 255
Abu-Salima, Tell, 178
Abu Tabaq, Khirbet, 402–3
Achish (king of Gath), 337
Ackerman, S., 150, 158, 163
Adad (storm god), 21
Ader, 389
Adullam, fortified by Rehoboam, 256
Aegean, Philistine material culture and,
    250, 263
Aelia Capitolina, 297, 299, 300–2. See also
    Jerusalem
  Cardo Maximus, 301
  Mount Zion, 296–98, 301–3
Agatharchus of Peloponnesus (physician),
    319
Agrab, Tell, 23
Agrippa and Berenice, palace of, 305
Ahab (king of Israel), 11, 204, 399
Aharoni, M., 171, 335
Aharoni, Y., 67, 171, 174, 188, 334–49
Ahaz (king of Judah), 56, 217, 259
Ahiram sarcophagus (Byblos), 25
Ahlström, G., 144, 420, 424
Ai, Acropolis Temple, 118

Aijalon, 248
  fortified by Rehoboam, 256
  Philistine settlement in, 257
  valley of, 248, 255
  archaeological survey in, 173
Ain Boqeq, 137
Ain Dara temple, 21, 23, 25
Ain Feshkha, 133, 135–37, 403
Ain el-Ghuweir, 135–37
Ain Jenin, Khirbet, 240
Ajjul, Tell el-, 88
Ajrud, Kuntillet. See Kuntillet Ajrud
Akko, Phoenician inscription, 96
al-. . . . See . . ., al-
Alalakh (Tell Atchana), 199–210, 293
  census lists, 115
  excavated by Woolley, 200
  Idrimi statue inscription, 201, 207
  texts from, 199–210
Alasia/Enkomi, 19
  Tomb 2, 24
Albertz, R., 159
Albright, W. F., 145, 150, 171, 345,
    366–67, 373, 391, 411
Aleppo, 200, 207
  Nur-Sin (prophet), 21
Alexander (bishop of Narcissus), 300
Alexander Jannaeus, 303
Alexandria (Egypt), 319
Ali, Wadi el-, 240
Alt, A., 262
altars, 147–48, 157, 363
  Arad, 148, 152, 162–63, 338–39
  Beer-sheba, 338–52

429

Index of Ancient Texts

BIBLE

Genesis

1–2	230
1:22	271
1:28	271
2:10–14	387
2:11–12	373, 387
3:10	27
3:24	24
6–9	370, 384
9:1	271
9:7	271
9:11	275
14:14	1
15	204, 205
15:2–3	203
23:5	202
25:8	90
25:17	90
25:24	233
25:25–26	233
29:18	203
29:27	203
30:37–39	23
32:3	233
32:26	318
32:33	318
34:12	203
35:11	271
35:29	90
36	216
36:8–9	231
36:21	231
36:31–39	233, 235
37	72

41–47	373, 390
48:13–14	203
48:14	203
48:22	203
49:3–4	203
49:16–17	5
49:29	90
49:33	90

Exodus

15	233
15:1–18	27
15:1–2	27
15:13–18	27
15:15	233
15:27	24
19:5	204
19:18	189
20:24–25	333, 339
21:2–6	208
21:5	208
21:26–27	208
27:1	338, 339
31:6	5
35:34	5
38:23	5

Leviticus

7:20	275
7:21	275
7:25	275
7:27	275
8:18–21	363

14:33–53	117
14:41–43	117
19:20	208
25	203
25:10–15	203
25:39–42	203
25:49	104

Numbers

1–4	114
3:9–10	360
4	359, 361
4:1–20	359
4:7–8	359
4:9–10	359
4:11–14	359, 360
6:22–24	156
9:13	275
20:14–21	236
20:18	234
20:20	234
20:24	90
22:24	111
24:18	231
26	114
27:1–11	203, 204
31:2	90
33:9	24
33:35–36	237
33:48–50	233

Deuteronomy

1:7	272
2:1–8	236

446

21	204	23:8	149, 152, 334	3	112
21:34	11	23:10	152, 154	7	114
22	196	23:16	157	7:61–65	114
22:10	8	23:16–17	153, 157	7:64	114
22:17	275	23:16–20	157		
22:47	153	23:19	11	**Job**	
		23:24	155	1:22	119
2 Kings		24:10–17	60	3:19	208
2:4–5	400	25:1–12	60	6:6	119
2:15–18	400	25:4	112	19:8	111
3:26–27	103	25:11	275	24:12	119
3:27	97	25:12	263	36:14	153
6:13–14	72			41:24	317
8:20	217, 235	**1 Chronicles**		42:15	204
9:24	317	1–9	117		
10:32–33	272	4:42–43	231	**Psalms**	
12:31	148	21:5	116	18:7	189
14:7	217			18:8–16	26
14:13	112	**2 Chronicles**		18:11	24
14:22	217	2:12–14	5	23:6	202
14:25	11	2:16	114	27:4	202
14:28	11	4:6	19–20	29	26, 27, 289
15:5	54, 208, 209	6:13	18	37:15	317
15:8	15	8:17	237	45:6	317
16:6	217	11:3–11	256	46	189
16:14–15	18	17:14	114	52:8	24
17:1	333	20:36	237	80:13	111
17:17	155	24:14	359	88:6	208
18:1	333	26:6	256	89	26, 27
18:3–6	55	26:11	114	89:26	21, 27
18:4	146, 333	26:16–21	189	90:10	194
18:9	333	26:21	208, 209	93	26, 27
18:10	333	28:18	256, 257, 258	92:13–16	24
18:13	59, 60, 333	29–31	55	99:1	25
18:13–19:37	55	30	16	137:7	216, 218
19:8	59	31:1	333		
19:15	25	32:1–23	55	**Isaiah**	
19:35–36	55	32:2–5	61	1:8	298
20:20	61, 62	32:5	64	1:23	54
21:1–9	146, 158	32:6	8	1:26	54
21:5	155	32:9	59	1:28	54
21:7	150	33:15	178	2:10–21	196
21:16–18	158			5:2	133
22:5	116	**Ezra**		5:5	111
22:9	116	2	114, 117	5:25	196
23	143, 144,	2:59–63	114	6:1–2	54
	146, 147,	2:62	114	6:4	196
	149, 158, 161	6:4	8	7:14	67, 68, 193
23:4	149, 153	9:9	111	7:15–16	193
23:5	148, 152,			7:17	54, 55
	153, 157	**Nehemiah**		8:1	68
23:6	150	1:3	112	8:1–4	67, 194
23:7	149, 150, 153	2:13	112		

7	54	8:14	13	**Tobit**	
7:1	54	9:1	190	2:10	312
7:5	54	9:1–5	190		
8:4	54			**Judith**	
8:10	54	**Micah**		3:9	72
13:3	46	3:1–4	54	4:6	72
13:8	317	3:5	111	7:3	72
13:10–11	54	3:9–12	54		
		3:11	111	**Sirach**	
Joel		4–5	67	38	320
4:16	197	7:11	111		
				1 Esdras	
Amos		**Nahum**		4:41–46	218
1:1	188, 189,	1:5	197		
	190, 195			**Matthew**	
1:2	190, 197	**Haggai**		1:23	67
1:2–2:16	190	2:6–7	197	19:27	306
1:3	272			23:27	119
1:4	190	**Zechariah**			
1:7	190	3:8	98	**Mark**	
1:10	190	6:12	98	14:1–26	307
1:12	190, 239	9	270, 271		
1:14	190	9–14	269, 282, 283	**Luke**	
2:1	41	10	270, 271,	8:1–3	306
2:2	190		273, 278		
2:5	190	10:7-8	271	**John**	
2:8	33	10:9	270	12:6	306
3:9	33	10:10	270, 271, 273	13:29	306
3:13–15	190	13	269, 273,		
4:1	33		274, 276, 278	**Acts**	
4:11	190	13:1	274	1:13	304
5:6	190	13:2–6	274	2:1–4	304
5:11	34	13:7	274, 275	2:44–45	305
5:11–12	32	13:7–9	274	4:32	306
5:18–20	190	13:8	275, 278	4:34–35	306
6:4	32	13:8–9	277	12:12	306
6:4–7	90	13:16	274	23:3	119
6:11	190	14	269, 277, 278		
7:4	190	14:2	277, 278	**1 Corinthians**	
7:11	54	14:5	189, 197	11:23–32	307
7:14	196	14:14	277		
8:4–6	32	14:21	277		
8:8	190				

ANCIENT NEAR EASTERN TEXTS
(*see also* inscriptions *and* seals/sealings *in* General Index)

Alalakh Texts		AT 3	201, 202, 204	AT 17.4–6	203
AT 1	201	AT 6	201	AT 18–28	202
AT 2	201, 204	AT 7	204	AT 29.11	202
AT 2 (seal)	204	AT 17	204	AT 30.9	202

QUMRAN LITERATURE

CLASSICAL, PATRISTIC, AND RABBINIC LITERATURE